POLITICAL ECONOMY IN A GLOBALIZED WORLD

Foreword by Surin Pitsuwan,
Secretary-General of ASEAN

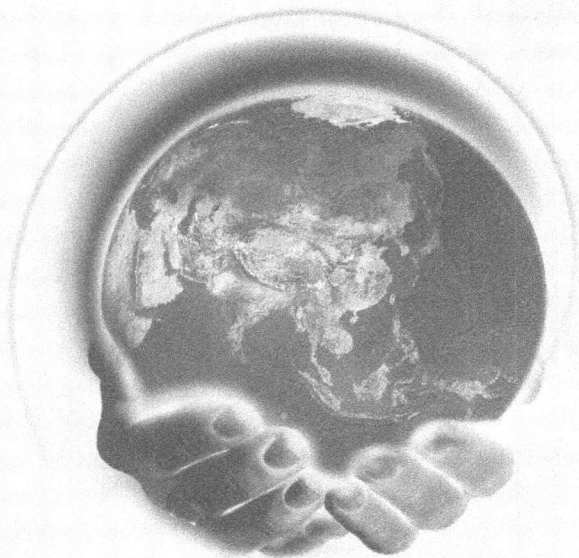

POLITICAL ECONOMY IN A GLOBALIZED WORLD

Jørgen Ørstrøm Møller

W **World Scientific**

NEW JERSEY · LONDON · SINGAPORE · BEIJING · SHANGHAI · HONG KONG · TAIPEI · CHENNAI

Published by

World Scientific Publishing Co. Pte. Ltd.

5 Toh Tuck Link, Singapore 596224

USA office: 27 Warren Street, Suite 401-402, Hackensack, NJ 07601

UK office: 57 Shelton Street, Covent Garden, London WC2H 9HE

Library of Congress Cataloging-in-Publication Data
Moeller, Joergen Oerstroem.
  Political economy in a globalized world / by Joergen Oerstroem Moeller.
    p. cm.
  Includes bibliographical references.
  ISBN 978-981-283-910-7 (pbk : alk. paper)
  1. Economics. 2. International relations. 3. Globalization. I. Title.
  HB75 .M59 2009
  337--dc22

                                            2009001776

British Library Cataloguing-in-Publication Data
A catalogue record for this book is available from the British Library.

To 'CURIOSITY' embedded in all human beings,
but all too often kept under strict guard.

Contents

Foreword

Professor Møller's book is a timely and welcome contribution to our understanding of the global economy and what it means for Asian countries and their citizens. The book contains essays about global political economy written over more than 10 years. His essays deal with many aspects of global political economy. The title itself is interesting, telling us that economics and politics are not separate items, but in fact are like two sides of the same coin.

The global economy had and continues to have a strong influence in shaping the economic behavior of Asian countries. As Minister of Foreign Affairs of Thailand from 1997–2001 I had witnessed the deleterious effects of this influence. Trade, services, investment and the movement of labor — skilled and unskilled — determine the scope for economic growth, narrowing the room for maneuver of the Asian countries.

We have also seen how the Europeans tried to manage their problems through a strong and robust European integration policy even if, from time to time, we hear how difficult it was for them to act in their collective interests by suppressing their individual sovereignty. But there is no doubt that Europe today is a much safer and stronger region with a better economy than it would have been if the Europeans had chosen to maintain the old nation-state approach.

ASEAN has just celebrated its 40th anniversary. The results achieved by ASEAN are by no means ordinary. The most important of these is the increased trust that exists among the ASEAN nations.

This has in turn increased the prospects for integration even if ASEAN has a long way to go when compared to the European Union. It is, however, not a foregone conclusion that economic integration in Asia must follow the pattern set by Europe. Each part of the world has its own background, traditions, and experiences and faces its own distinctive challenges. As we map our course and destiny we can learn from successes and failures of the European experience in regionalism.

Professor Møller's book can help us to do that. He is a noteworthy scholar and practitioner. He is a Visiting Senior Research Fellow at the Institute of Southeast Asian Studies and Adjunct Professor at both the Singapore Management University and the Copenhagen Business School. Prior to that he was, for over eight years, the State-Secretary in the Royal Danish Foreign Ministry, holding the portfolio that covered European integration, NATO, world trade and Denmark's relations with the US and Russia.

Many of his essays reveal new insights into the global system and how we can expect it to evolve under new circumstances. The relationship between the nation-state and the international community is currently undergoing tremendous changes. Many of the recent upheavals in the global economy are put under the microscope such as the sub-prime crises, the US economy, China and India and central bank policies. They offer valuable and frequently fresh views.

Professor Møller provides some interesting, even surprising and provocative, analysis about the new global paradigm unfolding before our eyes.

One of the most intriguing issues he has raised concerns climate change. Professor Møller offers several thoughtful essays about this problem and has given it a new dimension by comparing it to Malthus' theory about famine published 200 years ago. According to Møller, the world faces the prospect of a world of scarcities and he argues, persuasively, that the world does not face scarcities in some sectors only but in all sectors. In a way this is frightening, but the good thing is that this realization now opens the door for us to promote the right policies to reduce or eliminate negative impact on our societies.

Professor Møller is not asking us to agree or disagree with his analyses and conclusions. Indeed, what is important is that he has made us realize that in order to understand the globalized world and to manage the changes we need to start pondering about what is happening, why it is happening and what it means for us. This book is an excellent launch pad for our thinking, leading us towards our own conclusions and positions.

Surin Pitsuwan
Secretary-General of ASEAN

Preface

We live and thrive in an era of economic globalization weaving national economies into an international network. It is not the first time. The two decades before the outbreak of World War I constituted such an era, but the war turned internationalization into economic nationalization, ugly political nationalism and perverted racial theories legitimizing genocide. This underlines why economic globalization is not confined to economics, but indeed has strong bearings on politics and serves as a memento for all of us that more is at stake than just trade and investment.

Many people, especially the young ones, see economic growth and economic globalization as the only world order, broadly speaking a peaceful world even if there are limited armed conflicts. They may know from the study of history that "once upon a time" it was quite different, but they have not felt it. Hopefully they have picked up another lesson from history: these blessings cannot be taken for granted. The global financial crisis originating from the US housing market has brought this message home.

Economic globalization is unquestionably the best economic model to produce growth and wealth, but that does not mean it is beyond criticism and challenges. Indeed looking around and picking up political signals strong voices can be heard that economic globalization may be good, but it is not necessarily the only model and not necessarily a model benefiting everybody. Rising inequality both between richer and poorer countries and inside countries give rise to worries.

My interest in global economics or international economics as it was called in 1962 when I entered the gates of the University of Copenhagen arose from this combination of economics and politics. I was born in 1944, when Word War II still raged at full steam, and even if I do not recall the war, memories of post-war conditions has not been erased. In the 1950s and 1960s Europe underwent reconstruction and development but also entered a strong drive for integration — again combining politics and economics.

Since then uppermost in my mind has been the preoccupation of how we can safeguard an international, even global world against the many forces — extremism, protectionism, nationalism, and egoism — to name a few that would only be too happy to push us all back into the world as it was before 1945, i.e. dominated by nation-state rivalry swinging the door open for economic depression, political engineering thus casting the lives of millions of people in doubt, and ultimately war.

The only way as I see it is to deepen our understanding of economic globalization to better gauge what is going on and correct distortions and unwanted side effects.

During the 18th and 19th centuries, classical economists such as Adam Smith, David Ricardo and John Stuart Mill wrote about political economy. I have borrowed their label because it is much more telling than current economics which, regrettably, has fallen into the trap to operate in a mathematical context, frequently offering good opportunities to dig deeper, but at the cost of losing sight of the general view to combine various aspects. I believe in interdisciplinary analysis and almost all my essays fall under this heading instead of specialized economics. Some of my fellow economists may find that I tend to operate on thin ice, but the advantage is to draw other insight into the game than what pure economics offer.

A long service of 37 years in diplomacy combined with some academic activities gave me an opportunity to compare theory with how things are actually being done. This has been a fantastic opportunity.

Only a couple of months after my nomination as State-Secretary the Soviet Empire fell apart and Central and Eastern Europe wanted to join the European Union. China started to become an economic world power, raising the challenge of integrating that great country into the global economy. In 1992 the first economic reforms were launched in India. The framework for global trade was changed into the World Trade Organization. The Europeans moved towards a Single Market and a Single Currency. These are just a few of the vital changes I saw from my desk. They put their marks on my thinking. How could it be that a world dominated by a standoff between two superpowers suddenly changed into a totally different picture? Why did China change track and would it be successful? Could India make it into the group of countries with self-sustaining growth? What is going to happen to the nation-state, sovereignty, and domestic monetary policy? When the sub-prime mortage crisis struck, a number of other questions arose, among which the stability of the global system was the crucial one.

Now we see that scarcities are starting to dominate global economics. For more than 200 years we have lived in a world with growing wealth. Over the last 30 years a reduction of poverty in a scale unheard of and beyond what the large majority would have dared dream of has been achieved. But how do we adjust to climate change, global warming, food prices going up, energy in short supply and water not readily available?

For the last 25 years we have believed in the market forces, thinking they would get it right and lead the world into a sustained upwards business cycle. Since summer 2007 we start to question that philosophy, but at the same time we do not know how to retool the global model.

I hope the reader will enjoy the essays and form his/her own opinions about what needs to be done. All politics is the sum of the will of the individuals so it is up to all of us to shape the future of mankind.

Jørgen Ørstrøm Møller
Singapore, January 2009

Acknowledgments

The idea to publish my essays in a book came from Professor Euston Quah, Head of Economics at the Nanyang Technological University. I am truly grateful for his suggestion. On his recommendation I contacted World Scientific Publishing and have appreciated the professional way they produced this book.

Surin Pitsuwan, Secretary-General of ASEAN, whom I have known for more than a decade and first met when he was the Minister of Foreign Affairs of Thailand, graciously agreed to write the foreword. Glen S. Fukushima, President & CEO, Airbus Japan, former Under Secretary, US Department of Commerce Frank Lavin, and Professor Euston Quah — three good and trusted friends with whom I have enjoyed exchanging ideas over the years — volunteered to provide endorsements. Their kind help and the nice words they forwarded made me happy. Frank Lavin also offered many good suggestions about the presentation of the essays.

Over the years I have enjoyed exchanges of views with a large number of people. It would be impossible to name all, but without such an interchange of ideas I doubt very much that these essays would have been written. So many people have encouraged me to go on and write. We all stand on the shoulders of each other so actually the ideas incorporated in my essays are not my intellectual property, but belong to all my friends; and indeed, what is nowadays called the network. To all of them I would like to express deep and warm thanks.

My wife has put up with a husband who was sometimes lost in his own thoughts when he should have given more attention to family matters. Without her support I do not know what would have happened to me. She has all my love and affection.

Part 1: Future Global Trends

THE GLOBAL AGENDA FOR THE COMING DECADES WILL BE DOMINATED BY:

— scarcities putting burden sharing instead of distribution of benefits on the agenda,

— how to shape an institutional framework to bring the post World War II system up to date, and

— guaranteeing the moral and ethical standard achieved over centuries against extremists and terrorists determined to roll the evolution back

Many political and academic works have dealt with the challenge of scarcities, but few have put a coherent analysis together: food, energy, commodities, water, and clean environment. Rising population combined with growing income per head makes it virtually impossible to fathom a world without major scarcities, some of which will be physical ones and others economic scarcities working through the price mechanism. Global power balance will be affected as political negotiations turn into burden sharing connoting political fights. Any doubts are removed by the global economic crisis emanating from the financial meltdown in the US and negotiation positions concerning climate change and global warming. Our civilization enters into a new phase replacing more than 200 years of industrialization where nature's resources looked and were priced as if they were inexhaustible. We should have known better, now when we feel it, we do.

The rise of Asia is accompanied by strong growth in other developed parts of the world, changing the economic balance and consequently political power between what used to be called the industrialized world and the developing countries. History has many examples of such shifts in wealth and power and rarely did it take place in a peaceful and orderly way. What gives a ray of hope is the existence of international institutions serving as channels for decision-making and negotiations. Since 1945 international global institutions have had a hand in policy making, but actually served as a framework for an American dominated world. It has worked quite well primarily because the large majority of the world felt attracted by the American economic model, the American way of life, and partly at least also the basic American political model albeit that is less certain than the two other 'virtues'; what was attractive is fundamental freedom rights ingrained in the model.

As the world grows more global and the American dominance wanes the question arises whether global institutions can function in an environment where they have to act on their own and not as an instrument for American leadership. Many observers focus upon the glaring discrepancy between economic clout and decision-making in these institutions with countries like China and India being underrepresented. The veto right invested in the five countries since World War II in the Security Council of the United Nations is another case in point. These distortions may be corrected, but a pertinent question is to define what the institutions are supposed to do. A well-known sentence says that formalities cannot twist realities so even the most precise readjustment of decision making will not help much unless a clear objective combined with instruments are agreed upon.

Globalization is often taken for granted, but this is a dangerous stand. The same mistake was committed prior to World War I. Actually globalization is fragile when confined to economics, logistics, and transport and not yet having penetrated the mindset of the large majorities of people around the globe. A dangerous dichotomy is emerging with the elite being more and more global and the majority of people inside the countries being more and more skeptical. The growing inequality may be one of the main reasons. People acknowledge globalization as the best model to deliver growth and wealth, but see that it distributed inequitable, more and more making it legitimate for many people to ask whether the model benefits them.

The European Union has, for a couple of decades, been fairly successful in building a model based upon economic internationalization, cultural decentralization, and soft security policy. These three elements have combined to shape a unique European model framing development in Western Europe and cementing a peaceful Europe with a few admittedly acrimonious exception *inter alia* the former Yugoslavia. It paved the way and served as the foundation for integrating Central- and Eastern European countries into the European Union after the fall of the Soviet- and Russian empire in 1991. This model represents a political attempt to transfer many of the virtues of a national society based on the rule of the law onto the European and thus international level. It illustrates the conflict in the hearts and minds of many people between the logic of globalization with the feelings and emotions linking people to nationality.

Faced with the challenges and the likelihood of the transition of powers a fall back on the use of military power cannot be excluded. The threat can no longer be defined as aggression to conquer a slice of territory, but consists of attempts to jeopardize a country's ability to function thus removing the political system's legitimacy in the eyes of the citizens. The military in industrial countries has adapted to the new kind of warfare. This is good as long as the political objective is to protect advanced societies against attempts to disrupt social, economic, and political infrastructure. The war against terror is not predominantly a military war, far from it, but much more a struggle to lift people out of poverty, misery, and ignorance.

This raises the question of our mindset in a globalized world where cultural patterns criss-cross, interact and intercept each other. In such a world it becomes of paramount importance to show respect for others and their culture perceived as set of values. No one has the right *per se* to use military power. It can only be done justified by moral arguments and as a last resort. There may never have been so much power around, but it has never been so difficult to use it.

The Return of Malthus:

Scarcity and International Order

WHAT A DIFFERENCE AN ASSUMPTION CAN MAKE. SINCE THE INDUSTRIAL Revolution in the second half of the 18th century, a fortunate fraction of mankind has basked in a world of plenty. Living standards have risen exponentially as vast numbers of people escaped the dire poverty that had been the lot of their forebears for ages untold. The share of income spent on food in these revolutionized parts of the globe has fallen dramatically — in many industrialized countries to below 10 percent, and as low as 7.4 percent in the United States (as of 2006).

For most of the past two centuries, the denizens of plenty have assumed that the break with bleak pre-industrial poverty was a permanent one. They have often assumed, as well, that the ways of plenty would eventually spread to encompass the entire human family, and that when they did, most of the ancient misanthropies that have afflicted humankind would vanish from the face of the earth. The end of scarcity, it has been widely believed, would end the causes for greed and envy, avarice and war. War would no longer be "worth it", a presumption, it is fair to say, that lies at the very plinth of the Whig interpretation of history.

This is by now an old idea, but it is a sturdy one that has been propelled forward by the end of the Cold War and the cluster of phenomena known by the catchall phrase "globalization". Indeed, new and improved versions of the Whig interpretation have gained much credence since Herbert Butterfield coined the term in 1931. Thanks to globalization and the parallel spread of the received macroeconomic gospel, many millions more have been raised from dire poverty in the past two decades — a feat no amount of foreign aid could ever have produced. This unarguable achievement, many have claimed, could portend the end of poverty in our times. Add the comforting lyrical harmonies of democratic peace theory to the benign chorus of globalization and one gets a world veritably transformed very much for the better — perhaps even "the end of tyranny", as George W. Bush put it in his second Inaugural Address.

What if, however, the foundational assumption is wrong? What if the past two centuries, particularly the past two decades, have been not a reflection of the new rules of earthly progress, but exceptions to the old rules that once were and again shall be? In other words, what if Thomas Malthus turns out to have been right after all, and Adam Smith wrong?

For most of the past two centuries, few would have acknowledged even the possibility of such a thing coming to pass. Malthus was dubbed an intellectual fossil, a man who never understood how institutions and science could alter the terms of economic life. But alas, it doesn't take much to revive a wisp of doubt about the permanence of human material achievements. Food riots in more than two dozen countries stretching from Haiti to Egypt and a sharp increase in world food prices over the past three years are reviving Malthusian fears. Worrisome global financial instability, too, worsened in recent months by the subprime mortgage debacle in the United States, suggests serious structural flaws lurking in the international economic order. These developments have revived the question: Is the world really on a trajectory to escape poverty once and for all, or is it slipping back toward pre-Industrial Revolution conditions?

An Extended Debate

Is this a question we can answer in advance, before the verdict lands in our unsuspecting laps? The record suggests not. After all, pessimists and optimists have been going at one another for a very long time, and no one has yet won the debate. The modern version of it began with Malthus's 1798 *Essay on the Principles of Population,* in which he argued that "the power of population is so superior to the power of the earth to produce subsistence for man, that premature death must in some shape or other visit the human race." The roughly coterminous analysis of Adam Smith predicted a totally different future for mankind, however, and Smith won out in the hearts and minds of succeeding generations because history seemed to vindicate his view and condemn Malthus as a scientific failure.

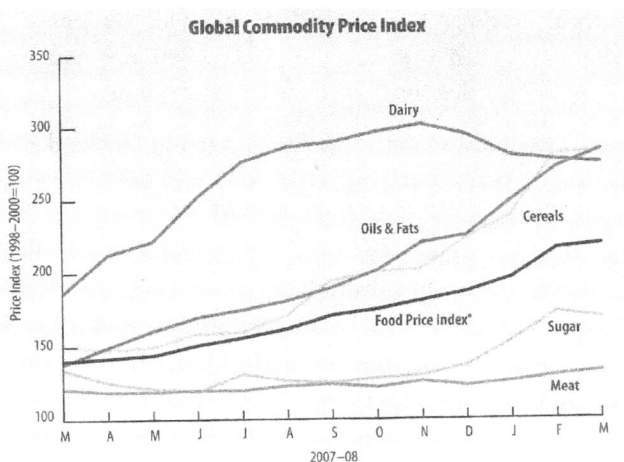

Source: *Food and Agriculture Organisation of the United Nations*
Food Price Index based on average of commodity price indices weighted by average export shares for 1998–2000.
Graphic by Thomas Rickers

Smith did not convince everyone, of course. There were and will always be doomsayers — it is part and parcel of human nature. For most of human history, doomsaying was an integral part of religion (hence the term "jeremiad"), but over the past century or so this tradition, like so many others, has been secularized and the analysis extended from Malthus's focus on food to the broader question of finite resources. Thus, the Club of Rome predicted in 1972 that limited availability of natural resources would stop economic growth. In a second report two years later, this unconditioned prediction was revised to say that some of the problems enumerated in the first report would be manageable after all, but the gist of the Club's pessimism remained and carried over into the Carter Administration. *The Global 2000 Report to the President*, commissioned by President Jimmy Carter in 1977 and released in 1981, stated:

> If present trends continue, the world in 2000 will be more crowded, more polluted, less stable ecologically, and more vulnerable to disruption than the world we live in now. Serious stresses involving population, resources, and environment are clearly visible ahead. Despite greater material output, the world's people will be poorer in many ways than they are today ... unless the nations of the world act decisively to alter current trends.

Wrong. The nations of the world in no way acted decisively, but after the twenty years spanning 1979 and the year 2000 the world's people were nonetheless much better off "in many ways". In the meantime, we were witness to some amusing side bets, like the one in 1980 between the optimist Julian Simon and the pessimist Paul Erhlich. (Simon won.) And CIA predictions made during the Carter Administration concerning the price of oil also turned out to be not just wrong, but ludicrously wrong.

If one looks at the key predictions of the Club of Rome, none of them has come true. To the contrary, the global economy has grown mightily over the past 35 years, and for most of that time the real price of oil and most other raw materials has stayed constant or has fallen. This has led a host of critics to charge that the essential view of the Club of Rome and its post-Earth Day supporters amounted to a late 20th-century manifestation of pantheism, an old romantic elitist ideal that is increasingly out of step with our dynamic world.

A Debate Extended

Despite the poor — embarrassing, really — showing of latter-day doomsaying, the idea that the past two centuries are the exception rather than the rule of economic reality never seems to go completely out of style. And well it shouldn't: Despite the record, attempts to revive Malthus may not have been mistaken, merely premature. So many times have little boys cried wolf that many are now persuaded there is no wolf. That could be a mistake, and it is certainly a possibility worth serious consideration.

All efforts to date to vindicate Malthus have proven wrong for four reasons. First, new territories have opened up to change the equation between the supply and demand for resources. Second, new technologies have arisen to make vastly better use of the resources we have. Third, the introduction and spread of the market economy has significantly improved the efficiency with which resources are used. Fourth, the modern state has been able to devise administrative machinery to help form, protect and regulate the market, and within this machinery there has arisen a transnational revolution in logistics that has enabled mankind to shift resources to alleviate imbalances and minimize scarcities on a global scale.

New Territories: Many textbooks in Europe present new territories opened up in Eurasia after 1800 as being most important economically, but four others have been even more so: North America, South America, Australia and New Zealand. These new territories in "New Worlds" delivered agricultural land to feed growing populations with lower food prices, while emigration to them reduced population pressures in the Old World. Real wages thus went up in newly industrializing countries, making a fool out of another celebrity doomsayer, Karl Marx.

Technology: The end of the age of sail brought about by the advent of steamships and the railroad made these new territories accessible. Otherwise, food grown there could not have made it to the metropoles, and little emigration would have flowed from Great Britain in the 18th and 19th centuries; catastrophes like the Irish famine of the 1840s–50s would have continued periodically, rather than being the last the West would see. Subsequent technological waves have enabled still higher productivity. After the advent of steam power came electricity, then the science of the green revolution, and then the information and communication revolution. And we are now witnessing a new wave with astonishing breakthroughs in bio- and nanotechnology. These inventions have progressively liberated us from the straitjacket of having to rely mainly on human and animal calories as sources of mechanical energy.

Markets: With Adam Smith and David Ricardo, the young Industrial Revolution found its high priests. Over the past two centuries, Smith's invisible hand and Ricardo's comparative advantage have constituted the foundations for economic growth around the world. This has been so because Smith, Ricardo and others not only described and explained how markets worked, but also showed individuals and governments alike how to keep them working.

Whether Smith and Ricardo discovered an objective reality or helped to create a social one is still open to debate. Either way, economic incentives and balanced contractual relationships replaced prohibitions and commands from on high. To the surprise of nearly everyone, nearly everyone benefited, and, more important, a shift of basic assumptions about social life took place as a result, leading the way from the advent of individual agency in the market to the idea of individual agency in politics.

The State: The emergence of the modern state in the latter part of the 18th century marked the transformation of small political units, which had characterized Europe for centuries, into larger and more viable economic entities. Had the petty princes and bishops of early modern Europe been able to constrain markets within political borders, the potential embedded in the new technologies of the Industrial Revolution would have come to little.

At a later stage, the modern European state itself became too small for its own economic britches, leading some elites to react by trying to expand trade, others to experiment with mercantilism and imperialism (best defined as deliberately imbalanced trade, armed). The need to enlarge the market to fit economic reality now leads states either to support free trade or to voluntarily construct even larger political-administrative units, the European Union being the most obvious example. The logistics revolution, meanwhile, has enabled some states to help others deal with scarcities, whether through food and foreign aid or with humanitarian relief efforts. In all cases the basic aim is the same: to enable, protect and guide the benign functioning of markets both within and among states.

Was it just a stroke of good luck that these four seminal shifts interacted and shaped a world so dynamic and so different from what had come before? Or is there something about human nature that can reassure us that this wasn't luck, but rather a sign of the human capacity for genuine achievement that can be replicated in the future? We are going to find out because, most likely, the world has now used up the breathing room that these four factors have provided, leaving us today in roughly similar circumstances to those of 200 years ago. Two questions thus come to the fore. Can we devise another set of escape hatches to ward off a Malthusian fate; and what might global politics look like if we can, or if we cannot?

The Wolf This Time?

The clouds of a Malthusian storm seem to be gathering. The world faces looming shortages of food, energy, raw materials, water and habitable environment. These shortages are not confined to the "known world", as was the case two centuries ago, but encompass the whole globe. To hold off the return of Malthus, we need some equivalent of new territories, new technologies, the further expansion and refinement of market efficiencies and, especially, new forms of political organization to enable markets to create the best balance of incentives for sustainable economic development on a global scale.

To match the aforementioned prospective shortages against the four categories of anti-Malthusian remedy is a project for a book, not an essay. A few selective and suggestive examples will therefore have to suffice as preliminary illustration.

For reasons both remote and proximate, food prices have been rising worldwide for some years, particularly so in the past three years. One reason is population pressure in general: There are more people, more mouths to feed. But this factor is, perhaps counterintuitively, the least significant of all in explaining the price rises of recent years. More important is the fact that people in many parts of the developing world are leaving rural areas for towns and cities, and rising wealth is enabling more people to want — and to afford — to eat higher on the food chain. It takes a far larger input of resources to produce the equivalent amount of meat calories than vegetable protein calories. More capital-intensive methods of growing food, which in some cases is responsible for helping to depopulate countrysides, require petrochemical fertilizers and fossil fuels. When the prices of those inputs go up, so do the prices of the outputs. The fact that much of the world market for food is denominated in U.S. dollars has also had an impact on prices; if the dollar weakens, by definition, it can buy less food per unit. If this were not enough, the use of foodstuffs to make biofuels has reduced the amount of food available, though experts argue over how much. If supply goes down as demand goes up, the inevitable result is higher prices.

Obviously, some of these factors are more amenable to intervention than others. Governments could, if they were ever to come to their senses, stop the foolishness of current biofuel programs, which are not cost-effective ways of meeting energy demand and which accentuate the basic unfairness of trading food in the mouths of the poor for fuel to run SUVs in the American suburbs. The dollar may not remain weak. The other factors, alas, are harder to change, but it is still worth examining what interventions in the form of new territories, new technology, market mechanisms and adaptive political organization we can expect to offset the factors pushing up the price of food.

There are vast swaths of the world that could be farmed but are not. Some areas used to be farmed but are farmed no longer, and new regions that have never been farmed might be if market incentives were right and state policies were enabling. In the former category are parts of Russia and most of Ukraine. In the latter category are parts of Africa. If global warming proceeds as most scientists predict, not all the effects will be bad — unpopular as it may be in some places to say this. Large sections of northern Russia and Canada that are now too cold to farm economically (or at all) might become richly arable in a matter of mere decades.

New technologies can also contribute to crop viability in colder climates, while other biotech innovations may increase productivity in lands already farmed. Of course, topsoil is in limited supply, no matter how efficiently technology improves and markets are able to function.

Even the most optimistic find it difficult to support predictions of strong upward trends for agricultural production — a second Green Revolution on the scale of the first. The likeliest prospect is not famine but higher food prices that will exacerbate social inequalities both among and within countries across the globe.

What about energy? Analysts agree that demand for energy is rising sharply worldwide, led by growth in China, India and other large developing countries. Prices will rise as demand outstrips the supply of "easy" oil, whose production has peaked. But the overall picture is not a simple one. As countries develop, energy efficiencies are bound to improve thanks to technological innovation, market efficiencies and deft political regulation. As was the case in the United States in the late 1970s, 1980s and 1990s, the global economy is now doing a much better job of squeezing units of gross domestic product out of one barrel of oil, and that trend is likely to continue. So prices will rise, but not in lock step with economic productivity. Economies can sustain higher energy prices and still grow.

In the slightly longer run, the issue will not be so much the price of oil but the overall composition of energy sources. Substitution from oil and gas into other energy sources will occur, but more likely than a major shift to renewable sources such as wind energy or solar energy will be a switch to coal and perhaps nuclear power. If coal plays the major role, the global economy's dependence on fossil fuels will be basically unchanged. Here, too, prices for energy will rise because of the need for large investments in infrastructure. The same can be said for other raw materials, despite some remarkable technical advances in materials science.

Shortages of these three elements — agriculture, energy and raw materials — will prove manageable. The global economy will not literally exhaust supplies, and price increases will not derail the global economy. Global growth under these circumstances will still be possible, though not at the levels we have seen in the past two decades. Political challenges may arise, however, from the fact that both resources and growth will be distributed in ways different from those to which we have grown accustomed.

The picture is less sanguine when it comes to water and environments clean enough to be habitable. The world has limited renewable supplies of fresh water, but the amount is great. The problem is not the absolute amount of water or some theoretical division problem involving gallons per capita per year. The real problem is that water is often scarce for agriculture and industry where it is most needed, requiring that it be transported and purified at considerable cost. China, for example, which has 25 percent of global population but only 7 percent of global fresh water resources, suffers from a lack of hydrological infrastructure, as do many developing countries. Low per-capita income makes it basically impossible to supply water on a commercial basis.

Water scarcity affects food scarcity in obvious ways and negatively influences other sectors of economic life as well, not least health. Like food, energy and other natural resources, water is a tradable commodity. To date, international trade in water is limited, but it is a safe bet that fresh water commerce will expand. After all, many industrial countries charge considerable sums not only for industrial uses of water, but also for household use in order to encourage conservation and to finance investment in infrastructure. It stands to reason that trading will become a growing aspect of the basic international economy of water. The problem is that water is very heavy and costly to move, so market mechanisms enabled by intergovernmental arrangements can only work once the replacement cost for water rises to a sufficiently high level. But some countries experiencing water stress will be too poor to pay such prices or to afford energy-intensive desalination alternatives.

Here again problems of equity, distribution and social stability broadly construed come into play. The difference with water is that the elasticity of demand is zero. People can do without meat, air-conditioning and copper pipes. They cannot live without water. This is why food shortages may cause riots, but water shortages may cause either wars or revolutionary efforts at cooperation to avoid them. Water is high-stakes stuff.

Having a clean, habitable environment falls into a category of its own. Food, energy, raw materials and even water are concrete, physical things. They can be seen, counted, measured and marketed in standard units. Inequities can be assuaged by arranging to literally move any of them from one place to another within rules established by political systems and calibrated by markets. Not so with environments. One cannot move, chop up or sell habitable environments in any practical way. And yet pollution and climate change can be generated by some countries to the detriment of others, with large overall economic implications. Environmental issues present a challenge to the global commons that neither new territories, technology nor the function of markets alone can solve. The only way to manage the threat of environmental degradation heralding the return of Malthus is to devise new forms of international governance.

So far, world leaders have not done a good job of this. The Montreal Protocol on ozone-depleting gasses is a notable exception to the general rule of failure. The Kyoto Protocol, on the other hand, illustrates the rule. Those who devised this Protocol made fatal political errors of judgment that have resulted in major parties being either left out (China and India, for example) or politically forced out (the United States) of participation. Just as bad, its key mechanism — cap and trade — does not address the real problem, which is the need to reduce global production of greenhouse gases. Kyoto's mechanism cannot ever hope to achieve the numerical aims of the agreement except by natural population decline in places like Russia and the European Union, for emissions track uncannily with demography once societies reach a certain level of development.

Everyone understands the basic problem here: State sovereignty protects polluters of all kinds from being called to task for the effects of their pollution on others. Sometimes these effects can be downright existential, as with the possibility that rising sea levels caused by global warming can drown whole island nations. In some cases, too, the effects can be deliberate — states can now wage environmental aggression on each other, and in the future this may become a more common form of aggression than traditional territorial grabs.

Nearly all the schemes propounded thus far to deal with this problem, however, are doomed to fail because they try to fix responsibility — and exact remuneration — on the sources of pollution.

Some favor emission quotas and some favor tradable quotas, but this will only cause market distortions and recession. Others want obligatory environmental standards written into all trade deals, even if enforcing them is impossible and the cost of goods would be highly inflated as a result. Still others advocate placing heavy taxes on multinational corporations that are polluters, but companies can move or disaggregate to avoid taxation. And others want to tax international transport, since emissions from ships and airplanes are considerable. But that will also further distort markets and raise prices, thus stifling growth.

The only sensible way to conceptualize the problem is to stop thinking about producers and start thinking about consumers. The ultimate cause of pollutant emissions is not the producer but the consumer. Demand is trump, not supply. A fiscal mechanism that shifts the burden to the consumer — some sort of Polluter Pays Principle (PPP) on the global level — seems therefore to be the least unfair, and the least bad, available solution. The basic idea is an old and proven one: Whatever you subsidize you get more of and whatever you tax you get less of. If you tax the consumption of products whose manufacture causes pollution, you'll get less pollution. If you subsidize the consumption of products that are carbon-footprint friendly compared to those they replace, you'll get more of them.

A PPP approach would not interfere with established comparative competitive advantages, and since it would be assessed against consumers, not producers, it will not affect geographical production patterns. If properly designed, a PPP system may even work as a strong incentive to reduce emissions if it rewards countries and/or companies that introduce new technology with a lower emission level per unit of fuel. As long as emission levels do not go up, the levy paid will be unchanged even if production does go up. One could even use revenues from PPP taxes to directly stimulate research and development of new environmentally friendly technology.

To get at the problem of environmental pollution with any hope of success, significant political accommodation — political engineering, so to speak — will be necessary on a global scale. The international order will have to change to keep Malthus at arm's length. Only an understanding that includes the major countries, beginning with the United States and including the European Union, China, Japan, Russia, India, Brazil and the oil-producing states, has a chance to succeed. And even then, implementation will be difficult, expensive, and take a long time to put into place. Who today would bet that this will happen? In short, if Malthus does return, he may do so not for wholly natural reasons concerning any inherent limits to growth, but because human societies prove unable to reorganize themselves to allow new frontiers, new technologies and new market designs to keep him at bay.

Winners, Losers and Big Losers

What might the world look like if we do not adjust, and Malthus does return? We cannot know for certain, but one way to think about the question is to postulate a world in which countries fall into one of three basic groups.

In this thought experiment, the first tier of countries would consist of North America and Europe, perhaps joined by Japan, Australia, New Zealand, Israel and a few other advanced states. These countries, or conglomerations of countries, do not face acute water shortages (Israel does but it has advanced desalination capabilities), and the agricultural sectors of most of them can be turned into genuine export bonanzas, reaping foreign exchange and providing large numbers of jobs, if they are willing to reverse 200 years of migration from the countryside to the cities. They are short of some raw materials and energy — Europe far more than North America, and Japan and Israel far more than Europe — but the larger ones sit on ample supplies of coal and all are rich and technologically advanced enough to turn scarcities of energy and raw materials into manageable problems by throwing R&D money at them. Indeed, if North America and Europe could combine forces, economically if not also politically, they would be in a position to dominate a Malthusian world.

The second tier is made up of China and India, where high growth over recent decades will be threatened by shortages in almost all areas except coal. Compared to North America and Europe, they may be forced into political choices about which problems to solve, or at least solve first, because they lack the money and technology infrastructure to finance a way out of all of them at the same time. They will need to prioritize dealing with water and food shortages, followed by energy and raw materials deficits — not to speak of what to do about maintaining environments clean enough for human habitation. Even if they make good choices, their political stability may be endangered. Parts of both of these countries are richer in resources than others, so as challenges mount, the richer areas may balk at supporting the poorer ones. In the end, it will be a race in which high growth and good governance are pitted against challenges and deteriorating conditions. With luck, China and India may make it, but it will be a close-run thing. If they do not, they may collapse into chaos. The stakes will be high. Whether the political leaders of the 2.3 billion people living there get it right will determine the future global system.

The poorer countries constitute the third tier, which unfortunately will not only remain poor but become even poorer. Some of them may escape the Malthusian trap if they possess energy or raw materials, but the large majority will tumble, fast or slow, into a Hobbesian abyss. Some countries in Latin America and many in Africa will fall into this category.

In a future Malthusian world it is clear that there will be a stark shift in relative prices in favor of energy, food and raw materials, and this will change global production and trade patterns. It will trigger new investment in infrastructure, logistics and transport facilities in the richer countries. Richer countries will be capable of delivering capital and resources to each other and to poorer countries, but poorer countries will not, and many poorer countries will not have the wealth or administrative coherence to receive and use what richer countries have on offer.

Clean environments aided by new technologies such as coal liquefaction and desalination will be enjoyed by the countries that can afford them; some poorer countries may have cleaner environments too, but mainly as a function of sharply reduced economic activity. In a Malthusian world, this would suit the interests of richer countries. It does pose what one might call a challenge of moral aesthetics, but the richer countries, if they really wanted to, could deliberately return to a time before CNN when the misfortunes of the poor were unknown to them. Whoever thinks this impossible suffers from a failure of imagination.

There is a good chance that the world can hold off Malthus, but in doing so it will come to be a different world politically from the one in which we live today. If that chance is lost, the world — or most of it — could come to resemble the dystopias of science fiction, or perhaps even a level of human degradation beyond novelists' imaginations. Even the "winners" in such a world would never be safe for long, for it is unlikely that the losers would leave off revolting against a world system that condemns them to seemingly eternal poverty and humiliation. When you think about it, Mr. Malthus is a man we should not want to meet in person. He is an unwanted guest, one well worth working to avoid.

This article was first published in *The American Interest*, Vol. III No. 6, July/August 2008.

The Importance of Global Institutions in Mediating between the West and Asia

LET ME START BY EMPHASIZING SOME BASIC PRINCIPLES ABOUT INSTITUTIONS, primarily how they work or do not work in an international context, but also valid for national and domestic institutions.

- Institutions cannot create or shape policies, nor can they lead to decisions if the political will is not present. They are channels or instruments to implement policies.
- They are not an end or a goal in itself. They serve a purpose and are mobilized only if a goal cannot be reached without them or is reached less efficiently.
- Formalities cannot twist realities. The substance dictates what we do and who is doing it.
- To be a suitable vehicle for decision-making, institutions must respect the balance of power, as seen by their member-states.
- To be effective, institutions must be perceived as being "theirs" by those they serve. A former Secretary-General of NATO had a sign above his desk saying: «The Secretary-General is the servant of the member states.»
- Institutions stop working effectively when their *raison d'être* disappears, but keep working inefficiently until that truth dawns upon the member-states.

The Post-War System

The Cold War ended in 1989–1991. Until the UN Security Council in 2003 failed to agree on the Iraq issue, the Cold War global system continued to function because the autopilot was switched on. No one really pressed for changes and no challenges popped up to disclose that the job it was designed to do had disappeared. The Iraq war did so for a variety of reasons and since then, the world has sailed on without a steering system.

Let us cast a glance on the post-World War II system, if for no other reason than that it served the world well for more than 50 years.

1) The system was comprehensive in setting up the UN, a trade organization (ITO/GATT, to be replaced by the WTO), a channel for funding reconstruction and development (with the World Bank designed to be the world's family bank), and a fund to help overcome balance of payments difficulties (the International Monetary Fund). Later, these institutions were supplemented by a host of other more or less specialized institutions, organizations and agencies. These institutions supported one other and where one could not help, another one was called in.

2) The institutions looked like multinational or international institutions, but were in fact a vehicle for the mightiest country, the US, to exercise power in conformity with its political priorities. The rest of the world not only acquiesced, but went along because the US resisted — not always but most of the time — the temptation to use the institutions to pursue narrow American interests. When the US acted alone, it acted … alone. The majority of the other member states were comfortable with sharing most of the set of values steering US policies and felt that they had joined the institutions for this reason. The institutions made it possible for the US to impose its will with some civility and most other countries saw themselves as its partners.

3) World opinion backed the institutions, perhaps not unanimously and not all the way, but to a large extent. It took a long time for pressure groups and NGOs to emerge as opponents or critics and when that happened, it was only half-hearted and aimed at part of the system or at isolated policies.

4) There was a dominating model, the American one, but there was still room for the socialist model to challenge it until 1989, when socialism collapsed and caused some developing countries like India to try their own model. The dissenters, so to speak, were not reigned in, but allowed to try their model.

5) In retrospect, that may have been one of the reasons it was only in the 1980s that the free market began to run amok. Before then, it was kept under control or might have kept itself under control because there was an alternative. So long as that was the case, aberrations were held in check. When the challenger disappeared, the economic model began to lose self-control.

How Does It Look Now?

Leaving aside, for a time, the question whether the institutions are looking at the right target, there is no doubt that decision-making is out of tune. Examples are the veto right in the UN Security Council being vested in the five victors from World War II; the composition of the Security Council, which leaves out India, Germany and Japan and which has no representative from Africa, the Middle East and Latin America; voting rights in IMF and the World Bank which, though adjusted, do not reflect the power balance. The WTO is based formally upon unanimity but in reality leaves decision-making in the hands of a few major powers, asking the rest of the world to endorse what they have agreed on. Bodies like the G-7, G-8 or G-9 reflect the idea of a directory, but are, in fact, a rich man's club that views the world from that particular angle.

People around the globe do not see the institutions taking consensus decisions but being moulded in the tradition of American interests, even if Americans sometimes appear to be their most vocal critical. There is a saying that a political compromise is a good one if no one is happy, but the same proverb cannot be applied to global institutions.

Those who shaped the institutions 60 years ago would probably have been pleasantly surprised if told that the institutions would still be there in 2008, but even more pleasantly surprised to see that all the rising powers have joined the system. It is one of the marvels of the past 20 years.

As a *quid pro quo*, the established powers should have stretched their hands out to welcome the new powers and made room for them by adjusting decision-making procedures. By not doing so, they have created a constituency of members which feel that the institutions are not really theirs but belong to the establishment. They did not join the institutions; they joined the global economic model and chose to live with the institutions set up to run that model.

The established powers, especially the US, apparently are unable to come to grips with the following dilemma:

- Either to welcome new powers, share decision-making with them and relinquish some of their power, but at the same time reap the benefit brought by the values guiding or controlling the system, which continues to be theirs. In short: You can shape a global system in your own picture.
- Or hold on to formal powers, counting on players to see things as they used to be, which will be the case for a time, perhaps a long time, but which sooner or later will change. When change occurs, it will do so in circumstances that will cut deeply into their influence and open the door for others to shape a world order.

What you cannot do is to do both — or neither.

Global System Out of Touch

The basic problem is not, however, that the decision-making procedures do not reflect the picture of the real global economic and political power, but that they have lost track of what happens in the world. This can be illustrated by five observations:

- The existing global model, which is the American post-1990 edition of capitalism, is not any longer accepted as universal.
- Free trade is being questioned by a number of countries, business (Warren Buffett!) and academics (Paul Samuelson!).

- The dissemination of information and the shaping of opinion is shifting. Facebook and YouTube have made interaction real.
- We are moving from an international environment of plenty and low prices for the whole range of commodities to an era of scarcities with high prices.
- The nation-state is gradually losing power to clusters, megacities, cross-border regions, and multinational or supranational companies. A whole range of new players has entered the fray without being integrated into the system.

The existing edition of globalization is out, another model is feeling its way in, but international institutions are caught by inertia.[1]

The system is out of touch, does not respond to current challenges and does not incorporate a number of important players. The contrast is striking with the post-World War II system, which was responsive and delivered the goods.

The new main topics for global action must either be incorporated into the existing institutions — alternatively, the institutions' objectives must be changed — or new institutions must be built. The world has seen this before — for example, in the post-World War II period — and knows how difficult it is. The drivers for this to take place should be the rising powers because they are the countries expected to benefit the most from new issues, but are newcomers in the game and lack experience.

It looks as if the US will still be the dominating power for a long time, with Europe presumably but not for certain to support it. But the US will not any longer be strong enough to design and impose a system on others. In other words, we are moving into an era with a strong power that is much stronger than the other powers, but is not strong enough to exercise undisputed leadership and impose its will and, if I read the signals coming from the US, has some self-doubts about where it wants to take the world.

Who is going to lead? The established powers are strong enough to block, but not to lead. The rising powers voice their discontentment, but are short of alternative suggestions.

Let me enumerate what I see as the topical issues that will shape international institutions in the years to come.

Issue number one. Regional internationalization

Coming from Denmark with the Lego bricks, I do not hesitate to tell you that a durable global model needs to be built by the Lego bricks method. We operate with several layers: national, regional and global. The nation-state is too small and the global level too diffuse. The regional level offers the prospect of tackling congruous problems in collaboration with adjacent nation-states pursuing analogous political objectives. The depth of regional institutionalization depends upon similarity of political objectives, political systems, economic model and governance in a broad sense.[2]

Regional organizations serve as vehicles for helping nation-states with problems confined to a region, for example currency cooperation in Europe or Asia, or freedom of movement for labour inside a region. Gradually, they take over safeguarding the interests of member-state at an international/global level. These regional organizations will gradually replace the nation-states and link together to shape a kind of global governance. Monetary cooperation will come first. In a not too distant future, we will probably see Europe and adjacent regions in a Euro Zone, North America and at least some of the rest of the Western hemisphere in a US Dollar Zone, and a large part of Asia uniting around a Yuan Zone. The rest of the world will choose one of these three currencies as its anchor. From there will emerge some kind of policy body to fix currency rates and control global economic policy and from that platform may emerge a new global body with wider competences.

The problem is that, so far, only one of the organizations, the European Union, has reached a level where it is capable of playing that role.

But the good news is that if we actually look at what is happening, we can see how regional organizations are growing in number and stature and gaining more clout in East Asia, Latin America, South Asia, the Middle East and in Africa.

Issue number two. Sovereignty

We have passed from the era of the nation-state to the era of inter-nationalism. The nation-state is fighting a tough rearguard battle — yes, it fighting for its life — but its days are numbered. How can a global steering system managing economic globalization be composed and controlled by nation-states? That is a contradiction in terms.

The hard core in all this is sovereignty.[3] In the former global model, sovereignty was the bulwark for the nation-state against what came from the outside world. It decided what it would let in and what it would block. The plinth of the system was the nation-state's right to defend itself against the outside world. In the era of globalization, it is the other way around. We have moved into an age where the international or global system reserves for itself the right to intervene in case it finds that the policies of a nation-state threaten global stability. For those in doubt, see what has happened over the last 10–15 years. Having digested that, just think of what would happen to globalization if we opted for a toothless global system allowing nation-states to disrupt international relations. We do not yet have a high priest or an icon as a whistleblower setting it out in specific terms, but we can see it happening.

If this is not intercepted by a global system, the next thing to happen will be the spread of coalitions of the willing — as we have seen.

The only thing that is not going to happen is that the international system sits back, adopting the cast of a lame duck. Formerly national economies could and did function on a domestic base and the international economy was seen as a potential disruptive force. Disruption came from external circumstances hitting the national economy. Now, the global supply chain, logistic networks and ICT must be secured against disruption emanating in one country and, *via* the global economy, making the other national economies fall like dominoes. Disruption originated nationally, putting the spanner into the works of the global economy. To mention a specific example, during the SARS pandemic in East Asia, the fear among several Asian countries was that the WHO would move to impose restrictions on travelling out of the countries/territories hit — not help the countries hit — to protect the international system

Sovereignty will be adapted to globalization, giving the right to intervene inside nation-states. An unconditional condition for this to be accepted is an institutional framework with rules and procedures, just as the world today has rules and procedures for how the nation-state can defend its sovereignty.

The intriguing question in the West-Asia perspective is that Europe, Asia and the US find themselves on different stages on the lifecycle of the nation-state, the guardian of sovereignty. Europe is dismantling the nation-state even if a host of people say the opposite. Asia is on the upward bend of the curve, with many Asian nations striving to build a national identity. The US may be at the beginning or the end of the curve, but is not near either Europe or Asia. A witty comment in *Fortune* (June 23, 2008) predicts that the US will fall apart with an oil price of US$1,000.

Issue number three. Burden sharing [4]

All the institutions are designed to distribute the benefits of economic growth or, alternatively, to support economic growth.

The game is changing. In the future, we are going to live in an era of scarcities, with high prices for commodities, pressure for pollution abatement and a focus on global warming/climate change.

The institutions we now have are not designed to do that and, although not impossible, it is unlikely that they can be turned around.

The future game will be a battle about burden-sharing, a brutal and ruthless exercise where everybody will try to pass the buck to somebody else. Politicians, be they national or international, have found it difficult to deal with distributing benefits. It is nothing compared to burden-sharing.

But if we do not succeed in shaping some kind of common policies to tackle this in an orderly way, the alternative is not to go on, but that large parts of the world will implode.

Issue number four. Interaction

International institutions probably, like national institutions, have not adjusted to the era of mass communication, dissemination of knowledge and information, how a consensus is shaped outside institutional frameworks and how to incorporate the new players in decision-making.

Just to give one example. When the London underground was bombed in 2005, it was not the authorities or the traditional mass media which were there first but people with their cell phones and cameras. The result was that before the authorities had had the chance to assess what had happened and how to shape public opinion, there already was a public opinion shaped by people themselves on the spot.[5]

Conventional communication *via* the authorities and/or by established mass media, which consider themselves to be part of the establishment — albeit, in some cases, being a pain in the neck for the authorities — is losing the game.

International institutions are delinking from national governments as a consequence of globalization and must accordingly build up their own channels to intercept this new trend on a global basis, take in the new players, and open channels on how to receive information and how to give information. This is interaction, not one-way communication.

Why Institutions at All?

Institutions are not perfect, but are the best instruments for delivering continuity, coherence, compromise/negotiations, transparency, legitimacy and accountability.

When international institutions are criticized — which, for example, is the case with EU institutions and the WTO — they are almost always compared to national institutions and not compared with an alternative global model.

The virtues above are well-known and not many would seriously dispute that institutions are better placed to deliver goods than, for example, bilateral diplomacy, where the mightiest powers either force their will through making less-powerful nations fear them, or show magnanimity to draw others into their orbit as client-states.

Let me finish by mentioning two virtues and two criticisms.

The two virtues are essential although their benefits may not at first glance be tangible and even less measurable.

First, institutions reflect a stage of political maturity, forcing countries into a negotiation framework instead of confrontational attitudes. It is easily forgotten, but until 1945 exactly such a framework guided global politics and the first attempt to change the pattern under the aegis of the League of Nations failed completely.

Second, institutions operate by rules and procedures. The virtue is that powerful and less-powerful nations both know the rules, and that a set of rules declares what is permissible and what is not permissible. The effect is not only transparency but also an improved basis for decision-making, so that the reaction of others becomes more predictable. Surprises cannot be ruled out, but will be the exception.

An extrapolation of this is the discipline imposed on member-states by the institutions and the self-discipline the member-states impose on one other. The trick, so to speak, is to make the member-states abide by the rules. That makes it unnecessary to bring enforcement into the picture

There are, however, two criticisms again international institutions that are somewhat difficult to deal with.

First, institutions normally are far away from the citizens they serve. This transforms them into faceless monsters regardless of whether they are or not monsters, because a citizen can go to the local community and talk with a person, but not to international institutions.

Second, when there is not sufficient trust among member-states, institutions will not enjoy trust, either. Country A has no trust in country B. An institution means that a citizen from country B takes decisions in matters of great importance for country A.

How these difficulties are to be overcome is an unresolved question that explains much of the public scepticism towards European institutions.

The somewhat disappointing observation is that we are still in first gear, where international institutions belong to the national government and nation-states. Hopefully, we will be able to move into second gear, where they start to belong to the people.

Endnotes

[1]See, for example, Bobbitt, Philip, *The Shield of Achilles*, New York: Random House, 2002.

[2]The European Union mapped out at the meeting of the European Council in June 1993 the Copenhagen criteria for accession to the union. See http://europa.eu/scadplus/glossary/accession_criteria_copenhague_en.htm.

The European Constitution, rejected by a majority of voters in France and the Netherlands in early summer 2005, contains for the first time an attempt to describe what the EU stands for and what keeps the member-states together. See Title I, Definitions and Objectives of the Union plus articles I-9, I-10, and I-11: http://europa.eu/institutional_reform/index_en.htm

[3]I have tried to take the analysis a bit further in the following works: Møller, Jørgen Ørstrøm, *European Integration-Sharing of Experiences*, Singapore: ISEAS, 2008; *A New International System*, Singapore: ISEAS, 2004; A New International System, *In The National Interest*, February 18, 2004; A Vacuum in Strategic Thinking, *The National Interest online*, November 2004.

[4]See, for example, Møller, Jørgen Ørstrøm, The Return of Malthus, *The American Interest*, Vol. III, Number 6, July/August 2008.

[5]See, for example, The New Media, Inc., co-author: Terence Chong, *The National Interest online*, October 30, 2006.

This article was first presented at the July 2008 symposium organised by the Asia–Europe Foundation for the book, *The New Asian Hemisphere: The Irresistible Shift of Global Power to the East*, Kishore Mahbubani, New York: PublicAffairs, 2008.

Fight Terror from Moral High Ground

LET ME START WITH DENMARK IN THE YEAR 1945. DENMARK HAD FOR more than five years been occupied by the Nazis. When my country was liberated by the Allies, the most acute, sensitive, delicate point on the political agenda was how to deal with those Danes having collaborated with the Nazis. I gather that the same was the case in all countries over Europe and to a certain extent also in Asia after the liberation from the Japanese occupation.

Denmark was split. One camp asked for revenge — pure and simple. Another camp which unfortunately proved to be in minority maintained that now the time had come to demonstrate why we fought the Nazis — why our political system was much superior to the Nazi system. We could do that and should do that by rejecting revenge, choosing magnanimity, even forgiveness, towards the sinners, so to speak, combined with a flawless application of the legal system for those whose crimes could not be overlooked and had to face legal proceedings.

Then, as now, the basic question is the same.

There are no short cuts to the moral high ground. It is like climbing a mountain. Upwards all the time, you have to strive to reach the summit, there is very little help, your marching equipment weighs you down — but when you get to the summit you feel deep inside your soul that it was worthwhile, that you deserved it, that you resisted the temptation to throw your equipment away. You have overcome temptations to degrade yourself.

Terror, as Nazism and Fascism present the most ugly face of human history. Respect for human lives, human dignity, the individual and other human beings are obliterated from the vocabulary. It is about raw, ruthless, systematic destruction of culture, human lives and values in a broad sense of that word. But above everything else: It is about the right to kill those having another opinion, another culture, another religion, belonging to another ethnicity. It is about stealing the monopoly to shape the world in the picture of a uniform way of thinking and behaving and selecting an unforgiving, bleak and dark model.

The fight against terrorism poses a dilemma for those taking up the gauntlet. Sometimes you feel tempted to use some of the methods applied by the terrorists themselves. It is so much easier. Shoot back!

But let me warn you. This is a short term recipe. It may admittedly give some easy results in the short term but in the longer run it blurs the divide between the terrorists and those fighting against terrorism. And this is exactly what the terrorists hope.

If we do not manage to drive the message home and stand firm on this issue, we will end up in not being much better than the terrorists.

For us there is no other way than the long haul — defending, standing firm, maintaining the moral high ground — never even opening the tiniest chink in our principles. The culture and civilization that we defend is based upon principles that cannot be negotiated. Only by choosing this road can we in the long run expect the people to rally to our banner. And be true to ourselves and what we believe in. If you surrender the moral high ground to the terrorists, you surrender your identity.

After these opening remarks, let me dig a little bit deeper to analyze an international system capable of and deserving to fight terrorism from the moral high ground rejecting all kinds of short cuts.

A viable international system worthwhile to defend for those inside the system and worthwhile to join for those outside should be built upon three key concepts:

— Self-discipline or self-restraint;
— Tolerance toward others and their set of values;
— Mutual respect and no double standards.

Self-discipline

An international system standing on the moral high ground should reflect:

— restraint exercised by the powerful actors, be it in politics, economics or business;
— an understanding of the need to shape a consensus for most, if not all, major issues even if the major player could force the chosen solution through;
— a mutual understanding that there is a place for others on the scene even if we did not agree with them.

Restraint and self-discipline are called for because in the international/global world, repercussions on decisions cannot be confined to the nation-state whose political leaders take these decisions. The stronger, more powerful and economically dominating a nation-state is, the more its behaviour radiates outside its own borders controlling the life of citizens in other nation-states. Exactly the same goes for the large multinational companies. Their decisions influence the daily life of ordinary people far away, offering those people little or no opportunities to raise their voice and state their case.

If decision-makers do not realize this but drive in the one lane, one direction tunnel designed to suit their interests only, the international system will work in a lop-sided way producing inequalities and harmful political and economic environments alienating people from the outside world.

Tolerance

Tolerance is not to open the floodgates for everybody to behave as they like. Tolerance constitutes the right to think and act differently from other people but within a mutually agreed framework. Tolerance defined in this way forces us to know precisely where we stand ourselves. Other opinions must be measured against our own opinion. We must know what we think and why we think in the way we do — what is our mindset and why do we have it and why do we think it is the right one for us? Thinking in this way opens the door for realizing that, what is best for us may not necessarily be best for others. And that gives birth to the crucial observation that the heart of tolerance is that, we care for other people's destiny even if we do not agree with them.

Understanding is the key to tolerance and the key to understanding how other people think and why it may be different from the way we think is communication. Unless we communicate and try to understand each other, there is no hope of comparing different ways of thinking with the ultimate objective of shaping a set of values to serve as the mutually agreed framework without which tolerance becomes a beautiful but empty shell. And without striving for that objective there is not much hope for internationalism.

Mutual Respect

Mutual respect constitutes the unseen ties making a community or a nation stick together. It requires a common set of values. Nationally a common set of values keeps the nation together, and if mutually agreed upon, and applied successfully, produces a solid even robust nation state. A common mindset presents an almost insurmountable obstacle to fragmentation, disintegration and disorganization. By upbringing and tradition, people react according to some kind of common denominator defined by the underlying set of values.

The question remains whether we are prepared to introduce a set of values on the international level to safeguard the identity of people irrespective of ethnicity and/or religion neglecting nationality as criterion for rights and obligations?

The first and indispensable step is to reject any kind of double standards. An international system in the true sense of the word must be based upon and reflect equitable rights and obligations. Equal to the law is not only a nice sentence nationally but must also apply for the international system — otherwise it is not equitable and if it is not equitable, how can we expect it to be attractive for all nations, all races and all religions, especially for those running for shelter from aggression.

As you may gather, I place the burden squarely on the shoulder of those:

— who has wealth;
— who possesses power;
— who is culturally at ease.

They do not only have the opportunity. They have the duty and the obligation to shape an international system worthwhile to join for the:

— not wealthy;
— powerless;
— culturally impoverished, downgraded.

Those on the sunny side of the world model need to share some of their wealth, show magnanimity, be parsimonious with use of power and get rid of preconceived ideas and prejudices.

They should heed the words and act in the same way as a Danish nobleman, Herluf Trolle, did.

When being advised by a fellow nobleman not to go to war and risk his life, Herluf Trolle answered: "Do you know why we are wearing chains of gold and being held in respect by fellow countrymen? Because we rally to the defence of the realm when called upon so that our subjects can live and work in peace."

He was true to his words. In 1565 he was killed in action as Admiral of the Fleet commanding the Royal Danish Navy.

But, there is an iron lining to this silver plate.

If an international model congruous with the principles mentioned above emerges, those not wishing to participate can choose to stay outside — and such a choice should be respected.

However, they cannot choose to attack, to disrupt even trying to dismantle by violent means the international system chosen and built by others just because it does not reflect a set of values preferred by them. The justification of violence and destruction is very rarely supported by the large majority of members of the same culture, ethnicity and religion — far from it. Violence is contradictory to and not in conformity with the teachings of all major religions.

The model should respect the rights of the minorities and prevent the majority from imposing its will on those having chosen to stand aside. But the mirror casts its spell in two directions. So nor should we accept that the minority prevents the majority from living in peace and stability inside a cultural framework chosen by them and for them.

If minorities and/or groups of minorities by acts of violence seek to destroy wealth, undermine economic and social stability, engineer cultural upheavals, such violence has to be resisted and, if necessary, by force. It then becomes a question of defence of the trend making seen for centuries towards a more civilized mankind. War, terror and fear have gradually been replaced by negotiations, civility and a genuine rule of the law.

In the fight against terrorism we must distinguish between the recruits and the officers.

The mindset of the recruits is not much different from fellow citizens. They want a decent life. They revolt against society because they feel they have got such a rotten deal that they have nothing to lose. For them terrorism is basically a social and educational problem. If we manage to root up poverty while at the same time provide education, we can squeeze the recruitment basis dry. But it requires a long-term effort with a substantial financial input. If Asia continues to enjoy high, or reasonably high growth, the prospect of a successful campaign to eradicate terrorism is promising. I have floated the idea that the modem secular world offers the Islamic world something akin to a Marshall plan for education but none listens.

The officers are another breed. We cannot negotiate with them, no compromises are possible. They do not ask for concessions. Their perception of the world is square-minded and single-minded. They want to destroy — wealth, values, ideas and people.

The recruits are social losers but they are told by the officers that they haven't failed. Not the fault of their upbringing, behaviour or education. They are innocent, they are acquitted. Somebody else or something else is the villain, the guilty one: Internationalism or Globalization. The officers use Islam as a rallying point for social losers. By mobilizing Islam they depict terrorism as a noble cause in a materialistic world — a refuge so to speak for many people having lost track of their identity in a hectic world.

What drives terrorism making it extremely difficult to combat is the constellation of social losers not knowing where they belong to without any loyalty to any existing society, being offered a meaningful existence — money, identity and belief — by a small group of fanatics shedding no means to achieve an objective inscribed in destruction.

Let me finish by stressing three points of singular importance for the international world in fighting terrorism.

First, no country, no nation, no culture, no civilization, no religious or ethnic group has the right per se to use power, be it politically, economically, militarily or culturally. The use of power must be justified by being weighed, measured and judged against the principles outlined earlier and the right to do so must be earned by self-discipline, self-restraint, respect and no double standards.

Second, the perception of the small-tiny-group of fanatics believing in terror can never be reconciled with our stance. Whatever offer we make, it will be rejected. But we can reduce, minimize and in the long run — let us hope we have the patience and stamina — estrange the recruitment basis. The way ahead is to improve the conditions for the followers giving them something to gain by joining our world and communicating that they have something to lose by staying with the fanatics. Following that track we may separate the few fanatics from their followers — those who support or even having joined the terrorists because they feel that our world has nothing to offer them and that we have let them down.

Third, challenged by terrorism we must counter-attack applying rules (written and unwritten) making it clear that we occupy the moral high ground. We must be adamant about this. No room for even the slightest doubt. It is precisely because our culture respects such rules that it is worthwhile to defend. If we resort to the same methods as the terrorists, they have already gained their most important victory by corrupting our mindset and let it be controlled by the same evil pattern as is the case for them.

I cannot find a better note to finish off than by quoting Sir Winston Churchill. He wrote as the moral of his book about the Second World War, another struggle between good and evil, and I quote:

> In peace, Goodwill
> In war, Resolution
> In defeat, Defiance
> In victory, Magnanimity.

This article was first published in *New Thinking on Peace*, Singapore Soka Association, 2007.

Wanted: A New Strategy for Globalization

GLOBALIZATION GIVES US AN OPPORTUNITY TO SOLVE PROBLEMS IN A new way — with a worldview of cooperation rather than conflict. But we are now seeing a backlash against the technologies and economic systems that further empower the powerful. Legions of disenfranchised minority groups, downsized workers, and others abandoned by the high and mighty are blaming globalization for their woes. To avoid a massive social uprising, the world's power elite must make a stronger case for globalization — and build stronger ties with the masses they hope to lead to future prosperity.

At the end of the eighteenth century, the world saw powerful new technologies destroying the social fabric of the agricultural and feudal society. The visible conflict was the Napoleonic Wars, but beneath the surface it was really a social conflict between a society based upon feudalism and the new industrial society.

A century later, a similar conflict was brewing and at last erupted in 1914 with World War I. The second Industrial Revolution introduced technologies of transformation — technologies such as electricity, which could turn night into day, now allowed humanity to transform its surroundings. But as with the first Industrial Revolution, social structures were ripped apart, unable to accommodate all those striving for opportunities and wealth.

The revolutions wrought by the new technologies of power and of transformation both created growing disparities with regard to income, wealth, education, and access to knowledge on an unprecedented scale. They created tremendous wealth outside the established elite groups or classes of society, accompanied by destruction of wealth inside those elite groups. This led to the emergence of new political forces shaping the evolution of societies.

The establishment is being crowded out by this onslaught of mighty economic and technological forces. The traditionally rich in society, having accumulated some sense of noblesse oblige or social responsibility, are losing influence as their wealth fades away. The new wealthy elite do not find it necessary to shoulder the burdens of society, their country, or the international community. Why should they? They believe they owe nothing to anyone other than themselves. The nouveaux riches have acquired their wealth by breaking away from the existing society, to which they feel no allegiance. Meanwhile, all those who lost jobs, income, or wealth do in fact belong to the core groups of precisely that society the new elite have abandoned. No reconciliation is in the cards. On the contrary, the nouveaux riches are distancing themselves from political and social responsibility, conveying the impression that this is not worthwhile and that those operating in these circles are losers.

One hundred years ago, we saw the working class coming to power. As yet, we have not seen a new determining political class, but we have seen well-established coalitions inside nation-states breaking up. In Britain, Margaret Thatcher ripped apart the post-World War II political consensus. She could work a new coalition while in power, but her successors cannot. In the United States, Ronald Reagan was the last president presiding over some kind of political coalition. Neither Bill Clinton nor George W. Bush has been able to shape a new coalition. Traditional and workable political constellations have been blown apart without any visible lasting and workable new structure rising to replace them. Political forces are ephemeral and malleable, not foundations for a lasting social and political consensus creating stability. There is growing uneasiness that this may pave the way for a decade dominated by nationalistic, maybe even populist politicians after the policy-oriented politicians in the 1980s and the management politicians of the 1990s.

Trends Portending Social Explosion Ahead

A new social explosion lies before us. Several dangerous trends are clearly visible, including the growing numbers of the disenfranchised and disadvantaged, the sacrificing of jobs and workers for the sake of creating wealth for the high and mighty, and the growing urge among minority groups to revolt against sublimating their cultural identity for the sake of economic progress.

The Elite Minority vs. The Abandoned Majority

The nation-state used to be a strong player in shaping national and international politics. It is now losing influence and power — and fast — especially in its own domestic political and social cohesion. To put it succinctly, the elite are going more and more international while the rest of the population is being left to fend for itself.

The elite minority takes its cue from global and international development. It buys international, it gets its information from international channels, it sends its children to internationally recognized universities, it communicates with the elite in other nation-states and not with the population inside the nation-states. The common identity linking elite and the rest of the population is fast disappearing.

The elite minority ought to lead the way and show that globalization is to the advantage of the nation-state as a whole; instead, it reserves all the advantages for itself and leaves the rest of the population to wonder about the advantages, if any, for them.

No End to Downsizing?

This is happening exactly at the time when business leaders are applauded by politicians and most of the elite have come to the conclusion that the best managers are those who retrench, laying off large segments of the workforce in the enterprises they are supposed to lead. For an economist of the old school, it is indeed strange to read business pages in the leading papers and journals. Column after column is filled with news of layoffs in this or that enterprise. That may or may not be necessary to survive in an increasingly competitive world, but the tone is that this is mighty good.

Formerly, economic science was about welfare and good living conditions for the majority of people. The objective of all economic activities was, or should be, consumption — what else? A whole string of pioneering economic theorists wrestled with the problem of how to increase welfare and consumption for the population as a whole. But the focus of late has been upon creating wealth, regardless of its distribution. The beacons of business became those who created more wealth for an enterprise or themselves by reducing wealth for a large number of persons being retrenched.

The Disenfranchised Begin to See Their Chance

This political, economic, and social challenge to stability is being aggravated by a cultural revolution breaking with almost 200 years of uninterrupted evolution: the revolt of disenfranchised cultural minorities inside nation-states. Potentially this may be the most dangerous threat to the political and economic architecture built since the Industrial Revolution. The nation-state was created to promote the industrial society. Minority groups were enrolled against their wishes, but they benefited just as the dominant groups did from the industrial development, which could not take place without the political, social, and technical infrastructure. This kept the Scots inside Britain, the Bretons inside France, the Catalans inside Spain, the people in Lombardy inside Italy, the Ukrainians inside Russia — the list is endless. They were willing to surrender some, albeit not all, of their cultural identity on the altar of economic progress. And so they did.

But now the industrial society is no longer necessary. Indeed, in many cases, it has become an obstacle to economic progress, so cultural, ethnic, and religious minority groups revolt. We see it most clearly in Europe, where the Industrial Revolution started. Minority groups are no longer ready to surrender part or all of their identity to belong to a nation-state that for decades, even centuries, exercised cultural imperialism, since it is no longer capable of furthering economic growth. In fact, many groups no longer feel attached to the nation-state at all and regard it as an enemy. Instead, they look to the international community as the midwife to deliver them. And, in many cases, the international community delivers.

Why Globalization Matters

Globalization is at the forefront of public attention because a rising share of economic transactions and dissemination of knowledge and information takes place at the international level. In the industrial society, most people could live a whole and active life without much connection to international economic transactions. Not so today. People are employed by supranational companies, they are being promoted or retrenched by companies with headquarters in other nation-states, and they get much of their information and entertainment from international channels. The sheer size of the global economy and its impact on nation-states guarantee that most people feel the consequences of the global economy.

But most people do not associate capital movements, trade, and transfer of technology with the global economy. Either they assume these activities are conducted at the national level or they consider them too abstract to care about. Rather, to them, the global economy and internationalism are represented by the institutions trying to rein in the activities of the supranational companies and constitute some kind of political framework — the European Union, the World Trade Organization, and the International Monetary Fund, just to mention a few. The majority of people aim their criticism and anger at these institutions, because this is all they read about and understand of globalization.

Most people still prefer the national political decision-making process, despite the fact that it has become more or less devoid of substance as the parameters that nations try to control have gone international. What they don't realize is that the global institutions they blindly criticize represent their only chance of gaining influence over the issues that affect them in the same way as they have in the national political system. This is why it is so difficult to move the political institutions onto the same level — international — as the matters they try to control, such as trade, capital movements, and technology transfer.

The forces resisting globalization are led by a powerful political coalition now being forged, including:

- A large part of the population in developing nations putting the question about globalization on the political agenda: "Where is the beef for us?"
- Political leaders from a number of semi-developed nation-states questioning the conventional wisdom that globalization is good for their countries.
- Political leaders from developed countries adopting a nationalistic or even populist policy.
- Globalization-rejecting activists, such as ATTAC (Association for a Taxation of Financial Transactions and for Assistance to Citizens).
- Pressure groups such as Greenpeace trying to curb the proliferation of economic globalization.
- A rising share of the population inside developed nations seeing globalization as a threat to their welfare and not an opportunity.

The dichotomy between the elite and the masses (comprising the retrenched, displaced workforce produced by supranational companies and myriad disenfranchised minority groups) boosts this political coalition. Those who want and are capable of delivering a strong defense of the benefits accruing to our societies from globalization constitute a silent group — having chosen to be silent. The elite do not really bother to take a stand and defend globalization. Why should they? They are doing quite nicely anyway, and probably feel that the threat toward globalization does not need to be taken seriously. Moreover, it is too burdensome to communicate with the population.

The supranational companies use the freedom of localization to shift production from country to country, thus aggravating the criticism against globalization. They demand more and more liberal rules and use them to wriggle free from efforts to control their activities.

The minority groups emphasize their cultural identity instead of economic progress as they used to during the industrial age. In many cases, we clearly see a willingness to prefer identity (culture, religion, ethics) instead of higher production, productivity, or competitiveness.

This last point may be a very dangerous one. In many parts of the world, political leaders confront these dissatisfied groups by saying that, if they do not accept enrollment in the programs offered by society to prepare for international competition, they may not be able to maintain a rising living standard. Until recently the reaction was grudging acceptance, but now the response is becoming, "That may be so, but we are willing to pay that price."

This reaction puts the proponents of globalization on the spot. If the minority groups are ready to accept a lower living standard to safeguard what they regard as their own cultural identity, there is no argument left in favor of globalization. The consequence will be a breaking up of many societies between the powerful elite, with part of the population taking part in globalization and the rest rejecting globalization because — in their view — it represents a threat to their cultural identity.

For those convinced that globalization is the best model, the challenge is to combine the benefit of economic internationalization with the right to maintain and even develop cultural identities inside nation-states. If we do not master that problem, nation-states will gradually break up, propelled by nationalism. This will herald not only the end of internationalism but also economic, cultural, ethnic, and religious confrontations of a very ugly nature. What we have seen in the Balkans for the last decade will not be the final chapter of political misconduct 100 years ago but a new pattern of international and national behavior.

What Leaders Must Do

It would help if political leaders perceived this threat as the greatest challenge to the world; instead, they are captivated by Cold War–era strategic thinking based upon military instruments and enemies vs. allies. The challenge today is to shape a system to facilitate global co-operation — to think and act like internationalists — and not to find out who is going to be the next enemy 20 years ahead and how we are going to prevent that potential enemy from growing stronger.

The political and economic infrastructure governing the Western world (domestically and internationally) since 1945 was shaped by the Cold War. The main characteristic of the international system, as it now emerges, is the end of the sovereignty of the nation-state. The Westphalian system, introduced in 1648 guarding the nation-state and making it the cornerstone of the international system, is out, dead, and gone forever.

Such a turnaround in problem-solving strategy away from conflict to finding common ground would entail the following:

- **Acceptance of and adherence to common values.** This is not what some call monoculture, or a misguided attempt to harmonize culture and behavior, but simply an idea of what is good and what is bad. Without such a set of common values, it will not be possible to reconcile the elite and the masses, nor will it be possible to avoid a clash between those who give priority to their cultural identity and those who favor economic progress. It served the world tremendously well after World War II that there actually was such a set of common values pointing to an increase in economic and social welfare as priority number one, with few if any dissidents. The main problem right now is that this common understanding is slipping away.

- **The creation of a tradition of cohesiveness.** Nationally, a common set of values keeps countrymen together and, if mutually agreed upon and applied successfully, produces a solid, even robust nation-state. A common mind-set presents an almost insurmountable obstacle to fragmentation, disintegration, and disorganization. By upbringing and tradition, people react according to some kind of common denominator defined by the underlying set of values. Globalization's supporters must be prepared to introduce a set of values on the international level to safeguard people's ethnic, religious, and other identities, irrespective of nationality as the criterion for their international rights and obligations.

- **Defining the moral use of power.** Collectively, the world must prepare to rein in the use of power and subject it to agreed rules and norms. Powerful nations must be counted upon to respect these rules in the interest of internationalism. Power in itself does not legitimize intervention. Only by maintaining the moral high ground can international use of power be warranted. An even more difficult problem involves reining in the use of power by the powerful while, at the same time, imposing rules of behavior upon violent minorities as a quid pro quo. The powerful majorities must recognize the cultural identity of disenfranchised minorities, but, too, those minority groups must exercise their distinctive character in conformity with and not against the grain of the community in which they live.

- **Redefining tolerance: Empathy for other people's futures.** Tolerance does not mean opening the floodgates for everybody to behave as they like. Tolerance means the right to think and act differently from other people but within a mutually agreed framework. Tolerance defined in this way forces us to know precisely where we stand ourselves. Other opinions must be measured against our own opinion. We must know what we think and why we think in the way we do — what our mind-set is, why we have it, and why we think it is the right one for us. Thinking in this way opens the door for realizing that what is best for us may not necessarily be best for others. And that gives birth to the crucial observation that the heart of tolerance is that we care for other people's destiny even if we do not agree with them.

Overcoming Fear and Suspicion

Doubts are cast over international actions even where a lot of good will is present. The International Monetary Fund was heavily criticized for its actions in 1997 and later to help Indonesia stabilize its economy, despite this unquestionably laudable objective. The NATO action in Kosovo aroused suspicion and misgivings in other parts of the world, though NATO governments felt that they were moving in to avoid genocide. In these and other cases, international action becomes more and more difficult, arousing suspicion, because it takes place without the implicit backing of a common set of values to remove any doubt about the purpose and motivations of intervention.

International intervention inside the nation-state becomes gradually the rule rather than the exception. But if or when intervention takes place outside an agreed set of values, the fear arises — warranted or unwarranted — that the yardstick is sheer power instead of a common set of values that allows the weaker nation-states to have their say in shaping and operating the international system.

Our political systems and our economic models are gradually moving toward value-based and value-controlled systems. This is a complete break with the past, where both systems were mainly guided and tested by economic considerations. "It's the economy, stupid," is no longer the case. It was the threat to the American homeland and the focus upon American values that helped George W. Bush-backed Republicans to win the mid-term election in 2002 despite a depressing economic outlook. In the same vein, it can be said that consumers are increasingly being guided by values when choosing what to buy. Enterprises are being pushed to produce not only economic accounts, but also environmental accounts, social accounts, and now value-based accounts — what do they stand for and what have they achieved in pushing their values?

Most people can identify themselves with the national political system even if it does not work as they would like it. But they cannot identify themselves with the international system. It is not theirs. It is not transparent, it does not embody accountability, and it loses legitimacy because it blurs the picture about who is actually responsible for which decisions. People feel that in the national system they can reward and punish politicians according to the scoreboard, but not so in the international system.

This is why political actions outside the normal pattern take place on the international scene. Nongovernmental organizations and other forums for pressure groups, plus the large supranational companies, have more or less given up pursuing their objectives by patterns known from the domestic political game. They do not find such patterns on the international scene. They then fall back on non-parliamentarian actions, which the national parliamentarians take as an affront. This produces a stalemate between the outworn national system, which has not been able to transfer its main instruments to the international arena, and the players in this arena, who demand channels to political decision making but unfortunately, time after time, find that they do not exist.

The world needs such channels to accommodate the international players, which sometimes, but not always, are the same as the players in the national arena. It is no longer any use to pretend that companies like Microsoft, pressure groups like Greenpeace, and minorities inside nation-states do not influence political and economic developments. They do. The system must incorporate them in decision making or it will undermine itself.

International organizations such as the United Nations, the European Union, and NAFTA must be better geared to draw the distinction between what they can usefully do and what they should definitely not do. A big conference to draw up a catalog of *dos* and *don'ts* would be the certain road to disaster, but the leaders of these organizations should build their moral compasses so that those in the lower levels of the political decision-making process are well guided. On matters demanding international action, the leaders of these supranational entities should engage in a dialogue with the populations affected by their decisions.

Most people are not against globalization or internationalization, or whatever it is called, as long as they understand and see the advantages — and see that the decisions are made collectively instead of individually by each nation-state. People refuse to take part when the advantages are doubtful, or absent, or serve only a handful of politicians and civil servants.

International actions can only be supported when the objectives they aim to achieve are themselves supported by a large majority of the population. That broad support can only be found when the politicians explain to the population what they are doing, how they are doing it, and why they are doing it. Unfortunately, this is rarely being done, because most politicians engaged in international decision making perceive the process as completed when they leave the meeting room. Indeed, this is where the real work begins, because now they have to go back to their constituencies to rally the necessary support.

What is in doubt, severe doubt, is whether this is the case for the present international system. Our common future depends on creating an international system built on a foundation of inclusiveness, cooperation, and consent.

This article was first published in *The Futurist*, January/February 2004. Used with permission from the World Future Society, www.wfs.org.

Towards Globalism:

Social Causes and Social Consequences

Prelude

Since the end of the Second World War, there has been an uninterrupted movement towards more internationalism and more globalism. The trade system has been liberalized. Capital movements flow freely between the major countries. Information and entertainment do not recognise borders. National seclusion as we knew it in the 1930s belongs to the past. Today our economic well-being and our knowledge base are firmly anchored in an international context.

A network of international institutions has been built to cope with the problems created by the nation state's failure to exercise control over economic, monetary, industrial and technological movements in its shift from the national level to the international. How can the nation state control these developments when they already operate internationally? The international system has been the response to this evolution, exactly as the British historian Arnold Toynbee coined the phrase "response to challenge" to explain the rise of civilisations.

Internationalism has for many years been taken for granted and viewed as an evolution that could only go in one direction. More internationalism and more globalism. The strength and magnitude of economic and monetary flows on the international level and the internationalization of industrial and technological activities have confirmed this belief.

Politicians, industrialists and scholars are all operating in the framework of ever greater internationalism. Politicians consider it self-evident that they have to perform inside this model. Industrialists plan on this basis. Scholars publish paper after paper setting out how globalism will change the world, for better or for worse.

And yet, behind this screen can be detected a growing discontent with globalism. The impact on individual societies and on groups inside individual societies does not seen to be as undeniably positive as was once thought. Widening social disparities lead many people inside the nation states to dispute whether internationalism and globalism really benefit them. A growing dichotomy between the élite and the rest of the population puts a question mark on the social cohesion inside many societies — a cohesion that has been and still is the foundation for stability.

The might of the large multinational enterprises, creating havoc with individual currencies, raises the fundamental question of who is really in charge — who is governing the world.

Basically the political system refined during the growth of globalism seems to have run out of steam. Many of the problems faced by the large majority of people in the countries engulfed by globalism are not addressed by the system — at least not in the eyes of the large majority.

There still seems to be strong support for globalism and internationalism but the support is not as strong as it used to be, and it continues to wane. Policy makers seem to be aware of this.

Gradually the following picture is emerging:

• An élite in most countries that is more international in the sense that is consumption pattern and its communication and information channels are more and more international, while the large communication and information channels are more and more international, while the large majority of the population inside nation states find it difficult to jump on the international bandwagon. The implication is a dichotomy inside the nation state between the international élite and the more nationally oriented majority of the population. There is no dialogue between the two groups. The élite hold dialogues with the élite in other countries. The majority hold dialogues inside their own caucus. The élite marvel in enjoying internationalism while the majority of the population start to ask themselves and the politicians, "Where is the beef for us?" Internationalism still rallies the majority behind its flag, but the ardour of the followers is cooling down.

- A social disparity, meaning that internationalization and globalism result in higher production and a higher gross national product per capita, but also in a growing social disparity. Even if everyone labours in the same stony vineyard, the fruits of the effort seem to be confined to a smaller and smaller part of the population. Everyone knows that total production is growing, but the large majority are not convinced, and sometimes with good reason, that their lot is. This constitutes the psychological and political problem.
- A market that is running full speed ahead without being aware of possible icebergs directly in its path. The political counterweights and the legal and constitutional frameworks controlling the market and protecting it from the worst abuses and distortions have disappeared in the aftermath of the end of the cold war. Market forces have become almost the saint of the century at the turn of the century.

The fundamental questions we face are:

- What are the effects on social cohesion in individual nation states?
- Can we expect globalism to continue in view of the impact on social cohesion?
- What are the policy conclusions to be drawn from the answers we find to the first two questions?

Technology, Culture and Organisation

The interchange between technology, culture and organisation determines not only which cultures flourish and which do not, but also which kind of society emerges as the foundation for the social structures.

For two hundred years we have been living with:

- An industrial technology focusing on manufacturing and the generation of power.
- An industrial culture which praised everything big and homogeneous.
- A model of organisation based on rules governing relations between individuals, organisations and nation states, which highlighted efficiency, precision and specialisation.

Together this interchange produced:

- The industrial society, and
- An internationalisation to promote and control the industrialisation.

For a large part of the period, the model produced the secluded nation state. Everything was based on the nation state. All industrial companies were national, all efforts to disseminate information were national, and the nation states sought to build fences with regard to trade and information to keep outside intervention away. The organisation aimed primarily at distributing the wealth generated by the industrial process. It did not envisage participation in an international framework.

During the past fifty years this picture has gradually shifted. Today we live in a semi-international world — one that tries to assimilate the industrial structure into the stream of new technology and culture, and to shape a model for combining the national organisation with the demands of a truly international society, while still trying to apply the industrial model to the new society. This has not, cannot, and will not be successful.

Industrial technology is being replaced by new technology based on information and biotechnology. Generation of power is of no interest. Now it is about creation, dissemination and controlling information and bioengineering, processes which the industrial mind is unable to grasp.

The industrial culture is being replaced by information, entertainment and adventure.

For both technology and culture, the crucial factor is that homogeneity and worship of all that is large are being replaced by diversity, imagination and all that is small and applicable in various respects. This society can be named the non-material society. Some scholars go a step further and talk about the dream society.

Organisation faces a new era where the rule-based society will gradually be accompanied by ethics, norms and values. People and organisations will behave and act in certain ways not because they are compelled to do so but because they know and feel that such behaviour is the right thing to do. And the right thing to do is what is in their interest and in the interests of society as a whole — at the same time. The broad concept of values appears as the guideline for society (persons, institutions and enterprises). People do not look in the book to know how to behave. They call upon their conscience and values engraved into their mentality.

The secluded nation state is on its way out. That also means that the nation state as a political infrastructure is dead and buried. We face the challenge of shaping a truly international or global institutional set-up able to respond to the problems, opportunities and challenges presented by internationalisation.

And that is where the problems begin. The nation states have built an infrastructure capable of operating inside the industrial society and inside the national framework without realising what internationalism really means.

The social structures are still predominantly national. But very few of the problems, opportunities and challenges originate inside the nation state. The vast majority come from the outside world.

Thus, we have a schism between the infrastructural set-up which is primarily national and the real world, so to speak, which is predominantly international. No wonder that we are running into "cul-de-sacs"!

The New Actors in the Great Game

During the industrial period the political and economic infrastructure was, broadly speaking, confined to the nation state. Once set up, it worked sufficiently well to sustain the development of the industrial society. On the international scene the nation state was the *jeune premier*, in the sense that it was the ambition of the nation state which called the tune. Only late in the industrial period did international institutions begin to emerge, but all of them except one — the European Union — had very limited powers.

As the generation of wealth and the distribution of this wealth are transferred from the national to the international scene, the same is happening for the political and economic infrastructure, which now has the control of this political game as its objective. The machinery to deal with social problems and social structures in our societies is becoming devoid of substance as long as it operates on the national level. It has to follow suit and jump from the national to the international arena. Thus once actor is replaced by a string of actors all fighting for a place in the sun.

The nation states are no longer *jeune premier*. They are performing the dying swan — sometimes with very little grace, but no other role is available in the script of history. Economics, trade, politics, security and social structure — all the elements forming the substance are operating internationally and do not recognise borders. Any form of legal framework to control these topics will prove hollow because the substance avoids any national legislative framework. The conclusion is simple enough: the defence of national interests has to move from inside the nation state to the international level, and that means participating in an international effort to shape conditions that provide possibilities for the nation state to forge and finance the society and the social structures it wants. This explains the emergence of international institution after international institution, and why sovereignty is being transferred so that nation states no longer take decisions in isolation but in common. An often-heard misunderstanding is that nation states hand over sovereignty to these international institutions. The truth is that nation states decide to exercise decision making in common. They do so not because they love it but because they need to. The alternative is "declaratory" decision making — decisions that look nice on paper but that have no impact.

Inside the nation state *the regions* are enjoying new-born freedom from cultural imperialism exercised for decades, even centuries, by artificial nation states. The regions go international in the sense that they feel more and more attached to internationalism and international institutions as a substitute for the nation state. Citizens in Europe feel more like regional citizens, European citizens, than citizens of a nation state. They try to solve their economic and social problems in the context of internationalism instead of through the nation states. The region has become a new actor trying to offer participation in the economic internationalisation and local cultural identity at the same time.

As if this were not enough, *cross-border regions* are appearing as actors in the power game. In Europe such regions can be seen on both sides of the Rhine, both sides of the Alps, both sides of the Pyrenees, in the triangle Vienna-Budapest-Prague, and in the Baltic area. There is more common interest between citizens in Denmark, Southern Sweden and Northern Germany than between citizens in the northern part of Germany and Bavaria or between citizens in Skåne and citizens in Norrbotten.

The enterprises grow bigger and bigger and assume great economic and information-based power to the detriment of the nation state. The nation state finds it increasingly difficult to provide its citizens with social services (welfare, education and entertainment): the enterprises take over. The employees in the enterprises no longer appear as employees but become "citizens" of the enterprise. They feel increasingly attached to the enterprises as they lose their attachment to the nation state, because the nation state can no longer deliver. The enterprises exploit the window of opportunity providing ethics and values to the staff and in doing so become the vehicle for the social security sought by the staff, not so much in economic terms but in terms of mental security. In a world becoming more and more stressful, people look for a safe haven with regard to their identity. They work in the enterprises not so much to earn a salary but because the enterprise and the staff have common values.

The international institutions become, one could say, the decision maker of last resort. This is where the broad framework is being laid down for the economic, cultural and social evolution inside as well as outside the nation states. Those who want to influence these rules governing our societies have to bypass the nation state and operate with the international institutions. The most striking example is that international courts of justice can force nation states to abandon national legislation if it goes against their international obligations. And who decides if that is the case? The answer is international institutions — not many people are aware of this added dimension to decision making.

The pressure groups and non-governmental organisations are among those who are. They have shifted remarkably efficiently the grain of their activities from the national to the international level. Why bother with these national governments and national parliaments when the real power is at the international level? It is far better to appeal to, for example, the European Parliament than national parliament. It is even better to appeal to international public opinion than to public opinion inside a nation state. There are several cases where pressure groups have managed, by playing on internationalism, to force a nation state to undo legislation.

The Impact of Globalism and Internationalism

Social Disparities

Few will dispute the consensus view — otherwise it could not be called a consensus view — that internationalisation and globalism have led to strong growth in gross national product per capita. Many will agree with the statement that at the same time, social disparities have risen. However, the reason for the latter is contested and it is even more contested if one goes a step further and blames it on internationalisation and — to call it what it really is — "a new kind of global capitalism".

The figures leave little doubt, however, about the state of affairs. The latest UNDP report brings to light the following facts:

• In 1820 the ratio between the richest and the poorest nation was 3:1. In 1913 it had increased to 11:1, in 1050 to 31:1, in 1973 to 44:1 and in 1992 to 72:1. These are burning figures.

- In today's world the 200 richest people have a fortune equivalent to the annual income of the group of least developed nations. Of these 200 people, 65 are found in the United States, 55 in Europe, 13 in other industrialised nations, 3 in Central and Eastern Europe, 30 in the Asia Pacific, 16 in Africa and 17 in Latin America.
- The OECD has shown that disparities, defined as income after tax (disposable income), in the decade 1980-90 grew strongly in the United States and Sweden, but less so in Australia, Denmark, Japan, the Netherlands, Norway and Belgium. There was no change for Canada, Israel, Finland, France, Portugal, Spain or Germany. Only in one country — Italy — could a decreasing disparity be spotted.

These figures do not prove that internationalisation is to be blamed *per se*. But it cannot be disputed that there is correlation between this growing disparity and the growing internationalisation of economics. One of the complaints heard from the transition economies in Central and Eastern Europe is that while they do not dispute — indeed they welcome — the strong growth in gross national product, they have to grapple with problems of social disparity hitherto unknown, or maybe kept hidden. One topic that pops up again and again in discussions about the Chinese economy is that while it is steadily producing growth rates between 7% and 10%, observers highlight the growing social problems inside Chinese society.

A *key question* is whether global capitalism can thrive without increasing social disparities inside nation states and between nation states. As the figures mentioned above show, the answer has so far been no. *Another key question* is whether such a pattern is sustainable and if not, what will happen. Or, to begin in a more positive mood, can the pattern be reversed, and is something to that effect already happening?

Attention is shifting towards preventive social policy and the concept of social capital. These concepts constitute the counter-attack.

Preventive social policy implies some kind of conceptual break with the past. In the industrialised world social policy and social welfare were conceived in an exclusively economic framework. If people were hit by the economic onslaught, they had the right to be paid by the state, making it possible for them to maintain some kind of life even if not at the same standard of living as before the event took place. Old age pensions, allowances in case of invalidity, and unemployment allowances are all examples of this kind of thinking. It could even be said that where a person was not able to contribute to the national product, he or she was paid by the state to stay away. What emerged here was a kind of external social diseconomy. It was cheaper for the nation state to remove superfluous persons from the productive part of society and pay them to stay away. By doing so, productivity could be kept high and competitiveness maintained. In other words, gross national product increased sufficiently to allow the rest of society to pay those in need or those without the necessary skill to quit the productive part of society and still be better off.

It is difficult not to conclude that it was a cruel way of thinking.

Preventive social policy means that efforts are directed at maintaining the overwhelming majority of the population — if possible, the whole population — inside the productive part of society, conveying the impression that everybody contributes and that everybody counts. This kind of thinking thus abandons the exclusive economic pattern and opens the door to the psychological side of social problems.

This can be done in a national economy. The problem is to do it in an international economy. How do we implement such policies in a world where there is incessant demand for higher productivity and competitiveness and the risk of enterprises, research and development shifting location — unless we keep pace with the pack in some cases even become the leader of the pack?

On the macro level this requires some kind of contract between the public sector and enterprises. The important thing is to make enterprises an active player in the game. The social system — in particular, the welfare system as practised in Northern Europe — saw the enterprises as outside the game. They did not contribute to welfare. They paid taxes, yes, but that was their contribution and they did not see their role as political or psychological. They felt little or responsibility towards staff laid off because of slimming down or cutting off unnecessary fat or whatever phrase was used to justify firing workers. It was the responsibility of the public sector to take care of those persons in society not employed by the enterprises. This climax was reached during the 1990s, and unfortunately was linked to internationalisation. Page after page of business news announces — often with trumpet fanfares — reduced payrolls and this or that enterprise reducing the number of workers by 5000 or 10000 or whatever number is relevant. One page later it says that the management of the same enterprise has allocated stock opinions to themselves leading to annual salaries of $10–50 million dollars. In this way, the schism between, shall we say, the ugly part of global capitalism and the staff is revealed. Participation in global capitalism opens the window to enormous gains in productivity, and thus profits, provided that a sufficiently tough line is being taken to reduce the number of employees in the enterprise. But how can staff and workers be expected to applaud the global capitalism bringing this about? Or the equation of reduced payroll leading to higher profits producing higher salaries for management? It looks as if management is being rewarded every time the staff is reduced and it seems that the vehicle for this development is globalism.

It is no wonder that the public sector in the nation state finds it increasingly difficult to cope with this burden. That is why there can be seen emerging, slowly but surely, a social conscience for what might be called social responsibility inside the enterprises. In the first place, many enterprises feel that they have a responsibility towards the staff. This goes for a great number of the social welfare benefits hitherto administered by the nation state. It also goes for entertainment and leisure activities. Such a policy makes the staff feel more attached to the enterprise. In fact what is seen emerging could be called a cultural profile of the enterprise providing identity as well as social welfare for its staff.

On the micro level a network is being built among citizens in the local communities and inside the enterprises. People try to support each other. This does not apply — at least not yet — to economic benefits where we are all still on our own without support from neighbours and colleagues, but it does apply to the psychological side of the social welfare problem. A support factor is being built which starts to operate in case of unemployment or other social problems, making the individual feel that he or she is sliding out of the active part of society.

In many enterprises, staff and management are working together to help individuals experiencing problems, *eg*, alcohol or not being able to assume a 100% job. Facilities are being provided that enable the individual to stay inside the active part of society and draw upon the network to support and assist. Special job functions labelled "protected work functions" are being set up. On the other side of the coin are conditions that the individual in question has to accept. In the old welfare system the person received money — and that was that. In fact the condition imposed upon the beneficiary was that he or she kept out of the way. The preventive social policy and the network only function if all the participants — those who help and those who benefit — assume obligations and responsibilities. This is new in the welfare concept. The beneficiaries are now faced with a little list of what they must achieve. If not, "something" will happen — "something" unpleasant. It is not a free ride. It works. The duties imposed upon the beneficiaries make them understand the system and activate them much more than just being placed at the receiving end of a money pipeline.

Lifelong education combined with flexibility and mobility is one of the most important instruments to move this development along. In the old industrialised society people were educated at a young age and that was that. In today's non-material society no education lasts for very long. It needs to be supplemented and to a certain extent replaced by new tools and, most importantly, by new ways of thinking.

The common interpretation of unemployment was that it was a cyclical phenomenon. So people unemployed today could be re-employed a couple of years from now in the same industry doing more or less the same job. Why waste money on re-educating or retraining workers? No need. A welder without a job because of a slump in the shipbuilding industry would re-enter his old job when the industry picked up. As long as unemployment was a cyclical phenomenon, this way of thinking was simple enough.

But now most unemployment is not cyclical, it is structural. People are on the dole because their skills belong to an industry that is dying. The welders in the British shipbuilding industry losing their jobs in the 1970s and 1980s saw the yards being closed down — one after another. Their skills could not be used any more. The 21000 Japanese workers declared superfluous by Nissan cannot expect to be employed again by Nissan or any other car manufacturer. Unemployment is a consequence of working in a sunset industry with an obsolete skill.

The way out of this is to introduce into the labour market continuous education. This means two things. In connection with unemployment, it means that people acquire skills that can be used outside their traditional job. Their chances of shifting to other jobs will greatly increase. The spectrum of job opportunities is widening. They can shift inside the same enterprise or they can shift from one job in an enterprise to another job in another enterprise. It also means that their productivity is increasing, thus reducing the risk that the enterprise will lose in the competitive game.

Lifelong education is thus killing several birds with one stone. It enhances skills, knowledge and the ability to handle more than one function, increasing the number of jobs or functions for the worker in question. It increases the competitiveness of the enterprise.

The drawback is that in the short run it costs money, and the problem is that the enterprise cannot be sure that if it invests in the worker, he or she will stay with the enterprise. This therefore calls for a combination of efforts encompassing the enterprises, the public sectors and the trade unions. Only by such a concerted effort will the chances for a successful implementation of lifelong education on the labour market be sufficient to warrant the big investment in human resources called for.

The key is to think and act to promote human resources. In the industrialised society labour was a production factor like machinery. In the non-material society workers are not workers, they are human resources to be developed. It is what is inside the skull — the small grey cells — that matters, and the ability to handle situations and find answers that constitutes human resources. Only nation states, institutions and enterprises thinking in this way will be able to jump from the old welfare system with unemployment allowances to the non-material society with preventive social policy and lifelong education.

We are moving towards what Joseph Schumpeter called *workfare* instead of welfare and workplace. This goes hand in hand with *social capital.*

Returning to the comparison with the old industrialised society, there were formerly three productions: raw materials including soil, machinery and labour. Later we discovered human capital instead of or as a supplement to workers. Now we discover social capital.

Taking the case of Russia for example, an analysis of that country's endowment with production factors should reach the conclusion that the Russian economy is strong and buoyant. Yet that is not so. Why?

Because there is no social capital. Mutual confidence between individuals and trust in the public sector and other service facilities in society were absent — totally absent. When this is the case people keep their knowledge to themselves. They do not share what they know or their hard-won experiences. The dissemination of skills and knowledge applicable in the productive part of society does not happen. An educated worker knows how to perform certain functions. He is the only one. He keeps it to, and for, himself. He is afraid that if he spreads his knowledge others will take the job away from him. People in possession of money do not put it in the bank. They keep it in gold or US dollars under the mattresses. So the financial system, if ever there was one, ceases to function. People are not paying taxes because the public sector does not provide them with any services, so if they need something they have to pay for it themselves and cannot do so if they have paid the money to the public sector. Society breaks down; there is no network. Everybody fences for his or her own good.

The opposite is a society where we have this trust and mutual confidence. Skills are spread around society not because people are ordered to do so, but because they know and feel this will increase production and productivity, thus making everyone — including themselves — better off. They put their money in the hands of the financial system, which uses it to finance production. They pay their taxes and the public sector rewards them.

Productivity is much higher in societies with a high capital than in societies with little or no social capital.

The key point is to understand the need for service functions to support the active part of society. In the old industrialised society we had the industrial or private sector and the public sector. In the non-material society, with the onslaught of globalism, the borderlines disappear and we see clearly that productivity in the industrial part of society can increase only if it is supported by a strong service sector, for which the public sector must provide the lion's share.

Globalism and internationalism are quite ruthless. No one can hide. Even the most remote corners of society feel the repercussions. Social structures become a consequence of how well we respond to these challenges. If we accept the need to operate internationally and if we understand or try to understand the patterns (opportunities and limits) traced by globalism, the manoeuvring room for the domestic social structures is available. If not, if we continue to think nationally and in terms of the industrialised society, we will be washed away by the strong current and we will then risk a backlash generated by the majority of people.

Communication and Information

The elite look to the elite in other countries for communication and information while the majority of the population are confined to national or local media. It has probably always been like that.

The difference now is the speed and the quantity of information pulling the élite are educated abroad (or at least receive some of their education abroad), they follow international news, they enjoy international entertainment, they adopt international fashion, they travel, they make friends in other countries, they marry across borders. In short, the framework for the élite is no longer the national culture or the national society. Their culture in the broad sense of behaviour in daily life loses the links to the national culture and the élite measure their behaviour against that of the élite in other comparable societies and nation states.

News channels like CNN epitomise this development, as does international entertainment controlled by tycoons like Rupert Murdoch.

On the other hand, the majority of the population are still confined to the national framework. They read national newspaper, they follow national news, they get their education and entertainment inside the well-known, established national pattern.

The implication here is a "dichotomising" of society. To paraphrase Karl Marx, the élite in all countries unite, leaving the majority behind in a national cave.

The dialogue inside the nation state is starting to break down. The sense of commonality disappears in the mist of globalism versus localism. The élite and the majority of the population may speak the same language but they do not mean the same thing in using the same words. Language stops being a part of civilisation. Instead it becomes one of several instruments for passing messages around.

The unwritten understanding that the nation state is governed by the élite in the interest of the nation state as such is not necessarily valid any more. A growing feeling, even suspicion, arises among the majority of the population that the interests of the élite are congruent not with the interests of the majority but with the interests of the élite in the other nation states. The establishment around the world of large international banks, the multinational companies, the behaviour of IMF and the World Bank all work in the same direction. The same goes for the preponderance of the United States serving as the focal point for the élite, and in the late 1990s without any counterweight.

This is one of the reasons why in many countries around the world we see a strong revival of traditional cultures and religions. The élite may or may not take part in this evolution. In fact the élite often try to prevent it and sometimes show that they hold the traditional culture in low regard. In most places the movement originates among the majority of the population. It begins as a bulwark against globalism and internationalism, a way for the majority of people to maintain their own lifestyle regardless of the mighty attack of the global and international flow of communication and information.

So the élite continue to enjoy the fruits of global communication and information while the majority of the population move back to basics. Social structures start to fall apart and homogeneity, if it ever existed, as replaced by layers of society more or less unable and unwilling to communicate with each other.

The concept of *mondoculture* has entered our vocabulary. What we see is some kind of mondoculture with regard to superficial information and entertainment. But behind this screen we also see a strong revival of traditional family cultures pointing well-established cultural patterns with deep roots in national or local communities.

The *first key point* in this connection is whether the superficial mass culture can coexist with the deep-rooted family cultures — the basic culture.

The *second key point* is whether those who get their information from international networks can convince those who want to be firmly anchored in local basic culture that the stream of communication, information and entertainment from abroad is beneficial to society as a whole and not only to the élite.

The answers to these two questions are still blowing in the wind. They will determine whether globalism and internationalism can continue or whether we will see a counter-attack mounted by the majority of the population to reintroduce a more — nationally — secluded communication and information system.

The Education System

The structure of an education system depends on the kind of society it serves — agricultural, industrial, non-material. The social structure determines how large a portion of population will get access to the education system.

In the industrial age the education system was intended to prepare people for the industrial workplace. It therefore taught people how to answer questions and provide solutions to problems. The high point was how to dig a ditch which in various guises accompanied the pupil from grade one to grade twelve. If two men can dig a ditch in four hours how long will it take one man? This related admirably and immediately, without any barrier, to the industrial society. On their way back home from school pupils could see people digging! The education system also turned pupils into specialists but at a later stage in their life in the education system. The industrial structures required mastery of all kinds of tiny mechanical details that had to be calculated and produced. So we had the specialist trained in answering questions and delivery solutions.

In the non-material society it is almost the other way round. The computer provides the calculations — cheaper and faster. So the challenges become how to ask the right questions, how to define the problems and how to choose between various alternatives offered by the computer. If we build a ferry boat the computer tells us that we can have it with a speed of 20 knots and space for 200 cars or space for 150 cars and a speed of 23 knots. What do we want? How do we trade off these alternatives? We need also to think and behave like creative human beings fulfilling the role that lies outside the performance of the computer. We need the generalist to do that, a human being who is able to combine all kinds of data into the concept needed just now (in short, able to conceptualise). Having done that once, the generalist may, a week or two later, have to conceptualise in a different way because our needs may have changed (another concept is needed). The digger has no place in this society; not only is the digging education system obsolete, but its value added is negative as it puts a roadblock — the wrong way of thinking — in the way of people and society.

Unfortunately, the education system tends to become more expensive. In the good old days, it was comparatively cheap and society could afford to pay for education for a large part of the population for a large number of years. Only the very élite educated in selected — self-selected — universities required the students to pay for themselves.

Now the principle of "pay if you can, or stay outside the learning process with disastrous consequences" is creeping into the heart and soul of societies. Apart from basic education, which to many observers is deteriorating in quality, the pay principle hits an ever-larger share of pupils. The implication is not difficult to grasp. The door of higher education is no longer open to everybody, but only to those in the population who can afford to pay. Gradually the principle of "either you are well off and well educated or you are not well off and not educated" dominates society. It is rare to find someone poor and well educated or well off and poorly educated.

This is where the social structure comes in as a determining factor. A low social mobility means that a low share of population gets access to the higher echelons of education, while a higher social mobility produces the opposite results.

Many people have for years heralded the social and geographical mobility of American society and criticized European societies for being petrified. Few if any would dispute the geographical mobility feature, but a similar picture is not detected for social mobility. One of the barriers in the way of ascent from the bottom or even the middle stratum in the United States is exactly that: the pay principle prevents these social groups from moving into the education system and thus into higher strata. There seems to be evidence that a limited share of the American population enjoys the luxury of access to higher education because the rest is not able to pay. The United States thus mobilises a comparatively small part of its *own* human resources. In the much-criticised European societies where the welfare system is practically ridiculed, social mobility is much higher because higher education is financed by the public (at least to a much higher degree than in the United States, even if this is not universally the case). You do not need to be well of to get into universities and stay there for the period it requires to get your BA, MA or whatever. The European societies thus mobilise a much higher share of their human resources. And with regard to social mobility they are much less petrified than the US system.

The *key point* is that social structures and social mobility determine the long-term competitiveness of nations by opening or closing higher education for a large portion of the population.

Now comes the *key question*: why is the United States doing so well in spite of this? Because the country is importing talent from abroad. And who pays for this? The talent-exporting nations? No, the élite in the talent-exporting nations!

The fact that English is the international language, the fact that the US universities rank among the best in all major areas, and the fact that they operate on the pay principle means that from all over the world the élite send their children to the United States to study. This provides the United States with an imported mass of talent which that country has not paid for, and the exporting nations with a smaller highly educated élite even if they paid for a larger one. It also increases the gap between the élite inside the nation state and the majority of the population.

It should in principle be good that higher education is becoming more and more international and more and more global. However, the question looms whether this is indeed so.

The *key observation* is that we have double dichotomy: inside the nation states, between the élite and the majority of the population; and outside the nation states, between the poorer nation states not able to finance high-quality universities and richer ones, in particular the United States.

Minorities

The social structure in many nation states tend to focus on the problem of minorities in terms of immigrants and sometimes in terms of refugees.

The élite become less and less rooted in their own nation and their own national cultures because they tend to be intellectual food in an international context.

The minority also tend to feel less attached to their roots because they often have their roots in another nation state. They are not always welcomed by the majority if they display their original race, religion and culture. The minority do not enjoy the luxury of the élite to choose between various cultures and where to live. The fact that they are torn between roots in the original nation or culture and impact in their new home nation or culture makes life very complex and sometimes uncertain in view of historical experiences that are not always positive.

The borderline between rich and poor often follows borderlines between minority and majority of the population. On top of the ethnic and religious problem there is also a social one.

Either the rich segment of the population belongs to a majority possessing a large proportion of income and wealth — this is the example of some nations in East Asia where the Chinese minority possesses considerable economic power — or the lower social strata are constituted by minorities, often immigrants or quest workers, having arrived to settle in the nation state in question but not being able to work their way upwards.

The *key observation* is that in both cases the combination of social structures and globalism tends to worsen instead of helping to solve the problems. The rich elite enjoy the fruits of globalism and transfer large sums of money out of the nation when problems arise, as was seen in Indonesia. They can only do so because globalism keeps the door open. Malaysia took a step in the direction of closing the door at least for a while when introducing restrictions on outward capital. The poor majority compete with the lower indigenous social strata for jobs in that category, and as seen in several European nation states this gives rise to social and political tensions.

The *key conclusion* is that it is very rare that ethnic and religious tensions are not accompanied by social tensions, and that globalism frequently either aggravates these tensions or makes them possible.

The Political Consumer and the Political Enterprise

As we all know, Adam Smith coined the phrase "the invisible hand", explaining how the market would guide economic activities and determine which producers were most competitive and which products were in strongest demand. Some may dispute that the market plays the role now, with the large monopolies and concentration of financial and technological power.

However, the market is coming into focus as the ruler of another process of selection: the selection of values.

The *key point* is that the consumers and enterprises assume some kind of leadership with regard to selection of values, and they do so by the market mechanism.

The political consumer is a consumer who is building into his or her preferences not only the usual and well-known economic criteria, but also the value factor. The product is being demanded or shunned because of values, ethics, etc. This has been seen for a long time with regard to the environment. What is new is that it is also seen in the area of true ethics — what is good and what is bad. Examples are legion, but to mention just a few: animal welfare, human rights issues and the question of ethnic minorities. Companies such as Shell know very well what it means to be up against a strong trend of consumer preferences based upon ethics.

The *key observation* is that the political consumer becomes a player in the power game — not in the traditional party paradigm but in a new paradigm where preferences select enterprises that have guessed the evolution of ethics correctly. More of the same. This game increasingly takes place at the international level where pressure groups throw their weight around and influence institutions.

There is feedback from the grass roots, and to a certain extent it works. And it uses the market mechanism by way of purchasing or non-purchasing.

Some observers talk about the internet as a channel for democratic expression in the future. They may be right or wrong. But they should instead focus on the already existing use of the market to influence political decisions.

Some would say that this is happening because the traditional political process does not work anymore. The feedback between the electorate and the politicians is becoming weaker. Politicians are being pulled away from the voter because he or she needs to be near the power centre, and in some cases this is international.

Thus, the emergence of the market mechanisms as a channel for political expression is another consequence of the dichotomy between the élite and the majority of the population. The majority and/or grassroots are not heard by the traditional political hearing aids. They then seek other ways and other channels to influence decisions of importance to them and their daily lives. And this channel is to go directly to enterprises and to push them toward the "right" behaviour.

This is natural because what we see emerging is the political enterprise. In today's world very few enterprises can exist, never mind expand, without becoming more and more political. This does not mean party politics in the traditional sense but political in the sense of showing the way ahead and putting forward ideas, ethical values and positions *vis-à-vis* the problems.

The *key point* is that ethical leadership is gradually being moved away from the political game as we used to know it and to the pitch of the large enterprises. Who is most important for the destiny of citizens in a middle-sized European or Asian nation state: its Prime Minister, or Bill Gates, or Rupert Murdoch? The answer is no longer self-evident. So what do we do to channel our views to this mighty person or this mighty enterprise?

The *key observation* is that we force them to adopt values and to put them forward to us. No enterprise is allowed to hide its head in the sand like an ostrich, and not say what it stands for. It is required to do so one way or another, not necessarily for all issues but for some of the major issues on the agenda. An enterprise wishing to invest in Burma will have to say where it stands with regard to human rights. An enterprise wishing to lay a pipeline in the Amazon will have to announce what it thinks about the ecology of the operation. An enterprise selling toys produced in some of the Asian countries will have to make clear where it stands with regard to child labour.

Gradually we see emerging another concept beside the political enterprise: *the cultural profile* of the enterprise.

And here we come to the *key conclusion*. Customers and staff are attracted to or repelled by the values the enterprise stands for. They wish to know them and they wish to express their attitudes. They form a social and cultural link to the enterprise. If the values are perceived as positive, consumers buy the products of the enterprise and staff are attracted to work for the enterprise. If the values are "negative", the customers do not buy the products and staff do not want to work for the enterprise.

Thus the emergence of the political consumer and the political enterprise goes hand in hand with the breaking down of traditional social structures where people are attached to the nation state which delivers social and cultural security. It does not do so any longer. The enterprise as a political enterprise with a cultural profile has not replaced the nation state, but it is among several players moving into the vacuum created by the disappearance of the nation state.

As consumer patterns and large enterprise operate internationally, this development contributes to sever the link between the international élite and the more national-oriented majority of the population.

Conclusion

Where do we go from here?

For many decades the political and economic architecture erected by the industrialized society and the industrial technology served us well. It no longer does so. Social structure based upon the nation state system is breaking down, and often faster than is imagined. During the nineties we have seen the market as an economic factor play the game without any opposition and/or any counterweights. The impact upon our well-known and well-established social structures has been almost devastating.

We face some awkward but crucial questions and political decisions. Do we want to accept an international system able to replace the old nation state system as a legal and political framework capable of controlling development? If so, can we design one? What will the main rules be, and who will be the main players? Do we want the market to continue its forward march without any parapet? Is the present and growing social disparity inside nation states congruent with stable development? Is the dichotomy between the internationally oriented élite and the large, more nationally oriented majority sustainable? How will emerging new players, such as political consumer and the political enterprise, make their mark on the future power game?

All these questions need to be addressed by the politicians. Some of them need to be answered, and fast.

Most, if not all, of the analytical part is readily available. What is missing is the political act — that is, a design similar in scope and determination to the one bringing the world forward in the late 1940s. That one was based upon the national welfare system, the concept of collective security and economic internationalisation.

The *new* design might feature:

• Less social disparities inside as well as between nation states.
• Another concept of social welfare focusing more upon the role (rights and obligations) of the individual.
• Economic and political institutionalising on the international level comparable to the domestic political and economic architecture that served the industrialized nations so well.

This article was first published in *The Creative Society of the 21st Century*, pp. 113–131, © OECD 2000.

The Growing Challenge to Internationalism

TENSIONS ARE BUILDING UP AROUND THE WORLD OVER THE INTER-nationalization of the world's economy. There may soon be a clash between the continued drive for internationalism — favored by the elite in countries everywhere — and the growing feeling of ordinary people that internationalism lets them down and fails to provide an answer to the problems they face.

If such a clash really happens — and the risks are larger than most people like to think — we will have to go back to the drawing board to redesign our basic models for future economic progress. A clash will also pose an acute security problem because it will rip apart the basic fabric of society, letting loose all the emotions that traditionally lead to war and conflict. It will be a major trend shift — one of the largest and most important in many decades.

We have all grown accustomed to internationalism, and we now take it for granted. Since the end of the Second World War, all major changes have gone in the same direction — more and more internationalism, including increasing trade, capital flows, investment, research and development, dissemination of knowledge, and persons moving across the borders, working and attending universities in other nations.

It has been taken for granted for so long that nobody seems to notice the gradually increasing signals that we may be in for a major shift in the trend. Waning support for internationalism may lead not only to a halt in further internationalization but a pull back toward nationalism.

The Rise of Internationalism

What has happened to the world in the last 50 years can be ranked as one of the great revolutions. The world has managed to live without major wars, and, at the same time, it has succeeded in building a sophisticated and effective political framework at the international level.

These achievements resulted from an alliance between the elite and the rest of the population in the various countries. The elite pointed the way. It persuaded the people to follow, regardless of the doubts that surfaced. The population went along, not because they share the long-term political objectives, but because the new division of labor (and other factors) brought about a higher standard of living. The economic integration of Europe took place in the midst of an almost unprecedented economic upswing, which increased people's standard of living year after year. The Asian miracle did the same, first in Japan, later in the Tiger economies, and finally in China. People everywhere assented to internationalism because it was obvious that everybody was better off. Or, to be more precise. The old prescription of an increase in welfare proved valid: Those who benefited could pay for those benefits to those who did not benefit and still be better off themselves.

As the basic economic factors such as trade and capital movement ascended from the national to the international level, the legislative framework to control the basic economic factors followed, albeit with a time lag. The Europeans set up the European Economic Community, which later became the European Union. In North America, a similar development resulted in the North American Free Trade Agreement (NAFTA). None of these institutions would have been created without a genuine and strong demand for international institutions to replace national institutions obviously incapable of delivering solutions to an international world.

But now a new shift is occurring: Around the world, ordinary people — not the political and intellectual elite — are asking whether the international system really delivers the goods. Are we better off participating in that system or would it be preferable to turn around and begin a nationalistic policy? This questioning of the predominantly Western international system often arises among ethnic or religious groups inside a nation that is fully participating in the international model and the international world.

Internationalism's Losers

The international world is highly competitive. Those who still gain from internationalism are the strongest and most competitive people. Those who lose are the weakest and least competitive. The situation becomes particularly dangerous in cases where the dividing line between those who benefit from and support internationalization and those who do not tends to follow ethnic and/or religious divisions.

In Europe, immigrants — often from Muslim countries — compete for lower paid jobs with native residents who are sometimes described as potential social losers. The two distinct groups are set against each other. In Asia, for instance, Chinese minorities in countries like Thailand, Malaysia, and Indonesia control a large part of the economy and may be resented by their non-Chinese neighbors.

To make matters worse, the international decision-making process is becoming more and more remote from the ordinary citizen. The elite may still follow what is going on and even take part in many of the decisions made on an international basis. But ordinary people recognize that they have little influence over decisions affecting their lives. They do not understand *why* the decisions are made or *how* they are made — that is, by whom and for whom — or *when* the decisions will affect ordinary individuals like themselves.

The audience of people ready to listen to criticisms of the international model is growing. In Europe, well-known politicians of the far right in France, Germany, and Austria are getting around 10% of the vote. In Australia, the One Nation party is imitating the European far-right parties. In Malaysia, Prime Minister Mahathir Mohamed echoes the same nationalistic trend by blaming the West for the financial crisis.

These politicians find an audience only because it is no longer obvious that people are better off inside than outside the international system, and because people do not understand the reasoning behind many of the decisions that apparently cost them their jobs.

Many people feel that economic and monetary development has escaped the control that the nation-states once exercised. The market has taken over, and the market produces profits by cutting jobs in multinational enterprises. Meanwhile, small wars and conflicts make the world seem increasingly dangerous, even though the risk of a major world war has been reduced.

The Ugly Internationalists

Supranational enterprises, which are becoming larger and larger, represent internationalism for many people. The fact that the large enterprises operate internationally means that they do not assume as much responsibility toward local communities as do the people living there. Furthermore, there is no channel for communication between the local people and the management of the large enterprises.

The supranational enterprises may also exhibit economic disparity and nontransparency, which are regarded by many as inevitable consequences of internationalism. On one page of a business paper there may be a story about the CEO of a supranational enterprise earning $25 million. On the next page there may be a story about the same enterprise laying off 8,000 workers. For many people this is unacceptable. It strengthens their belief that the elite takes care of itself and is totally unconcerned by what happens to the rest of the people. Anger is provoked further when, after thousands of layoffs, the plant is moved to another nation.

The rise of large, cross-border regions in Europe, in North America, and in Asia has exactly the same consequence.

These regions do not attract enterprises and undoubtedly contribute to a higher standard of living, but they operate according to the role of the market and without a political framework.

Economic integration presents a similar picture. The procedures of the European Union are not transparent, and there is little or no accountability. This is one of the most important problems for the future development of the EU.

The market possesses enormous forces that can quickly outflank established policies. In 1997, the market overruled exchange-rate policies in the Far East, just as it had done earlier in Europe.

There is growing disparity among many of the countries that have shifted from more or less national economic policies to join the international economy. Cases in point include Russia and Indonesia.

No one knows whether the collapses in these nations are due to internationalism or not, but the people in these countries believe that to be the case. They blame internationalism for having disrupted a social model that, while far from perfect, they could live with. Now they have a competitive international model that they do not understand and cannot live with.

A Russian or an Indonesian minister can negotiate with the International Monetary Fund (IMF) but for many ordinary people it seems to be wrong. They ask, What is the IMF? And to whom are the IMF staff accountable? There may be an answer — maybe even a good one — but people in a country like Russia or Indonesia do not know it. On television, they see mysterious people in dark suits being flown in and leaving a couple of days later, and then they read in the newspaper that these fellows have dictated this or that policy, with the implication that rise or bread will cost two or three times more. Internationalism in such cases appears at its worst.

Besides economic disparities, social disparities are growing for several reasons: First, the elite in each country prefer to communicate with the elite in other countries instead of communicating with nonelite elements in their own country. As a result, the nonelite part of the population feels rejected or forgotten. Second, the communication channels increase the division between those who follow international news and those who watch their local or national TV channels, which in turn causes the channels themselves to focus more on local and national news. Third, many elite universities are increasingly recruiting from elite schools whose students come from elite homes. The result is an exclusive world, since only elite parents can afford to pay the costs, especially the cost of sending a son or daughter to an elite university in another country. The result is a cultural and mental fault line that divides the elite from the nonelite and leaves little or no hope that the gap can be bridged.

Security Fears

Many people feel that the insecurity following the end of the Cold War is worse than the military standoff between the two major blocs. For one thing, ethnic and religious conflicts are growing within nations. A minority group revolting against the majority in a nation does not constitute a movement against internationalism. In fact, a minority will often look to the international community for help to loosen the political and cultural ties imposed upon them from the central government. However, that is not the end result. The process continues with three results:

First, the majority in a nation feels — quite rightly — that the international community takes the side of the majority. So the majority becomes anti-international and more and more nationalistic in its attitude. This is what happened in the former Yugoslavia.

Second, the minority finds that the international community is ready to speak loudly but carries a very small stick. So the minority will feel let down by internationalism, because it failed to provide the firepower for their drive toward freedom. The minority ends up more or less like the majority; that is, feeling very nationalistic.

Third, the international community may send soldiers to maintain peace, but only so long as it does not lead to casualties. If casualties result, emotions may run high against a venture that costs the lives of our sons.

So the bottom line is that ethnic and religious conflicts that could and should lead toward more internationalism often tend to produce its opposite.

Terrorism and Immigration

Besides ethnic and religious conflicts, terrorism — state-sponsored and otherwise — is a growing and constitutes a major threat to stability around the world. The ease with which terrorists can cross borders raises the question. Why are we being forced to open our borders so that these people can enter? For many, the answer is internationalism, so nationalism comes to be viewed as a way to protect us against acts of terror.

Immigration is also viewed as a threat. Large parts of the native population of a nation feel threatened by immigration and want the foreigners to go away. In France and Britain, sentiment against Muslims is strong in certain segments of society.

What these three themes — ethnic/religious conflicts, terrorism, and immigration — have in common for the citizen is that what is coming from the outside is dangerous, wrong, and a threat to ordinary citizens' everyday lives. When we combine that feeling with the uneasiness flowing from international trade and investment, we arrive at the uncomfortable conclusion that the international society and the internationalist model is not regarded as a model leading to stability, prosperity, and security. Rather, internationalism is seen as a model that may produce a higher level of total production but only at the cost of insecurity, social imbalance, and instability.

Looking to the future, a growing number of people seem to be concluding that is preferable to have a lower living standard inside a cultural framework established by the nation-state without annoying minorities — in short, a life and workplace that are foreseeable and understandable instead of a higher living standard in a multicultural world based upon internationalism accompanied by changes, challenges, and risks — a life where you must compete to find a suitable place for your talents.

Thus it appears to many people today that in the good old days we had political control and it worked — not perfectly, but it did work. Now, there is no political control; the market, with tycoons such as Rupert Murdoch and Bill Gates calling the tune, and unknown civil servants in the IMF are the ones dictating economic and social terms.

Paradoxically, it is rising nationalism that prevents international institutions from getting the political control needed to avert many unwanted outcomes. Another dilemma is that the domestic political process tends to become distorted: The elite, who want internationalism, pay for social welfare. The nonelite, who want nationalism, benefit from the social welfare. But how can a nation go on with a political majority imposing upon those who pay political model that they do not want? Probably not for long.

Politics now blurs who is actually responsible for decisions. People sense this and realize that the world has gradually slid into a system where accountability for political decisions seems to disappear in mist, and the transparency of the political process is lost in haze. This may not lead us toward dictatorship of the kind George Orwell envisioned in *1984*, but it may carry us toward some kind of nongovernance, even chaos, where the only stable factor in people's lives is some form of nationalism — ethnic, linguistic, religious or even tribal.

The Risk Ahead

The world is still moving toward internationalism, since the elite are still leading the way. But there is increased grumbling on the lower decks. People are not necessarily questioning where the elite is taking the ship, but they are demanding that the crew know where the ship is heading.

Unless the elite manages to achieve much improved communications plus a return to economic prosperity the odds will increase that the majority of the world's people will reject internationalism.

Since the elite will probably still hold on to the international model, there will be a clash between the international-minded elite and the nationalistic majorities within nations. It is not likely that the elite will win such a clash. And if it comes after a period of suppressed nationalism, chances are that the nationalism that emerges will be strong and ugly.

This article was first published in *The Futurist*, March 1999. Used with permission from the World Future Society, www.wfs.org.

The Remodelling of Armed Forces:

A Danish Perspective

BETWEEN 1949 AND 1989 THE BIGGEST MILITARY STAND-OFF IN GLOBAL history took place only 100 kilometres south of the Danish border but not a single Danish soldier was killed in action. The armed forces of Denmark were designed, trained and equipped for the territorial defence of the state against a conventional attack from a Cold War aggressor that possessed a formidable arsenal which was a mere fifteen minutes away as the crow flies. Since 1988, a total of 28 Danish soldiers have been killed participating in peacekeeping operations often far away from Denmark. Not a single one of these operations has had any connection with the defence of Danish territory. A platoon of Danish Leopard tanks fought a small tank action at Tusla in the former Yugoslavia in 1994 and inflicted severe casualties on the enemy. F-16 aircraft of the Royal Danish Air Force have flown combat missions in Afghanistan attacking enemy forces on the ground with laser guided bombs.

For Denmark, as for a growing number of European countries, security policy has been turned upside down over the past fifteen years. Security is no longer a question of defending national territory; rather security now depends upon whether the whole of Europe is secure. For example, the conflict in the former Yugoslavia in the 1990s had a spill over effect on Denmark's security as did the political crisis in the Ukraine in December 2004. As long as European security is in balance and stable, Denmark is unlikely to be exposed to any form of security threat. However, if a political or social crisis erupts somewhere in Europe involving the use of military force it will have repercussions on Denmark's defence.

The definition and perception of security by Europe as an international entity affects Denmark intimately. A parallel may be drawn with the process of economic integration in the sense that, for as long as the continental European economy flourishes, so too do individual national economies prosper. It is now almost impossible for a European country to adopt an economic policy that is contrary to the policies pursued by other members of the European Union. In short, in no other continent are the repercussions of the process of globalisation more spectacular than in Europe. Every individual European country contributes to economic stability and political security in the region. Globalisation blurs the distinction between military operations and non-military operations. This article examines how Denmark, as a European country, has remodelled its armed forces to meet the demands of a globalised world and goes on to make some observations about the likely shape of future military forces using a Danish perspective.

Territorial Defence Out, Intervention Abroad In

To meet new global security conditions, the Danish defence forces have gone through a full scale restructuring during the last fifteen years. Basically the Danish military has been remodelled away from a focus on territorial defence towards a force structure designed for military actions abroad. Thus, Danish security forces have participated in two wars against Iraq and provided a military presence to help rebuild that country. Danish military activity has also taken place in Afghanistan. In Europe itself there were combat missions of an offensive character under NATO auspices in Kosovo in Operation *Allied Force* and military operations were conducted over a number of years in the former Yugoslavia.

The most significant remodelling of the Danish forces has been in the army that has been completely recast in its character. The Danish Army is no longer expected to provide a classic battle line against a conventional enemy. Instead the land forces have been converted into a 'toolbox' from which the Danish Government draw out the various instruments required for operations abroad. A Dane would say that rather than depend on territorial defence forces, one now 'digs into a box of Lego bricks', in order to choose the preferred force model. For example, the acquisition of a number of wheeled fighting vehicles has occurred in order to give the army greater mobility than that provided by tracked vehicles. To reverse General Patton's statement, the aim is 'getting their firstest rather than getting there with the mostest'.

The Danish Navy has also been remodelled. Before 1989 the pride of the navy was its submarine force and missile boats which were responsible for patrolling and intelligence gathering in the Baltic Sea. Today, the Danish submarine force has been decommissioned and it is highly unlikely that any submarines will ever fly the *Dannebrog* (the name of the Danish flag) again. The decision to abandon a submarine capability was hotly contested in Denmark. Many Danes, including this writer, felt that Denmark had achieved a unique experience in NATO in handling submarines in shallow waters. It was a hard-won, exclusive experience that should not have been thrown away but which should have been put it to good use in naval operations around the world, not the least in intelligence-gathering. Despite these arguments, the submarine arm of the Navy was dismantled. In terms of defence policy, the view that submarines and missile boats were primarily combat platforms associated with territorial defence carried the day. Today, a whole new naval force has been developed around the concept of multiflex ships that are able to support operations far away from Danish shores. This offshore policy has delivered the Danish Navy its biggest ship ever, HDMS *Absalon*, a frigate type vessel with priority given to endurance, logistics and support capabilities. A variety of multiflex ships now constitute the backbone of the Navy.

The service least affected by change has been the Danish Air Force. The service has maintained most of its fighter element acquiring up-dated F-16 jets. The transport arm of the air force has also benefited from purchases of Hercules C130 aircraft. In masterminding the remodelling of the Danish defence forces, policy makers were assisted by two unique experiences. First, active Danish participation in peacekeeping operations since the Suez crisis in 1956 gave Copenhagen a useful understanding of what force elements were actually needed for overseas operations. Almost fifty years of active duty in peace operations provided the army with a considerable number of soldiers who had been exposed to the exigencies of overseas operations.

In December 1995, a Danish analysis led to the establishment on 15 December 1996 of the SHIRBRIG (Standing High Readiness Brigade) with seven founding members aimed at providing the UN with an instrument for urgent and vital peacekeeping action. The SHIRBRIG initiative reflects Danish thinking about the importance of peacekeeping activities and, as a result, the headquarters of SHIRBRIG is located in Denmark. Currently there are fifteen members of the organisation: Argentina, Austria, Canada, Denmark, Finland, Italy, Ireland, Lithuania, Netherlands, Norway, Poland, Portugal, Romania, Slovenia, Spain, and Sweden.* Seven other countries, Chile, Croatia, the Czech Republic, Hungary, Jordan, Senegal and Portugal, participate as observers. Hungary, has recently been accepted into full membership, and will ratify its membership of the SHIRBRIG in a signing ceremony in the near future.

Second, surveillance activities in the North Atlantic by Greenland and the Faroese Islands are the responsibility of the Kingdom of Denmark.[1] While both territories have home rule, their foreign and security policy falls under the competence of the government in Copenhagen. Danish defence forces have, for more than fifty years, carried out surveillance missions associated with the fisheries bound-aries for these two geographical areas. For the Navy, these respon-sibilities have provided valuable experience in operating ships for long periods away from Denmark in extremely rough and unfriendly seas. There are many incidences of helicopter pilots having rescued persons and being forced to execute landings in 'out of box' condi-tions. Similarly, the Danish Air Force has had to operate in uninviting conditions in the same area. Indeed, in 1996, the Danish Chief of

---

*It should be noted that Argentina has currently suspended its membership temporarily.

Defence was killed when his plane was caught by adverse winds while trying to land in the Faroese Islands.

The Army of the Future: A Danish View

The modern army of the future is likely to be composed of four layers: a 'bang for the buck' or spearhead force; a mop-up force; a special intelligence component; and an occupation component.

The 'Bang for the Buck' Force

A 'bang for the buck' force constitutes the spearhead of the current US Army. For example, it was demonstrated in Iraq in 1991 and again in 2003, that the choice for the modern armoured attack force is not between firepower and mobility but the combination of both elements. American operations are symbolised by combined mobility and firepower supported by all available forms of information sensors backed up by satellite communication. The weak point of such an integrated force is its high dependence on logistics. In battle, such a force consumes enormous amounts of ammunition and fuel, making it both cumbersome and time-consuming to deploy. Such a force is also vulnerable against an enemy who seeks to confront not its head but its tail by targeting its logistics support.

The high priest of German armoured warfare, Heinz Guderian, taught that an armoured force is invulnerable as long as it keeps constantly moving.[2] Yet, constant and continuous movement requires a tail of logistics putting a heavy strain on manpower and financial resources. And if the enemy actually manages to cut the supply chain, then, the spearhead changes from a lightning bolt into a sitting duck. The mobile 'fireball' directed by superlative intelligence, crushing and paralysing all before it can be extinguished by counter-attacking the thinly protected and often outstretched supply columns.

The US battle plan against Iraq in March-April 2003, was strongly reminiscent of the German attack against France in May 1940. Like the German assault of 1940, the US plan relied upon an armoured spearhead deployed far in front of the rest of the army sowing confusion among the Iraqi enemy and indecision among its leaders. The plan worked in both cases but it was something of a gamble for the US military in Iraq in 2003. An enemy capable of targeting the Coalition's supply lines might have jeopardized the whole ground operation. In terms of logistics, the weak links are 'gas guzzlers' such as heavy battle tanks, self-propelled artillery and other heavy pieces of equipment that may slow down the build up and the operation itself. In the future, thought will unquestionably have to be devoted to analysing how much durability the tracked vehicle offers in comparison to the much cheaper and faster wheeled vehicle.

The Mop-Up Force

After the main battle have been fought and won by the spearhead or 'bang for the buck force' experience from Iraq in 2003 and Afghanistan in 2001 demonstrates how vital it is to mop-up what is left of the enemy's forces. Without being contained and controlled, enemy forces may melt away or may regroup to stage some kind of guerrilla warfare or insurgency operation.

The threat of residual forces — potential or real — must be removed by disarming what is left of enemy forces, fast and unequivocally, by the use of mop up force elements. Such forces, especially their infantry, must be versatile and capable of fighting in urban warfare conditions that are reminiscent of Stalingrad and Berlin while exercising restraint in the choice of tactics and weapons. Human intelligence becomes the key in this phase. Human intelligence gathering must not only be able to detect groups of people and concentrations of vehicles, but must have some capacity to determine whether groups of people assembling behind a vehicle are preparing an ambush or whether they constitute a funeral procession behind a hearse.

A Special Intelligence Force

Having won the battle, and mopped-up enemy forces the job is now to find the political and military leaders of the country whose military forces have been defeated. As the hunt for leaders such as Karadszik and Mladic in the former Yugoslavia, Mullah Omar and Osama bin Laden in Afghanistan and Saddam Hussein and Al-Zarqawi in Iraq demonstrates accomplishing this mission is not easy. As long as renegade leaders are loose, the risk is that they may act as a rallying point and help to mastermind some kind of insurgency as indeed has been the case in Iraq.

The instrument to apply in decapitating resistance is some kind of special covert branch of special forces and intelligence officers capable of operating inside an enemy country before military action starts. Only by preparatory covert operations can a network of operative be created that is capable of striking fast in the slipstream of hostilities.

The Occupation Force

The most difficult component of an army is the occupation force. The need to hold ground is a lesson that filters across centuries of military history. In today's rapid mobile-firepower wars, one may not need to hold ground in order to win in the field but once operational victory occurs, an occupation force is required in order to win the peace. In a regime-change mission, it is essential to ensure that the majority of the population feels secure.

A traditional warfighting army is not trained or equipped to win the hearts and minds of the majority of a population. And, in modern conditions, there are often not sufficient numbers of soldiers available for such a task. The unpleasant but striking truth is that forces must be at hand who have experience in peacekeeping or similar activities and possess education and a deep knowledge of intercultural communication. This type of military component acts as a 'social neighbourhood police force' and guarantees security around homes and work places, repairs facilities destroyed during the fighting, provides basic medical care and participates in reconstructing the local economy.

No existing modern army is capable of performing such a range of operations. The US and British armies are trained and equipped for warfighting, but not for the occupation-style duties of phase four operations. Although the British army has been confronted with complex civil-military challenges in Northern Ireland, the circumstances cannot be compared to the scale of reconstruction now required in Iraq.

The question arising for Western militaries in the future that might have to undertake operations of the kind outlined above is whether their population and the politicians are willing to mobilize the manpower and devote the financial resources for occupation and reconstruction duties. If Western societies do not confront the full-spectrum of operations, the risk is that they will possess glorious hard-hitting armies capable of winning almost any battle, but which are incapable of winning lasting peace.

Armies Manned by Whom?

In the future who will constitute the rank and file of advanced Western armies? Based upon military history there are several military options open to any society. These options include creating professional army, calling up a conscript army or spending money on hiring a mercenary army. These three options have to be considered in the context of a socio-political and economic world shaped by a decreased willingness among democratic populations to serve in the armed forces and by privatisation and a tendency towards outsourcing government services, including security.

The 'bang-for-the-buck' or spearhead army will undoubtedly for a foreseeable future be composed of citizens of nation-states. However the growing costs of even limited wars and the constraints on manpower emphasize a need for coalition warfare in order to share the burden of security. It may be less and less likely that a superpower like US will find it attractive to fight a war like the one against Iraq in 2003 if such an operation must be undertaken alone. The second component of advanced armies, the mopping-up force might also be made up of citizen soldiers, particularly from armies in a coalition that do not possess the capabilities for high speed, firepower warfare, yet remain eager to contribute to operations.

The special intelligence force segment might become privatised since many of its activities might skirt on a legal knife-edge. The temptation of nation-states to disguise such operations might become irresistible. Such a course would, of course, create a contradictory situation in which national authorities seek to exercise control over privatised security while simultaneously seeking to avoid legitimisation or responsibility for the outcomes of their actions.

The fourth component, or layer, of the future military is the occupation army and it is in this sphere where outsourcing enters calculation. Despite reservations, Western nations may be forced to recruit foreign troops or mercenaries for military service. In the future, troops from developing countries may well be cheaper to recruit and retain by advanced nations than citizen soldiers. Such a comparison of military service with economic outsourcing may displease some readers but circumstances are increasingly congruous. In both economic and military outsourcing cases, large manpower savings make a substantial difference in human and financial costs. Moreover, in both cases, little transfer of sensitive technology or intelligence is likely to be involved. The challenge, of course, will be whether 'outsourced soldiers' will possess the proper military qualities called for to perform a successful occupation mission.

Conclusion

Armed forces establishments reflect the nations and the peoples they serve. They do not live a life of their own and in the course of the 20th century we saw two world wars being won by the side having the largest production capacity. Those great struggles of the first half of the last century were followed by fifty years of peace dominated by nuclear deterrence. In this era, the armies of the great powers, with the exception of a few limited wars were not called into action. In practice, the risk of mutual destruction made large-scale war largely unthinkable.

At the beginning of the 21st century, we are moving into an era that is increasingly shaped by two trends: globalisation and technology including information technology, nanotechnology and biotechnology. We do not know what impact these new dynamics will have on war as a concept. It is, however, tempting to see wars as an instrument of last resort at least amongst individual nation-states pursuing globalisation. The philosophy of war as an act of force may eclipse Carl von Clausewitz by not being about territorial gains or conquest but rather be aimed at making recalcitrant nation-states or trans-state organisations observe global peace. Safeguarding internationalism and securing the workings of globalisation are likely to be the objectives of future uses of force by most states. Pursuance of national interests has fallen victim to the intellectual dry cleaning of globalism and the analysis presented in this article may suggest the kind of armies that advanced states will required in the future to wage war.

Endnotes

[1]These two geographical entities are special cases when dealing with military security, strictly speaking, but however interesting or even exciting it falls outside the scope of this article.

[2]Colonel-General Heinz Guderian's book 'Achtung — Panzer!' is regarded as the first textbook in armoured warfare. Guderian proved the validity of his doctrines in the campaign against France in 1940 and against the Soviet Union in 1941.

This article was first published in the *Australian Army Journal*, Vol. III, No. 1, 2005.

The Future of Europe:

Economic Internationalization, Cultural Decentralization, Soft Security Policy

IN MANY WAYS EUROPE IS REINVENTING ITS PAST TO FORGE ITS FUTURE. It is difficult — not to say impossible — to form an idea of the future model of European integration without trying to understand European history and adapt its lessons to the challenges of the coming decades. One striking lesson is that it has never proved possible to shape a politically united Europe. Every time it has been tried, Europeans have met with stalemate or outright failure. However, European history also shows that, despite the barriers to political unification, strong economic and cultural integration has existed at several periods, promoting growth and cultural diversity.

Another lesson is that Europe, as such, has never been united. For most of its history Europe has been fragmented. Twice Europe has dichotomized: the first time during the Roman Empire and the second from 1945 to 1989. Both times the dividing line has followed almost exactly the same lines on the map.

A third lesson is that Russia joined Europe in the fifteenth century but has never really succeeded in gaining on Western Europe despite strenuous attempts to do so during the reigns of Peter the Great and Stalin.

A fourth lesson tells us that the European ship is manned by a motley crew. There are many minorities living inside nation states where they are not always liked or respected. In modern times, most European wars have been triggered by minorities revolting against the nation states in which they have been placed involuntarily.

Speaking about the future of Europe, our task is made easier because many of the tendencies shaping the future are not only visible on the horizon but already putting their stamp on European development. European integration during the next decades will be a hare compared to the tortoise of the 1980s and 1990s!

The reason many people have a flimsy picture of European integration is that they fail to divide substance and appearance. We read about crisis after crisis. But these headlines are always about situational infighting, e.g. does this or that proposal or procedure infringe on the powers of the European Parliament?

Behind this veil of institutional quarrels lies a steady, robust and determined drive to push the integration through.

European politicians have realized that "it is not only about the economy, stupid" but "the economy is international". The lesson they have learned is, that if they wish to exercise control over the evolution — and if they don't want to do that they are not politicians — they will have to transfer much of the legislation from the national to the European level. This triggers both a blurring of competencies between national and the European level and a power game involving 1) nation states versus the European Union; 2) national institutions such as parliaments versus European institutions such as the European Parliament (parliaments fighting not against other institutions but among themselves for power); and 3) pressure groups and citizens' groups shifting their clout to the European level to use European institutions against their own governments and their own parliaments.

This points to a totally new development in exercising power where pressure groups go international. They use international institutions such as the EU, the Council of Europe or the UN to exercise pressure on national governments and national parliaments. We may soon see Greenpeace or Amnesty International represented in the European Parliament but not in national parliaments. Beware, here lies one of the stronger and new power vectors of the future in the mix-up of national and international politics. The outflanking of national institutions!

Recently, we have seen important examples of this. Shell was forced to change its decision concerning the Brent Spar oil platform because of strong protests by pressure groups voicing their opinion in the European parliament and through a boycott of Shell products. This was despite the fact that Shell had a good case even if it seems still unclear which method (dumping or destruction on land) was less detrimental to the environment.

Greenpeace was drumming up tremendous support for protests against the French nuclear testing in the Pacific despite the fact that it was probably not detrimental to the environment and definitely not to the environment in Europe.

Amnesty International and Human Rights Watch play a significant role influencing the nation states in their evaluations of which nations seem to be safe enough to repatriate refugees.

Why is it that these tendencies are felt very strongly in Europe? The answer to that question is that it is exactly the patchwork of European decision making that provides a propitious ground for pressure groups going international and using some of Europe's supranational institutions.

Behind this cloud of institutional bickering, we have a tremendous machine for making decisions and solving problems — the European Union. Very rarely does a member state come to the Council of Ministers with a problem without a solution being found — often within a very short time. Contrary to the belief of some people, the European Union is one of the most remarkable problem solvers ever invented — combining national and international politics.

The problem it faces is that European populations put their feet on the brakes when the integration touches the symbols of the nation states: the flag, the currency, the monarchies, and citizenship. Every time some of these symbols come under fire, a question mark looms whether the politicians have the support of the populations. But that problem can be solved. Of course, integration can be brought about in Europe while maintaining these symbols and by doing so preventing the fears of individual European citizens from jeopardizing the European integration.

These symbols grow from the evolution of each individual European nation state. In Denmark, the Danes feel that they have a splendid welfare system which to their minds is second to none. It is irrelevant whether that is true or not. What matters is that the Danes think this is the case. So, every time the European integration seems to touch on the Danish welfare system the Danes put on the brakes. Even the remote threat of such a possibility triggers off a protest.

The British think that they have given the world the parliamentarian system. Apparently, their horror scenario is an evolution which transfers powers from the mother of all parliaments to the new and unproven European parliament at Strasbourg.

The Germans have given Europe, not to say the world, the Deutschmark and feel extremely uncomfortable to see it replaced by some new and artificial European currency not as solid as the D-mark.

The French are proud of many things including the Force de Frappe. When other Europeans criticize their nuclear testing they feel humiliated and fear that one of their accomplishments is being jeopardized by those they regard as their partners.

Without an understanding of this political and psychological picture, it will be difficult to push the integration further.

Without the economic internationalization, the European economy would be composed of a string of small and medium sized national economies that are not able to survive under the onslaught of American and Japanese competition. The programs consist of the single market — the economic and monetary union — and investment in infrastructure.

The single market introduced in 1985 was and is Europe's counterattack to win back market shares lost to American and Japanese enterprises. The Europeans have been partly successful in their endeavour. The single market has increased growth rates and employment the most important factor, however, is that it has forced European enterprises in the small and medium sized bracket to think, act, and operate on the European and later the international level. Without the single market, most European enterprises would still be national enterprises and thus fade away instead of having grasped the vital significance of competitiveness on the international, even global, market place. In the longer run, this may prove to have saved Europe from a major economic disaster.

The economic and monetary union has been ridiculed by many economists and politicians. Many claim that it will never materialize. They are wrong. It will come sooner than they think. We have already had economic conditions for more than five years among a group of countries numbering around 5–6 comparable to what an economic and monetary union would bring about. This may be formalized or not. If it does, it will probably not take place within the framework of the Maastricht Treaty but outside, grouping not all but a smaller number of member states. That can easily be done. And my guess is that it will be done. And will take place before 1999. I again warn against being fooled by formalities and institutions and thus lured away from realities. One of the realities is that the German Economy is still the largest economy in the European Union but not necessarily the strongest. Look at the forecasts. A decade ago an annual growth rate in Germany of 2.5–3% was compatible with a surplus on the current account of 1–2%. Now such a growth rate cannot be sustained without accepting a deficit on current account of about 1%. When markets realize this, and sooner or later they will, something will happen and that something could easily be very much like economic and monetary union.

The plain fact is that monetary stability belongs in the same category as security policy: it cannot be divided. It is simply not possible to imagine a single nation pursuing monetary stability regardless of the economic and monetary policies being pursued by other European countries. Either a critical mass of member states of the European Union adopts policies to this effect or everybody will be dragged toward higher inflation rates and depreciation of currencies. The German objective of monetary stability can be implemented in Germany only if a number of European countries pursue the same policy. This is what the economic and monetary union will do for Germany.

Add to this that almost all European countries have for some years had real interest rates about double the size indicated by economic theory. The explanation is that they are competing with each other and North America in order to attract savings from the Far East, which is the only place in the world where we find a surplus of savings.

Europe is promoting a large program of investment in infrastructure:

— traditional hard infrastructure to cope with the demands of the just-in-time industrial society; bridges, roads, railways, airports; modern plants require such big investments that spare parts and service must be available not just-in-time but NOW.
— semi-hard infrastructure in the form of communications networks and attached services. No enterprise, no country, no region can survive unless it has access to the international communication network. High quality and low costs are imperatives.
— soft infrastructure facilitates the transformation from the industrial society to the nonmaterial society focusing not upon physical goods but upon services, information, knowledge, culture, leisure and entertainment. All that demands some kind of infrastructure. The country or group of countries realizing this will be world leaders for the next century. My guess is that Europeans, in spite of all the shortcomings and narrowsightedness, are far ahead of the Americans and the Japanese in this respect.

The improvement of soft infrastructure falls neatly into line with the coming of the non-material society with emphasis on knowledge, information, and adventure. This is where we find the growth industries of tomorrow. Soft infrastructure helps to attract these new industries, because managers and researchers in these industries attach importance to the quality of the life surrounding them not only when they work but also in their spare time. As their work primarily consists of developing new ideas, they find it hard — almost impossible — to distinguish between work, family, and leisure. This blurring of borderlines promotes soft infrastructure as a new competitive parameter.

I now turn to cultural decentralization. That means that the political and economic architecture of Europe will be turned back to what it was more than 200 years ago. Most of us do not always realize it, but the political map of Europe based upon the notion of the nation state is the twin of industrialization. The nation state is the political infrastructure invented or rather born to promote industrialization of Europe. No wonder that is being undermined by the removal of the industrial society.

The old European regions reappear as entities for cultural identities subdued by the nation state. Let us take a quick look: Scotland and Wales in Great Britain; Bretagne, Alsace, Provence in France; Catalonia in Spain; Lombardy in Italy; Wallonia and Flanders in Belgium. The 16 German states offer themselves in this context. There is only a handful of genuine European nation states composed by one people with the same religion and the same language. All the others are artificial nation states encompassing several peoples with several religions and several languages. The nation state is simply not capable of offering a cultural identity to its citizens, because most of Europe's nation states do not have such a cultural identity. To mention just one example, there is an English cultural identity but not a Great Britain cultural identity. The search for a cultural identity is brought about through the global mass culture — an American invention communicating messages by a mixture of text and picture. This evolution brings forward the need to distinguish between family culture, work culture and leisure culture. Family culture is the one with a firm set of values giving the individual some kind of security in the face of the pressure of impressions produced by the global mass culture.

The next step is cross-border regions. We see these in Europe today as a very strong lever for removing the nation state from the scene of action to be replaced by a combination of European Union and regionalization.

On both sides of the Rhine, we see eastern France linking up with western Germany. On both side of the Pyrenees, we see the same for southern France and northern Spain. The triangle Vienna-Budapest-Prague offers third example. In the Baltic area we witness a stronger integration encompassing about ten countries. All these examples mean that regions move together regardless of national boundaries. Gradually, we will see that Germans living in Mecklenburg-Vorpommern have much more in common with the Danes than with fellow Germans from Baden, who in their turn do not find it interesting to know what Schleswig-Holsteiners think, but pay much more attention to the neighbors from Alsace or France Comté.

In Southern France, we see Occitania reemerge as a concept for culture, bringing together what has until now been different parts of France from Bordeaux in the west to Provence in the east. In the medieval period Occitania could have developed into a kingdom. Now it puts its mark on European history once again.

The European enterprises have themselves an important role to play as bearers of a cultural profile of their own, increasing the pressure on the nation state. However, it is even more noteworthy to draw some conclusions for the location policy of the cross-border regions. Enterprises operating in Europe will, of course, disengage themselves from the nation-based straitjacket to accept the cross border region as a framework for their activities. Very few will continue to operate from London to cover Great Britain, from Paris to cover France, from Düsseldorf to cover Germany, and so on. Many more will choose Copenhagen to control activities in the Baltic, Lyon, Stuttgart of Strasbourg to control activities in that cross border region; Barcelona or Toulouse in that part of Europe; Torino, Nice or Milan between France and Italy, and so on. Studies by geographers disclose that medium sized European cities have the strongest growth potential for the next decades. They have one thing in common. They already are or could be the center in a region inside a nation state or cross border region.

Let me point to decentralization in the United States: Asian-Pacific interests in the West and Northwest; Hispanic-oriented impulses in the South; repercussions in the North following the debate in Canada; and the Eastern seaboard becomes more aligned with European regions. Inside the states themselves, strong questionmarks mar future cohesion. The referendum in Quebec closed the chapter on independence, but probably only for a while. If or rather when it comes to the surface again it will be difficult — not to say impossible — to keep it away from the debate inside the United States.

On top of that, many indicators point to diverging developments of American enterprises and the US economy as such. Heavy deficits in the public budgets and the balance of payments go hand in hand with strong and rising profits for American enterprises. This points to a development that could hit the United States more than most other nations around the world; the emergence of the supranational enterprise, which does not feel attached to any individual nation state. The Wall Street index rising above the 5,000 mark at the same time as most people would characterize the US economy as weak is an omen of this development increasing the pressure on the US economy.

I now turn to soft security policy. The security problem in Europe today is the risk of not a major war, but minor conflicts triggered off by ethnic differences, cultural diversity and ecological problems. Traditional military instruments can do little or nothing to solve challenges of this kind. Conventional hard-security policy consisting of defending territory with military hardware is out. New soft security policy aiming at stabilizing adjacent regions by economic, commercial and cultural — human relations — instruments is in.

Three great empires — the Hapsburg empire, the Romanov (succeeded by the communist) empire and the Ottoman empire — have for more than 500 years played havoc with the peoples of Central and Eastern Europe. In a belt about 500 miles broad from Finland in the north to Greece in the south we have approximately 25 nations, 25 peoples, 25 languages. Unfortunately, this is not a chess-board, but an impressionistic painting. Geology teaches us that the risk for earthquakes appears where the great shelves meet. So it is in Europe today. The risk for conflicts is to be found where these three great empires met, creating ethnic and cultural tensions. Note, the problem is not a conflict among the great empires but conflicts in the buffer zones between them.

The security policy designed to keep the ambitious Soviet Union at bay — successfully doing so for 40 years — does not provide an answer to the present challenge.

The answer of course is to eliminate the buffer zones. That can be done by enlarging the European Union with the three Baltic States and the six Central and Eastern European countries (plus Slovenia). That would offer these nations exactly what they want: access to the international economy while safeguarding their cultural identities under attack for so long by the Soviet empire and the Russian empire. In short, it means economic internationalization and cultural decentralization. Being a member of the European Union would not constitute a military guarantee in the NATO interpretation of this word, but it would offer what we term an implicit security guarantee. The threshold for aggression would be much higher in the sense that a potential threat would aim at a European Union member state and not, let us say, at Estonia. This is what we term soft security policy.

Such a policy demands a European answer to four neighbors: Russia, Ukraine, Turkey and North Africa. That answer is not ready made, but the Union is working at it, again implementing soft security policy. Russia is gradually being seen as a privileged partner. Russia has always wanted to emulate Western Europe. Sooner or later Russia will be a great power again. It should be treated as such in the interim period. Russia today is where Turkey was 75 years ago as the core of an empire not wanting to shoulder the burden associated with the empire anymore. Ukraine has not gotten the support it deserves from the West — the US and the European Union. It is high time we begin to define a foreign policy about Ukraine.

Turkey has an association agreement with the European Union. The Union needs to make up its mind whether it wants Turkey inside as a member or outside. And if so, what it requires to maintain a country, which has received a no to its request for membership, as an ally in a very hot corner of the world. North Africa constitutes the third potential powder keg in the vicinity of Europe.

For all four we can safely conclude that hard security policy does not constitute the answer. Europe must primarily rely on soft security policy to stabilize the situation promoting political and economic reforms — not an easy task.

At the forthcoming intergovernmental conference, scheduled for 1996, there will be one overwhelming issue dwarfing all others. How does the European Union prepare for the enlargement with the Baltic states, the Central and Eastern European countries and Cyprus plus Malta? How do we go from 15 to 27 member states? This is what the conference will be about. Thus, the conference, even if it is not said explicitly, is about security in Europe for the next generation. The Europeans are trying to find the answer to solve the soft security problems primarily in Central and Eastern Europe and they look to enlargement of the European Union as the instrument to achieve that commendable but awesome objective. The stakes are high.

Some will observe that is it not really possible. We hear from time to time that the costs will be prohibitive. That is not correct. These countries will add about 115 million people to the 350 million already in the European Union. The European Union budget is running at about 1.27% of GNP. Maybe it will need to be increased a little, but compared to the prospects and the potential risks if we do not succeed, it is really peanuts.

If the Europeans are successful, and I think they will be, 5–10 years from now we will see a European Union enlarged with almost all European nations belonging to Protestantism or Catholicism. It underlines culture as the driving force.

In the 1940s, NATO provided security to Western Europe by applying hard security policy. In the 1990s, it is within reach to offer security for Europe as a whole by shifting the weight to soft security. In the 1940s, the US pulled Western Europe from the abyss of an economic catastrophe with the Marshall Plan. It is now within reach to spend economic growth across the Central and Eastern Europe including the Baltic states by enlarging the European Union while at the same time offering Russia a privileged partnership.

In a way it is all very simple. In the second half of the 1990s, the Europeans with the benevolence of the Americans have within their grasp the possibility to stretch political and economic unity in Western Europe to all of Europe. If successful, it will be the first time in European history.

Inside the European Union we will witness strong decentralization diminishing substantially the power of the nation states. The European city-state known from the renaissance period may be reborn. That will trigger off a new kind of feudalism, where the European citizen shifts his or her allegiance from the nation state to one or more of the following: a region, a cross-border region, an enterprise, a trade union, a non-governmental organization (citizens' network), a political party, or maybe even a strong personality.

Such a feudalism may be termed new, but it has in fact been seen several times before in European history. The Hapsburg Empire is a case in point. An even better illustration can be found by evoking the Holy Roman Empire. You may say that these examples point to a patchwork rug. The answer is yes, Europe is a patchwork rug. Fortunately, such a rug is often more lasting and more useful than beautiful tapestries.

This article was first published in the *Futures Research Quarterly*, Vol. 11, No. 4, Winter 1995. Used with permission from the World Future Society, www.wfs.org.

Part 2: Economic Globalization

SOME OBSERVERS ADHERE TO THE THEORY THAT WE LIVE IN AN ERA of the nation-state. Others take the stand that the nation-state is the player in the international concert, but behind the curtain other forces are the real drivers.

The picture is blurred for several reasons. First, the US has been and still is, albeit not to the same extent, the strongest power. The US is important for all other nations and a leading power in all global negotiations regardless of the subject; it is irrelevant to no one and an enforcer in global negotiations. Other nation-states have found it difficult to adjust to the American preponderance. Second, especially over the last decades new channels for exercising power have entered the arena and consequently changed the rules of the game.

The last half of the 20th century was unquestionably some kind of American empire. It was, however, another empire than the one history books teach. The US was not really interested in conquering and possessing territory. Its foreign and security policy was at least to a degree shaped by idealism going back almost 100 years even if the ability to project power may sometimes work like an aphrodisiac! The global institutions were built when the US was the unrivalled power and reflected the world as the US saw it and wanted it to be. It could not be otherwise.

Immediately after the fall of the Soviet- and Russian empire in 1990–1991, it looked like the US was reinstated in the same position immediately after the end of World War II, having within reach to shape a new world order in America's image projecting American values instead of power. This did not happen and from the late 1990s onwards surprisingly the problem put before the world has been to judge whether we see a decline in American power and if so how to deal with it. There are clear signals of temptations for the US to steer away from its hitherto strong and unequivocal commitment to world affairs and put America first. So far such tendencies have been kept at bay, but they are visible and no one can guarantee that they will not gain in strength. Policy makers and strategists need to think about repercussions for the world and for globalization if it happens irrespective of whether it looks likely or not. Political preparation aims at events upsetting the order of the day, posing problems and challenges; there is no need to prepare for uninterrupted continuation of existing trends, well-known and thoroughly analyzed.

One possibility is a movement toward what may be called world governance, not in the sense of a kind of world government, but perceived as more weight to global institutions in framing the development and decision-making on a global level. A look at what has happened in recent years does not give evidence whether we move toward more global governance or the US is still in the driver's seat or a challenge is posed to the US by countries with rising powers. This makes it exciting for the analysts, but somewhat like a nightmare for the policymaker.

It is not becoming easier when realizing the powerful influence cultural patterns exercise on globalization. The problems inherent in the immigration of people with other cultural roots and holding on to them in new home countries are evident. People care for their identity and are not willing to let it go. It is the case both for immigrants and for those already living in the country where the immigrants arrive. A reciprocal threat to identity risk conquers the agenda. As it is happening in many European countries which are not used to immigration and living with more rather than less homogenous cultures for centuries, conflicts have arisen which are capable of undermining globalization.

The role of the mass media is not as it used to be. It is gaining influence by interfering in the political game and establishing itself as a political power while at the same time depending on political decisions — a role not like the one we used to see.

The game is getting hotter as the burden sharing to tackle scarcities and climate change brushes away traditional and well-known issues on the global agenda thus monopolizing more and more of the time and effort necessary to ensure globalization's future.

Asia Looks Forward:

The Decline of the US Dollar

THE WORLD FACES A DEPRECIATION OF THE US DOLLAR, A PHENOMENON that will result in the transfer of purchasing power from the US to other parts of the world, specifically to Asia and to a lesser extent, Europe. An unprecedented economic decline for the US, never evinced in its history, is on the cards.

This is certain to happen. The uncertainty is when and whether it will be an orderly and controlled adjustment under the aegis of the authorities or imposed by a market that finds policy makers not up to the task of restructuring and rebalancing the world economy.

The basic problem on the agenda is not a reform of the global monetary system or more regulation in the financial sector. Although something has to be done in these areas, the real problem is much more daunting.

The US economy needs to be rebalanced. For years, demand has outstripped production leading to a deficit on the balance of payments resulting in debt weighing the economy down. As the US accounts for almost one-quarter of global Gross Domestic Product, a realignment of demand and supply supplemented by a reduction of debt cannot be executed by the US alone. The effect will ripple through the globe and affect everybody else, so it needs to be orchestrated by all the major economic powers. The entire global economy will enter a cataclysmic decline in the absence of a concerted effort at opening the door for countries to adopt divergent, and in some cases contradictory policies.

What is called for is a burden sharing arrangement not only inside the US among the various classes, but also globally between countries. This is something the world has not seen since the early 1930s, when endeavours to tackle a similar problem failed abysmally.

It is almost pathetic to read President-elect Obama talk about creating new jobs to stimulate the American economy by injecting up to one trillion US dollars. The money is simply not there. In good times, the US spent lavishly instead of preparing for weathering a storm many observes were predicting, albeit not on the scale that was recently witnessed.

If the US goes on to print money, and that seems to be the plan, debt will escalate. Some people say that increasing debt will not be a problem, but how can they say that knowing that it has to be serviced, putting an extra load on an already overburdened federal system? It can only be done if spending results in increased production and income, thus enlarging the size of the economy, and even this presumption cannot be taken for granted. Ironically, there are considerable risks that further spending will keep the economy in a stalemate.

Fiscal policy may prove ineffective, dovetailing Keynes' observation in the 1930s that monetary policy in a heavy recession is ineffective. Keynes saw that irrespective of low interest rates, corporations did not invest because demand was not there (the liquidity trap). Now we may see that irrespective of fiscal stimulus packages, people will not spend because they do not trust anyone.

Monetary policy has been used intensively over the past 12 months and rightly so. It has probably saved us from the worst, but it has not managed to turn the economy around. There is very little that monetary policy can do to stimulate demand. The interest rate is low, but nobody wants to invest. The liquidity is there, but nobody wants to lend, preferring to hoard money instead.

So the only realistic policy instrument available is to depreciate the US dollar. The caveat is that although the US dollar may fall, but the Asian economies, through improvements in productivity will wipe out much of the shift in competitiveness it should have brought about. If so, the global economy is back to square one, or even worse, if efforts to improve productivity entail keeping domestic demand in check, the foot may be on the brake instead of the accelerator. The end result would be a ceiling for global demand and growth, keeping the world on a low growth pattern for years.

A falling US dollar will depress real US incomes making the US poorer, transferring purchasing power from the US to other parts of the globe. A more competitive US will stimulate American exports and reduce imports, gradually putting the US economy back on a growth pattern, although not like the one we have seen the last few decades. Keeping in mind the need for a higher savings rate in the US, it is unlikely that domestic demand will improve.

Whichever way we turn the spotlight, the answer to where demand and growth will come from is the rest of the world, and that will be primarily in Asia. It is a misconception that increased demand in the US will bail out the world. On the contrary, demand in the US needs to be kept in check to allow a rebalancing to take effect. The global economy will only start to grow if domestic demand and private consumption begins to climb in countries like China and Japan.

The only way out of this policy dilemma is a coordinated policy response where the US brings its house in order gradually without disturbing the global economy including its own. In tandem, China and Japan acquiesces a real shift in competitiveness to their detriment, while at the same time beefing up domestic demand. Quite simply, the rest of the world must spend more while the US should spend less and save more and production in the US must go up, without boosting domestic consumption.

Such burden sharing would in the medium and probably long-term result in a visibly lower US share of global Gross Domestic Product and a larger Chinese one. The US will start to save and China will consume more. The accumulated US dollars held by China (and Japan) will — at least some of them — be spent, and both the US and Chinese economies will become more balanced.

This article was first published in *OpinionAsia*, 18 December 2008 (www.opinionasia.org).

Obama's Real Dilemma:

To Kill Globalization or Not?

THE RHETORIC OF INCOMING PRESIDENT OBAMA COMBINED WITH THE Democratic Party's tendency to lean into protectionism augurs a much more America-first policy. In all likelihood, President Obama will have to retract some of his promises about protecting American jobs and reexamining free trade agreements. But Asia might be in for a nasty surprise when it discovers what kind of protectionism a new administration prodded on by Congress may opt for.

In the 1930s, the world saw how the biggest economic powers succumbed to a strategy of shifting the burden of economic collapse at home to countries abroad. The US and Britain, the two economic superpowers, hiked customs duties. The US enacted the Smoot-Hawley Bill and Britain introduced imperial preferences. These measures proved counterproductive as other countries retaliated, but it took several decades to digest the lesson.

In those days, countries protected local production by shutting the door to foreign imports. Now the temptation will be to protect corporations by shutting the door to the purchase of such corporations, or a minority shareholding in the same.

The age of dissaving in the US has transferred not only purchasing power, but also capital to China and other countries in Asia, and to the oil exporting countries of the Middle East. Everything would look fine if these newly endowed countries would increase their imports by purchasing more goods and services from the US, thereby lifting

US exports, generating higher employment and recycling the savings into the real, productive part of the US economy — but they are not doing so. Asia can produce what it needs and does not want to buy from the US. The oil exporting countries have a limited capacity to absorb imports, putting a ceiling on what they want to buy.

From the US perspective, both Asia and the oil exporting countries could behave like good friends and just keep their US dollar assets in cash or bonds without making such a fuss about it.

But why should they do so? For years they have allowed US consumers and the US government to use their savings, waiting for a time when the accumulated cash and bonds could be turned from a sterile asset into something of real value, opening the door for a transfer of technology and management know how.

Now their time has come. The US financial system has collapsed and a string of American corporations can expect lower earnings in view of the recession, which may be longer than most observers think.

Many of these corporations will be desperate to find somebody willing and able to financially assist them over what they rightly consider to be a temporary problem. Fundamentally, these corporations are sound, and are able to generate revenue and profit for the owners, and jobs for their employees. But right now they are caught in the storm unleashed by Wall Street. If somebody else other than Wall Street had created this cataclysm, these same corporations would have cried out for help from Wall Street and this money machine would have come to the rescue. But with the potential rescuer playing the role of the villain, where to go?

There is only one place to find the money: Asia and in particular, China plus the oil exporting countries. It would have been their money anyway, but Wall Street would have worked out a temporary credit arrangement with no prospect for a transfer of ownership. But now, the creditor is asking for his pound of flesh, and it is a shareholding that is demanded, not an offer of a loan facility.

America's corporations will fall back on these cash-rich countries and they will be ready for America. The purchase price will be lower than expected, and the prize of ownership a reality hitherto only dreamt of. Ownership or influence over a considerable segment of the heart of the American enterprise system is a once in a lifetime opportunity. Asian capital will move from being an outsider to a main player, owning some of the crown jewels of the capitalist economic system.

Mid-September hosted rumours that China Investment Corp would increase its share in Morgan Stanley. And it is not just the US that is a target. In early August, similar rumours suggested that the China Development Bank was interested in buying Dresdner Bank, Germany's third largest bank.

Some of the capital may come from private investment funds with others from sovereign wealth funds, but it will not change the fact that ownership of American corporations will move into foreign hands and in some cases, into the hands of foreign governments.

Will America be willing to sell its family silver? Highly unlikely, but what then?

The strength and commitment to globalization will be tested. China and the oil exporting countries have played by the rules for several decades even if they may have questioned whether the road taken was really to their benefit. Now the tide has turned, and globalization has offered them real benefits. If that is deemed as foul play by the established guardian of the system, the US, because it is in an inferior position today, then there is a genuine risk that globalization will crack.

The adage that some are more equal than others is a phrase borrowed from political philosophy, but one cannot run a global economic model where the mightiest economic power sees fit to cast aside the rules when these do not suit it any more. For decades, the US has trumpeted the message that the debtor plays to the tune of creditor. This has been the recipe dealt out to countries in difficulties. But today, the US has no choice but to swallow its own medicine.

Sell the family silver to keep globalization intact or introduce restrictions on the purchase of corporations by foreign entities thereby throwing economic globalization into chaos? This is the critical dilemma confronting President Obama when he sits down in the Oval Office two months from now.

This article was first published in *OpinionAsia*, 6 November 2008 (www.opinionasia.org).

WTO Negotiations Crash: What Now?

THE DOHA ROUND OF TRADE NEGOTIATIONS HAVE TAXIED UP AND down the runway for seven years without taking off. The time for the end game had come. Convening the world's ministers a few months before a US presidential election, a year before the Indian general elections, with a lackluster global economy as a backdrop, provided an appropriate setting, considering that failure at Doha was cast in stone much earlier.

Optimistic projections on Doha focused on potential economic benefits, which arguably would have boosted the global economy between a hundred and two hundred billion US dollars. While certainly a figure of note, it pales in comparison to calculations by the International Monetary Fund that the subprime crisis entailed a write down of approximately one trillion dollars for financial institutions worldwide.

The economic repercussion of the Doha collapse will not shatter the global economy — in fact, this was one of the main reasons why the talks were allowed to falter.

The rub of the matter is deeper though. Failure at Doha may be the first omen indicating that the objectives of the financial institutions built in the immediate post-War II period and their decision-making apparatus, do not reflect modern realities and thus, cannot deliver. A hitherto powerful global system has moved into an age of impotence.

The US, and to a certain extent Europe is no longer strong enough to lead. Both suffer from mental fatigue, having shouldered the burden of leadership for more than 60 years. They are definitely not even strong enough to push developing countries and emerging market economies to toe the line as they see it. The latter countries and economies for their part are strong enough to block policy. Critically however, they do not seem to have not yet arrived at a stage in their political and economic development where the responsibility to lead and to burden-share influences their respective policy calculus.

A closer look at the main stumbling blocks over Doha reveal some new elements to be taken into account in future. Allegedly, several countries including China and India demanded farm import rules, which allow countries to protect poor farmers by imposing a tariff on certain goods in the event of a drop in prices or a surge in imports. This demand was rejected by the US.

Despite the obvious benefits and the strong dependence on exports as one of the drivers of developing economies, countries such as China and India chose to set the foot down and stop further liberalisation of the global economy. They were driven to that point because economic globalisation had increased wealth and income dramatically, but at the same time deepened inequality, giving rise to serious political and social problems at home. The Gini-coefficient — a yardstick for inequality — had risen consistently over the last 20 years for China and is now approximately 0.47 compared to an OECD average of approximately 0.31 (0.40 is routinely observed as the high-water mark that signals a worrying degree of inequality).

This explains why the Chinese government time and time again places the development of rural areas on top of its political agenda. During the last general elections that took place in India in 2004, the Congress Party replaced the BJP as the dominant party primarily because growth accrued to the urban districts had not benefited rural areas.

Western observers may not only be aware, but also, disinterested in analysing domestic politics in developing countries. But as the Chinese and Indian cases demonstrate, these countries have reached a level of political and economic development where domestic politics greatly determine the conduct of their foreign and trade policies.

Quite simply, large sectors of their economies have not really benefited from economic globalisation. If the roles were reversed and a similar situation faced the US or Europe, commitment to a global deal that threatened to aggravate inequality would be akin to political suicide.

Five or ten years ago, China and India would not have been strong enough to stop a deal being hammered out between the US and the EU, with the tacit approval from a large number of countries. But now, their share of global trade has reached a level where they can play ball, and even hardball.

However, this is neither the end of the beginning, or the beginning of the end for the WTO. In a year or two, an attempt will be made to pick up the pieces and the circumstances may have changed sufficiently to suggest an agreement.

But one condition must be fulfilled to keep hopes alive — a wholehearted commitment to respect existing rules. The cornerstone of the WTO system, the dispute settlement mechanism must be employed to avoid trade wars. If member states start to disregard rules — as regrettably was the case less than two months ago when the US failed to comply with a WTO ruling concerning cotton subsidies, and/or not referring cases to WTO — the entire regime will be in trouble. Consequently the effort right now must include rallying member states around existing standards, and to adamantly resist any dilution of the legal regime or to the lure of taking the law into one's own hands.

For the longer term, any failure to cut through the maze and get agreement to the Doha round may prove detrimental to world trade, at least in the form observed since 1947.

It will be difficult to achieve future liberalisation. As trade gradually turns away from manufactured goods liberalised through many rounds, to services not fully covered by the WTO, the goal of a status quo may actually amount to a decrease in free trade, forcing countries to look at other ways of securing access to markets.

These may take the form of regional trade arrangements where countries seek a partnership steered by common interests. It is not difficult to predict that such groupings will be formed around strong economies. Weaker economies, in particular, developing nations will be left stranded, since they will not have much to offer in any negotiation. If so, a dichotomised world trade system may emerge, which in reality will work to keep a lid on the weaker economies as the latter seek to upscale trade and production. It may yet be referred to as a world trade system, but certainly not a global one.

This article was first published in *OpinionAsia*, 5 August 2008 (www.opinionasia.org).

Institutional Collapse?

The End of Globalization

THE GLOBAL POLITICAL AND ECONOMIC STEERING SYSTEM HAVING FRAMED economic globalization for more than fifty years, is losing power and influence. The United Nations, the International Monetary Fund, the World Bank and the World Trade Organization all look like a racehorse on its last legs.

In September 2002, former Secretary-General Kofi Annan spoke to the General Assembly about there being no substitute for the unique legitimacy provided by the United Nations. These words reverberated even more so as they were cruelly ridden roughshod over a couple of months later. The United Nations found itself a spectator, having no influence on military action undertaken in the name of the international community. A coalition of the willing was formed and went ahead to do the needful in Iraq.

The basis of UN reforms — especially the automatic and exclusive right of veto for the five victorious nations in 1945 — pose the question: How it is possible to live with a directorate of the five mightiest powers in 2008? Possession of nuclear weapons is increasingly perceived as the ticket to influence. The Non-Proliferation Treaty (NPT), a cornerstone in international "legislation" from the cold war period, stand in the way of nations wishing to acquire nuclear weapons, appears to have fallen apart without much attention. Several countries have acquired the bomb — and have made it public. Iran, we are informed is apparently scrambling to do so. A number of countries are waiting in the wings. South Africa manufactured a handful in the bad old days of apartheid, only to give them up later. Today, aspiring nuclear powers reason in the same way: Influence comes with a posture that forces the US to take them seriously.

Among the powers with the right to veto, not a single voice comes from Africa, the Middle East and Latin America. China is the only power that represents a vast Asia. This is a paradox that defies logic because most of the problems discussed and negotiated in the Security Council occur precisely in these geographical regions.

The International Monetary Fund (IMF) was until early to mid-1990s one of the most powerful international institutions, instilling fear in countless Finance Ministers around the globe. It was the prime example of the influence of the international power elite. Today, it has become an institution operating in a vacuum with little or no demand for its services, desperately searching for a role. In 2003, outstanding loans amounted to almost 80 billion SDR. Last year, that figure was down to less than 20 billion SDR. Many countries simply do not want the IMF to step into their economies as they have lost confidence in the ability of the Fund to guide them through economic and monetary policies — regardless whether the economic aid is justified or not.

The former President of the World Bank Paul Wolfowitz, reinducted the Bank into the limelight, but questions about its role had long been simmering. The Bank had shifted its focus somewhat from pure economics to one with a quasi-moral and ethical ballast, seeking to root out corruption and nepotism. The philosophy of this effort was that such distortions constituted obstacles to future growth. Therefore an attack on them was in conformity with the Bank's objective of growth and development.

This was commendable, but many observers and many countries, even if they subscribed to these objectives, questioned whether the Bank had got the balance right between supporting and promoting investment projects on the one hand, and issues related to good corporate government policy, on the other. The World Bank has — unwillingly — put the same question that harassed on the IMF on the agenda: is it needed anymore? The challenge facing its new President,

Robert Zoellick, is to draw the lesson from business and private banking: you do not do a number of things which you are good at, you do one thing only and that is what you are best at. Concentration upon the core functions is the key to success in economic realm.

The World Trade Organization (WTO) has over the last few years fought tooth and nail to secure approval for further liberalization of global trade — the Doha Round. There are several reasons that account for the increasingly unpredictable terrain ahead. One is the obvious difficulty of switching from agriculture and manufactured goods to new sectors such as services, intellectual property, investment etc., a realm much less transparent and much more difficult to liberalise than the mere reduction of tariffs. The European Union ran into the same difficulties in the 1980s when establishing the Single Market, an enterprise only possible because of its unique structure as a rule-based organization underpinned by pooling sovereignty.

The WTO cannot boast a similar structure. The other reason is that the WTO like the UN, the IMF and the World Bank, hosts an out of date decision-making mechanism. Decisions are passed unanimously. For many years it worked, with "worked" akin to state of affairs where the EU and US agreed, and the rest of the world approved. This modus operandi is an anachronism in present day circumstances when countries like India, China, Brazil, Egypt, South Africa amongst others are not content to applaud, but regard themselves as legitimate decision-makers.

The new Director-General, Pascal Lamy, is trying hard to maneuver round these rocks to strengthen the global trade system. The wall to overcome became more onerous when the US Congress in mid-2007 decided not to renew the so-called fast track authority undermining confidence that Congress would not honour the commitments entered into by the Bush administration.

This new trend in US trade policy was highlighted when Senator Hilary Clinton told Financial Times late last year that she would ask hard questions on whether it was worth reviving the stalled Doha round of world trade talks if she were elected US president. She believed that the theories that underpinned free trade might no longer hold true in the era of globalization. In the same article Senator Clinton raised the alarm about sovereign wealth funds asserting that they posed a potential threat to America's "economic sovereignty".

Three current issues illustrate the need for leadership — leadership that no multilateral institution let alone the IMF, World Bank or IMF is likely to exhibit.

The US dollar's slide on the currency markets is of concern especially since it shows no signs of abating. So far, the markets do not seem unduly worried, but as events have proved so many times before, that may change in a few seconds. Asia, in possession of 2/3 of all global currency reserves has a vital interest in the stability of the currency markets and the future exchange rate of the US Dollar. If policy makers do not step in, markets may take over with incalculable and potentially damaging consequences. Economic history indicates that market driven adjustment tends to overshoot and bring along the unwelcome side effects of economic may be even political instability.

Sabre rattling from the US and the EU augurs the risk of a gradual reversal of global trade liberalization. Even if Asia is becoming a more self-sustaining economic area, it is dependent on access to overseas markets. The Asian economies are developing their expertise in mature industries with research, technology and innovation as drivers. If the momentum for trade liberalization is lost, the opportunity for mapping out future rules for these issues may fade away to haunt Asia a few years down the road. The danger for Asia may be even larger especially when the US and Europe starts to beat the drum, insisting that Sovereign Wealth Funds may not — at least not in all cases — be a welcome investor.

The evidence that global warming has emerged as one of, and perhaps the most important threat to global security and stability is growing almost with the same speed as disturbing reports about deforestation, melting ice caps in the Arctic and the diminishing capacity of the oceans to absorb emissions of carbon dioxides. The Europeans have taken a clear lead while the rest of the world so far continues to sit on the sidelines. The same applies for the US, at least until the presidential election at the end of 2008.

An acrimonious battle about burden sharing has already started, but irrespective of political and economic arguments against it, Asia has to step in and shoulder some of the burden. In such circumstances, it may be preferable to harvest a political point by taking leadership roles to draft new rules rather than to adjust what others may put forward.

Asia will suffer most if things go wrong. The established Western countries are discovering that rules instituted by them to govern the global system have started to work against them and in favour of emerging Asian economies. This calls for Asia to take the lead. If not for other reasons, then out of sheer necessity. If Asia does not, somebody else will and this will almost certainly not be in Asia's interests.

This article was first published in *OpinionAsia*, 3 March 2008 (www.opinionasia.org).

Is the Sun Setting on US Dominance?

Expect Asia to Replace the US as the World's Dominant Economic Force

SINGAPORE: JUST BEFORE OUR EYES A TECTONIC SHIFT IN THE GLOBAL economy is taking place — the Asian economies rising to replace the US as the dominating global economic power. Absolute figures may still give primacy to the US, but emerging trends suggest its grip on the steering wheel is slipping.

The most persuasive signal is that Asia has decoupled, with a decreasing dependence on the US. *The Economist* reported in February 24, 2007, that the increase in China's exports accounted for 2.2 percent of the country's 11 percent GDP growth in 2006, down from 2.7 points in 2005. The figure for 2007 was expected to shrink to 1.6 points. Statistics from the Asian Development Bank show that over the last five years domestic demand, primarily investment but also consumption, amounts to more than 80 percent of contributions to growth. The Asian Development Bank's outlook for 2007 reports that the US, Europe and Japan — the G-3 — accounted for 43.3 percent of Asia's exports in 2005 compared to 53.2 percent in 1985.

The world's savings also take place in Asia, excluding the Middle East and its petro-economy. Asia may not like it, but most on the continent have acquiesced in allowing reputable Western financial institutions to shuffle their savings around, investing them as deemed most profitable. However, most of Asia's financial institutions wisely did not embrace the risky financial instruments that included sub-prime mortgages originating from the US. The sub-prime crisis — triggered by increasing defaults as housing prices slip in the US and homeowners cannot afford rising interest rates — revealed that these venerable Wall Street firms are less than perfect. In fact, many firms sought rescue from Asia's growing wealth funds.

The list of Western financial institutions relying on support from Asia reads like a "Who's Who" in international finance: For example, Singapore's General Investment Corporation took a stake of US$9.7 billion in UBS, China Investment Corporation channeled US$5 billion into Morgan Stanley.

The support does not signify control or ownership, but does signal that global investment decisions can no longer be made without hearing Asia out. An augury of what the world can expect surfaced in February 2008: The mining giant BHP wanted to acquire its competitor Rio Tinto to create a juggernaut sitting on one-third of the world's trade in iron ore and the biggest producer of aluminum and coal. China feared that the new company would use its power to push up prices and stepped in to prevent the merger. With a war chest of US$120 billion, the Chinese aluminum company Chinalco entered the fray offering to bid for Rio Tinto.

Multinational companies originating in Asia, excluding Japan, not only emulate existing Western multinationals, but also forge their own path. Companies from small nation-states like Singapore are active, as can be seen with Singtel and DBS, both of which invest in other Asian countries, but still hold back from the global scene. Chinese and Indian companies demonstrate no such modesty: Chinese companies like Lenovo, Petrochina and CNOOC spread their wings globally, and Indian companies like Mittal Steel, Tata, Wipro and Infosys also enter the big game.

Asian companies are active in mergers and acquisitions, as seen with Lenovo's purchase of IBM's computer division. India's Mittal Steel bought Europe's biggest steelmaker, Arcelor, consolidating its position as the world's number-one steelmaker. India's Tata Group launches the people's car for US$2500 on its home turf and wants to purchase two British motor-industry icons: Jaguar and Land Rover.

Inexperienced compared with established Western multinationals, most Asian firms, particularly the Chinese companies, prefer the minority-shareholder route in this initial phase of going global. Industrial and Commercial Bank of China has taken a 20 percent share of South Africa's largest bank, Standard Bank, also operating in 18 other African countries, thus gaining a foothold in Africa. Two Chinese firms vie for 20-percent stakes of the West Australian iron-ore miner, Mount Gibson. India's biggest bank, ICICI, is present in 18 countries through wholly-owned subsidiaries, branches and representative offices. International operations account for about 23 percent of its consolidated banking assets.

The exciting question is whether a new corporate culture forged by the Asian way of doing business — more cautious, more network-oriented and not compelled to publish higher earnings on a quarterly basis — will emerge or whether the new multinational companies born out of Asia will adopt existing formulas.

The most likely outcome is a gradual transformation of corporate culture, depriving Western companies of their monopoly of not only doing business, but also drawing the lines in business culture. Admittedly, Japan, China, India and Southeast Asian countries have striking dissimilarities in business practices, much like the differences in US and European practices. Still the fundamental difference between Asian and Western business culture remains the Western focus on short-term profits, a factor that was instrumental in the Enron and WorldCom disasters.

The reaction of the Western world to Asia's rise is defensive in nature, bordering on protectionism. For decades, the Western world, in particular the US, praised the free market, free trade and all related principles. Now as newcomers like China and India use free competition to erode market shares of established powers, another tune is heard. The US imposed steel tariffs in 2002, Brazil disputed American cotton subsidies in 2005, and in July 2007 the US Senate Finance Committee voted 20-1 to allow US companies to seek anti-dumping duties on goods from any country that maintains a "fundamentally misaligned" exchange rate after being formally cited by the US. Final approval of the latter legislation is unlikely, but such moves signal a change of the tide.

The US and the EU criticize China for not appreciating its currency. More politicians question free trade as the best model in the era of globalization and talk about America's economic sovereignty. And even as sovereign wealth funds bail out US financial firms from their sub-prime mess, politicians and investors fret about the size and goals of the funds, determined to set limits, as was done when the US Congress put a stop to the takeover of US ports by a Dubai-based consortium in 2006.

Asia may well solidify its position as the largest and most dynamic economy in the course of 2008. It remains to be seen, however, whether Asia is willing or indeed allowed to shoulder the political responsibility that comes with such power. Will the US and Europe relinquish institutional power that no longer reflects realities? One wonders how long members of the G-8 can discuss the global economy without China and India as permanent members and how the IMF can continue to function with imbalanced quotas — 16.79 percent for the US, 5.88 percent for Germany, 4.86 percent for each Britain and France, compared to 3.66 percent for China and 1.89 percent for India.

Such imbalance between wealth and power is a recipe for a global stalemate paralyzing any efforts to put together a framework to take over after the one so wisely crafted almost 60 years ago giving the world the trinity of the International Monetary Fund, the World Bank and the General Agreement on Tariffs and Trade.

This article was first published in *YaleGlobal*, 27 February 2008, © 2008 Yale Center for the Study of Globalization (http://yaleglobal.yale.edu).

Asia to Follow Serfin' USA?

IN 1944, AUSTRIAN-BRITISH ECONOMIST FRIEDRICH HAYEK PUBLISHED *The Road to Serfdom* arguing that any form of collectivism — he targeted communism and fascism — would lead to the destruction of all individual economic and personal freedom. Under Hayek's banner, politicians such as US president Ronald Reagan and British prime minister Margaret Thatcher led the struggle against communism, socialism and the social welfare state.

It is one of history's strange paradoxes that unwillingly they and others sharing their philosophy have led us into a situation where the individual finds him/her in exactly the situation against which Hayek warned so eloquently and convincingly. Two illusions have emerged: the illusion of ownership through the boom in leasing and the illusion that one can live a risk-free, consequences-free life.

After the end of the duel between capitalism and communism in 1991, centralization of capital has put economic decisions in the hands of the few, turned free-markets and free competition into a relic of the past and removed any reminiscences of Scottish economist Adam Smith's theory of the market acting as an invisible hand.

Most of us looked forward to liberal values with the individual as owner of homes, cars and other durable consumer goods, but it does not quite look that way. A leasing economy has taken the place of the market economy. Financial institutions provide money to the consumer conditioned on de facto ownership until the loan is paid back. The operation of the debt market is based on revolving credits that serve to perpetuate themselves and protect the financial institutions rather than to truly serve borrowers and consumers.

The large outstanding loans indicate that payback increasingly fills the role as exception to the rule relegating individuals to leasing property and goods. Looked at in the terms of capitalism and communism, this is much more communism than capitalism, albeit with the difference that large funds instead of state-owned assets control economic activity. The owners of quite a few funds are anonymous and the funds are not always listed on the stock exchange and are not always subject to the rules of transparency. The public does not know who owns their homes through mortgaging or their cars through loans. A labyrinth of faceless intermediaries has replaced the age-old direct link between debtor and creditor.

Not many will step forward to defend the workings of centrally planned economies as they utterly failed, but you have to look for brave people to find praise for the workings of capitalism since 1990, it having delivered several financial crises and accumulated wealth and income into a few hands. The capitalistic model has proven itself as a superior growth machine, but has squandered the opportunity to allocate wealth in an equitable way and lay the foundation for sound and stable economic development. Furthermore, it is beginning to rub out the very core market principles that should have been its lodestar.

How Has It Come to That?

The property market in the US and parts of Europe, with rising prices and reckless lending by many financial institutions, is the obvious starting point. By offering very attractive loans, financial institutions lured potential homeowners to buy beyond their means. The loans did not draw interest or payback for an initial period. The lender and the borrower hoped that the value would go up, offering the opportunity to extend the loan or even increase the loan.

In many cases, elderly people joined this wagon by borrowing to finance their old-age consumption, not having a sufficiently large pension. They mortgaged their home with the result that after their death the home would not go to their children but to the real owners: the mortgage institution. The operation of the debt market weighs heavily on revolving credit that serves to perpetuate itself and protect the institutions behind it rather than to truly serve borrowers and consumers.

As the subprime crisis in the US shows, this was simply irresistible to almost the whole range of financial institutions entering this market, inventing new financial instruments to reallocate and resell the loans between financial institutions. Millions of people jumped into this frying pan, rejoicing in being homeowners without realizing that they were nothing of the sort, in reality transferring their homes from individual ownership to institutional ownership.

Even worse. As falling home prices do not yield sufficient money to redeem original loans, buyers depend on lenders to offer terms stretching over many years. They become serfs as Hayek warned, not of the state but of financial institutions with an obscure ownership having little or no interest in softening the economic blow for millions of people.

The stock market shows a similar pattern. In 1965, individuals owned the majority of US stocks, with 84% and only 16% in the hands of institutions/funds. In 2005, institutions owned 67% and individuals 33%. Ordinary common sense tells that control over the large part of corporations in the US has changed from individual stockholders to institutional ones with the inescapable observation that the whole panoply of measures to ensure corporate governance geared to the old model had to be changed. The misery of the individual is being almost completed by the credit card business. Outstanding debt is growing enormously and is now about US$900 billion, equal to 7–8% of current US gross domestic product. Each month, credit cards holders pay to the companies 16% of outstanding balances, but that figure covers those who pay the full amount as well as those carrying debt forward from month to month with an interest rate of more than 13%. This explains why it does not take long for some credit cards holders to run up an insurmountable debt.

Analysis of the subprime crisis tells that it is neither new nor special. Like all previous crises, solutions will be found. Debts and assets will be shuffled around between institutions. Some individuals, corporations and financial institutions will declare bankruptcy and after a while the debt will have been brought down to a manageable level.

But there is something new behind the veil. And that is the obliteration of individual ownership of homes and many durable goods with the individual replaced by the real owners the financial institutions and/or funds. Inspired by British statesman Winston Churchill, we might put it this way: never in the history of mankind have so few owned so much taken from so many who believed it was theirs'.

The present debt crisis suggests a need for the consumer to get back to the basic principles of individual responsibility plus accountability and for the financial system to reinvent ethics prohibiting products that through their complexity disguise risks and make the debtor and creditor unknown to each other.

If not, the unanswered question is what kind of society this will bring about. Certainly not a liberal economy and a market state with the invisible hand and the individual in the driver's seat. The world may enter an era of institutionalized economics with capital, money, ownership and power to steer the economy according to the wishes and preferences of institutions.

As recent experience suggests, that will tend to override signals from the market, open the door to accumulate capital value and make a virtue of short-term profits irrespective of long-term consequences. The potential for the individual to pursue his/her preferences and safeguard economic interests will be limited, very limited indeed. That is why Hayek's prophetic words may come true more than 60 years after he wrote them and inside the kind of society he thought would prevent this from happening.

Asia is still in the early phase of searching for an economic and social model. At present, it is a mixture of Western capitalism and Asian institutionalism. Further down the road, Asia may have to follow either the US and disown private ownership with all the consequences that implies for economics and social structure, or endorse the old-fashioned core virtues of the market economy. It would be one of history's whims if Asia swings towards the market economy and private ownership at the very moment these long-cherished assets lose favor in the US.

This article was first published in *Asia Times Online*, 10 January 2008 (www.atimes.com).

Post-Bali and Post-Kyoto:

Who Shall Pay for Climate Change?

A SEISMIC POLICY SHIFT NEEDS TO TAKE PLACE BEFORE THE IMPENDING environmental crisis can be addressed. Negotiations have to target the ultimate polluter; the consumer, regardless where production of the goods or services take place. Such a policy would also be consistent with globalisation.

A signal has been received to initiate what could arguably turn out to be one of the most pitiless brawls about global burden sharing since the cycle of globalisation began in the late 1940s. At the heart of this envisaged quagmire is the question of who is going to fund the reduction of emissions of greenhouse gases now on the agenda for a host of meetings to find a replacement or amended extension to the Kyoto Protocol, expiring in 2012.

The 13th session of the United Nations Framework Convention on Climate Change (UNFCCC) Conference of Parties in Bali has opened a race geared to finish in Copenhagen at the end of 2009. Ratification and implementation, among a host of other commitments, make it imperative that a new regime comes to force before the end of 2009 to ensure that the world is not left without any international framework covering greenhouse gasses after 2012.

The Kyoto-protocol was forged in the mould of yesterday's world — a world dominated by the nation-state and its pursuance of national interests. Quotas were specified for countries, albeit accompanied by a mechanism that allowed for the trading of certificates among nation-states. In principle, this should have led to higher efficiency as those who were able to pay, could buy quotas from countries that did not require them.

The ostensible reality, in relative terms, was that rich nation-states had capital, while the poor and newly industrialised nation-states did not. Given such a schema, the end result was that established producers could purchase certificates to 'monopolise' production. Or in other words, instead of flexibility channeling production where it is most efficient, it may bring about a petrified production structure where producers in established industrial nation-states purchase certificates, in effect, crowding out their potential competitors in less developed countries.

This is probably one of the reasons that some of the rising nation-states such as China vigorously reject most of the proposals on the table, propounding that rich nation-states having enjoyed a free ride in their industrialisation process many years ago, should now bear the brunt of the burden of halting and hopefully reversing climate change.

Many industrialised nation-states may not necessarily reject that argument, but are tepid and disagreeable to the second proposition — that they assume the lion's share of the burden in addressing climate change. These industrialised countries maintain that while they may have polluted the environment during their rise to power, the environment was not a problem then, as it is now. Today, emission levels have reached a stage where the problem is acute. And in the minds of the industrialised nation states — the rising economic powers are the culprits in chief.

The current dispute seems to overlook an analogous debate when environmental policies took off in some industrialised countries in the 1960s and 1970s. Then, consumers and industry were at each other's throat, trying to shuffle the burden around hoping that the burden-sharing fight would lead to a stalemate so everybody could be left off cheaply in the short term.

The Gordian knot was cut in those days — well, more or less — by the PPP or the Polluter Pays Principle which stated that the ultimate polluter was neither industry nor the public, but the consumer. The implication of this principle, transferred from theory to practice, was a number of taxes and levies designed to be passed to the ultimate polluter. In many industrialised countries water levies, taxes on solid waste, petrol taxes, have been introduced. And apparently, it worked.

A dramatic qualitative improvement in environmental standards and energy efficiency is noticeable in countries such as Japan and many of the European countries, especially in Northern Europe. This marked improvement can only be ascribed to the change in price structure — one that penalises polluters and rewards less pollutive goods or production processes mainly by way of levies and subsidies.

This hard won experience informs that one can only go some way with declarations and regulation. In the final analysis, what matters is to make the ultimate polluter feel the pinch on his or her purse. Only through such an emotive is there any prospect of green house emissions falling.

As long as the discussion revolves around quotas or regulations allocated to nation-states, the chance for an effective agreement is remote. The circus of accusations and counter-accusations are likely to continue. Having committed themselves so clearly and in some cases unequivocally, to mutually incompatible policy positions, it is close to inconceivable that many countries will have a change of heart in the short to medium term on how to engender positive climate change.

A seismic policy shift needs to take place before the impending environmental crisis can be addressed. Negotiations have to target the ultimate polluter: the consumer. That will make it clear that it is not the producer in China, the US, Europe or Singapore that is ultimately responsible, but the consumer wherever he or she is. The burden has to be passed on to the consumer regardless of where production takes place. Such a policy, fully in accordance with national application of PPP, turns the sometimes almost theological arguments about national quotas into a mirage. It would also be consistent with globalisation.

Just follow this reasoning. Outsourcing from the US or Europe to China would cause Chinese emission levels to rise. Global production and consumption is unchanged, but with a system based upon national quotas, China would have to 'pay' more. But such a state of affairs makes no sense when the consumer in both cases plays the role of the polluter or emitter. The shift to a geographical place of production should only influence the distribution of the burden if outsourcing also connotes a shift from a less pollutive production process to a more pollutive one. A mechanism to that effect could be built into a PPP model.

Such a solution would understandably put the newly industrialising countries in a bizarre quandary. A national quota model places them between the devil and the deep blue sea. Either ways, they absorb the cost reflecting rising production and emission levels. Or, their refusal runs the risk that rich countries will move towards some kind of 'coalition of the willing' ready to impose levies. And even if the new industralising countries try to pass on the cost to the consumer by increasing prices, they might undermine their own competitiveness vis-à-vis the already industrialised countries.

All three options appear problematic hence the call to develop an agreement that paves the way for the international community to pass on the costs to the ultimate polluter/emitter, in such a way that does not distort competitive advantages and influence relative production costs.

If such a road is not found, two outcomes, both of which look rather unpalatable, may haunt the global economy. The first one is a complete break down, leaving an international agreement on climate change hanging in the air. The second is a mix of political compromises that will probably force a cost increase on rising nation-states, introducing global inflation as those nation-states increase their export prices. That would be the last thing the world needs now with high oil prices, a continually unfolding sub prime crisis and falling growth in the US. Rich countries should not forget that it is due to cheap production from countries like China that global inflation has been kept low for the last 15 years. If global inflation starts to go up at this junction, the world economy is likely to jump from the frying pan into the fire.

On balance, the conclusion of a successful climate change regime, measures to combat global warming and the reduction the emission of green house gases must not undermine growth. A plausible solution would be to hive off a portion of growth and turn it away from consumption to anti-pollution measures without distorting competitive advantages or undermining globalisation. The Polluter Pays Principle meets this requirement — what needs to be done now is to develop the magic formula to apply it on the global stage.

This article was first published in *OpinionAsia*, 3 December 2007 (www.opinionasia.com).

Gale Warning, Global Burden Sharing

THE CARDS ARE ON THE TABLE; THE WORLD IS WARMING UP TO THE MOST brutal economic confrontation seen in many decades, perhaps centuries.

Simultaneously, four issues require answers. All have severe repercussions for distribution of global income, and in all four cases, the solution, if any, will reverberate through the global economy, reallocating economic power and political clout: global warming, rising agricultural prices, water shortage and, probably, but less certain than the other three, rising raw material prices, in particular oil.

Almost everybody agrees that something must be done to stop or, if possible, roll back global warming. Unfortunately there is corresponding disagreement on how to do it and who should pay the bill. The rich countries are the worst sinners, but the growth rate for emissions is manifold higher in newly industrialized countries, blurring the game. The rich countries grudgingly admit that the largest burden is on their shoulders, but their willingness to pay is a far cry from the expectations among the less rich countries. Developing nations fear global warming will be used as a racket to hold them back, an excuse for imposing restrictions or financial burdens. Hardening this standoff is a global shift of competitiveness in favor of newly industrialized countries; established manufacturing countries are wary of repercussions on competitiveness and dread surrendering control over the global economy to newcomers like China and India.

Economists float the idea of selling rights to emission targets. In theory, it looks fine. Certificates are put on auction, and firms win the right to "pollute" with the highest bid. If we accept the principle of the market mechanism, the highest bids should come from those representing the largest purchasing power, guided by the invisible hand.

But this is a misleading description. Such mechanisms favor existing industries with capital to make the highest bid. The blunt fact is that the plan would preserve industrial structure, complicating any reallocation of production among countries. The rich countries and their industries possess the capital to bid and would win auctions and the right to produce. Emission ceilings would constitute a barrier for rising production in the less rich countries, freezing the world's economic structure for a long time. The plan would reverse traditional policy of helping infant industries with temporary measures to overcome initial hindrances. In theory, the playing field is level; in practice, it's skewed in favor of established producers.

Another proposal — converting agricultural land or forests into crops suitable for bioethanol — has similar flaws. Two are obvious: First, converting forests risks elimination of large forest areas, wiping out the "lungs" of the world, ultimately worsening instead of improving global climate. This can be seen in Southeast Asia where a country like Indonesia has embarked upon such a course to produce palm oil. Second, an inevitable consequence of increasing bioethanol crops is a decrease in agricultural products.

The world is already on a collision course for rising food prices, favored by very few. As formulated recently by Lester R. Brown of the Earth Policy Institute before the US Senate Committee on Environment and Public Works, a contest is underway between 800 million people sitting behind a wheel in their car, many obese, and 2 billion people who struggle to make money for their daily food, many malnourished.

The UN forecasts that in 2016, less than 10 years from now, people in developing countries will eat 30 percent more beef, 50 percent more pork and 25 percent more poultry. Such production requires increasing inputs of grain, even as the world's stocks are at the lowest levels in 30 years. This equation can be solved only by steeply rising prices for grain and meat.

Global warming changes the pattern of food production; many of the well-known food-basket areas will be subject to climate change, dramatically modifying the production outlook. Even with cases of large countries spanning several climate zones, agricultural production will likely not take place in the same locations, calling for investment, mobility of labor and new infrastructures.

Water shortages, irrespective of global warming or not, aggravate this dismal picture. China, already threatened by water shortages, confronted a choice on allocating water to rural districts and cities. Apparently urbanization and industrialization won out, and the obvious consequence is China has been a net importer of food since 2004. Over the last year or so, drought in Australia has emptied the country's most propitious agricultural areas.

The water shortage may, like other shortages, be solved by higher prices, which would lead to higher food prices. In some cases where rivers flow through several nations — the Mekong River, the Jordan and the Nile — nasty negotiations about water rights may destroy prospects for regional cooperation and, in some cases, lead to armed conflict.

The fourth factor, rising raw material prices, is less certain. Manufacturing increasingly demands more input, but technology diminishes input per unit of any final product. The same trend can be seen with oil: Higher energy efficiency and switching to other sources may stop further price increases. No one knows for certain the impact of rising manufacturing versus more efficiency, but newly industrialized countries offer tremendous potential for savings per unit. As a rough estimate, China has improved its energy efficiency three times since 1980, but still has one third of the efficiency of the US and one fifth of Japan's efficiency. India figures are a bit lower than China's, but improve at a slower pace. (India is slightly more efficient than China.)

All in all, this augurs a major shift in political power and economic clout. Burden sharing will move to top spot of the global agenda. All nations will attempt to emerge from this "battle" by shifting the burden to other nations. Not all can be winners. National delegations will mobilize political and, to a certain extent, military power to show the other side that there is much to lose.

There will be two obvious losers: First, poor people primarily in developing nations, but also in the US, struggling to foot daily bills. The increasing inequality within nations, visible for the last two decades, will be deeper, aggravating social and political tensions. Questions from the poor about benefits flowing to them from economic globalization will grow louder, sharper and bitter. The second group is nations with agricultural production in one of the climate zones no longer suitable for agricultural production. Several major food producers are already fragile, vulnerable to even small alterations in temperature or rainfall.

This ugly fight will continue for the next decade, maybe longer. It may overshadow many present conflicts and create new ones. Confrontation between established and rising powers over rights to use resources will last for a foreseeable future — the rest of this century, maybe longer. Compared with similar transitions of power from established powers to rising powers — the UK to the US, the German challenge in the first part of the 20th century — this distributional fight revolves around shortages regarding food, water, clean air and maybe raw materials. Hitherto, we witnessed distribution of benefits, now we face burden sharing.

It is the first time in history that the world confronts a battle over income distribution. Transferring the burden to a group of underdeveloped countries, as was so convenient many times over the past centuries, cannot solve the equation.

The stakes are staggering.

This article was first published in *YaleGlobal*, 19 October 2007, © 2007 Yale Center for the Study of Globalization (http://yaleglobal.yale.edu).

The Prophet Muhammad Cartoon Episode and Implications for Europe-Muslim Relations:

A Danish Perspective

Introduction

In February 2006, the so-called cartoon case erupted into a full-scale international hot issue, drawing headlines all over the world. The case became a catalyst for a long awaited break out of a clash between strong and divergent views inside Europe. It started on September 30, 2005, when the biggest Danish daily *Jyllands-Posten* published 12 cartoons of the Prophet Muhammad. The Muslim community in Denmark reacted in a predictable way, but found little official support and no sympathy from the newspaper. Eleven ambassadors representing Muslim countries requested for an appointment on October 19 to meet the Danish Prime Minister, Andres Fogh Rasmussen, but he refused, responding that he could not infringe on the freedom of the press. Other Danish newspapers decided not to print the drawings. In the rest of Europe, the newspapers were also divided, some of them publishing as an act of support for freedom of expression, while others did not see any purpose in doing so.

In the beginning of December, a delegation of Danish imams visited Egypt, and the Egyptian government handed a dossier about the case around at the OIC summit. Later the same month, the UN High Commissioner for Human Rights announced that the UN was investigating racism of the Danish cartoonists. On 22nd December, former Danish ambassadors critized the Prime Minister's handling of the matter, and the Council of Europe also voiced criticism against

Denmark. In his New Year speech, the Prime Minister stated: "I condemn any expression, action or indication that attempts to demonise groups of people." That was an attempt to settle the matter. He did not succeed. Jyllands-Posten tried to calm the gathering storm by apologizing, not for the printing of the cartoons, but for hurting the feelings of Islamic society. It did not work.[1]

Saudi Arabia issued a public condemnation of Denmark and recalled its ambassador. Mass demonstrations in many Muslim countries, closing of Danish embassies — some of them attacked by mobs — and boycott of Danish companies in the Muslim world escalated. The incident was classified as the most serious Danish diplomatic crisis since World War II. It gradually petered out with the last statement coming from Osama bin Laden on April 24, 2006 calling for boycott of Denmark and punishment of the cartoonists.[2]

The case caught everybody by surprise and spread around the Muslim World and the Muslim communities like a prairie fire. It was, however, a catalyst for a long awaited eruption of a clash between strong and divergent views inside Europe where parallel cultures have emerged, challenging Europe's social fabric unprepared for this edition of 'cultural globalism'.

Some people take the view that the case validates Samuel Huntington's theory about a clash of civilisations. To my mind, we are witnessing a clash inside civilisations, triggered off by minorities versus majorities, fighting over control to guide Europe and the Muslim World — something entirely different. Neither the Europeans nor the Muslims have adopted a uniform or common stance.

An analysis taking this as its starting point reveals three strategic choices:

(1) Is Europe moving towards some kind of multicultural society and if so what happens to traditional European values that the Europeans neither can nor will sacrifice?
(2) What is the repercussion on Europe of the Muslim, or may be more accurately, the Arab world's apparent difficulty in transforming the economy to benefit from economic globalization?

(3) Should Europe and the Europeans in these circumstances opt for a head-on confrontation with Arab/Muslim fundamentalism or use their influence to support the modernizing forces in the Arab/Muslim camp?

These three seminal but awkward questions point to five strong schisms arising for Europe: (a) Europe's search for an identity, (b) Are the Europeans hardening their attitude vis-à-vis Muslims or will integration into European societies of the Muslim community be accelerated?, (c) Europe's role in the world, (d) How will the image of the Western world look after the cartoon case?, and (e) Most intriguing of all, what will it mean for European values?

Europe's Search for Identity in Changed Circumstances

As has been stated many times, the case demonstrates that what the mass media reports cannot be confined to a national or cultural enclave. It may attract international, even global attention. There is a new dimension to it. The keyword is the minorities. Some decades ago, a report touching on Islam and Muslim values in a Danish, or even European, newspaper would hardly have attracted attention outside Europe. That is the case now. The Muslim minorities inside Europe communicate to their home countries, to their cultural base so to speak, what is said about their values in another, for them foreign and sometimes perceived as not too friendly, culture. This is where the pickets have been moved. On the one hand we have the traditional Europeans behaving like they did some decades ago, not recognising the changes. On the other hand we have a part of the Muslim minorities sticking to their cultural roots, disregarding their new home country and feeling more at ease with the values in the country/culture they left than the country/culture they have chosen to live in.

Most if not all the European newspapers behave with a certain amount of restraint when exercising freedom of expression inside the established culture, but do not feel the same responsibility vis-à-vis other cultures. The attitude of some Europeans is that people adhering to other cultures should adapt quickly to the new home country's culture. Jyllands-Posten stated clearly in the opening phase of the case: No one and/or nothing is exempt from mockery.

One view is that the Muslim minorities must adjust and fast to the existing European culture/identity and the European societies do not need to broaden their outlook and help to merge foreign cultural values with traditional European culture. Those who live in Europe must subscribe to the European culture. They can practice their own religion even if not an established European one, but they cannot distance themselves from societal norms. Europe is not and should not be multicultural.

To understand this view we must recall that until a few decades ago, Europe's cultural minorities did not break away from European societal values. Immigrants were and are welcome and they can practise their own religion, but when it comes to societal values there is no way to escape the basic question of whether or not they accept European values. There is another view trying to integrate the immigrants (the Muslims) gradually, understanding the problems they face breaking away from their original culture, and having strong family links with the home countries. This policy focuses upon second generation Muslim immigrants. The aim is to facilitate integration, while at the same time acknowledging the wish of the Muslims to practise Islam.

In several European countries, the problem has not been solved but indeed aggravated by mistaken policies. The home country has, for a considerable time, allowed the Muslim minorities to live in enclaves and establish parallel cultures, without signalling that this was the wrong way. Suddenly when the problems become all too apparent, an abrupt change in policies follows. Understandably, that leaves a large part of the minorities baffled. This was a misunderstood and misguided leniency, pushing the Muslim minorities toward an untenable role in the European societies. It played right into the hands of those inside the Muslim minorities not wishing to integrate, and weakening the hands of those actually wishing to do so. The

European right wing political parties and the dogmatic part of the Muslim minority succeeded in depicting precisely the picture of the other side they wanted, starting a vicious circle.

The choice, an agonizing one the Europeans face now not to be skirted, is whether they want to follow the first option (cementing the traditional European identity) or adapt to make room for cultural minorities with the inevitable imperative to adjust traditional European values. Will a majority of the Europeans rally behind a more multicultural Europe? The decisive point will be whether the right balance can be struck between acknowledging religious freedom and European societal values. Can some kind of congruity be found between Islam (a traditional theocratic religion) and the secular European societies?

Speaking about Europe in this context may in some cases be misleading as individual European countries have chosen their own path defined by the distinct nature of the problem they face. The UK may be the European country moving furthest toward a multicultural society with — if judged by various analyses — mixed results.[3] France seems to be the European country having encountered the most visible difficulties.[4] The dilemma could hardly have erupted in worse circumstances with low economic growth, difficulties in reforming Europe's economic structure, question marks about Europe's role in the world, a rejected European Constitution stopping the integration in its tracks, and fumbling political leadership.

Europe's Aspiration: Old Europe, New Europe or Another Europe?

A clue to the answer may be found in the negotiations about the European Constitution. Here we find a summary of 'The Union's Values'[5]: "Respect for human dignity, freedom, democracy, equality, the rule of law and respect for human rights, including the rights of persons belonging to minorities. These values are common to the Member States in a society in which pluralism, non-discrimination, tolerance, justice, solidarity and equality between women and men prevail".

The hard core of the answer is that Europe cannot be expected to abandon or bend these principles. This is what Europe stands for in the eyes of the overwhelming majority of the Europeans. The challenge for Europe and the Europeans is to exercise tolerance and respect the rights of minorities. The challenge for the Muslim communities inside Europe is to realise the importance of these principles. The challenge for the Europeans and the Muslim minorities is to define in common the room of manoeuvre and compromise. This is after all what tolerance, solidarity and respect is about.

European Attitudes towards Muslims and the Challenge of Integrating Minorities

The extreme right in Europe has got wind in its sails. Europe is losing confidence in itself and its ability to find answers to the challenges posed by new technology and the rise of China and India. The right wing parties ruthlessly exploit the problems putting the blame on 'foreigners' without really specifying how and why. This is the bad news. The good news is that despite terrorism, Osama bin Laden and similar news on top of a running conflict between Christian Europe and the Muslim world in particular in the Middle East from around 800 to around 1750 A.D., the extreme right only gets around 15% of the votes.

Whether the Europeans will harden their attitude depends, to a certain extent, on the Muslims' willingness to integrate, and at least adopt some of the European values. The more the Europeans feel that the Muslim minority distances itself from the rest of society, the more likely it is that their attitude will harden. We cannot skip the role of symbols. The Muslims not wanting to adapt to traditional European societal values signal this by their choice of symbols, for example the headscarf and other visible demonstrations of 'standing apart'. Many Europeans regard this as a provocation more or less comparable to how many Muslims look upon the cartoons. They ask a simple question: Why do the hard line Muslims signal that they do not feel comfortable inside the home/host country's culture when choosing by their own free will to stay there?

For many Europeans the problem is not that they sense a request for equality with regard to religions but for special treatment of Islam — some sort of positive discrimination guaranteeing Islam and the Muslims not to be exposed to what in Europe is regarded as normal societal norms. That may be what the minority of the Muslims — the extremists and/or the dogmatists want — and they voice this stance with such vigour and use symbols so forcefully that, rightly or wrongly, it is perceived as the Muslim position. Equality would not be a problem, special treatment is.

What many Europeans do not see, and in some cases, do not want to see is the large number of Muslims actually having adapted, being integrated in society and successfully combining traditional European societal values with their traditional religion. These Muslims are mostly silent because they are often squeezed between their former kin so to speak and their new societies, thus not being fully accepted by either camp. It is hard for them to follow suit and tell where they belong as they feel at home in both camps, but unfortunately both camps want the 100% loyalty that they cannot deliver.

In the eyes of many Europeans, the Muslim view is almost exclusively being monopolized by the Imams and the hardliners. The press chasing confrontational views blow up this schism.[6] Much will depend on whether the Muslim societies inside Europe wishing to adapt, or already having adapted, will be able to wrest the right and even the monopoly to speak on behalf of the Muslims, away from the hardliners and the Imams, to present a much more nuanced and accurate picture of the Muslim minorities.

Implications for Europe's Role in the World

What does it mean for Europe's role in the world e.g. Turkeys bid to join the European Union, Europe's role in the Middle East, in North Africa and as a player in the game on the issue of a presumed nuclear weapons programme in Iran? Europe has traditionally tried to convey the impression of a moderate, tolerant and understanding player in the diplomatic game. This will be increasingly difficult and as the

Europeans do not have many other instruments at their disposal, inevitably Europe's influence in the world will suffer.

For many in the Muslim world, the events highlight two trends. Firstly, that the prevailing mood in Europe is replacing Communism and the Soviet Union as an enemy with Islam and the Muslims as the enemy. Secondly, if the above statement is not wholly true, that Europe and the Europeans practise double standards.[7] This will breed suspicion regarding any European initiative on foreign and security policy for a long time. Europe's scope to supplement and complement U.S. foreign policy with more subtle means will be almost non-existent. It will move towards a self-fulfilling theory, depicting the Western world as deaf to other cultures, relying more and more on military power to pursue its foreign and security policy objectives.

For Europe with a near abroad predominantly belonging to the Muslim world, this is as close to a catastrophe as it can be. North Africa has for a long time been a potential powder keg with grave social problems calling for a European effort. The Europeans have played a useful albeit, not dominating role in the Middle East. The question of Turkey's admission to the EU has been regarded as a litmus test whether Europe is a Christian club automatically excluding Muslim countries.

Iran's presumed nuclear weapons programme calls for strong international action. After the intelligence failure concerning Iraq's WMD, the Western powers need to act on solid and irrefutable evidence and seek the support of almost all countries in the Middle East whatever action is chosen. Iran has made it known that its objective is the destruction of Israel. This was a clever step to split the Arab political leadership from the Arab population. If it was difficult for the Middle Eastern countries to join a Western action against Iran, it now becomes almost impossible even if the Arab leaders know very well that an Iranian nuclear bomb aims at securing Iranian supremacy in the region. By taking a tough attitude in the cartoon case, the Iranians enhance this position. Iran, a traditional enemy of the Arabs, has managed to emerge as a champion of the chief Arab cause — the fight against Israel and Western values. Not many Westerners bother but watch carefully how the vocabulary is putting Europe, USA and Israel in the same box: the Western world.

Whatever foreign and security policies Europe may set in motion vis-à-vis the Muslims and in particular the Arab world, it will be looked upon with suspicion. The Arab/Muslim regimes will be drawn towards a more intransigent line towards Europe. The extremists, even the terrorists, will emerge in the mindset of many people as being right: "The Western world did not mean it when preaching co-existence. They despise us and look down upon us. Better to prepare for the inevitable conflict whatever form or shape it may take".

The U.S. is bogged down in its efforts to introduce democracy in the Middle East. Europe has demolished any room for manoeuvre it may have had to influence the Arab/Muslim mindset. The key to the future of the Arab/Muslim world is firmly in the hands of the Arabs and the Muslims themselves.

Image of the Western World after the Cartoon Case

How will the Western world look after the cartoon case? Will we see a divergence between USA and Europe, and will the Muslim world continue to look at the Western world as a monolith?

The initial reaction of both the U.S. and European governments was to distance themselves from the cartoons and express their view that other people's religious feelings should not be hurt. The U.S.[8], the UK[9] and France came out with critical comments against the publication, but did not voice any opinion on the position of the Danish government. This attitude became blurred as the violence directed against Danish embassies produced statements against official trade boycotts and violence. It is unclear whether the second wave of statements[10] also meant that the U.S. and European governments shifted their attitude with regard to the publication itself, or whether it was a reaction against violence and disturbance of normal international relations.

The U.S. may not, after all, have felt too unhappy by watching what was going on. For years, the U.S. preaching to remodel the Middle East — and what in the eyes of Washington was regarded as the militancy of parts of the Muslim and Arab world — had fallen on deaf ears in Europe. The Europeans had not responded as the U.S. would have expected them to do. Now they themselves could taste the bitter drink. No middle ground seems to available in what the U.S. regards as a seminal struggle. The Europeans were punished, and they deserved it.

There is, however, a crucial snag in this perspective. Those who use the cartoon case are extremists and those in the Muslim and/or Arab camp using it direct their animosity, even attack not against Denmark or Europe but the U.S. They want to fuel anger against the U.S. and see the cartoon case as one of many pieces in this puzzle. For them the enemy is the Western world, and the U.S. is the foremost representative of the Western world. Their real target may not be the Western world, but the political leaders in the Arab and/or Muslim world co-operating with the Western world. By depicting the Western world as not respecting Islam and degrading Muslim values, they want to discredit political leaders inside the Muslim world trying to lead their countries into the age of globalization by broadening links with the Western world.

In this respect, the coincidence in timing of the cartoon case and several other events could not have been worse. The following cases all seem to prove the Western double standard or, even worse, some kind of Western policy to degrade the Muslim and/or the Arab world:

(1) Pictures showing torture of prisoners in Abu Ghraib were published again and even if they were not new pictures, they conveyed the same impression as the original ones namely that American servicemen in Iraq do look down upon Arab/Muslim prisoners.

(2) An Austrian court sentenced the British historian David Irving to three years imprisonment for denying the Holocaust. Since the cartoon case exploded, many Muslims have repeatedly pointed to Europe's attitude towards the Holocaust in contrast to its attitude towards Islam as an illustration of double standards. Now they had proof.

(3) Australia's Prime Minister John Howard in a book, allegedly written earlier but published now, was quoted for making unfriendly remarks about parts of the Muslim community, and even if his remarks did not point at the Muslim community as such it was one more example[11] of western bias against the Muslim world.

(4) The uproar in the U.S. about the purchase of six American ports by a Dubai state-owned enterprise, claiming that such a purchase would jeopardize national security.

These cases may all follow the law in European nations and/or the U.S. and they can certainly be explained by logic, but it does not remove Muslim suspicions of the existence of a double standard. Even seen with European eyes, it makes mockery of the line taken by some Europeans that freedom of expression knows no borders. They unequivocally demonstrate that such borders do exist, but apparently not for insulting Muslims. It may be difficult to judge whether the cartoon case will move the U.S. and Europe towards or away from each other. It seems, however, obvious that in the eyes of the Muslim and Arab world, the cartoon case brings out into the open the notion that the Western world is united in applying double standards with regard to values, and Islam and the Muslim world rank at the lower end of the scale than Western culture.

The Europeans and the Americans may not think that they are in the same boat but the Muslim world perceives it as such. The Muslims are quite capable of distinguishing the European political and economic policies from the American, but for them the decisive question is the attitude towards Muslims, Muslim culture and Islam — and on that score Europe and the U.S. are perceived to have similar views.

Whither European Values?

Most intriguing of all: What will it mean for European values, such as freedom of expression confronted with responsibility for what is said and done? Freedom of expression guaranteed in Western countries, is not unlimited. Nor is it true that European, or for that matter Danish mass media, do not exercise self-discipline. The Danish newspaper Jyllands-Posten has itself admitted that a couple of years ago it refrained from printing certain images of Jesus Christ, as they were deemed insulting. In all countries, there are precedents and/or legal provisions setting limits for what can be said or shown. In Denmark, article 266B in the penal code has been used against people speaking degradingly about Islam and/or the Muslims. Article 140 of the penal code prohibits blasphemy.

On March 16, 2006 the Danish Director of Public Prosecutions decided not to institute criminal proceedings in the cartoon case. The decision[12] falls in two parts and a brief summary reveals the following: Part one deals with the specific case: *In Denmark criminal proceedings may only be instituted, if it with the necessary certainty may be assumed, that the offence is punishable.* The Director of Public Prosecutions has made a thorough evaluation of all material and jurisprudence relevant to this case and has found that it may not with the necessary certainty be assumed that the publication of the said article is a punishable offence.

Part two deals with the general question of blasphemy:

The Director states in his decision that although there is no basis for institution of criminal proceedings in this case, both provisions of the Criminal Code contain a restriction of the freedom of expression. Section 140 of the Criminal Code protects religious feelings against mockery and scorn and Section 266B protects groups of persons against scorn and degradation on account of i.a. their religion. To the extent publicly made expressions fall within the scope of these rules there is, therefore, no free and unrestricted right to express opinions about religious subjects.

The decision by the Danish Director of Public Prosecutions cannot be appealed to a higher administrative authority. This follows from Section 99(3) of the Danish Administration of Justice Act. As the decision by the Director of Public Prosecutions is based on a thorough examination of all aspects, which may have legal implications in this matter, the Danish Minister of Justice has no basis to change the decision. The heart of the decision is that there is restriction of freedom of expression, but the specific case did not warrant criminal prosecution.

For the Muslims having initiated this procedure, the decision can hardly have been satisfactory, however correct it may be from a legal point of view. According to the Muslim point of view, there certainly was mockery and scorn. According to the Danish point of view, based upon legal practice and earlier decisions, this was not the case. The question of multicultural society or not, equality among religions or not, different thresholds for different religions exploded into the open exposing the different perceptions between the Danes (Europeans) and how they see Christianity, and the Muslims and how they see Islam. The political and moral problem is the gap in perception of which values the legal system shall protect. The national legal system reflects the norms and values of society. The legal system was caught unaware and unprepared, being asked to rule in a case predominantly and overwhelmingly not legal but psychological, emotional, religious and above all political.

The case illustrates what is known from economic globalisation. National sovereignty has become an empty shell and is not anymore instrumental in governing nation-states' behaviour and safeguarding their interests. It does not really matter in this context whether it is legal or not according to Danish law to print the cartoons. That may be an interesting topic for academic debate, but bears no impact on realities. What is done and said inside a nation-state in conformity with its national sovereignty triggers international reactions. A nation-state cannot any longer do what it wants neglecting repercussions abroad.

The immediate effect will certainly be a higher degree of self-discipline by the European mass media. This is being denied by a large number of people, but is nevertheless true. Very few newspapers would want to test the limits again. The longer term effect may be some kind of international code or convention, inviting nation-states to amend their legislation making it a blasphemous act to hurt the feelings of people adhering to religions and going the necessary step further to define what blasphemy actually is. As long as different religions and different national cultures operate different thresholds, no solution is in sight.[13]

The Muslim World as Seen from the Western World

The western world has conveniently forgotten the glorious past of Islam and the Muslim word and the many scientific breakthroughs that have taken place in the Muslim/Arab world.[14] In Western eyes, the Muslim world is looked at as backwards and as former colonies not having been able to get their act together after the exit of Western powers. It is also conveniently forgotten that democracy is nothing new for the Muslim world. India, with the second largest Muslim population in the world, and Indonesia, after the fall of President Suharto in 1998, are genuine democracies, although admittedly they function under secular constitutions.

The Muslim/Arab world has not been able to find a place in economic globalization. There are many reasons for that, but in the eyes of the Western world, it is primarily the fault of the Muslims themselves. They have not adapted, they have not put in place modern institutions and their economic systems reflect half-hearted attempts to adopt market economies.

In the vocabulary of modern politics and economics, the Muslims have ended up in the unenviable role as losers in the global market place. They have not followed the export led pattern of growth chosen by Japan, the Southeast Asian countries, China and now India, but instead opted for a domestic and semi-protectionist economic policy. But this perception goes further. The large majority of guest workers in Western Europe come from Muslim countries and in many cases, do the kind of work the Europeans themselves shy away from, and often for low salaries. The first generation staying in their new home/host countries is often holding back on higher education for their children, keeping them in the same position as their parents. This may be right or wrong and statistics are used with political purpose in mind, but it is difficult to contest this view held by most Europeans.

Basically, to state the unpleasant and brutal truth the mainstream European view is that the Muslims are living in an old-fashioned world dominated by a religion standing rooted to the spot, and apart from oil exports outside the paradigm of economic globalisation, have only themselves to blame.

The Muslim World as Seen from Inside

Seen from inside the Muslim world, the spectacular point is that many Muslims and Arabs do feel that the Western model has been tried. It failed and did so primarily because it was not supported from outside. Egypt followed a democratic course for a considerable period of time until the middle of the 20th century. Iraq maintained a secular state for several decades. But none of these attempts were embraced by the Western world. The Western world criticizes the Muslim world and the Arab world for not modernizing societal norms, not introducing democracy and not adopting the secular model. "But we tried that", comes the answer, "and then you let us down". Seen through the Muslim/Arab prism this leaves no other way than the dogmatic and/or orthodox Islamic road. What else could be tried?

In the Western world, it is again conveniently overlooked that modernization and adaptation is a priority item on the agenda of the Muslim countries. Where the Organization of Islamic Countries (OIC) held its summit meeting in 200 in Malaysia's capital, Kuala Lumpur, Prime Minister Mahathir gave the opening address.[15] In the Western world it was mainly, if at all reported as an attack on Israel and he did indeed let loose some vitriolic words against Israel. But in the Muslim world, it was noted for its harsh criticism of the Muslims themselves telling them in Dr. Mahathir's blunt way that they had themselves to blame for being underdeveloped. On how the Western world looks upon the Muslim world the former Malaysian leader said among other things the following: "Today we the whole Muslim ummah are treated with contempt and dishonour. Our religion is denigrated. Our holy places desecrated. Our countries are occupied. Our people starved and killed".[16] On how the Muslims feel and how they should feel, he said:

> Some would have us believe that, despite all these, our life is better than that of our detractors. Some believe that poverty is Islamic, sufferings and being oppressed are Islamic. This world is not for us. Ours are the joys of heaven in the afterlife. All that we have to do is to

perform certain rituals, wear certain garments and put up a certain appearance. Our weakness, our backwardness and our inability to help our brothers and sisters who are being oppressed are part of the Will of Allah, the sufferings that we must endure before enjoying heaven in the hereafter. We must accept this fate that befalls us. We need not do anything. We can do nothing against the Will of Allah. But is it true that it is the Will of Allah and that we can and should do nothing? Allah has said in Surah Ar-Ra'd verse 11 that He will not change the fate of a community until the community has tried to change its fate itself.

On what the Muslim countries should do: "We must build up our strength in every field, not just in armed might. Our countries must be stable and well administered, must be economically and financially strong, industrially competent and technologically advanced. This will take time, but it can be done and it will be time well spent. We are enjoined by our religion to be patient. *Innallaha maasabirin.* Obviously there is virtue in being patient." Dr. Mahathir expressed what many Muslims feel. The time has come for adapting to the modern world and only the Muslims can do that. There is no room for self-pity and illusions.

The challenge to this view comes from three groups inside the Muslim world. Firstly, the clerics and what we may call the dogmatic circles, taking the stance that what is written in the Koran is valid once and for all and does not need to be interpreted or seen in the light of the times we live in. It is difficult to know how dominating this group is inside Islam, but judged by history, there certainly must be a debate also among the clerics about the future course for Islam. The clerics influence the Muslims by interpreting the religion, hence their influence is considerable, especially in a time where the importance of religion and Islam is growing.

Secondly, this growing importance of Islam for the Muslims can at least partly be explained by the new geopolitical situation after the fall of the Soviet Empire in 1990. From 1945 to 1990, the secular world was divided between, broadly speaking, the American/Western model cherishing democracy plus the free market and the Soviet/Russian model cherishing one party rule plus central economic planning. The Cold War was a civil war inside the secular world. As long as this civil war tapped the secular world for strength, Islam as the only existing theocratic model, was left in peace and did not feel any pressure or threat from secularism. When the Soviet/Russian Empire fell apart, the road was cleared for only one global model. Islam and the Muslim world suddenly felt targeted by the conquering and overwhelmingly powerful American style capitalism. The Bush administration's drive for democracy and the open talk of remodelling the Middle East was taken as proof by the Muslim world that this threat was real. If the Muslims yielded, there will be only one global model. That model would be secularism unacceptable to many Muslims.[17]

Thirdly, many Muslims both in Muslim countries and as minorities abroad realize that they are lost behind in the global economic race. The label social losers are sometimes used, even if it may be the wrong way to describe their social position. But while the majority of the Western world finds that the Muslims have only themselves to blame, the Muslims, not surprisingly, take quite a different approach. In their view, the Western model is to blame. They are forced to live and work inside a model designed and operated by people who think differently from them. The paradigm imposed upon them, so to speak, means that they are automatically left out. Regardless of what they do, the American/Western model will never permit an equal footing. For them the playing ground is not level. Thus, they blame the prevailing global model for alienating them. It is not their fault. Economic globalization perceived as American style capitalism is to blame.

Conclusion: Fundamentalism or Moderation?

The cartoon case reveals that inside the European camp, some parts of the political segment, the mass media and the public feel that the time has come to affront Islam. Muslim communities have grown in Europe without being integrated. The perception among many Europeans is that terrorist groups such as Al Qaeda have the support of parts of the Muslim world. Regrettably, the image of Islam as a world religion providing peace in the soul for hundreds of millions of people risks being erased. Not many Europeans are truly interested in knowing what Islam is about and what the religion actually teaches and stands for. They content themselves with superficial views, offered by the mass media and/or politicians pursuing their own agenda.

This paves the way for fundamentalists in Europe, as it can also be seen in the U.S. Such people are so convinced that their view is the only one and everybody else is wrong, that they have the right, and in some cases, the obligation to impose their view upon others, if necessary by force. The cartoon case also uncovers the fundamentalists inside the Muslim camp — people who decided to use it to pursue their course of action. Unfortunately, there are segments of Muslim society working to prevent the Muslim communities from participating fully and constructively in globalization.

In the European camp, the fundamentalist's argument is that freedom of expression cannot be contested, cannot be negotiated and that it means complete freedom. Those arguing for some degree of respect for other people's beliefs are brushed aside, and accused of abandoning several centuries of struggle to ensure freedom of expression. In the Muslim camp, the argument is that no insult to Prophet Muhammad can be tolerated and those trying to dampen the reaction are accused of not being true believers and abandoning the faith. In both camps, the fundamentalists have occupied the high ground, accusing the moderates of abandoning holy and untouchable principles — in short, being some kind of cultural and/or religious renegades.[18]

The future relationship between the Western world and the Muslim world will be determined by whether the fundamentalists manage to carry the day, or whether the moderates will be able to gain the upper hand. The moderates fact an uphill struggle.

Endnotes

[1] The official Danish position as set out by Prime Minister Anders Fogh Rasmussen at several occasions can be found at:

(a) Press Statement, Danish Foreign Ministry, 31 January 2006. http://www. um.dk/en/servicemenu/News/StatementByTheDanishPrimeMinister AndersFoghRasmussenRegardingTheDrawingsOfTheProphetMohammed. htm

(b) Prime Ministers interview in Al-Arabiya. Press release, Danish Foreign Ministry, 2 February 2006. http://www.um.dk/en/servicemenu/News/ PrimeMinistersInterviewWithAlArabiya.htm

(c) Prime Minister Anders Fogh Rasmussens opening statement in English at the Press Conference on 7 February 2006. http://www.um.dk/en/servicemenu/ News/PrimeMinisterAndersFoghRasmussensOpeningStatementInEnglish AtThePressConferenceOn7February2006.htm

(d) Comment by a Danish scholar, Professor Jytte Klausen, "Rotten Judgment in the State of Denmark", Spiegelonline. http://service.spiegel.de/cache/ international/0,1518,399653,00.html

[2] A complete timeline is available at Wikipedia 'Timeline of the Jyllands-Posten Muhammad Cartoon Controversy'. http://en.wikipedia.org/wiki/ Timeline_of_the_Jyllands-Posten_Muhammad_cartoons_controversy

[3] For the UK see for example Guardian unlimited, special Report, articles on: Islam, Race and British Identity from a Conference held January 21, 2005. http://www.guardian.co.uk/islam/identity/0, 1394762,00.html

[4] For France see the works of:

Roy, Olivier
— (2005) La Laïcité face à l'Islam, Paris, Stock.
— (2004) Globalised Islam. The search for a new ummah, London, Hurst.
— with Mariam Abou Zahab (2003), Islamist Networks. The Pakistan-Afghan Connection, London, Hurst, 2003.
— with Mariam Abou Zahab (2002), Réseaux islamiques. La connexion afghano-pakistanaise, Paris, Autrement.

[5] Part I, Article 1-2, Treaty establishing a Constitution for Europe (2005), published by the Office for Official Publications of the European Communities, Luxembourg.

[6] For repudiating these views see for example:

(a) President Susilo Bambang Yudhoyono, "Let's Try To Get Beyond Caricatures", *International Herald Tribune*, 11 February 2006.

(b) Hassan Wirajuda, Foreign Minister of Indonesia, Aljazeera 8 February 2006 'radicals exploiting cartoon backlash'. http://english.aljazeera.net/ NR/exeres/B9F7l476-D6A9-409E-8C01-FB0139746391.htm

[7]An interesting view is put forward by Emeritus Professor Mohammad Ariff Abdul Kareem, Comment: Lessons to be learned from the cartoon furore, *New Straits Times*, 18 February 2006.

[8](a) January 31, 2006. Former US President Bill Clinton stated that he feared anti-Semitism would be replaced with anti-Islamic prejudice and condemned "these totally outrageous cartoons against Islam". Source: Wikipedia Timeline.

  (b) February 3, 2006. A US Department of State spokesman stated "We all fully recognize and respect freedom of the press and expression but it must be coupled with press responsibility. Inciting religious or ethnic hatreds in this manner is not acceptable." Source: Wikipedia Timeline.

[9]BBCNnews February 6, 2006. A Clash of Rights and Responsibilities, http://news.bbc. co.uk/2/hi/south_asia/4686536.stm

[10](a) February 7, 2006. US President George W. Bush calls the Danish Prime Minister to confirm that he and the United States support Denmark during this crisis.

  (b) February 2, 2006. UK Prime Minister Tony Blair expresses his full support and solidarity with Denmark.

  (c) January 30, 2006. The European Union backs Denmark, saying that any retaliatory boycott of Danish goods would violate world trade rules. Source: Wikipedia Timeline.

[11]PM's Muslim Comments 'Offensive', *Sydney Morning Herald Tribune*, 20 February 2006.

[12]The Decision is published in English on the home page of 'The Director of Public Prosecutions' (file No RA-2006-41-0151 of 15 March 2006. http:// www.rigsadvokaten.dk/ref.aspx?id=890

[13]See for example Kishore Mahbubani, "The Opportunity of the Cartoon Crisis", YaleGlobal online, 9 February 2006.

[14]See for example: (a) Armstrong, Karen (1993), *Muhammad: A Biography of the Prophet*, New York: Harper Collins; (b) Ajami, Fouad (1998), *The Dream Palace of the Arabs*, New York: Pantheon; (c) Hooker, Virginia and Amin Saikal (eds.), (2004), *Islamic Perspectives on the New Millennium*, Singapore: Institute of Southeast Asian Studies.

[15]Speech by Prime Minister Dr. Mahathir Mohamad at the 10th Islamic Summit Conference, October 16, 2003: http://www.bernama.com/oicsummit/speechr.php?id=35&cat=BI

[16]For a similar approach see former President of Indonesia, Abdurrahman Wahid, "Right Islamic way to defeat radicals", *The Straits Times*, 17 February 2006.

[17]For an analysis of secularism in the present world see, Wang Gungwu, "The Future of Secular Values", published by Social Science Research Council, New York, http://www.ssrc.org/sept11/essays/wang.htm

[18]For a discussion of this theme see for example, Syed Farid Alatas, "Issue shows 'clash' of fanaticism, *The Straits Times*, 17 February 2006.

This article was first published in *Religious Pluralism in Democratic Societies*, ed. K.S. Nathan, Konrad Adenauer Stiftung and Malaysian Association for American Studies, 2007, pp. 159–175.

A Nationalist United States of America

Power in Today's World

The ability of nation-states to amass material wealth and wield hard power is historically unprecedented. Yet the utilization of power by well-established nation-states, such as the United States, rarely ensures foreign policy objectives are met, and often yields undesirable outcomes instead.

Transnational non-state actors like Al-Qaeda and Jemaah Islamiyah have taken advantage of this emerging paradox. Their objectives are to destabilize and undermine established Western institutions, norms and values. Fatalist worldviews held by terrorist organizations are meant to justify these non-state actors complete lack of political accountability to any nation-state. They are empowered by their disregard for any international rule of law, while nation-states must consider public opinion, domestic political opposition and global opinion in waging a defensive against terrorism.

In some cases, nation-states and non-state actors, both steeped in political or religious ideology, often follow self-centric policies that are meant to exonerate them from any responsibility to the global community. They even believe theirs is the right and duty to impose their ideology on those not "fortunate enough" to be born into the "right" cultural or national identity, whether religious or political in nature.

However, there is a crucial difference between the two. Non-state actors, such as terrorists, generally share the belief that the existing world order is against them. All their suffering is caused by "the system", and the way it is set up and steered by nation-states. More specifically, these actors are angry and they direct their anger at a world order highly influenced by U.S. foreign policy, a perceived exportation of American cultural hegemony and capitalism's sway over emerging democratic nations.

On the other hand, many institutional and nation-state actors have still not come to terms with these turns of events. For them, the current world order serves as a crucial global economic and political model with Western cultural values that have been refined over much of modern history. Faced by negative reactions, nation-states ask, "What is wrong with them?" But what needs to be asked is, "What is wrong with us? Why do our actions arouse so much anger when they are meant to be engaging?" These questions end in a mixture of sorrow, disappointment and deep resentment towards non-states actors.

It is for this reason that dialogue between states and non-state actors has not taken place: You cannot reconcile those seeking to preserve a system with those seeing it as their divine right to destroy it. To make matters worse, the traditional beneficiaries (natural born citizens) of the nation-state are threatened by globalization.

With regard to information communications, the Internet, satellite TV, blogs and alternative media have empowered individuals and groups to change traditional power dynamics. The power of global communications is no longer solely in the hands of the nation-state.

Changes in Power Creation

Power in the age of instantaneous information and images is the ability to forge and shape the mindsets of people, while earning widespread political support.

Under this definition, power and influence do not flow from the nation-state, but pour away from it. In fact, the United States efforts in Iraq were undermined by video footage from Abu Ghraib that showed prisoners being mishandled, beaten up and sexually abused.

And the whole world saw Saddam Hussein's hanging, which resulted in a colossal negative image of the Iraqi government and America. Non-traditional media outlets spread the images from these events widely. Meanwhile, the real-time images of the underground during the July 7, 2005 bombings in London were not disseminated by the mass media, but by people using their cell phones.

The agenda is gradually being set, not by nation-states or mass media, but by individuals on the spot — each with his or her own set of values, often diverging from those of the country in which they live. American soldiers at Abu Ghraib prison clearly did not act in accordance with U.S. military regulations or any society's moral standards. The wardens who used their cell phones to record Saddam Hussein's execution had their own agenda as well, probably that of revenge. For their part, institutions and nation-state actors are finding it almost impossible to cope with the swift and rather ruthless "hijacking" of news dissemination with values, norms and ethics differing from their own. When the news hits the fan, the media resorts to damage control, but in the process, they often aggravate the issue rather then limit its damage.

Who Are the New Beneficiaries?

Generally speaking, there are two groups — very different in origin and direction — that benefit from this shift in power creation. Of course, there are the violent non-state actors like Al-Qaeda, but there are also less obvious transnational organizations like multinational corporations (MNC), both of whom are held together by self-interested motives instead of a shared national identity.

MNCs ride on the back of economic globalization, which has brought about tremendous economic growth and unprecedented wealth for such entities. And the growing economic inequality within and between nation-states — driven by globalization — has engendered a strong backlash among the non-beneficiaries. Considering there are no international structures in place to ensure a more equitable distribution of wealth, many politicians find it difficult to manage further structural adjustment problems spawned from outsourcing as MNCs relocate their activities from one nation-state to another.

As MNCs increase technology transfers from one geographical area to another and fund research and development in other countries where the pool of talented people is larger, it may appear that they no longer act in conformity with the interests of their nation-state of origin. Their loyalty to the "flag" has decreased, even disappeared, and the world is their playground. But this privilege is not available to the nation-state and the large majority of its citizens.

The international political economy, since the age of industrialization, was designed to control economic activity and offer a politically acceptable distribution of wealth. Globalization has made many of those mechanisms impotent without replacing them.

Meanwhile, the role of the nation-state as an anchor of individual's identities is disappearing. Globalization, in a sense, has also led to immigrants flocking to new nation-states, not for their national appeal, but for economic opportunities. It is convenient to have a passport and to rely on the benefits provided by the nation-state, however, when it comes to shared beliefs, the answers increasingly point to cross-border affiliations that are held together by common values rather than by a shared national identity.

Non-state actors, such as Al-Qaeda, are an example of this development. Their ideology easily crosses national borders and is able to secure the loyalty of people from many different locales.

The Existing Political Structure

The nation-state used to be the sole agent that decided on the speed and direction of international politics. Today the nation-state is faced with many more constraints.

Efforts by the nation-state to control international economic developments generally have been futile. Globalization and the instantaneous dissemination of news, ideas and values have surpassed everything the nation-state comes up with. The nation-state's powers are derived from and confined to its sovereign borders, while the main beneficiaries of globalization operate outside and above these borders. And because nation-states, driven by mutual suspicion, are reluctant to relinquish any controls to supra-national political regimes, non-state actors are allowed to operate within a regulatory vacuum created by the absence of the nation-state.

Apart from the EU, the only genuine rule-based transnational organization, attempts to introduce political steering mechanisms on an international level have run aground. Many nation-states have preferred to hold on to the imaginary powers of sovereignty instead of opting to act in concert for the sake of facing mounting challenges.

Citizens of any given nation may still be loyal to their respective nations because the nation-state continues to be the framework for economic welfare, jobs, rising living standard and human security. But the nation-state is finding it increasingly difficult to deliver these public goods. Some challenges include the ability of MNCs to relocate and the threat to physical security from terrorism nourished from abroad. Now, these challenges may not defeat the nation-state, but they can definitely disrupt order and undermine its legitimacy and authority.

The United States as Superpower

Last year was disastrous for the United States' superpower status. It did not achieve a single one of its most important foreign policy objectives.

Despite its involvement in the Middle East, the region has become more unstable and dangerous, making violence and armed conflict more likely. An emboldened Iran and a resurgent cross-border Shi'a community spanning from Lebanon to India seem to be the only substantial changes and this can hardly be seen as a promising development for the region.

Moreover, North Korea has joined the nuclear club. The United States repeatedly warned that a nuclear test would be deemed unaccept-able, but North Korea went ahead anyway. And apart from sanctions, judged by most observers to be of little effect, no repercussions were dished out. The world's sole superpower was challenged by this "rogue nation" on one of the most important global security issues and America allowed them to get away with it.

Even Iran has chosen to neglect warnings from the United States about its nuclear programs. And while the UN Security Council imposed sanctions, the five permanent members do not appear to be wholeheartedly committed to their decision. Even worse, it demonstrates that the United States is unable to garner support for a global issue like non-proliferation, which affects every nation-state's security.

Nevertheless, the United States has been more successful than most people give it credit for when it comes to homeland security. Since September 11 there have been few high profile attacks and none on U.S. soil. The United States has also been relatively successful in pressuring nation-states to deny opportunities for terrorists to train, regroup and develop new tactics. This has crippled many terrorist organizations, pushing them back to small-scale attacks. Unfortunately, America's "good work" is overshadowed by the Iraq War, which has also tarnished its image as a superpower. In an ironic twist of political fate, the War on Terror has robbed the United States of its laurels won from improving homeland security.

The Iraq War has cost the United States it its centerpiece of foreign policy: Promoting the spread democracy.

The exigencies of war has also cost the United States the moral high ground in international politics and demystified the belief among other nation-states that it stands for principles worthy of emulation. The strength of a superpower is in its ability to lead and have others follow, not because they fear the consequences of not doing so, but because they want to. Only in this way can it avoid costly military actions that dampen its world standing.

The war in Iraq has also raised doubts over the utility of future U.S. military interventions in other theatres.

Facing rising powers, such as China, the United States is caught between the devil and the deep blue sea. Opening the door for potential rivals on the global stage is the price you pay for acknowledging new partners, but excluding them puts the whole burden on the United States, thus depleting its economic and military resources even further. The U.S. economy may not be strong enough to bear the burden of any protracted war, considering that its combined current account deficit is almost approximately 10 percent of GDP.

Thus the Iraq War is at least partly financed by China, creditor countries in Asia and oil exporting countries in the Middle East. While this presently serves their interests, this does not mean they support the United States in Iraq. The United States has made itself an economic hostage to foreign powers; some are allies and others are potential challengers. If alliances and preferences among the above mentioned group change, the United States might be forced into an agonizing reappraisal of its abilities to continue the Iraq War.

Suppose these countries are no longer willing to finance American debt and for various reasons begin offloading their accumulated dollar reserves. The dollar would be devalued even more than it already is and such an event would further highlight American impotence in protecting the value of its currency. It would certainly not paint an image of a strong United States capable of defending its own interests.

The United States used to lead on currency valuations, as in the case of the Japanese Yen appreciation in 1985. But nowadays the United States has to apply a mixture of threats and pleas to get countries like China to appreciate its currency. And when leadership is absent, other actors start to contradict and challenge the written and unwritten rules.

Consequences for the United States

Unfortunately, recent events will probably produce an unprecedented swing in American attitudes towards the rest of world. Since World War I American foreign policy has either been isolationist or internationalist in terms of world affairs. However, we may see a rise in U.S. nationalism — the pursuit of America's own interests coupled with neglecting global leadership.

The impact of September 11 on the American mindset pointed to a turn around from an open American attitude to a suspicious and inward looking America steered by fear about what comes from abroad.

The majority of Americans believed that the world praised the American model, admired the American way of life and looked forward to adopting a variant of its democratic political system. But now, Americans question all of this. This crucial change of mindset may lead Americans to withdraw from the world stage, instead of engaging global challenges.

It is not difficult to understand the loss of morale. The ordinary American asks why American soldiers should be killed and tax-dollars should be spent in places like Iraq if U.S. policy is seen by foreigners as some kind of misguided attempt to export an uninvited political model that causes people to react by attacking the United States, its allies and its interests abroad.

The Iraq War has been compared to the Vietnam War. There are some similarities. For example, a large majority of Americans justified both wars from a moral and political standpoint. The Vietnam War was seen in the larger context of the Cold War and the fight against Communism, while the Iraq War is perceived as fighting terrorism. Both the moral high ground and strategic explanations kept public support high, but then as the conflict dragged on, it became clear that these reasons could not stand up under closer scrutiny.

With American casualties mounting and the spread of cell phone photographs of the realities of war being sent home, the war may not be morally sustained by strong public support. Additionally, the strategic reasoning for "staying the course" is no longer attractive to the American public as a moral impetus, and until this is acknowledged, the Iraq War will never enjoy the support of a majority of Americans again.

The feeling that the United States is losing the scepter as the guardian of the moral high ground is accentuated by the fast waning international support for the Nuclear Non-Proliferation Treaty (NPT). The depletion of U.S. resources by the Iraq war makes it more and more unlikely that America is capable of putting a coalition together among the five permanent members of the UN Security Council to stop North Korea and Iran. In reality, the NPT has been replaced by a tacit acknowledgment that proliferation is unavoidable.

A string of other countries are lining up to watch how things play out. If Iran and North Korea are not forced to toe the line, the temptation for other countries to contemplate nuclear weapons may be overwhelming. This can be witnessed in Japan, where the government is opening the door for a nuclear discussion, which is perceived by many to be a quantum leap.

The U.S. response has been to develop a missile defense system. This policy is tantamount to turning its back on the world and failing to prevent more nations from going nuclear. It illuminates a shift in foreign policy thinking: let's spend less time on the world and concentrate on making the homeland safer.

This same mindset comes into the fore when the focus shifts to globalization. In the past, American jobs were lost to competition between other advanced economies like Europe or Japan. This was deemed as more or less a fact of life. Now, the villain seems to be a rising China, heightening economic insecurity. The perception is that China is either not playing by the rules and must be punished or that the rules are lopsided to the detriment of American workers.

But as long as the U.S. economy keeps trucking, the risk of an abrupt change in U.S. economic and trade policy will be unlikely. But if the United States heads into a severe economic downturn, the temptation to protect American jobs may be irresistible.

It may not be what the U.S. elite wants, but the combination of September 11, the devolution of the NPT and the pressure caused globalization may result in an American withdrawal from its role as the global superpower. Shouldering the responsibility for keeping the world on an even keel and doing so in accordance with American principles may be too costly, both politically and economically.

It may have been fashionable in many intellectual circles over the years to declare "Yankee go home." And this may now actually be happening. If it is, the world may realize that the United States is a superpower and one of the only saviors of the nation-state. It is certainly more desirable compared to that which may emerge in its place: Increasingly weakened nation-states, emboldened non-state actors and U.S. nationalism defending its own interests at the expense of global stability.

This article was first published in *The National Interest Online*, 10 and 17 April 2007. Co-authored with Terence Chong. (www.nationalinterest.org)

Asia and Europe Must Step Up to Bat

THE YEAR 2006 HAS SEEN A SHIFT IN POLITICAL ATTITUDES TOWARDS economic globalisation. Hitherto the full-fledged liberal edition of economic globalisation had been sacrosanct, with market forces regarded as an infallible conductor of the global economy. This edition of economic globalisation had after all delivered unprecedented global economic growth at almost 5 per cent over the preceding four years.

But now, growing economic disparities inside nation states and between them are attracting increasing political attention. The outsourcing of jobs and the concomitant falling share of wages in the respective gross domestic product of industrialised countries have become issues of concern to voters.

The following events point unequivocally in that direction: The mid-term elections in the United States last month, which saw Democrats regaining control of Congress; disagreement between the US and China over the exchange rate between the yuan and the US dollar; political trends in Europe; and the recent Thai intervention to stop the baht from rising further.

These events have two things in common: the protection of jobs judged to be in the danger zone, and the necessity of calming workers to ensure their political support.

Following the results of the US mid-term elections, the Democrats now glimpse a real chance to unseat the Republicans from the presidency. But for this, they need a united posture, and measures to accommodate workers and trade unions.

According to economic figures, wages in the US have not risen as much as they were supposed to do, resulting in a falling share of income for labour over the term of the Bush presidency.

The US attempt to pressure China into revaluing the yuan is essentially an attempt to shift part of the burden to Beijing. Washington feels that an unfairly low yuan rate makes Chinese exports too cheap and takes jobs away from Americans. Whether or not the perception is correct, it is gaining ground and is driven by job fears and lower wages in the US. This is a spectacular shift in sentiment from just a few years ago, when consumers revelled in the lower prices of imports from China and American multinational companies delighted in gaining new ground in the Chinese market.

In Europe, the same shift away from the free market is also discernible. In the United Kingdom, the likely successor to Prime Minister Tony Blair, Chancellor of the Exchequer Gordon Brown, is regarded as less enthusiastic about the market economy than Mr Blair, even if his tenure as finance chief does not warrant this conclusion.

In France, the two main contenders for the presidency in next year's election are talking about French national interests and less about France's role in Europe, and even less about its role in the global economy.

The socialist candidate, Mrs Segolene Royal, tilts towards the left wing of the party in her endeavours to keep the party united. Her likely opponent, Mr Nikolas Sarkozy, has spoken about reforming France and its economy, but has toned down this part of his programme, inviting observers to speculate on whether he actually wants to reform France or not.

In Germany, the grand coalition under Chancellor Angela Merkel is doing quite well. Growth looks good and business confidence is at the highest it has been in a long while. Still, not much reform has been carried through.

In Italy, Mr Romano Prodi has replaced Mr Silvio Berlusconi as Prime Minister. Mr Prodi belongs to the moderate left and can be expected to steer a course to the centre-left compared to his predecessor's centre-right.

The same goes for Spain, with a socialist government under Mr Jose Luis Rodriguez Zapatero approaching its two-year anniversary.

In Asia, the imposition of capital controls by the Thai authorities was meant to stop the baht from appreciating further. The driver proved again to be concern for jobs, especially in the export sector. In their attempt to protect local workers, the authorities aimed at international investors. Unfortunately, the move misfired, as the stock market almost crashed, forcing a spectacular reversal of capital controls.

Still, the Thai move showed how far a national government can be pushed when trying to safeguard its domestic economy and local jobs.

It also showed the weakness of economic integration in Asia: Such a step would obviously affect other South-east Asian economies, but apparently was taken without any consultation and coordination.

Malaysia, Singapore and Indonesia all experienced appreciation of their currencies this year, albeit not as much as the baht.

These signals point to one overall conclusion: The time when growth was uncontested king is over. We are now in an era in which income distribution will play an equally, if not more, important role.

Politicians must adjust policies to ensure a more equal distribution of income flowing from globalisation. Economists must amend their models of economic globalisation to tell politicians how to do that.

If these signals are brushed aside, the question may be raised whether globalisation is itself the best course for nations. And that will be quite another story.

There is one more conclusion to draw for the Europeans and the Asians: They cannot continue to count on the US as the global growth driver impervious to domestic economic inequalities. The run-up to the US presidential election in 2008 will encourage attitudes putting the country first and American voters at the very top of US priorities.

The lack of Asian integration was agonisingly visible during the recent Thai currency intervention. When China discussed the yuan-US dollar rate, it was a China-US discussion, ignoring the repercussions for the rest of Asia. But Asians seem unaware that there is a price to be paid in the future for the lack of integration, preferring to leave questions of vital importance to all member states to policymakers in individual nations. The result is there is no one in charge to safeguard Asia's global economic interests.

Current efforts to integrate, such as through the various Asean mechanisms and the East Asia Summit, are commendable and definitely the right things to do. But still the impression stands that when it really counts, each Asian country will fend for itself.

This situation is not viable when member countries are dependent on economic globalisation and even less so when economic globalisation does not look as robust as it used to, but calls for support from those benefiting from it.

The Europeans have just concluded a summit without paying much attention to these global trends. The time has come to find out where they want the still powerful European economy to go, and what role Europe can play in economic globalisation.

Europe and Asia can catch the spirit of the moment to strengthen their mutual cooperation, not against the US but to take some of the strain away from the shoulders of the — apparently weary — Americans to assume larger responsibility for running the global economy.

The Americans have shouldered this responsibility for a long time — so long that some stakeholders might have got the impression that free riders are allowed on board. Well, not any longer is the message from current events.

This article was first published in *The Straits Times*, 29 December 2006.

The New New Media, Inc.

THE RUN-UP TO THE MID-TERM ELECTION IN THE UNITED STATES DEMONSTRATES that the mass media has transcended its traditional role as a vehicle for aspiring politicians. Politicians see the mass media as a potential tool to outmaneuver rivals and mass media moguls expect politicians to help them gain competitive advantages in the market. We are witnessing a new, preponderant role for the mass media in an interactive game with politicians.

The dissemination of information and entertainment is becoming increasingly concentrated in the hands of a small number of companies and individuals. The TV channels looked at in Asia do not diverge much from those preferred by the public in North America and Asia. The media executives cast their net around the globe and offer their channels with a deep knowledge of consumer preferences

In principle there is nothing wrong with that. The market is king. Did Adam Smith not believe that the invisible hand would guide production towards consumer needs? Correct, but the coalescing of political and media powers narrows down individual choice. It is not so much that the mass media has failed to deliver choice but rather that it has succeeded in determining choice.

The media moguls do not confine themselves to commercial activities. In May 2006, Rupert Murdoch agreed to give a fund-raiser for Senator Hillary Rodham Clinton, the latest sign of cooperation between the conservative media mogul and the Democratic lawmaker who has often been a prime target of his newspaper and television outlets. An aide was reported to have told Murdoch, "She is going to the White House, so why not have a friend?" Murdoch controls the Fox News Channel, from which millions of Americans get their daily information and news. Murdoch also owns *The Sun*, Britain's best-selling tabloid. In 1997, Murdoch's British newspapers — *The Sun* and *The Times* — played a fundamental role in sweeping Tony Blair's "New Labour" into power.

Powerful media moguls have also been known to speak for the sovereignty of countries they are not even citizens of. Murdoch, a U.S. citizen, once asserted of a proposed European Union constitution: "I don't like the idea of any more abdication of our [Britain's] sovereignty in economic affairs or anything else. We'll have to see what's in the final constitution, if it's anything like the draft then certainly we'll oppose it."[1]

The separation between those creating the news — the politicians — and those disseminating the news — the media moguls — begins to be blurred. On top of this, a merciless battle is being waged over control of information and communication infrastructure in cable TV, licenses for 3G mobile-phone technology, etc.

The politicians become dependent on those who control the networks. The media moguls with this control determine both who is going to get air time and content of news coverage. That has always been so, yes, but the new factor is that very few alternatives are available, since it is enormously costly to operate a network and politicians often stonewall on granting licenses. The media moguls become dependent on the politicians for the right to build infrastructures and for licenses — with massive capital gains at stake

And in this new media, the individual becomes easy prey. Google is reportedly creating profiles for those using its search engines. Google and others could know more about each of us than we do about ourselves. It and others will undoubtedly use these profiles to attract customers' attention to products to bolster profits.

The method can also be applied to politics. It will be possible to follow the individual citizen to learn their political preferences.

A large part of campaigning will probably move from open media, with debates and live interviews, to closed media. Politicians can use the new media to give voters tailor-made information. Those in control of the infrastructure — the media moguls — can prevent counterarguments from reaching citizens.

There are several possible consequences.

First, the media will have to relinquish its role as Fourth Estate. As evidenced this electoral season, the increasingly obvious ideological alignment of major media networks with political parties will undermine the media's traditional role of defending the public interest within a pluralist liberal democracy. Instead, we will increasingly see the political branding of media networks, where citizens can consume unchallenged and ideologically palatable views.

Secondly, as politics and reporting become indistinguishable, the media will provide its own realities. Take Iraq — politicians and the media offset the absence of the original casus belli (weapons of mass destruction) by proposing Saddam's toppling as second best reason for war. Scott Novell, Fox New's London bureau chief, admitted rather openly that "Fox News is, after all, a private channel and our presenters are quite open about where they stand on particular stories. That's our appeal. People watch us because they know what they are getting."[2] News, like any other consumer product, is now packaged according to niche markets.

Finally, grassroots journalism is growing due to disillusionment, in the form of personal blogs, information from NGOs, mass e-mailings, etc. This reporting "by the people, for the people" will empower ordinary citizens, but it will come at a price: the inevitable cacaphony of views, facts, non-facts — ironically making it harder to decide what is real and what is not. Fox Interactive Media (FIM) of News Corp. has spent more than $1.3 billion during the last year buying Internet companies with user-generated content.[3]

The circle is thus completed. Citizens use the net to empower themselves and the media networks turns this into and economic asset.

Endnotes

[1]http.media.guardian.co.uk/rupertmurdoch/story/0,11136,1085544,00.html.
[2]http://www.slate.com/id/2119864/.
[3]http://www.businessweek.com/technology/content/may2006/tc20060502_
678266.htm.

This article was first published in *The National Interest Online*, 30 October 2006. Co-authored with Terence Chong. (www.nationalinterest.org).

New Economics Favour China and India

ONE OF THE FUNDAMENTAL LAWS OF ECONOMICS HAS BEEN TURNED upside down. For two centuries, conventional wisdom had it that the law of scarcity reigned supreme. What was scarce commanded a high price — gold is a case in point — regardless of its impact on and usefulness for the real economy.

This law has now been replaced by what I would label the law of abundance, explaining a good deal of what has puzzled economists for the last 15 years — that is high growth, low inflation and high productivity, at the same time and over a long period.

Consider the following examples.

A city has one million cars. The next car to be purchased may increase productivity somewhat for the owner but reduce productivity for all others, and on top of that bring along external diseconomies in the form of environmental damage augmenting anti-pollution costs. So all in all, the cost-benefit analysis leads to a negative result for society as a whole when one more car is purchased.

The same city has one million mobile phones, one million PCs and several hundred thousands on broadband and thousands on skype. What happens when one more user makes his/her entrance? Productivity goes up for that user, but productivity also goes up for all the other users of mobile phones, PCs, broadband registrants and skype users. The effect is the reverse of the car case in an industrial society, and there will be little if any external diseconomies. Those we see will be confined to recycling of batteries etc. which, if already in place, is not affected very much by the numbers.

The value of ICT (information, technology, and communication) gadgets increase with the numbers already in use. This positive effect applies to newcomers as well as to those already in operation. The larger the number, the higher the overall productivity for the economy as a whole. The smaller the number, the less attractive they are. Who would be interested in a mobile phone or a PC, if only a handful owned and operated these gadgets?

Further, investment in such gadgets is less burdensome for the economy than compared to industrial goods — no highways, no bridges and no need for hospitals to care for traffic victims, although base stations and repeaters stations do need to be built and positioned somewhere.

Many of the gadgets we talk about here are a mixture of consumption and investment. The person acquiring a PC or a mobile phone enters the game of blurring the division between work and leisure. Conventional wisdom posits, not surprisingly, that investment increases productivity, but the new observation is that high and rising consumption, focusing upon these sorts of consumer goods will actually do the same. Consumption goes up, so does productivity — a totally new phenomenon in the theory of economics.

The boom of the US economy over the last 15 years is very hard to explain if one is armed with traditional economic theory. Switching to the combination of high consumption as a productivity booster and the effect of all the new IT gadgets working their way through the economy - the pieces fall neatly into place. The law of abundance has given birth to this "miracle".

This phenomenon also provides a clue to the future shape of the US economy. As the panoply of IT gadgets seem to approach what may be termed a state of saturation, it is unlikely that the same positive effect will continue to control the economy. Even if one more mobile phone still means higher productivity for society, decreasing returns to scale will certainly be in evidence. This presages slow growth, lower productivity and probably also, a rising rate of inflation in the years to come.

The role of China and India in the global economy may soften the impact of a US economic slow down as they still are in the early stages of high consumption, combined with introduction of IT gadgets. China has a little more than 431 million mobile phone subscribers, rising 44.9% from a year ago, 123 million internet-users, up 20% from a year ago, and 77 million on broadband, rising 45% from a year ago. India is adding several million mobile phones every month.

These two countries have entered into a sustainable phase, where each new mobile phone, each new PC, each new subscriber to the internet (and especially broadband access) will increase overall productivity in the country as a whole.

When assessed against the impact of abundance on the economy, one cannot escape the observation that numbers matter. China and India stand at the door, ready to enter a new phase of economic growth promising rising productivity, high growth and low inflation.

The numbers game will be decisive. Conventional theory asserts that more capital and labour increases productivity, but less so than in the early days of economic development. China and India will for a long time, be located on the upward bend of the curve viz. increasing returns to scale of total productivity flowing from ICT. The large number of subscribers that ICT gadgets ride on, will generate a long and sustainable cycle of growth.

The world is not in for a "miracle" looking at future productivity growth in China and India. The logic of the law of abundance is actually quite simple. But it will change how we look at global economics.

This article was first published in *OpinionAsia*, 5 October 2006 (www.opinionasia.com).

A Vacuum in Strategic Thinking

PRESENT DAY STRATEGIC THINKING IS LOOKED AT THROUGH THE PRISM of the Clausewitzian model of crisis, conflict, confrontation and ultimately war. The primary power parameter is pursuance of national interests sheltered by the old-fashioned and outdated interpretation of national sovereignty. Globalisation as configured by the final decades of the 20th century thrives on exactly the opposite — co-operation therefore effectively destroying the Clausewitzian model. Strategic thinking and the way the world actually works are not only on divergent tracks. They are on head on collision course.

Globalisation is based on western ideas, rationalism, materialism, market economy, respect for the individual, democracy. Fortunately, the new impetuous national states, China, India, Brazil, have accepted the materialist model. They have joined the existing global system albeit demanding a revision of its mechanics reflecting their economic clout and political weight. They did not choose to rally the non-western world under the banner of an alternative model opening the floodgates for worldwide anarchy, autarchy and egoism.

Fundamentalists of all kinds have not, and neither have the rogue states and all those who find shelter within their frontiers. They have left the Clausewitzian model. They do not seek concessions from a beaten enemy but wish to eradicate, destroy and annihilate the existing global model — nothing less.

The sophisticated globalised world is so sensitive, so bound up with other political and economic units, that there is no place for outsiders, especially when these are bent on the destruction of the international system. International co-operation must therefore be global, not only geographically, but also conceptually.

As things are, this conceptual framework for new strategic thinking is absent, and so is respect for rules of accepted behaviour in international politics.

The confusion extends to the post-1945 great powers. They face a dilemma. To contain and defeat the rogue states and terrorism as only they can do they need the support of the new great powers. That seems simple, but is not, for the real long-term threat to the position of the post-1945 powers as they perceive it is not the rogue states and their allies, but the new great powers. If the established powers try to enrol them in the fight against terrorism offering concessions to that effect they undermine their own primogeniture. If they do not, the efforts and resources required to defeat the rogue states and terrorism will enervate them, thus jeopardising their control over global politics and economics paving the way for the new powers in an enhanced role. For the post-1945 powers operating in a Clausewitzian model it is like being caught between the devil and the deep sea. This is the dilemma that faces the new mega power, the USA, where Iraq, Iran, North Korea, and al-Qaeda are concerned.

An empire creates a world in its own image, in America's case the model is capitalism. History tells us that when empires fall, they take the model they established, which the surrounded world has accepted, with them.

Yet the USA is the first imperial power that can establish a real international society, a society which can survive and continue to function when the resources of the USA are exhausted. A condition for such an outcome, however, is that the USA exercises less power than its resources make possible. The reward will be a more durable international system created in conformity with American interests, but not fully reflecting the current values of the American empire.

Unrestricted exercise of the imperial power is the alternative. The probable consequence will be the generation of a new world view, but not one bearing the stamp of globalisation and internationalism, perhaps the opposite. It is an illusion — for some a beautiful illusion — to imagine a multi-polar world established against and not in conformity with US policy.

This defines the challenge for the EU. Keeping in mind historic ties, sharing of basic principles combined with the obvious common interests in maintaining globalisation EU is probably the only player having some leverage on US policy. The EU can choose to be a partner with the USA (more or less grumbling) or an independent operator on the international scene with a leaning either towards or against the USA, or even see itself as an adversary.

Or perhaps internal bickering will prevent the emergence of a common position and the individual states will pursue their own course at this critical juncture in world history, ending in the ditch themselves together with the international society of which they themselves were the progenitor and remain enthusiastic supporters.

The USA's dilemma shows itself in a combination of determination and fumbling to do the right thing in the right way against the rogue states. This is blurring the big picture for the Europeans, which in turn generates uncertainty in the attitude to the EU by the Americans and to the USA by the EU.

The EU's dilemma shows itself in the form of surprise, astonishment, and perhaps ignorance, about the real content and purpose of the USA's policy towards the rogue states, and a certain distance in attitude with regard to a common policy against them and terrorism, no matter how obvious it is that a partnership is in the interests of both parties.

The choices made by the USA will affect the Europeans, but this does not release them from showing their colours. The EU has the opportunity to influence the USA, and hence the great game, but can the Europeans see it and if so will they rise to the challenge? No better time to do it than now.

This article was first published in *In The National Interest*, November 2004 (www.inthenationalinterest.com).

A New International System

GLOBALIZATION HERALDS A SITUATION WHERE ACTIONS AND POLICIES OF one single nation-state may threaten the very survival of other nation-states and/or the international community. Unless actions are put in motion to force a change of policies upon the nation-state in question, the international system unravels as self-interest is paying off. In self-defense, the international community may even take the hitherto unprecedented step to intervene inside the borders of a nation-state against its will, thus violating sovereignty. To rally the overwhelming part of the international community, decisions to intervene must follow a pattern of transparency and accountability, just like in a domestic political system. Otherwise, the world ends up with interventions, yes, but carried out by the strongest power(s) — or coalitions of powers — nursing the root of suspicion that the objective is not the safeguard of the international community but to feather one's own nest. A more or less agreed upon set of values specifying what kind of misbehaviour warrants interventionism, in particular the use of armed forces, becomes the third, last and indispensable step in this new model.

Interventionism

Economic intervention. The International Monetary Fund (IMF) has steadfastly, without hesitation or the slightest doubt, intervened in national economic policies with the consent of its board. The protagonists expounded it as (self) defense of the international economy against disrupting forces. The critics have labelled that posture hypocrisy.

There is growing discontent that interventions are controlled by the creditors, shifting the burden of adjustment squarely on to the debtors. Already in 1945, John Maynard Keynes foresaw this risk. He tried — in vain — to forge the IMF in a balanced way, opening the door for stimulating policies in creditor countries as well as restrictive policies in debtor countries. The debtor countries have certainly felt the heavy hand of the IMF, but not much daring has been shown to force international responsibility on creditor countries.

The need for economic interventionism may be more acute than ever in the beginning of 2004. The US economy, with about 25% of global gross national product, is haunted by historically unprecedented debt burdens auguring a day of reckoning not far away. The much-welcomed recovery stands on a crumpling mountain of debt. Behind the veil, a seminal shift in purchasing power between the established economic powers — mainly the US — and the fast approaching new economic superpowers — mainly China and India — is taking place with very few pondering the impact on the world economic system.

Military intervention. Contrary to the preceding decades the 1990s stands forth as an era of international interventionism. Security policies were not swept under the carpet as an objective. Military instruments were openly brought into play. But neither objectives nor instruments were regularly inscribed in an orderly international decision-making process. Ad hoc approaches were the order of the day.

The first Gulf War, Kosovo, Bosnia, East Timor and Somalia illustrates what before 1990 and the end of the Cold War, would have been deemed totally unthinkable.

An interesting example took place in the beginning of 2000, when the European Union intervened in negotiations inside Austria to form a new government referring to the obligations in the preamble of the Treaty of Rome. The EU felt that the Austrian Freedom Party being invited to join the government called these principles into question.

The international community has gradually endorsed steps encompassing one or more of the five following measures:

1. Persuasion
2. Pressure
3. Economic measures
4. Isolation
5. Security policies including military actions

A close examination of the Iraq crisis shows that there was consensus among all major international actors that it was justified to take measures against Iraq, that the international community had the right to contest the Iraqi regime and that a whole string of measures could and should apply including, if necessary, military action.

The disagreement can be boiled down to one, albeit crucial, factor: whether it was justified to use force earlier or later.

The Iraq crisis demonstrates how far and how fast the international community has moved toward legitimizing intervention and not the other way around.

Institutionalization

Institutionalization appears as the logical successor to the demise of sovereignty. When nation-states abandon the right to exercise sovereignty, they stand naked unless or until another system emerges. And that other system could and should be the virtues of the rule of law propelled onto the international level.

Many nation-states, in particular those having recently achieved their independence, may be reluctant to follow this course of action. They confuse formal sovereignty with the power to shape the destiny of their nation-state.

In a global world, a nation-state has no, or at most limited, room for manoeuvre to introduce and implement legislation running counter to the path chosen by adjacent countries and the international community. It may do so and some have tried with the inevitable result that international investors shy them and steer trade and investment flows away towards other recipients.

To safeguard the domestic policies preferred by a nation-state, national legislation must fit into international rules and/or an international environment like a glove. In case of contradiction, two options obtrude themselves upon policymakers: either to change the international framework by negotiation or to abandon the proposed national legislation.

We may speak of a new kind of sovereignty. It is defined as the room for manoeuvre achieved by the nation-state to introduce national legislation in conformity with and not in contradiction to international rules and international norms. The more spacious room for manoeuvre achieved the more sovereignty that is encroached upon.

Different parts of the world may be in different stages of the development. The European Union is at the forefront. In the Western Hemisphere, steady development of NAFTA can be observed. In East Asia, ASEAN and various initiatives to establish Free Trade Agreements leap into the eye. The Asian-Pacific countries cooperate inside APEC and Asian–European countries inside ASEM.

What we glimpse is a picture of building blocks gradually — even reluctantly — taking shape but taking shape nonetheless.

Set of Values

A viable international system worth defending for those inside the system and worth joining for those outside, should be built upon three key concepts:

1. Self-discipline or self-restraint exercised by the powerful actors in politics, economics and business.
2. Tolerance toward others and their values while giving prominence to shaping a consensus on most, if not all, major issues — even if the major player could force its preference through.
3. Mutual respect and making room for alternative opinions — even if they run counter to the posture adopted by the powerful actors.

Restraint and self-discipline are called for because the more powerful and economically dominating a nation-state is, the more its behaviour radiates outside its own borders. Exactly the same goes for large multinational companies. Their decisions influence the daily life of ordinary people far away, offering those people little or no opportunities to raise their voice and state their case.

Tolerance does not mean opening the floodgates for everybody to behave as they like. Tolerance constitutes the right to think and act differently from other people but within a mutually agreed framework. Tolerance defined in this way forces us to know precisely where we stand ourselves. Other opinions must be measured against our own opinion. We must know what we think and why we think in the way we do — what is our mindset and why do we have it and why do we think it is the right one for us? Thinking in this way opens the door for realizing that, what is the best for us may not necessarily be best for others. And that gives birth to the crucial observation that the heart of tolerance is that we care for other people's destiny even if we do not agree with them.

Understanding is the key to tolerance and discerning how other people think. Unless we communicate and try to understand each other, there is no hope of comparing the different ways of thinking and shaping values for all. And without striving for that objective, there is not much hope for internationalism.

Mutual respect constitutes the unseen ties making a community or a nation stick together. It requires a common set of values. Nationally, a common set of values keeps the nation together and, if mutually agreed upon, and applied successfully, produces a solid nation-state. A common mindset presents an almost insurmountable obstacle to fragmentation, disintegration and disorganization. By upbringing and tradition, people react according to some kind of common denominator defined by the underlying set of values.

The question remains: is the world prepared to introduce a set of values on the international level to safeguard the identity of people irrespective of ethnicity and/or religion while neglecting nationality as a criterion for rights and obligations?

The first and indispensable step is to reject any kind of double standards. An international system in the true sense of the word must be based upon and reflect equitable rights and obligations. Equal to the law is not only a nice sentence but must also apply to the entire international system — otherwise it is not equitable and if it is not equitable, how can we expect it to be attractive for all nations, all races and all religions?

There is an iron lining to this silver plate. If an international model congruous with the principles mentioned above emerges, those not wishing to participate can choose to stay outside — and such a choice should be respected.

However, they cannot choose to attack or disrupt the international system chosen and built by others just because it does not reflect a set of values preferred by them. The justification of violence and destruction is very rarely supported by the large majority of members of the same culture, ethnicity and religion — far from it. Violence is contradictory to and not in conformity with the teachings of all major religions.

The model should respect the rights of minorities and prevent the majority from imposing its will on those having chosen to stand aside. At the same time, no minority can arrogate to itself the right to prevent the majority from living in peace and stability inside a cultural framework chosen by them and for them.

If minorities and/or groups of minorities, by acts of violence, seek to destroy wealth, undermine stability and engineer cultural upheavals, such violence has to be resisted and, if necessary, by force. It then becomes a question of defense of the trend making seen for centuries toward a more civilized mankind. War, terror and fear have gradually been replaced by negotiations, civility and a genuine rule of the law.

No country, no nation, no culture, no civilization, no religious or ethnic group has the right per se to use power be it politically, economically, militarily or culturally. The use of power must be justified by being weighed, measured and judged against the principles outlined earlier and the right to do so must be earned by self-discipline, self-restraint, respect and no double standards.

The Alternative

There is always an alternative. And the alternative to this new kind of internationalism may be found among the following models: The

United States as a global empire, a coalition of the willing run by the US, some kind of "three block" system with North America, Asia and Europe governed by competing centers, a return to the rivalry among nation-states or sheer and outright international chaos.

None of them represent the rule of the law, negotiations, mutual respect or whatever most of us would prefer. Instead they augur a back-pedalling to some kind of power play in a more or less repulsive form, unless of course we end up with some nice kind of chaos sending civilization back to the jungle.

This article was first published in *In The National Interest*, Vol. 3, No. 7 (2004) (www.inthenationalinterest.com).

The Coming World Governance

THE FIRST WORLD TRADE ORGANIZATION MINISTERIAL SESSION IN Singapore last December didn't appear to be a trend-setting event. Indeed, most observers found the process to be somewhat boring, and international media reports on the session did not even garner front-page headlines.

Yet the meeting brought to light a fascinating fact: The world is fast — and probably irrevocably — approaching a stage of world governance.

There will not be created a world government or world parliament in the foreseeable future. But what will gradually be transferred from the national to the international level will be that which matters most: The political debate about the optimal form of society. The meeting, which was ostensibly centered around trade issues, concerned itself more with the challenges of the rich versus the poor; the right of the have-nots to improve their lot on behalf of the have-too-much; distribution of international income; and the best means of generating more income to be distributed. Economic growth and income distribution entered the international political scene to be negotiated there.

Such issues have typically appeared on the national political agenda, rather than the international agenda. But the world must now shift its attention: International occurrences will soon become more important than domestic events.

The Europeans began this game in the spring of 1993 with their European Union. Jacques Delors, the former president of the European Commission, put forward his white paper, and it actually played an important role in the agenda of the European Council meeting in June of that year. Since then, it has become obvious to Europeans that time has run out for political parties and governments to shape their domestic political agendas isolated from the rest of Europe. The fate of the Economic and Monetary Union determines not only whether Europe will have a single currency, but which kind of society will prevail in Europe. It seems that the German model based on Bismarck's introduction of social welfare and Ludwig Erhards "Soziale Marktwirtschaft" (social liberal economic model) wins the race ahead of either the full welfare model, which is too costly, and the American-British pure capitalism, which did not strike roots in Europe.

Now to the WTO meeting in Singapore: Present were 128 nation states. The ministers delivered speeches of about five minutes to a plenary consisting of about a handful of delegates. This was solely for presentational purposes. Another forum was set up to make it possible for political pronouncements to be heard and perhaps taken into account as an agreement was hammered out. At these meetings, the audience was a bit bigger and somewhat more attentive.

Behind-the-scenes, a select group of countries and personalities worked to reach agreement. This group comprised the big trading partners and nation states with high profiles but ready to negotiate. The host country, Singapore, and the WTO-secretariat threw their weight in. Behind the veil, it was possible to discern names such as EU, NAFTA, ASEAN and APEC bringing out that the itinerary toward world governance has to build upon regional groupings of nation states already accustomed to compromise. Member states, even big ones outside these regional groupings and without the will or capability to negotiate, could state their views, and did so sometimes with great eloquence. But they were not rewarded with much influence. The key to success in this game is experience negotiating and compromising on the international level: An experience the

Americans have and can exercise if they choose; an experience the Europeans have excelled in during more than three decades; and an experience ASEAN-countries and some Latin American countries are now discovering the usefulness of.

Those who forged the outcome were typically participants who had done their homework, who knew what they wanted and who were ready to negotiate, having realized even before the meeting started that this was a negotiation. This is what augurs world governance.

The process toward agreement did not differ fundamentally from the domestic political process. Some of the nation states and/or regional groupings were very deft at playing the game of the media. They fed the media with information suited to their negotiating position, thus creating a favorable outlook for the objective they pursued. They made it known whether they would take a hard or soft position. Exactly as in the domestic process, they deviated from the media position only when seated at the negotiating table, but used the pressure exerted by the media to extract a higher price for concessions than would otherwise have been the case. Some governments even let it be known that they would fall from power in the national parliament unless they resisted particular proposals or received certain concessions: A very clever game, though difficult and dangerous.

The really new development, and what differentiates the Singapore meeting, is the role of international pressure groups (NGOs) and the supranational enterprises.

The NGOs have for a long time been front-runners and forerunners in the internationalization process. Precisely because they did not possess a strong national platform they tried early on to go international. Organizations such as Greenpeace and Amnesty International have for a long time been players at the international level. It has, however, been difficult for them to gain the necessary foothold because international decision-making was somewhat in the dark. As long as a number of ambassadors are gathered in a meeting room in Geneva, not very many people know what is going on. But assembling 128 ministers to negotiate a trade policy agenda for the future is quite different. Thus, this meeting and the preparatory work showed what will undoubtedly someday penetrate all international work: The role of the international NGOs operating both with and against the governments of the nation-states. For these organizations, nation-states are one of many players. They aim at the mass media — often preferable to the slow and unrewarding task of influencing government machines, the international organizations themselves offering a fertile ground, with officials searching for a role and supranational enterprises being attacked and exploited by the NGOs.

Not surprisingly, the NGOs were most active outside the pure trade policy area and instead concentrated their activities on new issues as environment, labor standards and the least-developed countries (LLDC).

This emergence of NGOs is one of the strongest and most far-reaching events on the international scene. The fact is that these organizations have never really been strong on the national level. They gain strength from the internationalization process and are thus an omen of world governance to come. In a domestic political context, where for various reasons there is direct parliamentary control, the NGOs find it difficult to go beyond a rather narrow political path. But internationally, where this parliamentary control does not exist, the NGOs (not being restrained by modesty) assume the role of some kind of democratic control in the sense that they are the only ones that truly express criticism.

In the same mold fall the supranational enterprises. At the Singapore session they imposed rules of their own upon the trade system for the first time, which occurred when the Information Technology Agreement (ITA) was not on the agenda at the Singapore meeting. This agreement brought about a considerable reduction of tariffs on information technology products. But the main actors and those who pronounced their views in the microphones were not the U.S. but Microsoft, not Germany but Siemens, not Sweden but L.M. Ericsson, not Finland but Nokia, etc. All these enterprises demanded such an agreement and they received it.

The trade minister of Malaysia, Rafidah Aziz, was correct to exclaim her bewilderment at being hijacked into negotiating this agreement, the subject of which was not on the agenda. Aziz gave way for several reasons, one being that Malaysia itself has tremendous interest in this matter as a major player in the trade segment of information technology.

Summarizing the meeting conveyed the decline of the nation-states (which were hardly present where it mattered and merely enjoyed themselves making statements) and the emergence of the regional groupings, the NGOs and the supranational enterprises. The chessboard will appear quite different several years from now at the next ministerial meeting of the WTO.

When the GATT — the forerunner of the WTO — held its last real negotiating session in Brussels in December 1990, the founding fathers of the post-World War II economic system were still very much in control and left little or nothing to the newcomers. The founding fathers were still able to craft a system and implement rules suited to their economies and industrial structure. Newcomers were listened to — politely or not — but their wishes were brushed aside as a somewhat irrelevant interlude.

The situation in Singapore in December 1996 could hardly have been more different. The founding fathers — the U.S. and Western Europe — did try to play the well-known game, but with scant success. They were being challenged by newly-industrialized countries and developing nations. These newcomers did not yet possess sufficient economic clout and determination to control the development, but they were now powerful enough to throw the gauntlet into the ring.

The majority of the founding fathers brought labor standards into this game. Apart from abuse of children and labor camps, this is really an issue of income distribution and not ethical values. The old industrialized countries find it more and more difficult to maintain high labor standards domestically in view of the economic internationalization. Their welfare systems are gradually being eroded by cheaper labor from newly-industrialized countries or developing nations approaching a comparable level of productivity and quality with a much lower wage level. They can respond to this challenge in three different ways:

One response is to try to suppress the wage level and labor standards. This is the British policy, which was epitomized by Margaret Thatcher and her wish to see Britain back again as a manufacturing nation. Not very many believe this policy can succeed. Anyway, the age of manufacturing is on its way out and not on its way in, at least for a country like Britain.

Another response is to trim welfare payments while safe-guarding the fundamental parts of the system. This policy is with some hesitancy being implemented in some parts of Europe, but it is a balancing act not yet being convincingly adopted.

The third response is to shift some of the burden to competitors in the trade system by imposing upon them comparable rules, and if they do not accept, resorting to retaliatory trade measures. What this means is in fact that the old industrial nations ask the newcomers to shoulder some of the burden for the welfare systems they have built during happier times. Not surprisingly, the newcomers resist and ask why they should pay for the preservation of a system to which they do not necessarily wish to subscribe.

Undoubtedly, this game is going to dominate the future work of the WTO and probably also some other international organizations because it goes direct to the root of the question: Income distribution. Which economic and social system and who pays for what? At the Singapore meeting, the old industrialized nations won the right to mention labor standards in the final declaration, but paid a heavy price for this "victory" in the sense that it was said that labor standards are the competence of the International Labor Organization (ILO).

The game went one step further with regard to trade and the environment.

Here the industrialized nations did not want to preserve something. For domestic political reasons they have chosen to change production technology aiming at reducing pollution and remove various environmentally-damaging production methods. Inevitably, that leads to higher production costs that are not accompanied by higher productivity or higher quality in the eyes of the end consumer.

That policy would of course make them uncompetitive, unless other trading partners came along. Again, the issues were income distribution and model of society.

The industrialized nations could no longer afford to continue in splendid isolation. That would have shifted production and employment from them to newly-industrialized nations and developing nations that use cheaper and less environmentally-friendly production techniques. To mold their societies in the way the industrialized nations wished, they needed to impose their rules on other trading partners and if they were not willing to accept that, then threaten to retaliate with trade measures to bridge the cost gap (regardless of the fact that this gap had nothing to do with trade or economic and industrial structure).

Labor standards was a contest to preserve the welfare state. Trade and environment was a game to create sufficient economic room of maneuver to develop one's own society. In both cases however, the industrialized nations invited the rest of the trading partners to share the burden arising from these countries' political choice, and not surprisingly the rest of the trading partners declined the invitation.

The founding fathers (primarily the U.S.) responded to this development by evoking a new item in the international trade system: Multilateral unilateralism. These words mean that the U.S. pursues its own interests with vigor inside the framework of the trade system, but not in conformity with the intentions of the system. This can be seen for new items such as telecom and financial services. Here there are no rules adopted by the system. Since 1994, the WTO has unsuccessfully tried to do so.

The U.S. wants the trade system to adopt rules tailor-made to exigencies of American-based supranational enterprises in order to keep these enterprises based in the U.S., the largest home market, while at the same time gaining access to other markets around the world. Most other nation-states resist this philosophy and strive to get rules also taking their interest into account. The American response has been to break off negotiations, implement rules in the decisive American home market, thus hoping that the sheer weight of the

American market would force the other nation-states to follow. It remains to be seen whether this strategy will be successful. The same pattern can be seen with regard to the Helms-Burton and D'Amato legislation concerning Cuba and Libya, where the U.S. pursues the course of forcing other nation-states to comply with American legislation, even if the administration for good reasons tries to hold back.

If this development continues, the trade system could well be in dire circumstances some years hence, because the future of the system depends to a large extent on how well it will be able to tackle issues such as telecom, audio-visual services and financial services. The agricultural sector and the manufacturing sector have had their heydays; their share of world trade falls, while the share of services rises steeply. This explains why the U.S. tries so hard to implement rules, while the U.S. economy is still preponderant. The role of the founding father shifts from manufacturing to services. There is nothing wrong with this policy: It is legitimate to pursue interest in the international game just as it is on the domestic scene. The problem is the approach chosen, i.e., multilateral unilateralism — meaning that the rules are not set by negotiating but are imposed.

Without it being generally perceived, the world has during recent years begun the long and arduous struggle to set up some kind of world governance. The U.N. security council takes decisions with regard to peace-keeping and peace-making.

There are summits on a number of policy issues such as environment, the role of women and social policies. All of them bring leaders together, and even if it is just to say that the result not always meets expectations, declarations pave the way for a greater international consensus.

Inside this cocoon, regional groupings actually create and implement policy. The European Union is the most obvious example.

The WTO is interesting because it appears to be the only example of a combination of all of these threads. The founding fathers of the old system are being challenged. Decisions are actually being made regarding such fundamental issues as income distribution. New players such as regional groupings of nation-states, Non-Governmental Organizations and supranational enterprises are emerging. Taken as a whole, it is not a bad augury.

This article was first published in *The International Economy*, May/June 1997.

Part 3: Economic Integration

ECONOMIC INTEGRATION IS THE RESULT OF A DILEMMA: THE NATION-STATE is too small to safeguard the interests of its citizens in the global economy and too big to care for policies close to the citizen such as cultural life, school system, and parts of environmental protection. It tends to fall between two chairs, an evolution striking roots with the phasing out of the industrial society and phasing in of the Information and Communication Society. The nation-state was the twin of industrialization.

The Europeans launched economic integration under circumstances special for Europe, which cannot be counted upon to sponsor integration in other parts of the world. There are, however, a large number of instruments, methods, lessons, and experiences that the Europeans have gained and sometimes paid a heavy political price for, which will be useful for other countries and/or group of countries contemplating whether they should make their own form of integration.

Obvious examples are integration as a plus sum game where everybody is better off inside than outside, capable of solving problems that member states find it difficult to tackle alone, and a step-by-step approach where a long term objective is set, but approached gradually by taking prevailing conditions into account and often stopping to wait for better times. The key is that economic integration has to prove its worth by offering solutions to problems which make the nation-state stalls when confronted with.

In exchange rate cooperation it took the Europeans 32 years from the first endorsement of an Economic and Monetary Union until the Europeans stood with a single currency, the EURO, in their hands. There were disappointments and a couple of times it looked inconceivable that such a union would ever be established, but it was. The combination of strong political will and superb technical craftsmanship turned a dream into realities.

The political invention is transfer or pooling of sovereignty. Quite often people speak about the members of the European Union (EU) having abandoned or given up or surrendered sovereignty. This is wrong. They have transferred sovereignty to exercise it in common with adjacent countries sharing analogous political objectives. By doing so member states enlarge their power instead of reducing their influence. Acting together with others, they can, in the era of globalization, shape international or global rules in conformity with their own domestic policies. Other countries live with the risk that such international rules force them to change domestic rules, thus encroaching upon their real sovereignty even if formally they still possess full sovereignty, only that it has turned into an empty shell.

Where the European model seems to have stumbled is in its attempts to convince citizens that the European political system is theirs in the same sense as the domestic political system is. Despite all arguments the Europeans do not feel like that, which explains the reticence about moving on with the so-called Constitution.

The European Union has come to stay. In every crisis it proves to be more resilient than its critics expect, but also a bit slower moving than its supporters prefer.

In the world the EU has found its rightful place as the biggest global trading partner and an important player in peace keeping and crisis management including humanitarian assistance. It does not harbor ambitions to project military power abroad and this limits its performances especially when up against countries not adopting similar moral and political patterns for use of power.

How the EU Saved the World

AS THE GLOBAL FINANCIAL CRISIS REACHES ITS CLIMAX, FOR NOW, MANY commentators have pointed to the impotence of the European Union and its apparent inability to step in and provide solutions to the predicament faced by member states.

The United States took action and Britain followed with a much cleverer package, but not the EU.

The sceptics seized on the argument, heard before, that the EU was conservative, slow-moving and behind the curtain, the member states disagreed much more than they agreed.

The 27-member EU — of which 15 have embraced the single currency, the euro — couldn't possibly agree; instead they would succumb to temptation, transfer the burden to other members and throw European solidarity overboard.

Well, it might have looked like that for a time, but the conclusion was hasty and the analysis superficial.

Over the weekend of October 11 and 12, the 15 European Union members met to hammer out an agreement to tackle the financial crisis — a milestone in international cooperation.

Some years ago, they gave up their individual currencies in favour of the euro. Now, they have closed ranks to fight a crisis that was not of their own making.

Asia is looking on its own integration so it may be worthwhile to look at how the Europeans got there. The hard-won experiences may be helpful in shaping Asia's own integration.

Three things were pivotal: The European Central Bank (ECB), which proved to be as competent — some would say more so — than its American counterpart, the Federal Reserve; the Continental European banks had followed a more prudent policy than the American and British banks; and the resilience of the euro.

The ECB was watched closely when the single currency was introduced in 1999. It took over from a prestigious central bank (German Bundesbank), which had established a reputation almost on a par with — some would say one a stature better than — the Fed. The ECB manoeuvred deftly and gradually managed to step into the shoes of the German Bundesbank, earning a reputation as a suitable successor.

Until a couple of weeks ago, the ECB had managed to stem the tide by pumping money into the financial system. The mass media has reported one bankruptcy after another among US and British financial institutions, but the victims in the Eurozone have been limited. It helped that most of the Eurozone's financial institutions have followed a policy of more traditional banking than the US and British institutions.

Many European banks did not favour deposits from other banks and were thus less vulnerable to a banking crisis. That policy had previously been depicted as old-fashioned; now it is regarded as sensible.

The euro was introduced almost 10 years ago. When the financial storm came — arising from a meltdown of the American financial system, not Europe's — the euro provided the stability.

Before the euro's arrival, upheavals on the financial markets would immediately trigger off a currency crisis among European currencies, with the weaker ones coming under attack.

But not this time. There were no national currencies for the speculators to play with. It is worth noting that not only was Europe shielded from wild swings among national currencies, but the biggest financial crisis in 80 years has also left exchange rates between the three major currencies — the US dollar, euro and yen — broadly unchanged. Without the euro, the outcome would have been even worse.

Last week, when it became clear that things were running out of control, France, as current chair of the EU presidency, took the lead in rallying other members around a solution based upon a British action plan to help banks to resume lending among each other, thus avoiding the credit crunch.

A coordinated effort that transcended borders — with individual member states pumping money into the banks — could not have been achieved without mutual trust. It once again illustrates the EU's resilience in the face of a crisis.

Britain, not a member of the eurozone, was invited to participate in parts of the meeting. That opened the door for the Europeans to feel their way towards one European economic-social model as a replacement for the last 20 years when the British model was closer to that of the US than to that of France and Germany.

This is not the time for criticism or recrimination, but this much can be said: If the ECB and the euro ·can survive this crisis — and so far they have — the euro will have developed into a truly global currency and the ECB a truly international central bank.

Europe may still be caught in the maelstrom, but if that happens, blame it on Wall Street, not the euro.

This article was first published in *Today*, 18 October 2008.

The Resilience of the European Union

THE EUROPEAN UNION IS THE ONLY EXAMPLE OF SUCCESSFUL, rules-based international economic integration; it has even managed to move from economics into foreign and security policy and open the borders between member states without jeopardising security for the almost 500 million citizens of its member nations.

This remarkable project of international political engineering rests on a sense of common destiny and mutual trust.

At first glance, the pooling of sovereignty might look like a loss of power and influence, but in practice, it works the other way round. But political leaders from all member states have worked to deepen and increase the level of integration. Why should they do so, if it was not because they felt a wielding of greater influence?

In a globalised world, economic activities — whether trade, capital movements or technology transfer — take place at the international level. But governance or political control rests with nation-states, which makes it less effective. The key to the riddle is to lift governance up to the same level as the economic activities it is supposed to control. The EU does nothing more than project governance from the national to the international level.

Today, the EU boasts a single market, a single currency, a single capital market, a common foreign and security policy (which has some flaws, but should not be waved away), as well as common policies regarding freedom, security and justice, just to name a few of its achievements.

But it has not always been plain sailing. In 1965, France boycotted the EU by not attending meetings. In 1974 the new Labour government in Britain demanded and got a renegotiation of the terms of entry brokered in 1971. Only five years later, former Prime Minister Margaret Thatcher rocked the boat again by demanding "her money back" after finding out that Britain had paid more into the EU than what it received from the EU. A compromise was found after several years of horse-trading where every penny counted.

When the EU looked to be preparing for a new Europe with the Maastricht Treaty in 1992, following the end of the Cold War and the break up of the Soviet Union, a majority of the Danes put a spanner in the works by rejecting this treaty. It was back to the drawing board to find a compromise.

The dreams of a single currency, the Euro, first laid down in 1969, looked within reach in the beginning of the '90s. Then the currency market went amok and, instead of fixed rates, the member states had to live for a short period with fluctuating rates. But the EU got back on track — the Euro became the medium of exchange in 1999 and was physically in the hands of its citizens on Jan 1, 2002.

The scene was set for a jump ahead with the EU's so-called Constitution, designed to be a framework setting out a number of principles, while solving outstanding problems in the day-to-day process of decision-making.

Everybody looked happy and content but French and Dutch voters delivered a "no" vote in 2005. A revised treaty, the Lisbon Treaty, was drawn up, skirting the sensitive issues and it was submitted to the member states for ratification.

The "no" vote for the Lisbon treaty at the referendum in Ireland last week was certainly a serious setback, but not an insurmountable one. First, keep a sense of proportion. Only 28 per cent of Irish voters said no, the rest voted yes or did not show up. This does not warrant statements by commentators that the European population has dealt the politicians a bloody nose. A way out of this dilemma will be found, even if things look obscure now.

These examples show that integration is not a highway allowing member states to cruise at 100 kmh. Rather, hindrances have always been overcome, which shows how risky it is to underestimate the resilience of the political and economic forces driving the integration.

Over the last 15 years the EU has been much more conscious of the need to address the preoccupations of its citizens in their daily life.

People now travel freely across borders without controls or harassment; they do not even have to stop. Common rules from the chemical industry prohibiting toxic materials have been agreed. More than 2,000 institutes of higher education have opened the door for students from member countries, and 1.5 million students have said "yes, thank you" to these programmes.

Only a few weeks ago, the French energy giant Gaz de France was informed that the European Commission had initiated an investigation about the alleged abuse of a dominant market position.

Its German counterpart E.ON was sent a similar letter. In fact the Commission is on a warpath to force 16 out of 27 member states to comply with rules aiming at liberalising the energy market.

Without the EU, its rules and its institutional set-up, any hope of restructuring Europe's economy would be dim indeed. It has become conventional wisdom to criticize the EU for bureaucracy and red tape. On closer analysis, the conclusion is the exact opposite: The EU and its executive branch is the staunch driver of liberalisation and deregulation — not the member states. The true revelation is that the EU is still moving ahead despite setbacks and disappointments.

The two major recent policy initiatives on top of the agenda right now are a massive programme to improve Europe's competitiveness as well as an ambitious programme — yet to be launched by a major country — to reduce emissions of carbon dioxide by endorsing the goal of a 20-per-cent cut in greenhouse gases by 2020, compared with 1990 levels. They seem to be the right priorities.

This article was first published in *Today*, 20 June 2008.

ASEAN's Relations with the European Union:

Obstacles and Opportunities

The European Union (EU) and ASEAN have over the years have come to appreciate each other as important and reliable partners sharing the same basic outlook on global politics and economics. Gradually a mechanism for consultation has been built up and it seems to work well despite some problems. Nevertheless it is puzzling why the relationship has not moved from a consultative one to a more substantive one. One reason may be that trade and investment flow smoothly without a formalized framework. This is, however, not a convincing reason. It is more likely that the EU and ASEAN have never really fully understood each other, what their respective objectives are and how they work. In 2006 the EU finally opened the door to negotiations for a free trade agreement with ASEAN, something, which had been on the ASEAN wish list for a number for years. Hopefully this will pave the way for a relationship not only rich in declarations and good intentions, but also of substantial character.

Introduction

Over the years diplomacy has gradually taken on a more multilateral character and few nation-states handle their relations with other countries and/or groups of countries outside a multilateral framework. This augurs a new ball game not only for diplomacy, but also for defining, pursuing and safeguarding national interests. For European countries as for countries in Southeast Asia, the regional organization of the European Union (EU) and the Association of Southeast Asian Nations (ASEAN) fulfills the role of a vehicle for participation in global politics and economics. A multi-tiered system spanning global, multilateral, regional and bilateral ties has developed as explained by Rüland (1996, 1999a, 1999b). The relationship between the EU and ASEAN is thus not only an academic issue, but is also of vital interest for the two regions. In a wider context, this relationship is an interesting case study of how two regions, each having built an institutional framework to suit their purposes, approach and tries to understand each other. It illustrates how much effort is needed to gauge what exactly the other party thinks — especially when operating outside the well known national box and looking across the table at a number of nation-states choosing to act in common instead of individually. The EU and ASEAN are well placed for an analysis focusing on how difficult it actually is to bring about mutual understanding because history, experience and traditions open the door for easy reciprocal understanding and yet it has proved difficult to move from talk to substance.

Despite the fact that, broadly speaking, the EU and ASEAN share a common outlook on global politics and economics, tangible and visible cooperation has been lacking. This article offers the thesis that this is due to a lack of understanding of each other's position arising from the EU's inability to comprehend the three dimensional stability and security sought by ASEAN, a certain degree of disunity among EU countries, and the establishment of the Asia-Europe Meeting (ASEM) in 1996 that has had the effect of taking some of the wind out of the EU-ASEAN sail.

Endeavours to Shape Genuine Cooperation

ASEAN and the EU have had ministerial consultations since 1978. Informal relations between the two organizations go back to 1972, and 1977 is generally regarded as the year when relations really started. The first EU-ASEAN agreement was concluded in 1980 with a cooperation agreement.[1] The agreement was useful as a political signal to highlight the interest both parties had in deepening economic cooperation and trade relations. It limited itself, however, to a declaration of principles and a statement of good and positive intentions, without putting much flesh on the skeleton. During the 1980s, the agreement gradually led to a political dialogue, which until the Myanmar issue arose, actually produced some tangible results, among other things concerning the plight of Indochinese refugees (Rüland 2001).

However, the political will on both sides was not strong enough to bridge the gap in perceptions. During the 1980s and 1990s, the dialogue was kept going, but it did not lead either side to prioritize closer and deeper relations. The EU was satisfied with the agreement and did not see any need to upgrade relations with Southeast Asian countries. The latter may have wanted to do so, but strong and vibrant economic development made them less dependent upon the EU. Both parties were caught in a kind of "steady as she goes" mentality, pronouncing themselves in favour of doing more without really putting in the effort to achieve it. This gave rise to a fundamental question: why do we need each other and what are the common objectives, ideas, and goals, which should be pursued. No appropriate answer was found, and as long as that was the case the 1980 agreement continued to function. And so it did without much dissatisfaction from either party.

In the mid-1990s, however, a strange kind of vacuum emerged making both parties feel that the relationship needed a boost. A group of eminent persons was asked to table a report mapping out how cooperation could be strengthened and deepened.[2] The following rationale was cited for the group's work: first, that the end of East-West confrontation had brought radical changes to political and economic relations; second, there had been a decade of unprecedented economic and political development in the ASEAN countries; and third, the on going changes in the EU. The main recommendations included, inter alia:

- Pursue the liberalization of their own markets and support the World Trade Organization (WTO);

- Alert business and industry to the potential of trade and investment;
- Deepen the substance of discussion in various existing forums about political and security matters;
- Encourage greater contact and exchange concerning the cultural dimension.

These recommendations sounded very much in line with existing arrangements and while useful, they were certainly not path breaking. In any case it all came to nothing for two reasons: the 1997–98 Asian Financial Crisis and, simultaneously, the emergence of the Myanmar issue on the EU-ASEAN agenda, called for a new approach.

The next attempt to kick start the relationship came at the turn of the new century, when the most severe effects of the financial crisis had subsided. In 2001 and 2003 the European Commission (EC) published a policy document[3] classifying ASEAN[4] as key economic and political partner for the EU. The EU mapped out six strategic priorities for its relations with Southeast Asia:

- Supporting regional stability and the fight against terrorism;
- Promote human rights, democratic principles and good governance in all aspects of EC policy dialogue and development cooperation;
- Dialogue incorporating issues such as migration, trafficking in humans, money laundering, piracy, organized crime and drugs;
- Invest dynamism by launching a trade action plan called Trans-regional EU-ASEAN Trade Initiative (TREATI);
- Support the development of less prosperous countries;
- Intensify dialogue in specific policy areas.

All of these points are useful and gives the EU a platform in Southeast Asia. At the same time it reveals one of the weaknesses of the EU in its relations with the outside world: the lack of a strategic vision of the long-term relations between EU and its partners. This cooperation conveys the impression either of a piecemeal approach or an attempt to do everything without prioritizing — none of which would encounter opposition from negotiating partners, but none of which conveys the impression that the EU knows what it wants to achieve.

A deeper problem is, however, the lack of an EU policy platform and doubts about whether it wants to nurture a long-term presence in Southeast Asia. This is most clearly seen with regard to trade and economics. During the Asian Financial Crisis, European countries actually contributed a larger share of financial assistance through the International Monetary Fund to the countries in need than the United States, but the EU and/or its member states were simply not capable or willing to capitalize on this aid politically. The United States has negotiated free trade agreements with several countries in the region, while the EU has offered closer trade arrangements, but stopped short of offering a free trade agreement until April 2005 when the Commission floated the prospect of an EU-ASEAN free trade agreement.[5]

This proposal opened the door for deliberations by an EU-ASEAN vision group established in 2005. The group reported in May 2006.[6] The key sentence concerning an EU-ASEAN Free Trade Agreement reads as follows: "A strong case for such an agreement, suggesting that it would boost trade in goods and services and help attract new EU investment to ASEAN, as well as encouraging ASEAN's increasing investment in the EU."[7] Two years before that conclusion, Willem van der Geest (2004) pointed out, convincingly, that the first best solution (global trade liberalization) might not be available. Under these circumstances, the absence of the EU from the network of ASEAN's FTAs with the United States, Japan, China and others would be detrimental to the interests of EU business as competitors would enjoy better market conditions helping to build a stronger long-term position.

Van der Geest makes the interesting and pertinent observation that benefits negotiated in an EU-ASEAN FTA could gradually be extended to other trading partners thus contributing to a successful global liberalization and not as some skeptics feared reduce the incentive for global liberalization. The main problem seems to be reluctance on the EU's part to move the EU-ASEAN relationship into the category of a strategic partnership. In the 2003 EU policy document, the word "strategic" and "partnership" appear 26 times each, but never in the same phrase. The concept of turning EU-ASEAN relations into a strategic partnership is never floated. The vocabulary that comes closest is "Strategic Framework for Enhanced Partnership".

One should always be careful not to put too much into words. In an EU context vocabulary and the precise wording, however, frequently reveals substance and is far from coincidental or irrelevant. This is underlined by the observation that the EU is operating strategic partnerships with such diverse groupings as the North Atlantic Treaty Organization (NATO), the Mediterranean, and the Middle East, and Latin America plus countries such as China, India, Russia, Brazil, Ukraine, Japan and the United States.[8]

The Commission is currently considering the proposal for a "strategic partnership". The main problem seems to be that there is no agreed definition of the term, nor is it always used consistently. In most cases a "strategic partner" is a country (sometimes a region) with which the EU has regular summits. The EU-ASEAN relationship does not satisfy this criterion as relations are at a ministerial level. It is, however, odd that the term is being linked to the label and/or the institutional set up instead of the importance and/or the depth of the cooperation. As a partner, ASEAN may rank at the same level, or maybe even higher in importance for the EU, than several of the countries or regions enjoying, this coveted and prestigious label.

Institutional Set Up

Institutionally the main vehicle for consultation and cooperation has been the ASEAN-EU Ministerial Meeting (AEMM), which is scheduled to meet at least every two years with the foreign ministers of ASEAN and the EU in attendance. This schedule has been respected except for interruptions caused by the Myanmar issue.[9] In recent years regular consultations between Ministers for Economic Affairs from both groups and between ASEAN Ministers for Economic Affairs and the EU Trade Commissioner have commenced.[10] The EU also takes part in the ASEAN Regional Forum (ARF) process, which discusses security issues and encompasses not only the ASEAN countries, but also 26 other countries including the United States, China, Japan and South Korea.

The institutional set up cannot be characterized as an unequivocal success, and both parties have voiced disappointment. In particular the ASEAN side has criticized EU ministers for their low attendance rate, leaving it to junior ministers or civil servants to represent their country. According to ASEAN, this diminishes the importance of the meetings. The ASEAN side looked forward not only to mutual briefings, but also discussions, which have been less fruitful because the EU was not fully represented at ministerial level. The EU side often pointed to the common position being mapped out at earlier meetings among the EU ministers, which could not be deviated from.

Irrespective of how the matter is approached, a low turn out of ministers reflects the lack of priority given to these meetings by the EU, and that again reflects the difficulty the EU faces in thinking strategically. It is confining itself to a rather narrow outlook in the framework of the agreements instead of perceiving EU-ASEAN relations from the long-term perspective of building up political ties with Southeast Asia.

The point has been made by Abbott and Snidal (2000) that the channels for communication look impressive but are in fact rather shallow and rarely if ever lead to binding obligations. Part of the problem is that the two organizations perceive these institutions through their own prisms. The EU sees them as a vehicle for decision-making more or less in the EU mould, while ASEAN perceives them as a forum for consultation and getting to know each other, possibly leading to actual decision-making in the future.

The Vital Role of Stability

ASEAN was born at the height of the Cold War, and it was fear of communism that had brought the five founding members together. As an American withdrawal from Vietnam became more and more likely, the angst of being the next "domino" to fall reverberated in the ASEAN capitals. The key to understanding ASEAN's attitude towards the EU is the concept of stability, bringing into play a three dimensional perception of what that means judged from the prevailing circumstances of ASEAN's birth.

The first dimension of stability is to protect the region from outside interference by major powers: the Soviet Union during the Cold War, and now the United States, China and maybe also Japan. Instruments such as the ARF, the Treaty of Amity and Cooperation in Southeast Asia (TAC) and the Treaty on Southeast Asia Nuclear Weapon-Free Zone (SEANFWZ) have been adopted and implemented to this effect. They are not aimed primarily at strengthening and deepening cooperation among the Southeast Asian nations; their purpose is to hold outside partners at arms length and define limits for their potential and possible operation in Southeast Asia.

The second dimension of stability is to promote economic growth, offering ASEAN citizens an increase in living standards and thus cementing the existing social fabric, reducing the risk of insurgency, but also other potentially destabilizing influences in Southeast Asia. In the early phases the risk was almost exclusively seen in the form of communist insurgencies, which afflicted several ASEAN countries. Political events in Singapore in the 1950s, the insurgency in Malaya/Malaysia during the 1950s and even 1960s, and in the Philippines during the same period offered further proof that ASEAN nations faced a threat that had to be taken seriously. In recent years, the threat emanates from Muslim extremists in Indonesia, the Philippines, Malaysia, Thailand and Singapore. The terrorist attacks in the United States on September 11, 2001 and its perpetrator Al Qaeda found some resonance in the region with organizations such as Jemaah Islamiyah (JI), Abu Sayyaf and the Moro Islamic Liberation Front (MILF). Even Singapore was threatened by terrorist groups leading to the arrest in 2001 of a JI cell which had planned to attack Western interests in the city-state including multinational companies and visiting US naval ships. This kind of terrorism might not have threatened nations in the traditional sense of losing territory or being defeated, but they constituted two threats: the nation-states' effective control over its territory and the well functioning of their societies. In both cases had the terrorists succeeded, it would have undermined the legitimacy of the political system's vis-à-vis its own citizens starting a destabilization process. Insurgency and terrorism might have destabilized Southeast Asian countries thereby jeopardizing the conditions for sustained economic growth. If so political stability would have been endangered. Stability has been a cornerstone in attracting foreign direct investment so vital for making the export oriented economic policies adopted by the ASEAN states a success. High economic growth has been instrumental in cementing stability. It is sometimes overlooked that for most of the second half of the twentieth century one of the ASEAN countries' assets was political stability, which was not, far from it, common among developing nations.

The third dimension of stability is that each Southeast Asian nation had the right to forge its own political system without outside interference — a kind of pledge among the member states not to interfere in each other's internal affairs. At least two explanations spring to mind. Most of the member states had recently achieved independence, which not surprisingly made them vigilant towards outside interference. In addition, almost all of the ASEAN states were multiethnic, with a variety of religions posing the risk of a spill over from groups in one member state to minority groups in another with obvious risks for destabilization. This is why ASEAN in its relations with the EU focused upon non-political issues such as the economic and trade sector combined with consultations and exchange of views on global political questions, but did not really want to enter into a dialogue about topics related to political systems and/or human rights.

From the ASEAN countries' perspective the question was how relations with the EU fitted into the necessity of stability. From the EU point of view, the question was how much common ground could be built on these premises.

The EU response to the first dimension of stability was that it had no grand strategy to intervene or interfere in Southeast Asia and so on the surface the EU attitude fitted nicely into the picture. But in reality this was not really the case. The Southeast Asian countries' interpretation of non-interference went beyond strict interpretation of that word and included some kind of counter balancing between the major powers. In a stability context non-interference meant that no outside power was sufficiently strong to dominate the region and exercise unwarranted influence. As the region itself was militarily weak — and still is — stability rested upon the assumption that other major powers would react if an outside power went too far.

The EU was neither capable nor willing to play such a role. After the British withdrew "East of Suez" in the early 1970s, Europe no longer had a significant military presence in Southeast Asia except for a small UK military presence in Brunei, which continues until today. The near absence of a European military presence as a potential force to intervene is of course welcomed by the Southeast Asian countries, but the fact that the EU is not among the players to maintain some kind of balance of power among the Great Powers makes the EU much less interesting as a partner, with negative spill over effects on economics and trade.

There is no better illustration of the lack of an EU security role in the region than the ongoing debate on how to reduce piracy and sea robbery in the Straits of Malacca (SOM) and secure Southeast Asia's shipping lanes against a potential terrorist attack which might have devastating effects on the global economy. The United States, Japan, India and even China have all offered to help the littoral states (Indonesia, Malaysia and Singapore) with capacity building efforts — but the EU, and major European powers, have done very little except express concern at the situation despite the SOM being of vital importance to Europe's trade with Asia. The EU could, as is the case for other powers have offered support for capacity building as a symbol of the interest and engagement, but it has not done so. This underlined the limitations of what the EU can or will do in Southeast Asia.[11]

With regard to the second dimension of stability, the European Union is a "super power" in Southeast Asia with regard to trade and investment. The EU is ASEAN's largest overall trade partner, with bilateral trade in 2005 amounting to 116 billion Euro[12] (the figure for the US was US$148 billion). The problem is that the EU does not behave as one unit. For many policymakers in Southeast Asia, Europe is still synonymous with one of the three major European powers — Germany, France and Britain — plus a couple of minor countries that have managed to carve out a name for themselves. The EU thus does not have the prominence it deserves in terms of its economic profile in Southeast Asia. One of the reasons for this is the sceptical and reluctant attitude towards jumping on the bandwagon of free trade agreements (FTA) with individual ASEAN members or the organization as a whole. For several years the EU perspective was that FTAs did not offer anything more than what was expected to follow from the Doha Round organized by the WTO. That may be right or wrong and European industry certainly did not exercise any kind of pressure to get one, but the point is political. Southeast Asian countries were interested in FTAs as a symbol of Europe's interest in the region, and has negatively contrasted the absence of an FTA with the EU with other countries and regions that have willingly entered into numerous agreements. ASEAN has concluded that the EU lacks interest in Southeast Asia. The EU is simply not capable of thinking strategically, unlike the United States or China, and pursuing the organization's long-term interests. This has resulted in the perception in Southeast Asia that the EU is an unreliable partner. During the 1997 financial crisis, the EU offered substantial assistance through the international lending agencies, but this support was never registered in the region.

The EU fared better when the threat of terrorism emerged. Consultations aimed at strengthening cooperation between the EU and ASEAN to combat terrorism led to increased information exchanges. At a ministerial meeting in January 2003 the EU and ASEAN adopted a Joint Declaration on Terrorism affirming their commitment to work together and to contribute to international efforts to fight terrorism.[13] Most of the declaration refers to both parties' commitment to support and strengthen international efforts under the auspices of the UN, but one paragraph recommends

"Exchange of information on measures in the fight against terrorism, including on the development of more effective policies and legal, regulatory and administrative frameworks".[14] This agreement marked a substantial step forward in turning consultations and declarations into substantive cooperative efforts. For the EU it was an eye opener that Southeast Asia was of strategic importance outside the realm of economics and trade. For ASEAN it signifies that the EU was finally coming to realize the importance of Southeast Asia in the context of global security.

Regarding the EU's response to the third element of stability, in 1995 it decided that "all association agreements as well as partnership and cooperation agreements with third countries should contain a clause stipulating human rights as an essential element in the relations between the parties".[15] More than 120 agreements entered into by the EU contain such a clause. In case those human rights principles are breached the EU may take appropriate measures, including suspension of the agreement. EU policy, therefore, went in the opposite direction to ASEAN's principle of non-interference. The EU felt that it had an obligation — for some a moral obligation — to promote human rights, including the obligation to interfere in the domestic politics of other countries.

The ASEAN attitude was that interference could destabilize political systems, and as stabilization was among its most cherished political goals, it had to be rejected (Palmujoki 1997). It is difficult to escape the observation of mutually incompatible political goals, but it is also fair to say that the EU and ASEAN and their respective members have done their best to maintain cooperation despite this framework.

Myanmar became the contentious issue.[16] In March 1997 the EU suspended Myanmar from receiving any benefits under the General System of Preferences (GSP) scheme,[17] strengthened sanctions against the regime in October, and, at the end of the year, refused to participate in the EU-ASEAN ministerial meeting if Myanmar was present on an equal footing.[18] The cancellation/ postponement of a ministerial meeting — repeated several times — has cast a shadow over EU-ASEAN relations. In 1999 Germany refused to issue a visa to Myanmar's foreign minister to attend a meeting scheduled in Berlin, as it would violate the EU's sanctions against that country.[19] For some time it looked as if the Myanmar issue would impede further development in EU-ASEAN relations. This did not happen, however, as ASEAN began voicing its anxiety over the political situation in Myanmar,[20] and while the EU rated Myanmar as an important issue, it did not consider it so important as to prevent the two organizations from pursuing mutual cooperation. As a result, the Myanmar issue did not lead to a crisis in EU-ASEAN relations. While perhaps the EU may never have really grasped how important non-interference in domestic politics was for the ASEAN countries, it gradually realized that Myanmar could jeopardize links between the two organizations and criticism of Myanmar had to find other outlets. ASEAN helped the EU by starting to voice concern at developments within the country, thus moving cautiously away from the principle of non-interference. The ASEAN realization that there was a problem also for ASEAN and the image of ASEAN[21] came to the forefront when Myanmar announced at the ministerial meeting in Vientiane in July 2005 that it would relinquish its turn to be the Chair of ASEAN in 2006.[22]

So much has been written on the issue of Myanmar in EU-ASEAN relations, the most recent summary by Magnus Petersson (2006). In this context, the point is the initial difficulties in reconciling opposing views gave way to mutual understanding and a desire to overcome this obstacle and not let it block what both parties wanted: stronger cooperation.

The Asia-Europe Meeting (ASEM) Process

ASEM was initiated in 1996 by Singapore's then Prime Minister Goh Chok Tong. Since then there have been six summits (Bangkok 1996, London 1998, Seoul 2000, Copenhagen 2002, Hanoi 2004 and Helsinki 2006). In some ways, EU-ASEAN relations provided a model on which ASEM was based, and yet transcend it, as ASEM achieved what EU-ASEAN relations never did: summits with the participation of political leaders. In a way, one could say that the much sought after strategic partnership between the EU and ASEAN has materialized in the larger institutional framework of ASEM. Even if the Europeans have committed the sin so often seen in EU-ASEAN meetings of not always being present at the highest political level, this has been less of a problem in the ASEM context than in EU-ASEAN relations. The role ASEAN played in crafting ASEM reflected the pragmatism that ASEAN leaders exercised in seeking engagement of different players to attain regional stability. With the establishment of ASEM, participating countries shifted their attention from EU-ASEAN dialogue to ASEM.

Yeo Lay Hwee (2003) notes that a variety of interlocking factors provided the backdrop leading to ASEM. She mentions the wish of ASEAN to find another forum for cooperation with the EU as EU-ASEAN suffered from the Myanmar issue and for the EU a broader contact with Asia that it had laid out in its New Asia Strategy.[23] Julie Gilson (2005) emphasizes the EU's use of inter-regionalism and the opportunity for East Asia to appear on its way towards a regional political and economic entity. She notes that ASEM enshrines the notion of "equal partnership" that the EU-ASEAN cannot deliver.

It is still too early to say whether ASEM will overshadow EU-ASEAN cooperation. Over time both dialogues may find a role to play, interacting and supplementing each other. For the ASEAN countries it is a crucial point that their own integration to a large extent is driven by their role and ASEAN's role in Asia. European interests and engagement in ASEAN may depend on whether ASEAN manages to carve out a role for itself inside and not outside a broad Asian integration.

The Future

The future of EU-ASEAN relations seems to revolve around three crucial questions none of which have found an answer. First, how far and how fast will ASEAN move towards closer integration? Second, will a EU-ASEAN FTA be concluded and if so how substantive will it be? Third, will the EU move closer to understand the background for ASEAN's integration combined with willingness from the ASEAN side to be more active in shaping the rules of globalization in view of the obvious advantages for the Southeast Asian countries of an open and market orientated international economic system (be one of the stakeholders of the system).

ASEAN's adoption of a blue print for closer integration — the ASEAN Community 2015 — is an important step forward for the organization, but seen from the EU perspective, ASEAN is still in the very early stages of integration. This is especially the case for institutions and the decision-making process. This disparity makes the two organizations unequal partners. When they meet at the negotiation table the EU speaks with one voice as member states have mandated the Commission to negotiate on their behalf while the ASEAN countries may have agreed to ad hoc common positions, but in principle are still in control of their economic, industrial and trade policies.[24] If and when the EU negotiates with individual countries in Southeast Asia this may not make much difference, but it does when the EU and ASEAN enter into negotiations as two organizations.

The ASEAN countries do not need to pool sovereignty to exercise it in common as the EU does, but the organization and its member states need to go a significant step further to empower ASEAN or its Secretariat. This requires a considerable amount of homework and preparation, and a new form of negotiating skill based upon trust. A stronger ASEAN may not only further economic integration in Southeast Asia, but also make ASEAN a more important player enhancing the possibilities for safeguarding the interests of the region in a global context.

In a way negotiations between the EU as an integrated organization and ASEAN moving towards integration may turn out to be a litmus test whether ASEAN and its members can mobilize the political will to overcome obstacles for their own integration. An FTA may prove decisive. This negotiation takes place at a time when the future of the world trade system around the WTO is in doubt. That poses two major problems for the EU and ASEAN. First, how far can and will they go with regard to issues such as the service sector, intellectual property rights, competition, and investment etc, which should have been dealt with under the Doha Round, but was left in suspense? Second, how will the EU and ASEAN strike a balance between regional, or rather region to region, FTAs and continued support for the global trade system? These are fundamental issues and even if they are not tackled head on the negotiations will reveal the attitude of the two parties.

The economic challenge for the EU and ASEAN is to do their homework and steer the negotiations towards sectors that will ensure both groups will benefit from liberalization. Negotiators must resolve to ensure that liberalization is achieved in sectors fulfilling criteria from international trade theory to increase welfare for both parties.[25] This does not happen by itself and some resistance can be expected on both sides especially from domestic producers enjoying some degree of protectionism. However, unless negotiators and their political masters muster the will to achieve such an outcome, an FTA may not offer much scope for increased welfare; disappointment over lack of tangible economic benefits may erase possible political achievements.

If the circumstances are right, an FTA between the EU and ASEAN may benefit ASEAN strategically. Negotiating with a much stronger economically integrated entity may expose its weaknesses, forcing the member states to realize the necessity of deeper and faster integration. That may open the door for ASEAN as a player in global economics. There are many indications that the United States is turning into a tired chorus leader of the global economy. Fresh blood and vigour is needed. Some of it may come from regional organizations such as the EU and ASEAN.

Even if an FTA has nothing to do with monetary integration, it may actually guide ASEAN countries towards some kind of currency cooperation without at this stage defining the end goal. An economic and monetary union is a goal that cannot be attained in the foreseeable future and maybe it is not the right thing for ASEAN, but currency cooperation to stabilize currency markets is certainly a commendable objective and within reach. For ASEAN an FTA with the EU might provide a glimpse into how the latter tackles and solves many problems connected with non-discrimination for trade in goods and services. As the EU has discovered, the easy part of non-discrimination is trade in goods while trade in services is much trickier.

There are two long term and far-reaching benefits for EU-ASEAN relations flowing from an FTA. The first one is the interest of both in Asian integration as argued by Paul Vandoren (2005). The second is an increased ability to tackle non-conventional and common threats to stability and security. Technically these two benefits may be attainable without an FTA, but politically an FTA is indispensable.

The fact that ASEAN has concluded or is negotiating FTAs with so many other partners makes it difficult to see EU-ASEAN relations deepen and strengthen without such an agreement. For ASEAN an FTA with the EU may provide a platform for adjusting the competitive position of member states, making them more capable of carving out a platform for competing with Asia's two giants: China and India. Most ASEAN countries face fundamentally the same problems as the Europeans and Americans: namely that they can no any longer compete on costs, but need to switch the competitive parameters to other issues such as corporate governance, legal system, protection of intellectual property rights, design, quality, performance. Many of these issues are not adequately dealt with in the present international set of rules under the World Trade Organization (WTO), which is why they find their way into FTAs. If ASEAN and the EU manage to include such items in an FTA, ASEAN's members will be much better placed to enhance their competitiveness vis-à-vis China and India in areas where they already enjoy a competitive edge instead of being forced to catch up with the two giants in areas where they are very unlikely to match them. ASEAN may be turned into a stronger organization, thus improving its credentials for pushing Asian integration. The three big Asian countries — China, India and Japan — may all have their own agenda, but for ASEAN it is of vital importance in the long run to appear united negotiating with these giants. A EU-ASEAN FTA will be an acknowledgement that the two organizations trust each other and would like to extend their cooperation into other areas. One such area will be addressing transnational security issues. But if the EU and ASEAN cannot achieve enhanced cooperation in trade and economics, dealing with more complex issues such as security issues will be impossible.

Conclusion

The EU-ASEAN relationship illustrates what the two organizations can do, and what they cannot or will not do. The EU is a good dialogue partner, and in many specific areas useful common projects can be launched and implemented. The scope for mapping out where the EU and ASEAN can support and help each other based upon common views and interests is quite large. The EU often finds it difficult, however, to address sensitive questions and make hard decisions. The EU system is geared towards consensus and has not yet reached the stage where interests are weighed against each other to decide which issues to delete from the agenda and which ones to pursue.

ASEAN is a useful and effective organization within the limits it has set for itself of which the most important is its character as an intergovernmental organization as opposed to the EU which is a supranational institution. ASEAN can use the relationship with the EU as a stepping-stone to deepen its own integration and enhance its role in the East Asian integration process. Besides that comes access to lessons from the EU's experiences with regard to principles, mechanisms and tools in the process of integration, which ASEAN may embark upon after formulating a Charter at the end of 2007.

The opportunity exists itself to turn the EU-ASEAN relationship from a consultation mechanism into a platform for pursuing common and analogous interests as genuine partners in global politics and economics. The flywheel could be a Free Trade Agreement and better acknowledgement of threats posed by security problems such as terrorism, energy and environment as demonstrated by global warming, piracy and lack good governance.

Endnotes

[1]Official Journal L 144, 10 June 1980.

[2]Report of The Eminent Persons Group, "ASEAN-European Union: A Strategy for a New Partnership", June 1996.

[3]The latest one from 2003 is Commission Communication, "A new partnership with South East Asia", Com (2003) 399/4 available at <http://ec.europa.eu/comm/external_relations/asia/doc/com03_sea.pdf>.

[4]For the ASEAN presentation of its relationship with the EU, see <http://www. aseansec.org/5612.htm>.

[5]In a speech by Commissioner Peter Mandelson, 29 April 2005, at a WEF Asia Forum meeting in Singapore available at <http://72.14.235.104/search?q=cacheGUVt7tRHeHEJ:europa.eu/rapid/pressReleasesAction.do%3Freference%3DIP/05/511%26format%3DPDF%26aged%3D1%26language%3DEN%26guiLanguage%3Den+eu+asean+free+trade+agreement+mandelson&hl=en&ct=clnk&cd=7&gl=sg>.

[6]The full report is available at the European Commission's website at <http://trade.ec.europa.eu/doclib/docs/2006/may/tradoc_128860.pdf>.

[7]Press release IP/06/624 of 16 May 2006 available at <http://europa.eu/rapid/pressReleasesAction.do?reference=IP/06/624&format=HTML&aged=l&language=EN&guiLanguage=en>.

[8]The list is not exhaustive.

[9]The 16th and most recent one was held in Niirnberg, Germany, 14–15 March 2007. The Joint Co-Chairmen's Statement is available at <http://www.eu2007.de/en/News/download_docs/Maerz/0314-RAA2/0315ASEANCochair.pdf>.

[10]The sixth and most recent one was held in Ha Long, Vietnam, 27 April 2005. The Joint statement is available at <http://www.aseansec.org/17440.htm>.

[11]It is interesting to note that in 2007 the Standing NATO Maritime Group 1 (SNMG-1), a navy flotilla built around warships from Canada, Denmark, Germany, the Netherlands, Portugal and the United States, made a foray into the Indian Ocean. *Sahara Time*, 6 October 2007.

[12]<http://ec.europa.eu/external_relations/asean/intro/index.htm>.

[13]<http://www.aseansec.org/14034.htm and http://www.aseansec.org/14030.htm>.

[14]Paragraph six enumerating a whole string of measures.

[15]<http://ec.europa.eu/external_relations/human_rights/inro/index.htm>.

[16]For a while East Timor (now Timor-Leste) was also on the agenda.

[17]The decision was accompanied by the following policy statement "The Regulation … will remain in effect until practices impeding human rights

and democracy have been brought to an end". See <http://www.iie.com/
Research/topics/sanctions/myanmar2.cfm>.

[18]<http://www.iie.com/research/topics/sanctions/myanmar.cfm>.

[19]For an ASEAN view, see paper presented to the Asia-Pacific Roundtable
held in Kuala Lumpur on 1 June 1999 by Dr Termsak Chalermpalanupap
Assistant Director for Programme Coordination and External Relations
ASEAN Secretariat. Available at <http://www.aseansec.org/2833.htm>. The
EU was more laconic. At its meeting 21–22 March 1999 the conclusions
read "The Council was informed about the Presidency's efforts to organize an
informal meeting with ASEAN in place of the cancelled Ministerial meeting.
It looked forward to continuing to work with ASEAN". Available at <http://
ue.eu.int/ueDocs/cms_Data/docs/pressData/en/gena/06776.EN9.htm>.

[20]The Joint Communiqué of the 39th ASEAN Ministerial Meeting (AMM)
Kuala Lumpur, 25 July 2006 states, "We expressed concern on the pace of
the national reconciliation process and hope to see tangible progress that
would lead to peaceful transition to democracy in the near future. We
reiterated our cells for he early release of those placed under detention and
for effective dialogue with all parties concerned". See <http://www.aseansec.
org/18561.htm>.

[21]The feeling of the other member states are expressed by the following
sentence in the communiqué, "We also express our sincere appreciation to
the Government of Myanmar for not allowing its national preoccupation
to affect ASEAN's solidarity and cohesiveness". See <http://www.aseansec.
org/17592.htm>.

[22]<http://www.aseansec.org/17592.htm>.

[23]<http://ec.europa.eu/external_relations/asem/asem_process/com94.htm>.

[24]The EU can only negotiate if there is a common position. EU member
states cannot negotiate economic, industrial and trade matters on their own
as they have pooled sovereignty in these sectors.

[25]This happens if the agreement allows the most efficient producers to
flourish on the expense of less efficient producers. An ageement for market
access in sectors where the economies are complementary will normally fulfill
that criterion, as competition among enterprises will crowd out less efficient
produers. If the agreement opens up for market access in sectors where the
economies are supplementary, no competition will take place and a less
efficient producer from one of the member countries will take the whole
market.

References

Abbott, Kenneth W. & Duncan Snidal. "Hard and Soft Law in International Governance". *International Organization* 54, No. 3: 421–56.

Gilson, Julie. "New Interregionalism? The EU and East Asia". *European Integration* 27, No. (September 2005): 3207–60.

Palmujoki, Eero. "EU-ASEAN Relations: Reconciling Two Different Agendas". *Contemporary Southeast Asia* 19, No. 3 (December 1997).

Petersson, Magnus. "Myanmar in EU–ASEAN relations". *Asia Europe Journal* 4, No. 4 (December 2006): 563–83.

Rüland Jürgen. *The Asia-Europe Meeting (ASEM): Towards a New Euro-Asian Relationship?* Universität Rostock: Rostocker Informationen zu Politik und Verwaltung, heft 5, 1996.

————. "The Future of the ASEM Process: Who, How, Why and What". In *ASEM. The Asia-Europe Meeting, A Window of Opportunity*, edited by Wim Stokhof/Paul van der velde. London and New York: Kegan Paul International, 1999a, pp. 126–51.

————. "Transregional Relations: The Asia-Europe Meeting (ASEM) — A Functional Analysis". Paper prepared for he Internatonal Conference on "Asia and Europe on the eve of the 21st Century". 19–20 August 1999*b* in Bangkok at Chulalongkorn University.

————. "ASEAN and the European Union: A Bumpy Inter-regional Relationship". ZEI, Discussion Paper, 2001.

Van der Geest, Willem. "Sharing Benefits of Globalisation Through an EU–ASEAN FTA?" *Asia Europe Journal* 2 (2004): 201–19.

Vandoren, Paul. "Regional Economic Integration in South East Asia". *Asia Europe Journal* 3, No. 4 (December 2005): 517–37.

Yeo Lay Hwee. *Asia and Europe: The Development and Different Dimensions of ASEM*. London and New York: Routledge, 2003.

This article first appeared in *Contemporary Southeast Asia*, Vol. 29, No. 3 (December 2007), pp. 465–482. Reproduced here with the kind permission of the publisher, Institute of Southeast Asian Studies, Singapore, <http://bookshop.iseas.edu.sg>.

Asia Has a Model in the Euro

THE GLOBAL CURRENCY MARKETS ARE RULED BY TURMOIL, WITH THE US dollar at an all-time low against the euro and statements from China casting doubts on its willingness to maintain the composition of its currency reserves.

This raises the issue of Asia's capability to ensure currency stability inside Asia and at the same time make it less vulnerable to destabilization from outside. It can be expected to play a significant role when Asian leaders in various groups meet from November 18–22.

A valuable starting point is to digest how the Europeans fared after launching plans for an economic and monetary union 38 years ago and how they actually managed to get from loose plans and sketchy ideas to an established and reputable international currency.

On January 1, 2002, the euro was introduced as the single currency for 12 members of the European Union. It looked like a snap with the fingers, just like that. In reality, it was the result of a long, arduous, hard, difficult and sometimes tumultuous endeavor starting December 1969, almost 33 years before the euro was in the hands of the European citizens. Few people know the tortuous road traveled by the party before arriving at the end.

There was no shortage of good advice to abandon an ambition looked on as ostentatious by the outside world. When sizing it up, academic experts with few exceptions were unanimous in the verdict: not feasible. To make it feasible the academic world prescribed a fundamental change of the European model into a free market model analogous to the US.

An economic and monetary union worked in the US, by implication the economic conditions prevailing there should be copied by the Europeans. Change your societies to make it workable, sounded the verdict and the advice. Otherwise the euro could not be accomplished, and if it did, it would not last, and if it did last, it would soon look like a major and decisive disaster. But the Europeans acted like the bumblebee that according to aerodynamics cannot fly, but unaware of this it just keep flying!

It may be too soon to declare victory. Five years after its introduction we are still in the early days of the euro and much can happen, but it is not too soon to brush aside the skeptics. The euro is here and definitely intends to stay. It has already weathered significant swings in its exchange rate against the US dollar.

Since its inception as a unit of account in year 2000 at a rate of US$117.89 to 100 euro, the exchange rate has fluctuated between a low point of US$82 and a high point of US$145 per 100 euro. Presently it is about the latest figure. This is a swing of approximately 80% against the supposedly strongest currency and the global reserve currency par excellence. The market has not lost confidence and belief in the euro. On the contrary. There is anecdotal evidence of a rising interest in reallocation foreign exchange reserves from US dollar to euro in the portfolio of both official and private funds.

But what about the European economies? Didn't they turn into low growth at the very moment the euro was introduced? The mass media report about low flexibility, low mobility and resistance to changes. The European welfare model is too expensive, keeps people away from work etc. The Euro Zone is in the doldrums, while the free market US economy is thundering ahead. Maybe the verdict that only the US model was compatible with economic and monetary union was right after all?

There is an element of truth in much of the criticism. A comparative analysis published by The Economist shows, however, that the main difference between the European and American economy is not due to the models, but to one and only one factor: higher population growth in the US. Somewhat astonishing figures reveal that:

- From 2001 to 2005 gross domestic product per capita grew at an average of 1.4% in the Euro Zone and 1.5% in the US.
- From 1996 to 2005 employment grew stronger in the Euro Zone than in the US albeit the difference is small. It is equally true if the 10-year period is broken up into two five-year periods.

Nobel laureate Robert Mundell comes to the same basic conclusion — that the main difference between the US and Europe is population growth — in an interview in September 2006 stating, "Some say that Europe has performed badly compared with the US over the past 10 years, but they forget that Europe has zero population growth and that European per capita income isn't much below the US figure."

This is not to say that the European economies are doing phenomenally well, they are not, but they are in much better shape than the popular presentation of sick European economies leads the observer to believe. Add to this the Euro Zone's performance on balance of payments and public budget compared to the almost calamitous imbalances distorting the US economy actually threatening the global economy.

Growth prognosis for 2007 and 2008 supports this view. According to the International Monetary Fund, US economic growth is decelerating from around 3.1% in 2005 and 2.9% in 2006 to 1.9% in 2007 and 1.9% in 2008. The Euro Zone is accelerating from 1.5% and 2.8% to 2.5% in 2007 and 2.1% in 2008. One swallow does not a summer make, and the European growth is still below US trend growth, but keeping in mind the points about population growth and imbalances the difference can hardly be said to be significant.

The critics and/or the skeptics point to growing disharmony among the euro members. The new French president calls for less independence for the European Central Bank, Italy is apparently fighting hard to regain competitiveness and Ireland has had to adjust uncomfortably. Such conflicting views should by no means be disregarded. But how easy to forget the running battle in the US about economic policy and the all too obvious difficulty for Japan in finding a suitable balance between fiscal and monetary policy.

The Euro Zone is not the only example, far from it, of an economic area where the central bank is under attack or faces political pressure to adopt a monetary policy preferred by politicians. The mass media report the dilemma the Reserve Bank of Australia faces with regard to its interest rate policy in light of the views of the government and the upcoming election.

Hopefully this suffices to warrant a conclusion that irrespective of all its weaknesses the euro has come to stay, and what we see in Europe of problems are not in any way different from what is seen elsewhere — do not ask more from the Euro Zone than already established national economic and monetary unions deliver.

It is thus legitimate to pose the question of how the Europeans got there. It is interesting not the least because currency cooperation is attracting increased attention in Asia. Very few would dare to take the view that the time has come for an economic and monetary union in Asia, but equally few, hopefully, would discard the view that Asia may gain by exploring how far and how fast cooperation about currency rates can go.

The lessons can be summarized like this.

A firm political will to start and keep going. An economic analysis may tell that the conditions are not at hand, but such an analysis is based on present conditions and currency cooperation is dynamic and changes the circumstances.

It must be realized among political decision-makers that currency cooperation is not emerging by itself calling for a subsequent political framework. It is the other way around. First the political decisions on the basis of political ambitions, then economic advantages may follow. The political leaders must want to do it.

There will be crises, turmoil and upheavals down the road. They may temporarily derail the whole enterprise. It happened for the Europeans in the 1970s and again in 1993 where for a period Europe had to resort to fluctuating exchange rates. When markets had stabilized, the Europeans went back to the drawing table and continued the road towards the goal.

The markets must be convinced that the political will is present. Member states must be willing to pay a price in crisis to maintain the currency cooperation and get the message across. The pound sterling was forced out of the European exchange rate mechanism in 1992 because the market was convinced that the British government would not pay the price to defend the currency rate.

Member states must pursue, broadly speaking analogous economic policies. They do not need to be 100% the same, but the overall design must be congruous. In Europe the German low inflation model labeled stability policy was adopted by France and the other European economies in the beginning of the 1980s.

In the same way member states must have come to the conclusion that exchange rates are not a suitable instrument to redress imbalances on the balance of payments. That happened in Europe in the course of the early 1980s after having been tried repeatedly and unsuccessfully in the 1970s by several member states including France, Belgium and Denmark. The reasoning was quite simple: if exchange rates are not regarded as suitable instruments in economic policy, why keep the option open instead of drawing the logical conclusion to establish an economic and monetary union and reap the benefits hereof.

The members of the Euro Zone have been criticized for not respecting rigorously the criteria in the original treaty about public deficits (3% of Gross Domestic Product) and public debt (60%). But the world does not stand still. There must be flexibility to adapt as circumstances change.

The ground must be prepared meticulously and with a clear eye for what is necessary. The Europeans established a number of common policies like the Common Agricultural Policy, the Common Market and the Common External Trade Policy. Later it was supplemented by the Single Market. Liberalization of capital movements followed. When all these policies were established, the time had come to move towards an economic and monetary union — not before. Looking at the European economies it strikes the observer that intra trade had grown to more than 2/3 of all external trade and the business cycle among the potential members moves in synchronization.

All in all the conclusion is that the Europeans got the euro by moving steadily, slowly and step by step towards the goal, taking the jump after careful scrutiny of the conditions telling that the time had come.

Whatever course Asia and/or individual Asian countries may choose towards currency cooperation, these valuable lessons are worthwhile to have in mind.

I do not intend to weigh pros and cons for currency rate cooperation in Asia or among the Association of Southeast Asian Nations countries, but offer the following observation: when the Europeans started the voyage in 1969 towards the euro everybody else than those who initiated this step deemed it absolutely impossible. The decision-makers went on to prove that political will and sound economic judgment can turn what looks impossible into a reality. That is perhaps the most important of all the experiences gained.

This article was first published in *Asia Times Online*, 13 November 2007 (www.atimes.com).

Integration — Yes or No?

OVER THE LAST DECADES, MANY REGIONAL ORGANISATIONS HAVE GROWN up. They were invented to frame economic cooperation, promote political consultations, improve human security, and help to counteract terrorism and international organised crime. Asean finds its place among these organisations, having earned its own brand.

Three salient features constitute the key to grasp the depth of cooperation or integration: the purpose of the integration, trust and the extent of analogous policies. Asean was established in the harsh climate of the Cold War. Anxiety for repercussions from the Vietnam War reverberated through South-east Asia. The initiative was political more than economic and fear of the unknown was a driving force.

The changed strategic situation has shifted the focus to challenges and opportunities presented by the economic rise of China and India. Asean members must define and improve their comparative advantage. At the same time these new giants offer a unique opportunity to get a share of economic wealth. No individual Asean country can mastermind this process alone. For Asean and its member states, it can be a plus sum game provided they stick together, implement analogous political objectives and take steps to prevent economic clashes inside Asean.

The European Union (EU) has moved faster and created a significantly deeper integration. The EU has pursued political and economic goals in tandem. It played an indispensable role in restructuring Europe after the end of the Cold War. The single market, single Currency (euro) and the move towards a common foreign and security policy stand as remarkable achievements. Over the last decade, human security has been incorporated in the integration. Trust has been the catalyst for a path-breaking model pooling sovereignty to be exercised in common instead of each member state safeguarding its own interests. A sense of common destiny forged by tradition, history, common interests and analogous policies have been instrumental.

Recently, the EU was on the verge of adopting a Constitution. It was rejected by a majority of voters in two member states, underlining how difficult it is to take the integration to such an advanced stage, but it also shows how far the EU had gone. The philosophy of the EU is reflected in the preamble of the Treaty of Rome on "an ever closer union among the peoples of Europe". It is an ongoing process, setting long-term goals but approaching them step-bystep, overcoming setbacks, failures and disappointments.

There are similarities between the EU and Asean. Adaptation to changed circumstances and an endeavour to take the cooperation beyond pure economics and trade and the pivotal ones. The main difference is found in institutional structure and decision-making.

Presently, Asean does not contemplate a pooling of sovereignty. As long as this is not the case, integration can be pursued but it will spread to fewer issues and be less deep than the European one. This approach limits the depth and width of the integration.

But Asean looks more lively and determined to move ahead than most other regional integration. NAFTA — the free trade agreement between North American countries — is confined to free trade and does not augur further integration and consultations among the member states. Judged by critical voices about benefits for the members, it is highly doubtful whether they feel the same degree or idea of commonality that Asean is striving to create.

The same observation catches the eye, looking at regional integration in South Asia (for example, the South Asian Association for Regional Cooperation) and in South America (for example, Mercosur). These are useful organisations, but they find it difficult to move beyond economic and trade issues.

The idea of a charter for Asean points to a rising sentiment of shared challenges, problems and common solutions to meet the preoccupation of all members — a feeling that together we may overcome the problems, alone we fail. The problems are not confined to economics and trade even if those are the most important. They touch on the whole spectrum of security, human security and large parts of social life.

This singles out Asean from many other regional organisations. It remains to be seen whether some of the basic principles from the EU model will be modified to suit Asean's purpose or whether another edition of integration will emerge in Asia.

The Asean countries can opt for distinctive, even in some cases singular, economic systems or strong economic integration. Both are legitimate political goals with advantages and disadvantages, but both cannot be pursued simultaneously. The Europeans chose economic integration leading to common, even single, rules for economic life.

Somewhere down the road, Asean countries have to choose where to go — integrate or be on your own? Maybe the degree of mutual trust and a feeling of sharing the same destiny will determine the outcome.

This article was first published in *The Straits Times*, 8 August 2007.

ASEAN Charter:

A Significant Step in the Right Direction

ASEAN'S EMINENT PERSONS' GROUP (EPG) HAS COMPLETED ITS REPORT which will form a basis for the drafting of the ASEAN charter. The charter will hopefully take shape when ASEAN next holds its summit, which will be in Singapore in November.

The EPG's report is a realistic attempt to push the integration of South-east Asia further. Considering that 10 persons with different backgrounds had to agree, the suggestions in the report strike a reasonable balance between what is desirable and what is achievable.

Much of the debate so far has focused on the thorny question of membership — expulsion, suspension or withdrawal. That is understandable, but regrettable. It may be politically desirable, even indispensable, to include this issue in the charter, but it is not the main issue for the future of ASEAN.

Integration should be based on mutual trust and a political will to succeed together. If one or more member states do not enjoy the confidence of the others, or one or more member states do not confide in the others, ASEAN faces a political more than a legal problem.

Globalisation means that many economic challenges are now better tackled together with adjacent countries than individually. This is the basic idea of economic integration. It is what justifies it in the eyes of citizens less interested in political designs than in its impact on their daily lives.

From this perspective, what can ASEAN do for its member states, for the international community, and for their members' citizens? What is the value added?

The report deserves unqualified praise for what it says about objectives and principles. There is neat balance between facilitating growth, developing societal norms, and providing a platform for ASEAN in the international community.

ASEAN will have to face tough questions from both its citizens and the international community in the coming years: Is ASEAN the right vehicle for cooperation? Does it focus on the relevant problems? Are the appropriate instruments available?

Citizens have to see that ASEAN is relevant to them. The international community must see ASEAN as a stakeholder in the international system. Integration will lose credibility if a gap opens up between intention and reality. The scoreboard must correspond to the ambitions.

The Lure of a Single Market

The report's suggestions about substance are the right ones. Endeavours to establish a single market need to be speeded up. A strong, vibrant and deep integration ensures purchasing power and economic clout in the region. Only a strong integration placing ASEAN firmly in the international picture would make South-east Asia an interesting partner for the three large Asian economies: Japan, China and India.

A supply chain is building up in East Asia, and one of the most important tasks for ASEAN — maybe the most important — is to carve out a place for South-east Asian economies in that chain.

Three specific areas are of particular importance in the coming years: international trade, energy and the environment.

The international trade system is not as well established as it used to be. The Doha Round aiming at further liberalisation is in a critical phase. The main point, however, is that the system may undergo changes in the coming years, possibly taking into account the widespread popularity of bilateral agreements.

Given these circumstances, individual countries may find it hard to defend their interests, lacking weight compared to the big players such as the United States and the European Union. Regional integration can provide the South-east Asian countries with a stronger platform — if they wish to use it.

Environment and energy — and probably a combination of these two questions — will dominate the international agenda in the years to come. The recent report by the United Nations about global warming is the starting point for international action on an unprecedented scale.

The ASEAN EPG report was written before the UN move. ASEAN countries should look at the necessity of beefing up the charter on these two items.

The main point is — again — that it will help the South-east Asian countries move ahead. Unilateral actions may be difficult, as they have a negative impact on the countries' respective competitive positions and put the lead country at risk. Taking measures in common obliterates this fear, as the European experience with integration so clearly shows.

On top of that, ASEAN may be able to influence the upcoming international rules and regulations about energy and the environment. The international agenda in the coming years will be dominated by these topics; it is not too soon to be prepared, mapping out what South-east Asian countries would like to see happen instead of being surprised by initiatives from other countries.

It is encouraging that the EPG report, albeit a bit timidly, opens the door for decision-making without unanimity. Time will show how it will work in practice.

The point, however, is that such a rule makes member states more disposed to move towards agreement, knowing that in the end one or two of them could be isolated and a decision taken despite their opposition.

This is how the European Union works. Qualified majority voting is the norm for most items, but rarely used as member states are eager to enter into negotiations to safeguard their interest instead of putting up barren opposition that leaves them outside a compromise.

Lack of Institutions a Weakness

The weak part of the EPG report is the one on institutions or rather the lack of institutions. Regional integration can go some of the way without institutions, but there are limits; and ASEAN seems to be close to these limits.

As it is now, everything rests upon trust among member states supplemented by a Secretary-General responsible for calling member states into line. This is better than nothing, but not good enough in the longer term.

Institutions offer two indispensable things: the role as driver of the integration, and the watchdog ensuring that obligations are respected. Without a neutral body entrusted with powers and competences in these two areas, the integration may be pushed somewhat further, but not much further.

ASEAN is now 40 years old. It has arrived at a crossroads. It can choose between transforming itself into a substantial vehicle for integration, offering solutions to the South-east Asian countries, and struggling to prove why it is there.

The EPG report, hopefully being transformed into a charter, is a step in the right direction and a significant one, but there should be general recognition that it is a step and not the end of the road.

This article was first published in *The Straits Times*, 10 February 2007. Co-authored with Rodolfo C. Severino.

EU's Lessons for East Asian Integration

THE STRAITS TIMES (SINGAPORE) ON MAY 26 QUOTED MINISTER MENTOR Lee Kuan Yew as saying that it would be difficult for Asia to be one community like the European Union because the countries of Asia are not as 'comfortable' with one another as are the nations of Europe.

'To have one currency, a borderless community, I don't see that. Not yet. Maybe after 50, 70, 80 years, we can look at the matter again,' he was quoted as telling a largely business audience in Tokyo.

True enough; which is why it is quite unfair to criticise East Asia, or the smaller, more compact region of South-east Asia, for not achieving the degree of union or community that the EU has attained.

On the other hand, it would be wrong to conclude from the dissimilarity between East Asia — or ASEAN — and the EU that East Asia or ASEAN has nothing to learn from the European experience.

For East Asia and ASEAN can learn much from the EU in three areas: the imperative of regional economic integration, the feasibility of the integration process and the EU example in specific sectors.

It is generally recognised that East Asia — especially South-east Asia — can sustain high economic growth rates if its economy is integrated as a region, so that it provides one production platform and an efficient supply chain. An integrated economy would give East Asia and South-east Asia more weight in international trade negotiations, largely in the World Trade Organisation, and in global financial discussions, as in the International Monetary Fund.

The European experience has given proof of this. Although a number of European economies are sputtering at the moment, it should not be forgotten that, from the start of European integration in 1958 to around 2000, the member-states of the EU achieved rapid economic growth and gained considerable economic strength.

At the same time, the process and achievement of integration have enabled Europe to transcend and relegate to the past the conflicts that had devastated the continent so many times in history. They have allowed the EU to absorb peacefully the Central and Eastern European states from which Western Europe had been estranged for decades.

To be sure, European integration was driven by the chastening experience of war and the necessity of Franco-German reconciliation. It was built upon Europe's traditions, the strong interdependence of the European economies and a common culture rooted in Christianity. It was tailor-made to the challenges that Europe faced in the second half of the 20th century and constituted a model suitable to Europe's needs and the European way of tackling political and economic challenges.

Nevertheless, many elements, principles and mechanisms that the Europeans marshalled with such great success can be mobilised to promote integration in other parts of the world, including Asia.

The European model is a combination of ambitious goals and a step-by-step approach. When the process of integration was launched, the goals were clear — a common market, a common agricultural policy and a common external trade policy.

In 1958, these were ambitious goals, so ambitious that few believed they were realistic.

However, the treaties that set these goals provided for a step-by-step process, including a timetable. Since then, the Europeans have used this model again and again. First, they agree on an ambitious goal, and then they implement it, in a laborious and often tedious process, but never questioning the goal itself.

Today, 12 EU countries are members of a monetary union, having replaced their own currencies with a single European currency, the euro. The euro was adopted as the single currency in 2002, but the

EU's leaders had approved it as far back as 1969. It took almost one-third of a century for the euro to go from idea and ambition to reality and use.

One important lesson that can be learned from the European experience is that the process and achievement of closer integration can cultivate in the member-states the mutual trust that is essential for lasting peace and stability.

Another is that one country cannot hope alone to deal with many challenges in today's globalised world, such as transnational crime, international terrorism, environmental degradation and communicable diseases. Nation-states can defend and promote their political and economic interests much more effectively together than separately.

A third lesson is that the Europeans have always ensured that they pursue regional integration in a win-win manner, that all EU members feel that they are better off inside than outside. The union has to serve as some kind of problem grinder for the member-states, never rejecting an individual member presenting problems, but trying to make that member comfortable by working out solutions.

These are lessons that transcend cultural and historical similarities or differences; they are applicable to all regions.

In the same way, there are lessons to be learned from the EU experience in terms of specific measures for integration, be they in the realm of customs procedures, product standards, environmental protection, public health, transport and communications policy, energy or the prevention of anti-competitive behavior. These are measures that work and should not be rejected out of hand just because they are practised in another part of the world.

Europe and East Asia are different and always will be, but this does not mean that East Asia, or at least ASEAN, is not driven by similar political and economic imperatives of regional economic integration as Europe was, or that the EU process cannot be replicated to some significant extent in East Asia.

This article was first published in *The Straits Times*, 30 May 2007. Co-authored with Rodolfo C. Severino.

Happy 50th, EU

FIFTY YEARS AGO, ON MARCH 25 1957, POLITICAL LEADERS FROM OLD rival European countries met at the Capitol building in Rome, which symbolised the glorious past of the Roman Empire, to launch Europe on a new venture.

They approached the Capitol under the watchful eye of Roman emperor Marcus Aurelius (AD161–180) in the centre of a small oval square designed by Michelangelo.

The philosopher emperor had consoled himself by committing his innermost thoughts to paper, in a renowned book known as *The Meditations*. It was to be almost 1,800 years before there was a resurrection of the prosperity and stability that had reigned in his time. But when it came, it was a victory for magnanimity and tolerance.

Between 1870 and 1945, Germany and France tried to destroy each other three times. Some historians call these wars the European civil wars, others Europe's suicide attempts, while yet others point to the harmful effects of nationalism and fanatical political ideologies.

What today is the European Union — in its first phase, it was called the European Economic Community — has given global politics and economics three major breakthroughs.

The first is that old enemies can and should forgive each other. France, one of the victors in World War II, took the initiative to include Germany in the construction of post-war Europe. Both countries realised that further bloodshed or even economic rivalry would harm them, while cooperation would open the door to a peaceful, stable and prosperous Europe.

Over the years, the two countries have quarrelled over the distribution of economic advantages and burdens within the EU, they have disputed the EU's foreign policy and they have competed for markets for their products. But both have stayed together as drivers of European integration.

The second is that confrontation, crisis and conflicts can be replaced by cooperation, consensus and compromise. What the Europeans achieved was a brand new idea in international politics: negotiations not geared to gain advantages for particular countries, but to enlarge the sum of potential benefits for all. The Europeans invented a plus-sum game.

The third may be rated by history as the true political invention. Not only is the EU a rule-based international venture, but it is founded upon the pooling of sovereignty.

There are many explanations for this bold invention. Europeans realised early that when politics and economics become more and more global, individual countries stand little or no chance of safeguarding their interests in splendid isolation.

Just think of capital movements. What can a European country, even the bigger ones, do alone against the market? As was seen in the second half of the 20th century, nothing.

What at first glance might have seemed to be a reduction of the nation state's room for manoeuvre was in fact the opposite. The nation state enhanced its capabilities of defending its own interests by pooling its sovereignty with others. Do not be mistaken. States have not joined the EU to give away power; it is the other way around.

These achievements speak for themselves. The first stage of the EU's evolution gave it a common market, a common agricultural policy and a common external policy. This was all done in under 10 years.

Next came the single market, designed to remove the remaining obstacles to trade and to gain the advantages of an enlarged market.

The most obvious example of the EU's path-breaking nature is the creation of its single currency, the euro, in 1999.

Many observers overlook the fact that it took the Europeans 30 years — from 1969, when the idea was first mooted, to 1999 — to get from the drawing board to reality, but they got there.

Despite all gloomy predictions, the euro has been with us for eight years now. And a number of central banks around the world are busy switching some of their US dollar-denominated assets into euros.

The Europeans are also trying to sketch a common foreign and security policy. In many respects, they have. But there are shortcomings. When having to take a stance with regard to crucial issues such as the Iraq War, the Europeans have not risen to the occasion. National interests, prejudices and old ingrained attitudes have surfaced.

But look at the tangible results the EU has achieved in the Balkans, in Aceh and in Africa with peacekeeping operations. Maybe Europeans will move towards a genuine common foreign and security policy like a crab — sideways and sometimes backward, but always going forward.

As judged by history, the EU has made fantastic progress. Yet it seems to be in crisis. The proposed Constitution was rejected in 2005 by a majority of the voters in France and the Netherlands. Does that mean the EU is facing a major crisis?

Let me give three answers to that question.

- The work to adopt new European legislation has not stopped. Recently, the EU agreed to important new legislation on the opening of markets for services.
- After the French presidential election next month, a determined and serious attempt will be made to agree on a new treaty as a replacement for the proposed EU Constitution.
- In the long run, popular support is indispensable for the EU, and the key to popular support is to show that standards of living, human security and daily life all benefit from integration. This is a tall order, not the least because the problems people see in their daily lives vary from member state to member state.

In Ireland, which has full employment, not many give priority to improved conditions for employment. But in France and Germany, where unemployment is at 10 per cent, they do.

The insecurity over identity introduced to the Europeans by immigration is another sensitive and emotional issue.

The challenge for Europe's political leaders is to switch the focus of integration from the grand designs of yesterday to the problems that ordinary people meet in daily life. We will see whether Europe today has political leaders of the same calibre as 50 years ago.

This article was first published in *The Straits Times*, 22 March 2007.

Towards an ASEAN Charter:

Lessons from the European Union

SOME KEY POINTS WITH REGARD TO THE EUROPEAN UNION (EU) THAT ASEAN could make use of are as follows:

Main Principle of Economic Integration

a. Integration had to be a positive sum game for all so much so that it would always be better for a member state to be in rather than out of the union. Politically: stronger influence and better possibilities to shape and implement domestic political preferences. Economically: higher and sustainable growth rate leading to a higher living standard.

Two defining instances can be listed such as in the 1965 incident concerning France (boycott of institutions for six months) and when Margaret Thatcher in 1979 demanded "money back" given the sentiments that Britain was financing the EU at too high costs without hopes of returns. In both cases the "recalcitrant" member state was accommodated by a special political and/or economic arrangement.

This underlines that the objective(s) for the integration applies for all, but special arrangements, i.e., of transitional nature can be agreed for one or more member-states. They all get there but not necessarily by the same road and at the same time. Looking at the state of the EU today, this is still the case. UK stood outside the Social Charter in the Treaty of Maastricht, several member states are outside the EURO and the Schengen arrangement regarding free passage at borders.

It is thus pertinent for the Charter to be drafted in such a way that such difficult situations do not occur.

b. It was important for the organization to be a problem grinder. There must be common acceptance that integration is for the good of the member-states and for the population and that no problems are irrelevant. All member-states must come to the EU confident that their problem will be dealt with. And the population must feel that this is the case — the EU being relevant for them in their daily life and not only a political exercise at a high level or even worse an irritant.

c. A visible political objective should exist. In the EU case, this includes the 1950s free trade to boost economic growth and to counter the threat posed by the Soviet Union. Later came the Single European Act, Single Currency and Enlargement. It should target a clear political problem that the people understand and feel is relevant. And it is advisable to highlight why these problems cannot be solved without the integration.

The failure of the proposed Constitution in two member states was precisely because politicians did not manage to get across to the population and explain why the constitution was needed — they failed to communicate which political project demanded a constitution, what the existing treaties could not do.

Impact of Globalization

On the one hand, there is a need to ensure that the organization's own goals as well as those of the nation-states would be non-contradictory to rules set by multilateral organizations such as the WTO. At the same time, it is necessary to be aware that actions of one country have important impacts on its neighbours, i.e., economic policies and environmental rules such as building a nuclear power station close to an adjacent member state.

Economic integration makes it possible for a nation-state to punch above its weight by letting the regional integration (EU as a case) put its position forward. On the other hand the integration imposes certain obligations that may work as constraints on the nation-state.

For the nation-state it is of vital importance to adopt an offensive approach taking an active role in international institutions to be sure that rules and decisions adopted by them are in conformity with its own interest. It thus pushes the burden of adjusting to international rules/decisions on other nation-states. At the same time it creates room for manœuvre for itself, knowing that no domestic policies will run counter to the international set of rules.

The defence of the nation-state's room of manœuvre to shape its domestic policies starts at the international negotiating table and not by national legislation being more and more eroded as a bulwark by globalization.

Clearly Defined Roadmap

On how to proceed, the suggestion would be to proceed a step at a time. A roadmap would have to be clearly defined, starting from the basics before adding on in an incremental process. This would allow for changes and reversals.

The EU started with a customs union, a common agricultural policy and a common external trade policy. They were all visible and easily understood as steps to promote growth.

When tangible results are achieved the next steps can be taken.

The EU experience shows that of the so-called four freedoms — goods, services, capital, persons — goods do not pose much difficulties, services and capital are more difficult to handle, but it can be done, while freedom for movement of persons is a very sensitive issue.

In addition, so as to alleviate negative impacts, special instruments also had to be in place on several fronts such as provision of social funds, etc. Otherwise the disadvantaged member states and/or regions feel that they are left outside and deprived of benefits.

Decision-making Process and Institutions

A choice between intergovernmental and supranational decision making had to be made — the latter would require the pooling of sovereignty and be a legally binding act.

The question of sovereignty was often misrepresented in the debate. Economic integration does not imply that member states abandon or lose sovereignty. They transfer sovereignty to exercise it in common with adjacent nation-states pursuing analogous political goals. By doing so they adopt an offensive approach creating space for domestic policies and policies pursued by the group of nation-states forming the integration.

Again, this would be done in an incremental manner and while some parts remained intergovernmental, there are parts that go under a supranational decision-making process.

A well-defined, specific platform as well as a pilot project in a specific area should be taken up.

The most difficult step for the EU has been to engage the population and convince people that the EU institutions are not distant and far fetched institutions but institutions "for them", where they are represented. EU institutions are still not regarded as part of the political life in the same way as the national political institutions. The result is a gap of confidence and lack of trust between the institutions and the European population.

The population still does not see or agree that the ultimate objective for the economic integration is to move the decision-making process to the same level as the economy. Goods, capital etc, have jumped out of the national context to operate internationally. Economic integration is basically an attempt to catapult the political decision making to the same level. That is why the key words are the same for the national decision-making: legitimacy, accountability and transparency.

The members of the Commission (in principle one for each member state) are nominated by the member states but pledge not to pursue national interest (the President of the European Commission has to be approved by the European Parliament after a debate about his programme — this is no formality). The officials of the European Commission are recruited and promoted on merit. Every year exams rather like the Chinese mandarin system take place for candidates wishing to start a career as "eurocrats".

Building Trust

It is of the utmost importance to build trust among the members. Feedback and proper representation of the population are also most necessary. In the 1970s and 1980s the Europeans created the foundation for what later became EUROland by classifying national economic and monetary policy as a policy of common interest. Countless meetings were organized to map out a common approach and member-states looked to the EU for support when in difficulties.

Finally the 3 Cs, namely Coherence, Consistency and Continuity, are of paramount importance to ensure the smooth running of the daily work. The member-states must know the policies pursued by each other to prevent surprises undermining confidence and trust.

This article first appeared in *Framing the ASEAN Charter: An ISEAS Perspective*, compiled by Rodolfo R. Severino, pp. 53–58 (2005). Reproduced here with the kind permission of the publisher, Institute of Southeast Asian Studies, Singapore, <http://bookshop.iseas.edu.sg>.

ASEAN Can Become More Like the EU

GLOBAL TRADE AND INVESTMENT DWARF NATIONAL ECONOMIC FLOWS and thus diminish the scope for individual and national policies. When that is the case, runs the argument, why not get together and institutionalise the cooperation — form a group of nations strong enough to safeguard the interests of each nation state, enhance their capabilities to shape national policies and even put an imprint on global developments?

The Europeans have in selected areas pooled their sovereignty. Contrary to expectations, this has not reduced but enhanced the power of individual nation states to pursue national objectives.

They have become better able to control the impact of economic globalisation and, to a certain extent, better able to shape its processes instead of being its passive subjects.

Wealth and prosperity rarely flow from national economies. They depend on how the nation states turn global economic developments to their advantage.

Two recent developments give credence to this line of thinking — the uncertainty about the future of world trade after the unsuccessful Doha round of talks and the discussion about an appreciation of Asian currencies, in particular the Chinese yuan compared to the US dollar.

Small nation states heavily dependent on international trade and investment are, more than bigger nations, subject to the vagaries of trade and currency fluctuations. The future of ASEAN will depend on its ability to define a role inside a larger and more powerful East Asian or Asian economic body.

This is not impossible. Asia's trade figures suggest that Asia could become a self-sustaining economy. South-east Asian countries can carve out a platform for themselves in this economic powerhouse built around China and India.

Secondly, it may be worthwhile to build an ASEAN identity, not in conflict or competition with the national identities of member states, but as a value-added factor. In Europe, many Europeans refer to both their nationality and their European identity when asked how they identify themselves; some even include the region they come from, such as Scotland, Bavaria or Catalonia.

For ASEAN, perhaps the time has come to sketch some guidelines, some ideals and some ambitions for member states.

Closing Loopholes

A degree of common understanding of what is good and what is bad behaviour would come in handy. A nation state should behave like a good citizen vis-à-vis its partners and vis-à-vis its own citizens. But some common ground must be established.

The notion of solidarity goes hand in hand with the idea of a common identity and common destiny. It strengthens the bonds between not only the member states but, and even more importantly, between the populations in the member states. Solidarity must be shown in helping and assisting other member states when hit by economic problems or natural disasters.

The goal of an ASEAN economic community by 2015 is an ambitious one but ambitions are indispensable for moving ahead. Without a timetable or a road map sketching when to do what, there will be too many loopholes left open. ASEAN needs, in one way or another, to pin member states down not only on the goals, but also on how to get there.

ASEAN should scrutinise its competitive parameters to see how they compare against China's and India's, and strengthen those where it is already in front.

As production moves towards higher value- added goods and services, the safeguarding of intellectual property rights — just to mention one example — will tend to determine who wins. ASEAN could and should capitalise on governance, legal systems and the qualitative environment as competitive parameters.

The time may not be ripe yet for coordinated economic policies, but the time is ripe for deeper consultations and information sharing about national economic policies.

There is talk of exchange rate cooperation in East Asia but no one knows how far and how fast it will go, and/or how successful whatever is put in motion may be. Steps to move national economic policies towards convergence instead of divergence are necessary first steps in preparing the ground for possible currency rate cooperation.

Like it or not, individual nation states are confronted with a whole range of global issues, such as trade policy, global warming and energy. It is fair enough if ASEAN member states do not adopt the same stand on all these issues, but steps to find a common position could be initiated. That will increase awareness of how ASEAN could influence global negotiations. It will also enhance the sense of identity, common destiny and solidarity.

International terrorism, international crime and infectious diseases constitute a sinister triangle threatening globalisation. ASEAN is in a position to contribute to the global debate on how to combat these evils.

Reaching Out to the Public

Despite integration being at a far more advanced stage, the European Union (EU) has found it difficult to rally continued support from the public. This underlines the necessity of reaching out to the public to explain why integration is a good thing and what advantages it offers for the majority of people. People want to know how it actually improves their daily lives.

Within Europe, passports indicate both the holder's nationality and his or her membership of the EU. The same may be considered for ASEAN. It will be tangible evidence of an ASEAN identity.

In schools, the curriculum could be used to develop an ASEAN identity. In the long run, children will be decisive in forging that identity. In Europe, it was the so-called "Inter-Rail generation" travelling around Europe on cheap railway tickets that led to more awareness of other EU member states.

The whole panoply of measures in the EU to facilitate study in other member states falls in the same category. Indeed, the French and the Germans are working on a common history book and have recently set up a common Franco-German university.

ASEAN cannot be compared to the EU or even to any particular stage in the process of European integration, but in one respect a parallel may be drawn. If nothing happens and the integration gets trapped in a stalemate without producing results and/or progress, support among politicians, business people and the general public will start to wane. It is often said of European integration that it can be compared to a bike: It must move ahead all the time in order not to lose balance.

In the globalised world it is cold to be alone, but cosy to be among adjacent and likeminded countries.

This article was first published in *The Straits Times*, 28 September 2006.

Template for Sino-Japan Peace

IN THE PERIOD BETWEEN 1871 AND 1945 — LESS THAN TWO generations — Europe was ravaged by three wars in which Germany and France were at each other's throats.

After 1945, an astounding and historically unique European integration was born out of a reconciliation between the same two countries.

As Asia now faces its own process of integration, it is natural to ask: How was the reconciliation between France and Germany brought about, what are the basic principles, how does it work and what are the results?

These questions are relevant for reconciliation between Japan and China, still waiting in the wings but without which any Asian integration looks fragile and half-hearted.

The first and indispensable step is having the political will. After the end of World War II, French and German political leaders concluded that war between them should never ravage the European continent again. They decided to trust each other, forget rivalries and forsake recriminations.

In short, to put history behind them and look forward.

France did not repeat the disastrous policies it had taken after World War I to 'punish' Germany politically and economically, but offered cooperation instead.

Germany's reckoning with its own past was sincere, as the denazification process illustrated, and was perceived as such in the rest of Europe. The Federal Republic of Germany emerging in 1949 should not be held accountable for the crimes of the Nazi regime and, most important of all, made every effort to dissociate itself from the Nazis.

In 1970, Federal Chancellor Willy Brandt, himself an exile during the Nazi regime, knelt in sorrow and repentance when visiting the ghetto in Warsaw where Nazi troops crushed a rebellion in 1943.

This unforgettable gesture said more than thousands of words could about Germany's own soul-searching.

Leaders of the two countries have constantly taken care to express the political will to deepen the reconciliation and bring the two nations closer together. In 1984, 70 years after the outbreak of World War I, President Francois Mitterrand of France and Federal Chancellor Helmut Kohl from Germany met to hold hands — a symbol of how far the reconciliation had gone.

They chose the French fortification of Verdun where a battle in 1916 incurred 400,000 French and 300,000 German casualties.

The contrast between German and Japanese is stark: From the German side we have official and openly voiced repentance, even by statesmen who suffered under the Nazis, while on the Japanese side there are leaders continuing visits to the Yasukuni war shrine, semiofficial attitudes to the Nanjing massacre that downplay its horrors, and textbooks that give a glossy picture of Japan's role in the war.

Preventing Rearmament

The Franco-German reconciliation was initiated in the late 1940s. The two countries decided to put the two key industries of coal and steel under supranational control in the European Coal and Steel Community (ECSC) that came into force in 1952. By giving up national control over these two industries, unilateral rearmament became impossible.

The ECSC grew into the incubator for the European Union which now has 25 member states, a single currency and a Common Foreign and Security Policy.

Under the Elysee Treaty signed in 1963, political leaders of the European Union meet three times a year in the European Council. It is well known that Germany and France coordinate their positions before the meetings. Mutual trust is deep enough to allow one to speak on behalf of both, even during negotiations about difficult political problems calling for decision-making at the highest level.

Indeed, Franco-German reconciliation goes beyond the political level and is firmly rooted in an extensive network of contacts between the peoples of the two nations. Facts on the ground reveal a deeply rooted mutual wish among the French and the Germans to bring about a special kind of commonality.

The official network is not limited to government level. Regions in both countries (in France les regions and in Germany the lander) have instituted a network of cooperation. An illustration is the network between the French region Alsace, that from 1871 to 1918 was a part of Germany, and two of Germany's western lander, Baden-Wurttemberg and Rheinland-Pfalz. The French region Lorraine, also partly German from 1871 to 1918, has formed a network with the German lander of Saarland and Rheinland-Pfalz.

There are also more than 2,000 twinning agreements between French and German cities.

Similar cooperative arrangements exist between research institutions and business organisations.

The two countries also established a Council for Culture in 1988. One of its outcomes is ARTE, a bilingual French-German television channel.

An organisation for bringing youth in the two countries closer was set up in 1963 and, since then, millions of young people have been involved in exchange programmes. About 200,000 take part each year.

After a pilot project, the two countries agreed in 1994 to launch a common German-French high school certificate called the AbiBac after the German Abitur and the French Baccalaureate. More than 30 high schools in both countries offer AbiBac to students.

In 1999, a German-French university was founded, with its administrative headquarters in Saarbrucken in Germany. About 3,000 students are enrolled in about 100 courses there leading to a bi-national certificate.

The lessons to draw from reconciliation between Germany and France?

Reconciliation cannot be achieved without a political will radiating mutual trust and putting the past solidly behind the countries in question. The political leaders must constantly drive home the point that they want the reconciliation to succeed, be deeper, include more societal layers and be sincere.

It helps if reconciliation takes place inside a broader geographical integration such as the European Union, bringing along other countries with a shared history and desire for peace, stability and prosperity.

The repentance of the nation that committed war crimes — in Europe, Germany; in Asia, Japan — must be felt as sincere.

Symbols and gestures to bring this message home must be found by politicians who earnestly believe that what happened during the war warrants repentance.

It is not enough to operate on the political level. A determined effort to mobilise the population is necessary.

The process can get a kick-start from politicians but it can succeed as a lasting element only if driven by genuine popular support.

Civic society must feel that it is the right thing to do.

This article was first published in *The Straits Times*, 20 January 2006.

Toward a United Europe

When the Soviet Empire crumbled in 1989/1990, observers also expected major upheavals in Central- and Eastern Europe (CEE). Fortunately, none of these calamities materialised because the prospect of joining the EU kept conflicts at bay.

In his essay, Ambassador Møller recounts the momentous decision taken by the EU to begin negotiations with the CEE countries for their entry into the former. He clarifies several common misconceptions about the implications of the enlargement process and also offers a prognosis about the future of an enlarged EU.

When the Empire Crumbles — The EU Steps In

The European Union (EU) is right now undertaking one of the greatest feats of political engineering ever attempted: the unification of Western Europe with Central- and Eastern Europe (CEE). It will reshape and change the political landscape in Europe. The single market and the euro will be strengthened. Europe will face the challenge and at the same time the opportunity to ensure peace and stability in this part of the world. This new situation will confront the EU with the expectation of a European voice in international concert.

When the Soviet Empire and the Russian Empire crumbled in 1989/1990 most observers would have put their money on strong economic, political, and social upheavals in Central- and Eastern Europe (CEE) making what happened in Yugoslavia look like a picnic.

From Estonia in the North to Slovenia in the South we find about ten nation-states but more than 25 peoples and languages and at least four main religions. Traditionally the minorities in one nation-state could be expected to call upon its brothers/sisters in an adjacent nation state to escape cultural imperialism exercised by the government in the nation-state where it lived. Civil wars with interference from outside were a realistic threat. Quite a few predicted major bloodshed.

None of these calamities materialised. Twelve years later we can look back upon strong economic growth combined with peace and stability. The potential conflicts were kept at bay by the prospect of joining the EU. At an early stage, farsighted statesmen in the EU put forward this as a long term objective for all CEE countries. But there was a condition. And that condition was respect for minorities and human rights in the candidate countries. The EU would stand by the pledge given during the Cold War to receive the CEE countries as full members provided that these countries managed to solve their conflicts among themselves, by themselves.

This turned out to be a brilliant piece of foreign policy. One tends to forget the risks and problems so obvious in CEE in 1990, how fragile these newborn democracies actually were and how painful the restructuring of their economies away from centrally planned economies toward market economies turned out to be. If the EU had hesitated, if the prospect of future EU-membership had been in doubt, it is possible that the courageous political leaders master minding the transformation of their countries in extremely difficult circumstances would not have succeeded. They might well have succumbed to non-democratic forces more or less as it happened in the inter-war period for most of these nation-states.

A Step-by-Step Process

The EU and the CEE countries got there through a step-by-step process. The EU used its panoply of measures and policy instruments and tailored them to new circumstances. Trade agreements were transformed into what was labelled Europe-Agreements. There was an Association agreement with the prospect of membership in due course, and in the early/middle part of the 1990's, country after country filed an application for membership.

Two steps need to be singled out. The first one was the meeting of the European Council in Copenhagen in June 1993 where the CEE countries were promised full membership provided they met three conditions. Their political systems should be democratic, based upon the rule of law, stability of institutions and protection of minorities. Their economic systems should be market economies. Their administrative systems should be able to cope with the rules and regulations of the EU including the objectives of political, economic and monetary union. The second one was the laborious and cumbersome examination of each country undertaken by the European Commission to see whether they fulfilled the conditions. Again, country after country was listed on the positive side. There were doubts, of course, but the reports were all giving the same message: They were eligible for membership but the timetable was up for discussion.

The momentous decision was taken in the middle of 1990's to start negotiations with all ten CEE countries more or less at the same time. This was done without promising to finish the negotiations or to fix entry into the EU at the same time. This recipe kept the door open for all. It responded to the basic political fact that they all wanted to join but also wanted to be treated as individual sovereign states. They were all given the same chance. It was up to them to grab it or lose it. The EU did not discriminate. It would have been disastrous if some of these countries had been singled out as worthy ones while others would have been rejected without even given the chance to present their case.

The European Council in Copenhagen in December 2002 finished the job. The EU envisages to welcome the following ten countries as new members from May 1, 2004: Cyprus, the Czech Republic, Estonia, Hungary, Latvia, Lithuania, Malta, Poland, the Slovak Republic and Slovenia.

Negotiations with Bulgaria and Romania continue looking for 2007 as the date for these two countries' membership.

Turkey is often being mentioned as a special case. That is not correct. And this is borne out in the conclusions from the meeting in Copenhagen. It says unequivocally that the same criteria will apply for Turkey as for other countries applying for membership. In December 2004 the EU will examine the situation in Turkey and decide whether the criteria are fulfilled and if so enlargement negotiations will start.

Enlargement with such a large number of countries require equitable, transitional arrangements taking into considerations the new member countries' economic, industrial, social and administrative problems. It is a misunderstanding often heard that negotiations running over a considerable length of time are about changes and/ or amendment to the basic treaties. This is wrong. The new member states accept the treaties as they are but they are granted transitional (temporary) derogations.

This is being done to preserve the objectives and the working of the EU despite the enlargement. It was exactly the same in 1973 when UK, Ireland and Denmark joined, in 1980 when Greece joined, in 1985 when Spain and Portugal joined, in 1995 when Sweden, Austria and Finland joined. The new comers join a club. The club does not change its rules. The new member states adapt to conform to these rules as they are but they are granted time to do so.

The Implications of Enlargement

What does the enlargement mean for some of the vital parts of the EU, and what are some of the myths about the implication of the enlargement — for the EU and for the new member states.

1. It is often stated that the costs of the enlargement are enormous. This is clearly nonsense. Based on present calculations, the total cost over three years (2004–2006) is about 0.10% of EU's total Gross National Product (GNP). And this is less than one euro out of every one thousand produced in EU every year. Calculated into tangible amount we get to about 25 euros per year per capita in the existing EU 15 member states. Just compare it with the so-called peace dividend (reduction in military expenditure) in Europe

after the end of the Cold War. Most EU members states have seen a reduction of the magnitude of at least half a percentage point (and that estimate is in the lower range) every year — five times as much as the enlargement will cost the EU. The real problem is not the costs for the EU but that the EU in its endeavours to save money has been so parsimonious that some of the new member states or rather a majority of their population comes to the conclusion that the deal is not good enough.

2. Some people fear that the enlargement will be the end of the CAP. The gap between farmers in the existing EU and farmers in the poorer new member states is too large. If the existing rules are applied forthwith to the farmers in the new member states costs will skyrocket. If not the CAP will drop the word common and instead become a dichotomised policy. This explains why the EU and the new member states agreed on transitional measures stretching to 2013. But again, this is not the real problem. The real problem is that the CAP badly needs an overhaul. It is not so bad as some people outside the EU insists. But the Europeans have to face the unpleasant fact that the CAP is too expensive and too costly. It takes about 40% of total EU budget while only about 4% of the EU population is employed in this sector. And the overwhelming part of the CAP expenditure goes to small and inefficient farmers not competitive and not economically viable in the present global economy. Seen from a Singapore perspective the CAP is a very visible obstruction for a more liberal trade policy pursued by the EU to give the EU more credence among developing nations.

3. The fear is sometimes being voiced that the free access to the labour market inside member states will lead to an avalanche of migration from the CEE countries to the present EU. Three counter-arguments to put the problems in the right framework. First, transitional periods of up to seven years have been agreed but each EU member state can decide whether they wish to apply a transitional period or apply existing EU-rules vis-à-vis the new member states from day one. Second, the economic situation in

Europe poses quite a different problem. Europe today needs more geographic mobility of labour to compete with the US, not less. A good many economists have pointed to the conventional wisdom of economics telling that EU as such cannot survive unless labour starts to move more freely around. Third, Europe is seeing a new pattern of competitiveness already visible when Spain and Portugal joined in 1985. The labour intensive industrial production is being outsourced. Not to developing countries but to the CEE countries. For Europe it is good that we preserve jobs inside Europe even if the distribution of jobs become more and more lopsided with the highly skilled jobs in the existing EU and the low skilled ones in the new member states.

Let us look upon the likely changes regarding economics, foreign policy and institutions following in the slipstream of the enlargement based upon the — likely — assumption that all major adhering countries vote 'yes' to join the EU.

The single market in goods and for most of services will function after the enlargement without much delay. As the existing agreements signed since 1990 have already introduced a large measure of free movements of goods and services there will be few but not very substantial immediate repercussions on the European economy and on the economies in individual member, including, the new states. However, in the long run the larger single market will work in favour of European competitiveness. As mentioned earlier exploitation of the possibilities to move production around will work in this direction.

The Common Trade Policy will have to take into account the interests of a larger number of member countries of which some will ask for more protection than the existing and more competitive member states. It is an open question how that will influence the EU's trade policy. The same concern was voiced when Spain and Portugal joined in 1985 but had not really materialised.

There are no transitional measures for the Economic and Monetary Union (EMU). This does not necessarily mean that the new member states will join the euro from day one. As mentioned earlier there will be transitional measures for some capital movements. With

UK, Denmark, Sweden outside the Eurozone the same possibility is open for the new member states even if it is not said explicitly. The argument that an economic and monetary union cannot work properly unless the regions included are more or less of the same economic nature is simplistic. Experience from economic and monetary unions around the world (examples: USA, Australia, China and in Southeast Asia, Malaysia) indicates that different economic structures and different economic levels among the various regions are compatible with such a Union.

The argument that the costs of integrating the Central- and Eastern European economies in the EU will be so large as to undermine future economic prosperity as it happened in Germany after 1990 may also not be fully substantiated. First, the subsequent development of the German economy was in the cards before the German unification and would have taken place during the 1990's even without the unification. Second, the size of the economies in CEE is manageable for the EU. Third, as outlined above there are also advantages for the European economies associated with the enlargement. My own assessment is that in the short run the enlargement will not create much change in economic power but rather that the European economies will benefit in the longer run from the larger market and better possibilities for outsourcing inside the single market.

The changes will be more visible for foreign policy. Two things have happened in Europe after 1990. Territorial defence is out. Soft side of security policy is in. It could be rephrased in a more conceptual form by saying two other things: First, security in Europe has become indivisible meaning that either Europe as a whole is secure and peaceful or Europe as such faces a security problem. Security in one part of Europe is a concern for all of Europe. Second, threats to security in Europe if any does not any longer appear in the form of potential aggression from one European country directed at another European country. Either it arises inside nation-states or from outside Europe.

In today's world the EU faces a threat and a challenge. The threat consists of the minorities inside individual nation-states. They can destabilise the political environment. EU faces a challenge by having to shoulder a responsibility for security in adjacent geographical regions and assume some responsibility for the global development.

The enlargement should and hopefully will mean that the problem of minorities in CEE will not weigh down the political agenda. The European model having served Western Europe so well since the 1950's will now also apply to CEE: economic internationalisation and cultural decentralisation.[1] This model implies that the key to participation in the international economy does not any longer rest with the central government but have moved to the EU. And the EU does not demand allegiance to the culture of the majority in the nation-states as a quid pro quo for opening the door to the global economy. The minorities will have a free run to pursue their own culture without trepidation of cultural imperialism exercised by the central government. This is what has solved or rather prevented potential conflicts inside the Western European nation-states. Witness the Scots in Britain, the Bretons in France, the Catalans in Spain, the Lombards in Italy — the list is almost endless. The same lies in the cards for Central- and Eastern Europe.

But the enlargement also means that the EU has got some new neighbours. Russia, Ukraine, the Balkans while North Africa lies just outside its doorstep and the Middle East looked toward the EU for attention.

In some of these countries the main security problem is exactly the same as it was in Western Europe and still is in parts of CEE — ethnic and/or religious minorities. Such internal problems cannot be confined to the countries directly involved. Exactly because security in today's Europe cannot be divided they will destabilise Europe as a whole if allowed to run their course. EU will be forced to apply preventive diplomacy. Thus, one should see a more active and engaged EU in adjacent countries exercising security policy, not to pursue its own interests per se, but to maintain stability and security in Europe as a whole.

What happened first in Western Europe, then in CEE and now being tried in adjacent countries are a remarkable and unique example of foreign- and security policy focusing upon the soft instruments of economics, trade and culture.

Europe cannot escape however the inevitable and uncomfortable question of bang for the bucks — a common defence and military policy. I do not see EU projecting power abroad more or less in the same vein as the US. Not now. Not in a foreseeable future. May be never. My view is that Europe and the Europeans have crossed the line. We may still see, and maybe increasingly so, European military forces participating — in some cases even being the major shareholder — in international military intervention. But we will not see a major European military action far away from Europe.

To sum up concerning foreign policy — EU will for some time confine itself to the soft instruments of foreign and security policy and be relatively successful in adjacent countries. A genuine common foreign-security and even more military policy is in the embryonic stage. It will come. When it comes it will rely much less heavily on military muscle than is the case for the present American foreign and security policy. Hopefully the world develops in a way compatible with such a reluctance to use force commendable in itself but also relying on a similar attitude gaining ground around the globe.

Needed Reforms to Accommodate Enlargement

Enlargement will force changes through with regard to the institutions and decision-making. No illusions. This is where the original and present EU will yield to a new and different Union. Early summer 2003 the so-called Convention under the presidency of Valery Giscard d'Estaing delivers its report on precisely these questions and problems. The Convention is expected to produce a blueprint for a European constitution.

All this augurs a fundamental change in the powers vested in the institutions and the balance between the member states. My own reading for what it is worth point to the following:

i) A weaker Commission because supranationality is not any longer in the vogue. ii) A stronger Parliament because there is an obvious need to strengthen the links between the institutions and the people of Europe. The Council will probably be left without much change. iii) The voting system will have to be adjusted to make it more difficult to block decisions. iv) A President chosen to lead the work of the Council to ensure better continuity and more political power than the present system of rotating presidency provides.

It has been a salient factor since the European integration was launched that the small member states were over-represented. This question has been on the agenda on several occasions. But changes have always been successfully resisted by the small member states even if the four enlargements since 1973 brought in two large members states and seven small or at best medium sized ones. We may now expect an amendment of the voting weights and what constitutes qualified majority becoming the rule rather than the exception. It may not be said explicitly but the objective will be to reduce the over-representation of the small countries. This is politically manageable. Among other reasons because it can with justification be said that the whole exercise aims at restoring the balance between small and larger member states to what is was in the early stages of the integration. The real battle will come over how to handle the balance between small and larger member states in cases, where not all member states are represented in an institution at least not at the same time. In this category falls membership of the future Commission, the rotating presidency and the ideas of replacing it with a permanent president. The flywheel will be whether the larger member states will open the door for a mechanism ensuring the smaller member states that they will be represented from time to time. Or whether they will insist upon some kind of voting system feeding and in some cases confirming the suspicion that they will use such a mechanism to rotate representation among themselves keeping the small birds away from the institutional breadbasket.

The European Union is the greatest problem smasher ever invented. It does so for the member states and it does so without interruption. No member state has ever taken a problem to the EU without seeing it addressed by the EU-institutions and the other member states.

Four Pertinent Issues for the Future

Trying to make a forecast my eyes fall upon four main topics.

1. The future of the euro. The euro has come to stay. The rise of the euro in recent months can be explained in many ways but one of the explanations is probably that some, may be many, of the Asian central banks are diversifying their currency reserves from US dollars to euros.

   But when will the euro be a real international currency? We will have to wait a while. Confidence has to grow. The European economies and the enlargement have to stay the course. EU to show a bit more dynamics. The ECB (European Central Bank) to establish itself as a partner among the peers in central banking. But it will come. Just give it time. The world needs and wants an alternative to the US dollar and there are not many candidates around.

2. The European economies need restructuring. Will it happen? Well, that is a good question. We still need mergers across borders, we still need the full exploitation of the single market now being enlarged. The mindset of European businessmen and politicians are still too secluded. A robust turnaround has yet to occur.

   My own guess is that the European economies will get back to a growth pattern somewhat higher than what we have seen in recent years but not much above let us say 2.5%–3%. The drive for reform and restructuring will not be sufficiently strong to push Europe back on the dynamic growth pattern but a little bit less can probably do it. Here as in other areas the Europeans will choose their own model. And that model means that a combination of lower growth and higher degree of social welfare/social security is preferable to a combination of higher growth pattern and less social welfare/social security. And this European preference has its merits. Among other things there are strong reasons to believe that it mobilises a large share of Europe's human resources while the American model does not do so but compensates by attracting human resources from abroad.

3. Will the integration encompass all member states to the same extent or will we see what is termed a Europe with several speeds that is not all member states taking part in all aspects of the union? One for all and all for one or take your choice and pay accordingly?

It is more likely than not that the vital parts of the treaty will emerge as obligatory and apply to all member states while other and less vital parts for the daily functioning of the union will be optional. This is in fact what we have seen for quite some time with UK, Ireland, Denmark, Sweden outside some chapters of the treaty. They have opted out of different chapters proving that such a model can work.

If this happens it will be supplemented by two policy prescriptions. Firstly, the member states being outside may accept that it is not forever. Secondly the said member state(s) will not the have same rights as the other member states.

In other words: The convoy is still moving in the same direction and toward the same port of destination. But not all the ships move with the same speed.

The revival of the Franco-German axis end 2002 and beginning 2003 should not be ignored. It is still in its early days and judgement may have to await more tangible evidence but what has hitherto been a theoretical issue has moved somewhat up the ladder of political options: A more closer Franco-German partnership even resembling some kind of union within the union. It would be a grave mistake to classify the present political and popular sentiments in these countries as an ephemeral phenomenon.

4. Relations to US. A difficult almost painful question especially right now. Let us face the facts. EU and US share the same basic principles with regard to political culture. There are a lots of arguments to be put forward supporting a continued alliance. But another fact is that the EU and US do not any longer face a military threat so obvious and lethal that it forces them to ignore and disregard the differences in opinions and policies which evidently are also present.

The Iraq war has shown what was known well in advance indeed even before UK joined the coalition, that UK is more favourably disposed toward US than France and Germany. If such a policy discrepancy remains in the long run and especially if it remains concerning the main question of euro and common foreign- and security policy (CFSP) something will have to give.

As we have seen recently there is no doubt that some of the EU member states will try to forge ahead with a CFSP including a military vector. The question remains however whether they will muster sufficient clout to shape a credible force. The answer depends to a large extent on whether they will put up the money — a lot of money — without which such a force cannot be build. And a political decision-making procedure without which it cannot be used.

The Iraq war has split the Europeans and put the movement toward a CFSP encompassing all the member states on hold. The victim in this regard is primarily the military vector but that part of the CFSP has always been doubtful.

In a strategic sense it means that EU can no longer be taken for granted as an ally of the US regardless of the challenge we have to tackle. It creates strategic room of manoeuvre for the Europeans and the Americans to find out how strong the Atlantic partnership shall be under the new circumstances. And it focus upon the main points which are how much the US values European partnership in the future and how comfortable/uncomfortable the Europeans feel with an America able to do without their support. In short: We will see how strong the common principles and ideas — the common set of values — are when confronted with divergent tactical interests instead of convergent strategic threats as under the cold war. They may be weaker than most of us thought.

Endnote

[1]This model is set out in the author's book *The Future European Model: Economic Internationalisation and Cultural Decentralisation* with a foreword by The Honorable James A. Baker III. Published in 1995 by Greenwood Publishing house, Westport CT.

This article was first published in *Singapore Institute of International Affairs Reader*, Vol. 3, No. 2, July 2003, pp. 47–60.

Part 4: Global Financing

THE GLOBAL FINANCING SYSTEM REFLECTS THE CURRENCY IT IS BUILT around: the US dollar and consequently the US economy. For a decade or even longer the anchor of the system has shown signs of frailty and vulnerability.

The US consumed and China produced is a crude characteristic of how the system worked. The nexus was a higher demand than production in the US. That can go on for a while and when we speak about the anchor currency for a long time — but not indefinitely.

The monetary policy of central banks in particular the Fed in the US and the Japanese central bank contributed to an overflow of liquidity finding its way into assets and pushing up prices. It had to burst and it did. What was surprising was the size of the bubble and the revelations of mismanagement of credit policies by well established financial institutions, throwing away reputation gained over more than 100 years in the race for short term profit inside a model the managers must have realized was untenable.

A considerable part of the blame goes to the central banks, which did not fulfill the role of supervising the system and built in check and balances. Maybe their attention was diverted by their joy over a long period with low inflation attributed to inflation targeting policies. This was, however, a misreading of how the system worked. The inflation was low because China stepped in with low cost manufacturing and thus acted as a global brake on inflationary tendencies directly by cheap exports and indirectly by keeping wage demands in industrialized countries down. The rise in prices for commodities only arrived over the horizon in the second half of the decade.

There was little understanding of how exchange rates had lost effectiveness as economic policy instruments. Outsourcing to low cost manufacturing countries such as China changed relative prices much more than exchange rate adjustments of 10 or 20% which used to be the norm.

When the bubble burst the weaknesses of global finance was revealed for all to see. The conventional wisdom was that the global financial chain distributed risks among a large number of institutions all having their share of a financial transaction. The truth proved to be the exact opposite. All of them had the same risks as they had passed it on instead of sharing parts of it.

Asia with the world's savings in its pocket suddenly became a major player. It was not a crisis Asia wanted as all three major Asian countries — China, Japan, and India — had to cope with their own domestic economy, but when it broke because of the imbalances in the US economy all eyes turned to Asia to see how the saving would be mobilized. Asia emerged as a large active international investor to control its own savings as capital to be invested by global financial markets. This is a seminal change even if it will take some years for it to work its way through the system.

It is not certain that the financial crisis is over. There are still question marks over the solidity of the new instruments born since the deregulation in the 1980s among which the investment funds having bought what used to be public services may be particularly vulnerable. It is most likely that the world at the beginning of 2009 moves from a financial crisis into a recession, threatening to become some kind of depression although not of the same magnitude as the one harassing the world in the 1930s.

The present debt crisis suggests a need to get back to the basic principles of responsibility plus accountability. The new financial instruments behind the calamities did not specify who the ultimate creditor was and who the ultimate debtor was. Nobody along the long chain of repackaged and restructured instruments actually knew the solidity. The financial system must reinvent ethics by prohibiting products that through their complexity disguise risks and make the debtor and creditor unknown to each other.

Most important of all is the need to restore the balance between demand and production in the American economy. That requires a transfer of purchasing power from the US to Asia. The end result will be a US with a lower share of global Gross Domestic Product. Fiscal and monetary policies have lost their room of maneuver because of misguided economic policies over the last decade, aggravating the adjustment process and raising the prospect of risky and/or ad hoc policies.

Protectionism has, unquestionably, its attractions in the eyes of politicians. Such policies shift the burden to other countries leaving the world as such worse off. The risk of traditional protectionism for barriers for trade and services may be rather low as the lessons from the 1930s are hopefully digested. It may be higher for capital movements and in particular foreign purchase of domestic companies especially in the next year or two where low profits will make many companies cheap and below their genuine value.

Hazardous Path Out of Crisis

THE GLOBAL FINANCIAL CRISIS LANDS AN ACUTE CHALLENGE ON THE table for policymakers in Asia, as it is the only place in the world having room to maneuver for active economic policies and is in possession of the world's savings.

For some time, the question was open as to whether deregulation and privatization — the policies of president Ronald Reagan and prime minister Margaret Thatcher — were permanently shifting the paradigm of the global economy, or were just another cyclical wave of political preferences. Now we know. It was a cycle.

For the past 30 years the world has lived under the spell that the market gets it right. This was the basis for economic and financial policies first in the US, then Europe and after that most other countries. Bastion after bastion of well-established and renowned enterprises, many of them public utilities, were transferred from public ownership (service to the population) to private ownership (where the priority is profit). The philosophy was that profit would ensure efficiency and that would guarantee the high-quality service the public looked for. The global financial crisis demonstrates that if left alone, the market tends to get it wrong — not right. When the assumption has been proved wrong, the policies cannot and will not be kept in place unchanged.

More international regulation and control will certainly be included on government agendas. That does not necessarily mean that deregulation and privatization will be rolled back completely, but it does mean that more deregulation and privatization is unlikely to take place and that some of the privatized enterprises probably will be brought back under public ownership.

It is noteworthy that US mortgage guarantors Fannie Mae and Freddy Mac have been nationalized — deprivatized, so to speak — and insurance giant AIG is in reality undergoing a similar process. Forced by circumstances, a US administration judged to be the least likely to nationalize and deprivatize has ordered two of the most spectacular and far-reaching nationalizations of financial institutions the world has seen. This lesson will not easily be forgotten.

Second, a new wave of concentration of financial institutions is under way. The Bank of America has bought Merrill Lynch and there will be other mergers and acquisitions. The days where genuine competition ruled between the mayor financial institutions are gone and will not come back.

The world will be left with a few mastodons so powerful and in possession of enormous financial might that they soon will throw their weight around with regard to economics and politics. We witness the gradual phasing out of specialized financial institutions, crowded out by the mega institutions without healthy competition and where wrong decisions may cause havoc because of their size. Until recently we could hope that if a financial institution got it wrong, the other ones might have got it right — not so anymore. Out of this may not come a more robust system, but a more fragile one.

Third, deregulation and privatization gave birth to investment funds. Many having enjoyed themselves during a spending spree buying public utilities one after another, they now may face a rough time.

Many operated on the assumption that the valuation of the assets (bridges, toll roads, airports and so forth) would continue to rise, allowing them to expand by increasing borrowing using new loans to repay former loans. Now these assets are starting to fall in value, with the inevitable consequence that it won't be long before we read about such investment funds in difficulties.

They excelled in complicated and opaque financial operations selling and buying among each other, sometimes between different subsidiaries inside the same mother company, and often publishing obscure annual reports. Their owners were sometimes pension funds, which did not want to undertake such risks under their own name.

Fourth, it has so far primarily been the American and British financial systems that have been in the firing line, with some Japanese banks also exposed. We cannot be sure that the rest of Asia and the eurozone continue to be relatively unharmed. It seems, however, a reasonable fair assumption that, if they are drawn in, the repercussions will be smaller than for the US and the UK.

One wonders what the consequence of that will be for the future global financial system. It is difficult to see the US regain its former position after having demonstrated such incompetence. For years, observers have amused themselves by pointing out that the eurozone was no match for London as a financial center. Perhaps perceptions will change. Perhaps investors will start to feel more at ease investing via more cautious, more conservative, and less sophisticated but also less risky financial institutions in the eurozone, and perhaps financial centers in Asia will start to emerge for real.

Fifth, the world needs a financial system ready to take calculated risks; otherwise many investments will not be undertaken. The virtue of a good financial system is that it knows how to weigh pros and cons and gets it right most of the time. For the next years, the global financial system will tend to be cautious and the risk for the global economy is that it may be too cautious, always thinking of 2008 and fearing to repeat mistakes.

Human nature indicates and history shows this kind of behavior. After a period of assuming unsustainable risks the world may move into a period with a financial system that is too risk-aversive. Many developing countries and newly industrialized countries will feel the pinch, and this may lead to lower global growth.

The global authorities face a challenge to tell the financial system that even if it is understandable in view of the 2008 crisis that they prefer to avoid risks, continued global growth requires some risks and accordingly it should not be too cautious. The balance must be found. The world may end up with a financial system being extremely solid because it does not dare to lend, which is why it is there. A strange outcome to a crisis started by reckless lending.

The present crisis is due to one single factor and nothing else: high and persistent imbalances in the US building up over decades and culminating in explosive growth of these during the past eight years. The US government's liabilities and long-term commitment stands at almost US$50 trillion — four times total annual production. The total federal debt is more than $10 trillion. Next year, the budget deficit will probably surpass $500 billion. The balance of payments has been in deficit for years.

Total demand can surpass production for some years — as it has — but not indefinitely. The longer it lasts, the more painful the alignment will be. It has become a global crisis because the US was and still is the largest and most powerful economy, with one-quarter of global production. Consequently, a solution must be a global one defining the burden-sharing between the US and the rest of the world.

Restoring balance for the US economy requires lower demand or increased production and/or a combination of both. Demand can be reined in by restrictive economic policies, but that will deepen the recession. Stimulating policies can be applied to combat recession through an upswing, but will aggravate the imbalances. The policy implication is that US fiscal and monetary policies cannot be applied effectively.

Years of irresponsible policies have removed any room of maneuver. It is good to hear plans of expansionary economic policies, but where does the money come from? More borrowing, and if so from whom? Private households already dissaving, a business sector facing alarming falls in profit, a maimed financial sector? The rest of the world is already up to the hilt with Treasury bonds, it definitely does not want to accumulate more of these.

That leaves us with two not very attractive policies: depreciation of the US dollar and/or protectionism.

They can do at least some of the job by reducing real incomes, thus cutting total demand and enhancing competitiveness and thus stimulating production through exports. It looks fine, but it isn't.

What the US gains the rest of the world loses. These policies redress US imbalances by shifting them to other countries. Only if other countries are willing to accept this will such policies work. And they can only be expected to do so if the US is ready to enter into some kind of arrangement ensuring that their burden is accompanied by a comparable effort by the US.

Irrespective of which policies are set in motion, the result is a transfer of purchasing power from America to other countries and a lower real income for the US — a lower share of global gross domestic product (GDP). The US can scream or squirm or whatever it likes, this is going to happen.

Here follows a sketch about how to manage adjustment and minimize the negative repercussions:

First, the US undertakes to reduce oil consumption, in particular in the transport sector. For an incoming administration, the opportunity arises to introduce a new energy policy. The political question is whether the American people, having resisted such measures for years, are now finally ready.

Second, a commitment by everybody to refrain from protectionist steps, thus guaranteeing continued free trade and international investment banning any attempts to solve one's own problems by shifting them to other countries. There is talk about relaunching the Doha-round, and that would be wonderful, but let us have both feet on the ground and not jump for the moon however desirable it looks.

Third, policymakers announce guidelines for a US dollar depreciation, signaling that a falling US dollar is the preferred option and thus removing the risk that such a policy triggers speculation. Major economic powers must align domestic monetary policies in particular interest rate changes so as not to open windows for speculators to exploit any differences.

Fourth, measures to stimulate domestic demand in countries having room to maneuver to do to uphold global demand. The recently announced Chinese stimulus package amounting to $586 billion and composed of three elements — loose monetary policy, tax reductions and investments — is a step in the right direction.

Fifth, a US commitment to follow economic policies in conformity with guidelines normally laid down by the International Monetary Fund (IMF) for countries needing assistance to sort out economic imbalances. The interpretation is limits for deficits on the public budget and the balance of payments.

Sixth, the top 10 or 20 global economic powers (not G-10, but the 10 countries with the largest share of global GDP) agree to co-ordinate economic policies to better synchronize the global business cycle.

Seventh, a keen awareness of the risk to the global economy of countries that may not be able to weather the crisis sliding into political anarchy and economic chaos, thus joining the list of failed states.

This is where the world really needs preemptive and preventive policies. The normal blueprint imposing restrictive economic policies will not do in these circumstances; something more imaginative is needed to keep the economy going. The IMF should step in, but the IMF does not possess money itself. It borrows from member countries to lend to other member countries. Only if creditors find it attractive or necessary will they place the necessary funds at the disposal of the IMF, and global leaders must create an atmosphere in which they are ready to do so.

These seven steps look like a tall order, and other methods to rebalance the US economy without too much harm for the rest of the world may be available — but they are not easy to spot.

This article was first published in *Asia Times Online*, 20 November 2008 (www.atimes.com).

How to Save the Financial World

THE CALAMITIES ON THE GLOBAL FINANCIAL MARKETS HAVE REACHED A point where a global summit is about to be convened to deal with the problems. It seems like good news, but there is a caveat. Such a summit raises expectations of leadership and ideas about how to turn the boat around. If these expectations are not met, it may prove counterproductive.

The first step should be to consolidate the global financial system and prevent the crisis from spreading further. With luck, we can see an end to the financial problems — even if risks are still ahead. But the onslaught on the real economy is still to come.

The last thing that the world needs right now is fluctuation between the US dollar, the euro and the yen, plus a couple of other important currencies such as the yuan. Therefore, world leaders should decide that they stand ready to hold the currency rates at more or less the level where they are today.

Potential 'speculators' have been so busy hoarding cash to escape the credit crunch that they have not had time to think of moving funds around, but this luck will not last. If speculation arises, the central banks must swing into action to assert their authority. In itself, currency rate stability conveys that the crisis is getting under control and its positive impact may help radiate confidence.

Obviously, China and some other Asian countries with total currency reserves above US$3 trillion will have to be partners in such a scheme. The time has come to invite them inside as members of the small group of countries, which control the global economy. No one can be less interested in seeing the crisis develop further than China, which needs a growing global economy to sustain its own domestic growth. The price for Chinese contribution may be a stop to recrimination about Chinese cheap products undercutting production in industrialised countries.

Consequently, currency stability must be accompanied by a strong pledge that protectionism is not the way ahead. No country can solve its problem by shifting the burden to others. The best would be an agreement about the stalemated Doha Round trade negotiations, but that may be too much to ask for, so a pledge not to go protectionist will do. The presidential campaign in the US gives rise to worries in that regard and a policy shift away from free trade under a new president would be disastrous. Recall how the US in the 1930s with the protectionist Smoot-Hawley Bill led the world into depression.

This time, the risk may focus more on capital movements and less on goods and services. If the US and/or Europe starts to block direct investment in industries, severe doubt would be sown about the system itself. How can you expect countries to accumulate reserves and play according to the rules if other countries break the rules and put barriers and/or conditions on how they can invest their reserves?

Some of the weaker developing countries may collapse financially. Economically, that has been seen before and is manageable; but if it takes place at the same time as the system itself is in deep crisis, it may undermine any attempt to get the global financial system back to work and the global economy going again. The richer countries need to set up contingency plans to bail out weaker countries regardless of all the arguments that can be forwarded — that it is financial irresponsibility that led these countries into difficulties. Exactly the same can be said about the US. This is no time for self-righteousness.

The challenge is to bring the world through the crisis and not prove the point about responsible financial behaviour. That can be done afterwards.

The problem here is that the money to save these countries, of which we may see more than a few, does not lie with the US and/or international institutions such as the International Monetary Fund (IMF) and the World Bank, but with some of the Asian countries and the oil exporting countries in the Middle East.

They need to be mobilised in a global effort. The difficulty is to convince them that it is in their interest. The second step should relaunch the global economy on a growth track. The solution is not difficult to spot. The oil price was instrumental in turning the financial crisis into a recession. It rose from about US$60 to about US$140 in less than two years. Now, it has fallen to about US$70. If it is kept at that level or ideally steered towards an even lower level, the risk of a deep recession or even a depression would be reduced. It may be too much to ask from the oil exporting countries, but there is no real alternative than convincing them of the need for a lower oil price to tow the global economy through these stormy waters.

The US has very little leverage to increase demand in view of the growing federal deficit and public debt. Europe may have some, but not so much, and countries such as China and Japan might pitch in with an effort. Again, the political problem is that the US can contribute very little to find the way out of the problems it has led the world into. Many countries ask the simple question: Why should we do it? The answer is age old and sounds like this: you may be right, but that is not the point. If you do not do it now, you may teach the US a lesson and rub your hands in joy, but it won't last long before the bill comes home to you and it will be higher.

We are living in a global economy and those countries being asked to make sacrifices now are those who benefited from the US consumer boom over the last 10 years. The US must deliver its pound of flesh by promising to put its house in order after the end of the crisis by running its debt down and reducing its deficits.

If the crisis has proved anything, it is that we no longer live in a world where there is one rule for economic behaviour for the world and another rule for the US, allowing that country to run an irresponsible economic policy.

The third step is the most difficult one, but also the least pressing one: reforming the system. The unanswered question is: what to do and how to do it? In any case, reform cannot be achieved as long as the present system is in ruins and fighting for its life, it can only be done when it is up again and running.

As with many other models or systems caught off balance, the basic problem is not the model itself but how it was applied. The special edition of capitalism growing out of Wall Street may not survive unscathed, but there is no viable alternative to capitalism. We should not forget that capitalism has brought about a tremendous economic growth over the last decades and lifted hundred of millions of people out of poverty.

The model may need retooling, but this is not the time for jumping into the unknown or already known alternatives such as socialism or protectionism, which has been tried and proved unworkable.

Capitalism supposes a market and a market supposes competition. What happened before the crisis and is about to strike roots is lack of competition because of the concentration of capital in a few hands. Compare the number of financial institutions in Wall Street 25 years ago with the situation today. Mergers & acquisitions have put many financial institutions together under same ownership and same management. Institutional investors have pushed individual investors aside and now account for about two-thirds of all shares in the US. It may sound old-fashioned, but even if authorities have fallen back on some of the big banks to help bail out the weaker ones, the 'reward' should be to break them up afterwards. If not, the next crisis is only a bus stop away.

There has been much talk about more international regulation. What needs to be done is establishing a higher degree of transparency which forces financial institutions to reveal the risk the creditor runs by buying assets. International rules stipulating that the issuer of financial assets be required to know who the ultimate debtor is and being able to explain that to national regulatory bodies would help to prevent similar incidents from happening again.

It is good to look at the future global economic system, but let us repair the present one first before we venture into an uncertain world.

This article was first published in *The Business Times*, 23 October 2008.

Protectionism Goes Into Reverse

FOR MORE THAN 60 YEARS THE WORLD HAS LABORED IN THE SAME stony vineyard of dismantling import barriers. Now we are almost there, few of these restrictions still harass international trade. Just when celebrations were due, a new monster is emerging to disturb things and distort international trade: export restrictions and export tariffs. Asian countries are in the forefront as potential major players in this new game.

They are in fact the twins of the new age of scarcity. For decades, even centuries, the world has basked in an era of plenty. Enough of everything and at low prices. It was a buyer's market to set conditions, terms and prices; the seller had little choice but to comply. Buyers could — and did — play suppliers against each other and took advantage of the situation to exercise downwards pressure on prices. Just ask producers of raw materials, food and to a certain extent oil how they fared and you will know.

Now it starts all over again, but in reverse, with an increasing scarcity of food, raw materials, energy, water and clean environments. There is not enough to feed growing populations, expanding economies, more factories and consumers all wanting cars, refrigerators and other energy-consuming gadgets and having the money to buy them.

It is no longer a buyer's market. It is becoming a seller's market. Those who think that international trade policy will remain unchanged are in for a nasty surprise. Economic textbooks mention as a curiosity export restrictions and tariffs as the contrast to import restrictions and tariffs, but they have never really analyzed them and there are few cases to build empirical analysis on. They may have to start doing so now.

The first shot has been fired. Over the first half of 2008, Cambodia, Indonesia, Kazakhstan, Russia, Argentina, Ukraine, Thailand, Vietnam and India have all introduced restrictions on exports of all or selected agricultural goods, justifying those measures with scarcity at home. These countries are not just anybody. Thailand and Vietnam, restricting export of rice, are the world's number one and two rice exporters. Importing countries suffered when the supply of vital foodstuffs was curtailed. Riots resulted in several countries.

Russia took similar steps at the end of June by imposing export duties on raw timber, a step that may cost 16,000 jobs in neighboring Finland's paper-processing industry and sour ongoing negotiations for a renewal of the existing agreement between Russia and the European Union.

This is nothing compared to what we may expect over the coming decades.

Most economists subscribe to the view that since the middle of the 19th century the terms of trade for commodities has deteriorated. There are many reasons for that and economic models offer various suggestions as to why it came about, but it is difficult to escape the conclusion that real income has been transferred from raw material producing countries to manufacturing nations.

The tide is turning and those who suffered will try to get back what they lost. There is no reason to expect countries in possession of scarce goods to hold back. Why should they? Trade policy will be one of several quivers in their arsenal.

As we have seen, export restrictions can and will be used Economics spell out that if supply goes down, prices go up. Raw-material producers may follow in the footstep of oil exporters to hike the price for exports of commodities while keeping the price for domestic consumption low. Export earnings will boom and lower real wages compared with other countries will improve competitiveness.

This is rewinding the past 100 years or more, when manufacturing nations enjoyed low food prices keeping wages down. The British economic boom in the 19th century is worth studying. Until 1846, the Corn Laws prohibited import of corn when the price was below a certain minimum. When the Corn Laws were repealed, prices started to fall and hit less than half of the earlier level in the 1880s. Imports took up more than 50% of total consumption compared with almost nil previously and real wages improved for British workers at the expense of corn exporters abroad, who were squeezed.

In reverse it will look like this: commodity exporters impose restrictions. The price goes up boosting export earnings. Low domestic prices on commodities financed by the higher export earnings enhance competitiveness in other economic sectors. Importing countries such as Britain, the rest of Europe, Japan, to a certain extent China and India and the US will see competitiveness eroded by higher prices pushing wage levels up and a deterioration of terms of trade eating into national income.

A cartel such as the Organization of Petroleum Exporting Countries (OPEC) works more or less like a combination of export restrictions and export tariffs. By agreeing to a high price guaranteed by manipulating output, demand forces prices up and the importers pay a higher price. OPEC was established when certain conditions, which we are going to see for a number of foodstuffs and raw materials, prevailed in the early 1970s: demand outstripping supply and a limited number of countries in control of output.

The world better brace itself for a totally new paradigm for international trade and trade policy triggered off by commodity exporters starting to play the game used against them to their advantage. Isn't fascinating that a decade or two from now item number one on a new trade round might be efforts to reduce restrictions and tariffs for export of commodities?

There are two more twists to it. According to reports, oil rich countries having no agricultural sector themselves are starting to buy farmland around the world to secure supply of food and avoid future high prices.

Saudi Arabia and the United Arab Emirates (UAE) are looking to Asia and Africa as opportunities for agricultural investments, Agence France Presse (AFP) reported this month. UAE President Sheikh

Khalifa bin Zayed al-Nahayan was quoted as saying his country was interested in Kazakhstan "to diversify its sources of food supplies". The UAE imports about 85% of its food, the report said.

The UAE is considering buying more than 40,470 hectares of Pakistan farmland worth US$500 million, AFP said, citing press reports, adding that private firms such as Dubai-based Abraaj Capital have also reportedly been buying agricultural land in Pakistan.

It won't last long before the target countries in question guess the intention and it is unlikely that they will accept the consequences. After all it will deprive them of what could turn out to be the family silver. But how to prevent such investments in a world where international capital movements are free of restrictions? The answer is not far away; they may start to question the rules.

Australia has floated the idea to cap foreign investment in the country's resource companies at 49.6% obviously to maintain control over those valuable assets. There may be several reasons behind such considerations, but one of them could be that Australia wants to secure the option of export restrictions/duties if or when it is deemed suitable.

Domestically, food producers suddenly discover that scarcity endows them with power they did not enjoy in the past. Beginning in June, Europe saw fishermen blockade harbors in a number of countries and German farmers stopping the supply of milk. If you think these are isolated and one-offs events you will have to think again. They signal a power shift.

A tremendous battle of redistributing wealth and income inside and between countries is gaining momentum and will rule the domestic and international agenda for years even decades to come.

This article was first published in *Asia Times Online*, 24 July 2008 (www.atimes.com).

Inflation Woes: Is the Global Economy in Need of Retooling?

AFTER A HIATUS OF DECADE OR TWO, WITH INFLATION LARGELY ABSENT, this unwelcome phenomenon has reappeared to dominate the global economic policy debate. The US and European Central Banks, the Fed and the ECB have been most vocal, not the least because their monetary policies, underpinned by inflation targeting have failed.

Now the International Monetary Fund and the Asian Development Bank have joined in the chorus. Some observers even speak about the dreaded combination of inflation and stagnation (stagflation). Central banks see this as a nightmare because lower interest rates may stimulate the economy but boost inflation, while higher interest rates may dampen inflation but also deepen the downturn.

The rise of inflation masks an even bigger problem that economic trends among main economic powers highlight — the lack of any genuine attempt to shape coordinated economic policies. With some justification, it can be said that the non-existence of global coordination viz. economic policies represents one of the villains pulling inflation out of the dark and into the limelight.

The world is now in a multilayered transition: the Euro has replaced national currencies, emerging market economies have acquired greater clout and confidence as compared to the US — the latter, continues to be harassed by the fallout from irresponsible economic policies coinciding with a forthcoming presidential election. An event which rules out new policy initiatives for the next six to nine months.

Demand pressure cannot explain the inflationary development because inflation has accelerated while global growth has dived. The culprit is likely to be found in the supply side and commodity prices are the first to catch the eye. The index of 19 major commodities jumped 29% over first half 2008 — the highest figure in almost 50 years.

While it is academically interesting to dissect the causes of the present inflationary wave, the rise in commodity prices has taken place and is behind us. It looks a safe bet that commodity prices will take a breather or fall over the next six to nine months. If so, the present supply generated inflation has run its course and economic policies should be designed, not to counteract what has happened over the last six to twelve months, but to prevent a new supply-generated inflation wave that strikes in a few years time. That makes it worthwhile to toss up a few ideas about how to extricate the global economy from the present trap and build in some mechanisms to achieve a better balance:

Firstly, although global demand is falling the prospect of global recession, albeit remote, cannot be ruled out if an erroneous policy mix is put on the table. Predictions for global growth in 2008 have steadily been lowered and hover around 3.7% — the final figure will probably be even lower. Admittedly, the danger of inflation calls for action, but decision makers should be ahead of the curve relative to timing and responses to counteract inflation now, without jeopardising future growth prospects.

Secondly, there is an urgent need to rebalance the global economy by bringing the large American deficit on balance of payments and public finance into line. This can only be done by reduced real income in the US. Such a prospect only seems palatable if combined with higher growth. Americans must produce more and consume less. This is going to happen. The question is when and how. If the US does not agree a policy mix with other major economic partners, the market, probably via a falling US dollar, will do it, and the ride may feel like jumping onto a roller coaster, not knowing when it stops.

Thirdly, the huge windfall profits accrued by the oil exporting countries must be recycled into the global economy. Purchasing power is removed from the global economy as long as these funds are sterilised.

Fourthly, the experience gained over a number of years point to adjustment imperfections in industrialised countries and probably also in some emerging market economies, explaining rising prices. Macroeconomic policy such as fiscal policy and/or monetary policy are simply not suitable instruments, while microeconomic or sectoral/structural policies have a much better record as corrective mechanisms. Examples include less rigid employment rules, a more effective and efficient capital market, measures to improve productivity and life-long learning.

Fifthly, steps to coordinate global economic policies have to be much more effective than is the case today. It is strange to see the International Monetary Fund completely out of the game instead of seeking to establish consistent policy measures among the five or six major economic powers. The fundamental problem is that both international institutions and the major economic powers see national economic policy as an issue not to be influenced by other states. How they can take this line in the era of economic globalisation is hard to fathom.

Finally, the use of the US dollar as the denominator for global prices of commodities including oil, is a remnant of the past when the US economy was the undisputed leader and therefore market for these products. There is an alternative. It is a basket of currencies comprising the US dollar, euro, yen and perhaps the yuan and rupee. With such a basket, commodity prices would be more stable than now with one currency as the denominator. Since 2004, the US dollar has depreciated approximately 15–20% against all other currencies. It is possible, even likely, that at least some commodity exporting countries/companies have acted to counterbalance the fall in the $US, thus complicating an already difficult situation.

A basket would politically signal that we live in the era of globalisation and it would draw a number of countries into the picture as responsible for the global economy. Economically it would reflect the reality, which is that demand (and price) for commodities is not dependent upon one, but a number of countries and the risk of spillover to commodity prices and economic (including exchange rate) policy would be reduced.

Often the argument is heard that the market is pushing prices up or down. That is only true as far as appearances are concerned. Free competition in the economic sense has long since given way to a situation where prices are set by a limited number of big suppliers without fear of newcomers as the initial cost of entering into global business constitutes an almost insurmountable barrier. Commodity prices including the price of oil is in general set by a few major suppliers. While these entities take demand and supply into consideration, they retain considerable scope for maneuver nonetheless.

What the world needs to do is to take a hard look at the realities to understand that the global economy is different from the picture defined by conventional wisdom. If the major players do not change track to adjust, the global economy will be driven in circles for some time yet.

This article was first published in *OpinionAsia*, 7 July 2008 (www.opinionasia.com).

Slide in the US Dollar:

What It Means for Asia

THE SUB-PRIME CRISIS HIT THE US ECONOMY WHEN IT WAS IN THE FIRST stages of an adjustment process to redress the large deficits in balance of payments and public budgets. These disturbances would on their own have steered the economy towards a slowdown, but the coincidence in the timings raises the spectre of a recession while at the same time turning an American problem into a question mark on the solidity of global capital markets. The US dollar is destined to bear the brunt of adjustment, but a dollar fall hides two obvious drawbacks. First, neither fiscal nor monetary policy in the US has been geared to suppress the purchasing power to bring it into line with the fundamental — weaker — economy. A falling US dollar means that real income is falling, but this way to realign demand and production capacity calls for more time than available to avoid a recession. Second, the sub-prime crisis undermines confidence in the US financial system, luring countries and overseas financial institutions to convert US dollars into other currencies like the euro and the Japanese yen, thus starting a self-sustaining downward spiral for the US dollar.

As things are, the most likely outcome is a US recession whose depth and, more important, length is difficult to predict, especially because repercussions on global growth are uncertain. So far it seems that Europe is less hit than feared and Asia much less, but as time lags have shifted over recent years, it is too soon to come to a final judgment.

It looks a reasonable bet, however, that Asia largely has decoupled from the US economy, at least compared to previous business cycles in the United States.

An analysis of recent events calls for three observations.

The first is that currency rate changes do not any more influence flows of goods and services to the same degree as one or two decades ago. The reason is quite simple: goods and services competing on prices have been outsourced to China and other countries, primarily in Asia benefiting from a wage level often less than 10 per cent of what is the case in the US and Europe. Compared to that, a depreciation of the US dollar with 10 or 20 per cent is small money. Therefore, exports do not rise much and imports do not fall much to redress the imbalances by increased production, pre-empting a recession.

This is why growth forecasts continue to fall for the US and remain high for China, irrespective of the falling US dollar and the rising yuan.

As changes of relative prices are neutralised as a policy instrument, the adjustment process shifts from a price cycle to a volume cycle. A price cycle mainly works by restructuring the economy in countries out of tune (currently the US) from domestic to foreign demand, keeping growth at a high level and in most cases stimulating it. A volume cycle suppresses economic activity until demand is reduced sufficiently to match production capacity. The major snag is that during the process, production capacity itself falls as the lower demand reduces incentives to invest.

Demand and Output

Total demand and production capacity come to match each other at a lower level, and experience tells that it takes much longer for a volume cycle than a price cycle to do the job. This phenomenon is often seen in the property sector where prices can stay at a high level for a long time, irrespective of falling demand waiting for lower supply of new housing to reduce the surplus.

The lesson to learn is to prevent imbalances from arising by a much higher degree of economic policy fine-tuning. Economic globalisation and outsourcing have changed the rules of the game and even the US cannot, with a snap of the fingers, hope for a quick realignment of demand and production capacity.

Once in the hole, it may take quite a while for the volume adjustment to work its way through the system.

The second observation is that contrary to conventional wisdom, changing relative prices affect international capital markets for two reasons: countries having accumulated large currency reserves become interested in using these assets in a more profitable way than just running up cash or treasury bonds and multinational companies from emerging countries boost transnational mergers and acquisitions.

In both cases the price of the game is one of the determining elements and the fall in the US dollar implies that American companies or companies having most of their assets denominated in US dollars become cheaper in the eyes of the rest of the world. While a 10 or 20 per cent fluctuation of price is insignificant for goods and services, it is almost of phenomenal importance when analysing an international investment and/or merger and acquisition.

What has taken off in the course of 2007 is foreign purchase of American enterprises and/or enterprises linked to the American economy. Instead of selling more goods to stimulate production, the US is selling more of its productive assets to finance continued over-consumption.

The Europeans may be a bit reluctant to enter the game for various reasons, but the Asian countries are not. So we see a shift not only of production capacity from the US to Asia in these years, but also a transfer of wealth in the form of full or partial ownership of US companies in the goods and services sector. The purchase of minority shares by Asian investors in US financial institutions has been the most visible sign, but is far from the whole story. It was only recently that the news surfaced that Sinosteel intends to buy the West Australian mining company Midwest for about US$1.2 billion.

Alternatively, the Asian companies are winning the competition to invest in companies around the globe as the decline of the US dollar increases their wealth compared to that of American competitors. The Chinese insurance company Ping An is on the brink of taking a 4.18 per cent share in Fortis, a Dutch-Belgian-owned European giant in financial services, making Ping An the largest shareholder.

The third observation is the beginning of a strong concentration of global financial power. After the start of the sub-prime crisis the world has seen how several financial institutions have been bought or forced to welcome a determining minority shareholder in order to survive.

The most recent example is JPMorgan Chase's purchase of the investment bank Bear Stearns — once a rival. The deal will cost JPMorgan a fraction of Bear Stearns' value only a couple of weeks ago. It is even better for JPMorgan. The US Federal Reserve is taking off approximately US$30 billion of Bear Stearns less liquid assets, thus actually helping JPMorgan (which by the way is paying with own shares removing any need for it to fork out 'real money').

Bailing Out Banks

The Fed has previously come to the rescue of banks, but this is the first time the umbrella is put up for a global investment banking, securities trading and brokerage firm.

Apparently, the Fed deems justified bailing out financial institutions, which have chosen to take on risky operations instead of giving them a dose of their own medicine.

The only explanation is a conviction that default in one segment of the market would spill over and threaten the financial market as a whole. But if the Fed takes the view that segments of the financial market have been so closely weaved together, it spells the beginning of the end for specialised financial institutions.

It is not difficult to discern the future financial system as made up of fewer institutions with much higher capital. The new mergers come after years of consolidation with JPMorgan Chase and Bank One merging in 2004, Chase Manhattan's buy of JPMorgan in year 2000 for US$36 billion and Morgan Stanley's merger in 1997 with Dean Witter, Discover & Company.

For Asia, as a comparatively newcomer in the game, this offers unique opportunities. It should not be overlooked, however, that the rules of the game and the game itself is going through a tectonic shift.

This article was first published in *The Business Times*, 3 April 2008.

Another Looming Crisis:

A Whistle-blower in Centro?

THE SIGNAL THAT ALERTED THE WORLD TO THE ASIAN FINANCIAL CRISIS is often said to be the devaluation of the Thai baht in July 1997, but many observers point to the bankruptcy or near bankruptcy of three Korean companies between January and March 1997 — as the original whistler-blower of what turned out to be a regional disaster. Hanbo Steel Co. collapsed in January 1997 with a debt of approximately five billion US dollars and Sammi Steel followed in March 1997 with debts of slightly under two billion dollars. Only frenetic interventions from a number of banks prevented Jinro, a distillery company, with debts of 3.6 billion, from joining the other two. The heart of the problem constituted financial behaviour that was ultimately mimicked in many parts of East Asia — brought to light when industry heavyweights experienced a tumultuous period, cleaning up their balance sheets for reckless borrowing and overextension. Had the warnings from Korea been heeded, the Asian financial crisis would probably still have haunted Asia, but repercussions less severe and fissures not only within economic structures, but also, the social fabric, less deep. This hard won experience compels policymakers to be on their toes for any signs of the subprime crisis from spreading to other sectors, especially those known to be vulnerable because of risky and fragile financial transactions. So far, it is becoming clear that segments of the financial sector have cast aside prudent corporate governance; exemplified none more so than the mushrooming panoply of funds in various disguises, moving in to make fast kills in the financial sector with no intention whatsoever of retaining a longer term presence and/or running viable business. The middle of December 2007 bore witness to a financial disaster that threatened to mimic the temporarily localised meltdown of the three Korean companies about ten years ago. A catastrophe struck the Australian Centro Properties Group, which was apparently unable to refinance loans amounting to 3.4 billion dollars. After having slumped on the stock market for a couple of days to the tune of 85% of its share value and shedding 3.8 billion dollars as a result, fear is growing that the reverberations from this summer's credit crunch could worsen and destroy the company. Centro is a well established owner of some 700 shopping malls in the US, even if it is an Australian company. According to news reports, Centro's operations were marked by expanding vigorously, some would say aggressively over the last decade and gambling on rising asset prices to extend or renew loans through revolving credit mechanisms, rather than genuine assets. Centro was known to sell a part of each shopping mall into a complex network of managed funds, a complicated procedural practice that kept most of its debt off the balance sheet making its fragility unknown and the extent of its debt non-transparent. Finally, the loans that Centro needed to buy most of its shopping malls were packaged into commercial mortgage-backed securities (CMBS), sold by JPMorgan Chase and the Credit Suisse Group, according to Merrill Lynch analyst Roger Lehman. Quite shockingly, Centro geared its financial operations above any known measure of normal financial behaviour. It is estimated that its debt amounted to 83% of its equity capital, in an industry where the average hovered around 36%. As things stand now, two scenarios are on the cards. The first, albeit less likely outcome is that other financial institutions step in and rescue Centro. The second, emerging scenario suggests that Centro will go bankrupt and its assets sold, which may take place in near panic depressing prices especially if executed prior to bankruptcy, as a last ditch effort to avoid such an outcome. Competitors — in this context, predators — are waiting to snap up assets estimated at 2.6 billion Australian dollars. The spokesperson for one of them, GPT Group, has already entered the fray with a less than cryptic announcement, "we look at any opportunity that meets our business model and strategy and that is across opportunities in the market place." If this happens, there will be a tangible spill-over effect. Psychologically at least, some people, especially investors will ponder about similar funds. Are any of these in the same danger zone? As seen so often, a number of people stand ready with assurances that this is not the case, Centro is unique, and other institutions have not followed the same reckless pattern. Such a response ostensibly points to the reverse, potentially heightening the anxiety, that there are other funds in similar situations. Why should Centro be the only one? Financially, a number of other institutions will be hit and will be forced to reveal their engagement in similiar operations further downgrading confidence in their management and their ability to steer a course around the looming disaster. Centro is not some unknown fund or a small fry in the zoo. It is the fifth largest mall owner in the US. What accentuates the worry for other funds is that looking back, Centro received almost unanimous praise. Its business model was regarded as almost exemplary. Three of Australia's well known banks are reported to have invested heavily in Centro with a stake between 5 and 10%, with one of them likely to hold a stake exceeding 10%. The three are the Commonwealth Bank of Australia, Barclays Australia and UBS. It was reported that as late as 4 December 2007, Barclays raised its stake in Centro from 4% to 9.3%. It goes without saying that if Centro does not weather this storm, part of the buck will be passed to these investors. The losses are undoubtedly surmountable for these three banks, but if other funds are facing similar difficulties the cliff may suddenly look so much steeper. It is worrying, deeply worrying, that the same managers who steered their bank into buying shares in Centro, have also been at the wheel, directing other investments. If they could be so wrong about Centro, what assurances does anyone have that similar mistakes do not dominate other investment opportunities and other funds? And why should this misjudgment be confined to one company? The Centro episode is quickly turning into one of those cases where observers ask how the company could get away with it, why professional analysts did not blow the whistle, and why investors were lured into what looked like a palace, but was a rotten hut. One hopes that Centro is an isolated case. But hope is very different paradigm next to reality. What should occur now is these well paid analysts cut their losses on their reputations and come clean and inform whether other funds are in similar positions. If so, the sub prime crisis may take on an ugly face; if it does not we may well have to say thank you to lady luck.

This article was first published in *OpinionAsia*, 26 December 2007 (www.opinionasia. com).

Recovering from the Sub-Prime Debacle:

The Coming Crisis

THE FINANCIAL MARKETS ALL OVER THE WORLD SEEM TO BE IN JUBILANT mood that timely central bank intervention has prevented a major crisis. It may well prove to be a short respite.

The sub-prime crisis was predictable in two ways. Firstly, all the analysis over the last years revealed disturbing imbalances in the US economy revolving around dis-savings in the household sector. Something had to give; the question was what and when.

Secondly, sub-prime lending reiterated lending behavior time and again leading to financial upsets or crisis: the collateral is neither the debtor's income nor existing assets, but future increase in asset prices allowing the debtor to repay old loans with new loans. Every time asset prices go up, the debtor takes new loans or increases existing loans to reduce the debt burden of the original loan. Repayment of old loans conveys a sense of solidity to the outsiders obscuring the fact that total debt is actually going up.

This works wonderfully under the assumption that asset prices continue to rise, but creates havoc in the market when asset prices stagnate or start to fall. And this is what happened in the course of 2007. US property prices did not rise anymore; they started to fall, throwing a spanner in the works of the above-mentioned mechanism.

It is not possible to predict with accuracy when the next crisis will announce its arrival and threaten the global financial markets, but it is a fairly good bet to predict what will take over from sub-prime as the spoiler — the new investment funds, which have sprung up like mushrooms over the last 15 years overshadowing respectable and reputable established funds.

It all started in the late 1980s with deregulation. A large number of public utilities and public services were privatised. Toll roads, water supply, bridges, and airports — you name it. In the initial phase the market was hesitant: institutional financial investors did not feel confident knowing their limited experience in evaluating the income potential and even more their limited ability to run such services and utilities. But it did not last long.

Investors sensed potentially large profits and moved in to set up new investment funds designed to buy these services, now so conveniently on the market. Existing pension funds and investors who held back in the first phase did not take long to spot this glorious opportunity and recognised the new funds as suitable instruments. The new investment funds, however, financed a large part of their operations through borrowing.

Public assets put on the market were under priced, because no one had a good idea of what they were worth, therefore playing it safe. The potential for a strong increase in asset prices were at hand and it duly materialised. That allowed investment funds to repay the initial loans with new loans. As long as asset prices continued to rise, it worked exactly as sub-prime operations: old loans were repaid with new loans. Expanding their business opened the doors for the investment funds to climb upward all the time. Their revenue rose and so did the impression that they were running a lucrative and forward looking new business.

Furthermore they often borrowed with the proviso that interest payments on loans were small sometimes extremely small in the initial phase to rise exponentially in the last phase of the loan's duration. Not surprisingly profits looked handsome for these companies making the financial markets believe that here was really something worth investing in. Share prices rose majestically opening another channel for capital.

Profits jumped upwards. The funds did not see themselves as long-term investors or long-term owners and even less, as custodians for the services/utilities they had bought. Their interests in long-term maintenance were not the same as had been the case when the service/utility was under public ownership.

There is a big difference between the public running utilities/services in the general interest of the public and an investment fund running them to rein in a profit. Compared to the results under public ownership the impression soon spread that the new owners were financial wizards. And so they were, but not necessarily as originally perceived.

The next phase consisted in complicating the financial structure by creating more companies out of the single one starting this business. Another mushrooming took place with financial operations inside the investment fund and its various subsidiaries making it very difficult and in several cases impossible to know who exactly owed what to whom.

None of these operations were illegal or contradicted regulations, but they obfuscated the picture of how big the debt burden is and to which extent risk taking has moved into the dark zone where prudence gives way to recklessness. In the same way as sub-prime, these operations rest on the assumption of further expansion. If the investment funds can enlarge their operations by buying new services and utilities and if services and utilities continue to rise in price everything will be all right.

The appalling thing is, however, that the whole mechanism is designed in such a way that if these conditions do not materialise, the whole house of cards will come tumbling down. With lower asset prices, new loans will not be sufficient to repay old loans and the funds cannot fulfill their obligations. The argument is sometimes advanced that public utilities/services offer a steady cash flow being less sensitive to the business cycle classifying it as a 'sound' investment. That is correct, but a steady cash flow is not enough if the price paid for the purchase is based upon either a rising cash flow or rising asset prices.

No one knows for sure how long it will take for this to work through the financial networks put up by the funds. They may be able to hold on for a while or they may collapse suddenly. The competition to acquire utilities/services has risen significantly recently as more and more funds enter the game exercising aggressive biding, pressing asset prices downwards thus undermining the business philosophy of the first comers.

Investment funds have one more common denominator with sub-prime. The former is a business which has been allowed to run out of control although one can visualise what is happening, not to mention, the embedded risk for global financial markets. As was the case with sub-prime debacle, the US seems poised to fall into this trap although deregulation in other parts of the world such as Australia and Europe clearly point to the reality that this is a global business, complete with all its attendant implications.

This article was first published in *OpinionAsia*, 10 September 2007 (www.opinionasia. com).

Markets in Disarray? Don't Sweat Over the Fever, Cure the Disease

A UNANIMOUS CHORUS OVER THE LAST TWO WEEKS HAS BLAMED SUBPRIME housing for the turmoil in the international financial markets. It would however be a grave mistake to mix up cause and effect, and neglect the factors that have given rise to jitters the world over.

The real cause for the tension can be identified within three fundamental weaknesses in the global economy: the growing imbalances in the US economy, the central banks' illusion that inflation targeting is a workable policy, and the asymmetry between global economic forces and the institutional frameworks that determine rules and regulations. Steps by central banks and monetary authorities to help stabilise markets may alleviate the temperature, but sweeping measures are needed to cure the patient.

One fundamental sources of market chaos has been US overspending over many years. Deficits on the public budget, and on the balance of payments have been financed by the rest of the world. The US consumer sets sail in a sea of debt, heading into the well-known danger zone of dis-savings. Such state of affairs was always going to be untenable over an extended period.

Curiously enough, no real action had been envisaged, even though many market watchers realise something was going to give way. Creditors were more than ready to accumulate US assets fearing the negative effects on global growth should they stop doing so. After all, the US consumer was the locomotive pulling the rest of the global economy along. For many years it was difficult to see what should fill a vacuum left by lower US consumption. The rest of the world acquiesced and the US itself saw no reason to act.

The going was good, or as some said — what's the problem? If there was one, it might be solved down the road. The political fallout from what may have appeared as a premature intervention to adjust the domestic economy seemed too costly. In the US' perspective, foreigners, in particular China, was welcome to dump its dollars on the currency markets. An appreciation of foreign currencies, principally the yuan, which had been item number one on the US wish list for a long time, would take place.

And so, the global economy lived with a strange equilibrium: the US over-consumed, China over-produced, the Federal Reserve System and Japan's central bank oversupplied the world with money, and the show was financed by Asia.

This tenuous equilibrium was never going to be sustainable, and the subprime housing crisis whatever technical reasons lie behind, has acted as the whistleblower. Its message to policymakers is simple. Redress these imbalances, if not, the market will. The current crisis may be solved and the wounds plastered over, but the respite will be short.

The quandary is not over whether the US balance of payments will be righted — they will, eventually. The issue is whether policymakers will allow for such a course of action to be implemented in an orderly and organised manner with costs spread over a number of years, so as to be politically manageable. Or if the market, as it has signalled, will do it in a brusque and pitiless way, without any consideration for the political consequences.

Central banks have over the last 15 years been seduced by inflation targeting. They pursued a policy of not more than about 2% inflation per year. All major countries have achieved that target and central banks claimed credit even though they had very little to do it with it. The main reason has been singularly down to the low-cost of production in China.

Convinced about the efficacy of their own diagnosis, the central banks looked at the low inflation figures convinced that everything was fine and kept printing money. As the money supply was too lavish, asset prices started to rise, stocks, property, minerals, and gold — you name it. There was nothing else to use the money for.

The world moved into a strange zone of low inflation rates for goods and services while hosting tremendous asset price rises. Consumers mortgaged their properties and spent the money on consumption. In normal circumstances prices would rise, but not this time. China was capable of delivering an endless stream of goods at low prices. The carousel kept running and yet, central banks did not sense that something could be amiss.

The same central banks and primarily the Fed stoked the growing imbalances because they pursued inflation targeting instead of looking at the whole state of the economy. Looking back, monetary policy should have been tightened earlier than summer 2004 when the Fed started to raise interest rates.

The policy of inflation targeting is understandable to some extent as central banks always have two eyes on price stability, but in one of the strange paradoxes of economics, it allowed the serious and threatening economic imbalance to run wild distorting the US economy.

Globalization is a fantastic growth machine. Trade in goods and services, capital movements and investments all move across the world without noticing the lines on the map detailing which national boundaries they operate within.

Financial institutions lived happily with this model. They knew that risks were growing, but took comfort in the belief that a large number of financial institutions shared the risk. One key sentence frequently heard was that globalization made it possible to spread risks making the financial system more stable and secure. But this philosophy backfired.

Risk spreading did not work to calm nerves in the preliminary stages of the recent crisis; it spread anxiety to a large number of financial institutions around the world. When it dawned upon them that a crisis was brewing, all of them opted to get out of risky assets, triggering off a storm instead of dousing the fire.

This is where one would expect international institutions to act, but they proved to be little more than paper tigers. Little has been done to put up the firewalls, ready to be activated if or when financial turmoil arose. The international community proved toothless when confronted by market forces.

The institution which should rise to the occasion, the International Monetary Fund, was in the midst of changing its managing director and has been absent from the stage even though it was the incumbent for the lead role. The European Union and other countries have pointed to the obvious need to act, especially since well-known credit rating agencies apparently got it completely wrong in explaining the aforementioned omissions or mistakes. The European Union, however, is only one player in the global concert.

Unless financial institutions, central bankers and politicians address these problems, subprime housing is only a bad omen for a series of financial crises to come — these in the long run may threaten the present version of economic globalization.

This article was first published in *OpinionAsia*, 3 September 2007 (www.opinionasia. com).

Heed the Warning

A NEARLY UNANIMOUS CHORUS BLAMES SUBPRIME HOUSING LOANS FOR the turmoil on international financial markets. It would, however, be a grave mistake to mix up cause and effect.

The genuine cause for the calamity is that the global economy has three fundamental weaknesses: the growing imbalances in the American economy, the central banks' illusion that inflation targeting is a workable policy, and the asymmetry between global economic forces and the institutional framework laying down rules and regulations.

The main problem is American overspending, which has gone on for many years. Deficits have been financed by the rest of the world. This simply cannot last.

The question now is not if the American economy will be balanced. It will.

The question is if policy makers will do it in an orderly way, which allows the costs to be spread over a number of years, or if market forces will do the balancing in a brusque way without any consideration for political consequences.

Unless financial institutions, central bankers and politicians address these problems in a comprehensive way, the subprime housing crash will be the omen of a series of financial crises to come that in the long run may threaten the present version of economic globalization.

This article was first published in the *International Herald Tribune*, 24 August 2007.

Tackling the Asymmetry in Financial Markets

LAST WEEK'S TURMOIL IN GLOBAL FINANCIAL MARKETS REITERATED A number of lessons from economic history. The first is that the only thing new under the sun is human forgetfulness. Though the current crisis has its own specifics, previous financial crises are all too easily recalled.

Financial institutions entered into too-risky investments, not because they wanted to, but because of too lavish liquidity. Under normal circumstances, they would not have touched a significant part of the current loans even with a barge pole. As the market is now, however, banks with a more prudent investment policy could lose customers and market share.

Market watchers, and probably also central banks and financial institutions, comforted themselves by saying that globalisation would spread the risks. No one would succumb if debtors defaulted, as lending was shared by a number of institutions. Financial institutions in many countries could help one another out, minimising the individual risk.

It turned out the other way around. Knowing that many financial institutions carried a part of the risk, each and every one assumed a larger burden than sound judgment would have dictated. When the bubble burst, risk spread like a prairie fire around the globe. Instead of rallying to the rescue of those in trouble, financial institutions tightened their screws and clamped down on lending.

Yes, globalisation means capital moves in enormous quantities within a few seconds. We had a live demonstration of what this means last week.

In pre-globalisation days, the losses within that small segment of the market, sub-prime housing in the United States, would have been confined to that sector. But not so now.

Financial institutions were caught off-guard because competition had pushed them to disperse investment over several sectors, sometimes outside their normal branches of activities. Not only did the credit squeeze spread globally among institutions involved in sub-prime housing, but it also jumped to other parts of the global financial market.

The next sector to be hit had similarly exposed itself to too-high risks. Mergers & acquisitions (M&A) have grown explosively recently. 'Predators' bought at overvalued prices, reckoning that global growth in the vicinity of 5 per cent would continue for years to come. The assumption was plausible, even likely, but it was not a given.

In the first half of 2007, M&A reached an estimated value of US$3 trillion (S$4.5 trillion) globally. But the financial institutions that had been quick to finance them just as quickly passed the burden — and the risks — to other investors by issuing bonds. These institutions functioned, shall we say, as intermediaries offering bridging loans.

This worked only for a time. Believing the ultimate creditor to be some other party, banks did not feel exposed to much risk. But when the sub-prime market imploded and investors pulled in their horns, the banks were suddenly left with huge amounts of unsold bonds. All at once they were converted from intermediary to ultimate creditor, a role they had never wanted and were not prepared for.

The paradox in the crisis is that, almost overnight, the world moved from having too much money and chasing too few investment opportunities to having too many debtors screaming for money to pay off their debts.

What next? In plain and unpleasant words, there will be losses for a number of financial institutions, companies and individuals. Some of them will default under this burden.

This will happen whether we like it or not. The pain will stop only when bad debt has been worn down to a sustainable level.

The game is about whom, how much and for how long.

Globalised world or not, the anatomy of a financial crisis has not changed. Bad debt has to be flushed out through a painful process, the sooner the better.

Globalised world or not, private financial institutions were simply doing what they have always done: pursuing profit and increasing market share. They used globalisation for these purposes. It was entirely predictable. No one can blame them for what they did.

The potential risks to the economy, and even more the global economy, are not part of the equation guiding the behaviour of market players.

This is where the Asian financial crisis of 1997-98 and the sub-prime housing crisis are similar.

The virtues of the free market are praised by many. All too often, however, it is forgotten that unless a suitable regulatory framework is in place, what former Federal Reserve chairman Alan Greenspan called 'irrational exuberance' will tempt financial institutions into deep water.

Time after time, events have shown that financial institutions pursue their own interests. They do not see why they should take the burden and responsibility of stabilising the market off the shoulders of central banks and the monetary authorities.

When you factor in globalisation, the dilemma becomes starker. Markets work globally; globalisation fosters stronger and harsher competition, pushing financial institutions towards riskier investments.

Monetary authorities, and their financial supervision and control mechanisms, are still predominantly national.

Unless this asymmetry is addressed by policymakers, last week's crisis will not have been a singular event, but an omen of a series of crises harassing future globalisation.

The US Federal Reserve was apparently caught by surprise, but acted quickly to prevent the market from imploding. It would, however, be unwise to count upon similar luck or adeptness every time in the future.

Strengthening international institutions and regulatory frameworks, taking into account what globalisation means for international financial markets and capital movements, looks a better bet.

This article was first published in *The Straits Times*, 14 August 2007.

Unconventional Wisdom on Exchange Rates

CONVENTIONAL WISDOM HAS FOR AGES EXTOLLED CURRENCY DEPRECIATIONS to correct deficits and appreciations to correct surpluses on trade balances.

In 1971, the world, spurred on by the United States, went from fixed to fluctuating rates. The applause was almost universal. Economists may have disagreed about the length of the time lag before exchange-rate changes had worked their way through the economic system and whether better instruments were at hand, but the very principle that eventually they would work was not questioned.

But something strange has happened. Exchange-rate changes no longer affect trade balances, at least not significantly. When mobilized to redress imbalances, they prove without much effect. Conventional wisdom is thrown out of the window.

The US is exercising pressure on China to appreciate the yuan, presumably in the belief that it will work wonders on the US trade balance. But will it?

When Japan was forced to appreciate the yen in 1985, the effect on the Japanese respective US balance of payments was difficult to spot.

In the 1980s, the European Union came to the conclusion that exchange-rate changes were no longer suitable as economic-policy instruments. That was one of the major economic reasons to establish an economic and monetary union.

There is much talk of a dollar slide to turn the US deficit on the trade balance around. The plain fact is that the US dollar has depreciated considerably over recent years, but without much effect on the trade balance. Calculations by the Bank for International Settlements reveal that the nominal effective exchange rate of the dollar fell from the beginning of 2002 to the end of 2005 between 15% and 25% depending on calculation method, the euro has risen about 20%, the yen has been comparatively stable, and the much vilified yuan has fluctuated but ended at the end of 2005 a little more than 10% down compared with the beginning of 2002.

Economic theory says this should improve the US trade balance, but it hasn't. Organization for Economic Cooperation and Development figures show not an improvement but deterioration, actually from a deficit of US$424 billion in 2002 to $716 billion in 2005 and $767 billion in 2006.

As the US and European economies are operating at the same level and broadly speaking are of similar structure, a comparative analysis may be rewarding and may correct an overall picture contradicting what you would expect.

But it doesn't. It gets even worse. From 2000 to 2005, the exchange rate of the euro rose from about $82 to $120 for 100 euro. This is, even by historical standards, a very, very large swing — a 50% depreciation of the dollar. The trade balance between the US and the European Union did not adjust in favor of the US as economic-policy prescription said it would. Quite the contrary. The bilateral deficit went up from about $32 billion in 2000 to $91 billion in 2006.

The fallback position for economic theory is to look at differentials in economic growth. If US growth was higher than in Europe and the growth differential between the EU and US rising, US domestic demand would outpace production, triggering growing imports from abroad, in this case the European Union. But again the figures disappoint. The growth-rate differential rose from 0.7 percentage point in 2002 to 2.1 points in 2004, whereafter it fell to 1.7 points in 2005 and 1.5 points in 2006.

Had exchange-rate movements and economic growth differentials worked in conformity with theory, an improvement, indeed a strong improvement, for the US trade balance vis-à-vis the EU should have materialized, while in fact it has steadily deteriorated.

The inescapable conclusion is that exchange rates do not much influence competitive positions or redress trade imbalances. Looking at the global economy over the past decades, the reason is all too obvious, even if it may be difficult to see the forest for trees.

Global outsourcing has moved most of the cost and price-sensitive production from high-cost producers to low-cost producers. Comparing hourly wage compensation, productivity and potential exchange-rate changes between the US and China or the EU and China, wage differential dwarfs the impact of exchange-rate changes. Even 50% depreciation over five years cannot compare to the long-term advantages of moving most labor-intensive production to China.

The main competitive advantages for developed countries such as the US, the EU nations and Japan have shifted to high tech, quality, design, style, branding, after-sales service and several other factors, which set up a unique position in the market delinked from costs and prices. The most interesting among them are accompanying services such as upgrading, maintenance, and training of staff, all of which are difficult to deliver by a newly industrialized country. But they are in the arsenal of developed nations and are brought into action to shift the competitive game away from prices and costs.

When US Treasury Secretary Henry Paulson cries buckets over the so-called undervalued yuan and President Nicolas Sarkozy of France attacks the European Central Bank for allowing the euro to rise, they are off the mark. It matters very little for the US and French trade balance and domestic production what the exchange rate is.

In globalization, macroeconomy and exchange-rate changes slip away from the policymakers. What has been labeled labor arbitrage takes over as the fact determining where cost-sensitive production takes place.

What is left for policymakers is a much more difficult and challenging task: to analyze their own competitive, non-price-sensitive advantages and strengthen them. A new paradigm for national economic policy makes established policies obsolete and puts the onus on a much more sophisticated formulation and implementation of policies.

Tomorrow's winners are those intercepting this and adjusting first and fastest. The key ideas: concentrate on what you are best at, skip the rest; do not try to climb the ladder, but focus on maintaining the one or two positions where you are in pole position.

It is likely that a number of Asian countries will start to look in earnest for cooperation about exchange rates. The Chiang Mai Initiative of 2000 must not be underestimated. It aims to create a network of bilateral swap arrangements among the 10 member states of the Association of Southeast Asian Nations plus China, Japan and South Korea to address short-term liquidity difficulties in the region and to supplement existing international financial arrangements.

This is good and commendable. If done in the right way, it will help Asia to weather new storms on the currency markets or a financial crisis like the one we saw in 1997–98. To be successful, however, the Asian countries should take a hard look at how the global economy has changed the effectiveness of exchange rates and the impact of the shift of competitive parameters.

This article was first published in *Asia Times Online*, 7 August 2007 (www.atimes.com).

Warning: Financial Chaos Ahead

AFTER RELATIVE CALM ON THE CURRENCY MARKETS OVER THE PAST 15 years — albeit interrupted by a couple of hiccups — sustained financial turmoil may be lurking.

An international monetary crisis is not a new phenomenon, but this time the extent, depth, violence and speed of capital movements chasing short-term profits may surpass anything the world has yet seen.

The central banks will step in to exercise damage control but, as in earlier crises, they may be caught on the wrong foot defending a system the market no longer believes in.

The post-1945 international monetary system falls in three stages. The first one lasted from the end of World War II to the early 1970s based upon fixed currency rates.

The second one ran from the early 1970s to the early 1990s with fluctuating rates in various editions, of which "managed floating" was the best known.

We are currently in the third stage, wherein central banks pursue inflation targeting, leaving the currency rates to the market and depriving them of their traditional role as economic-policy instruments.

The 1945-to-early-1970s model served the world very well. The markets took it for granted that rates reflected comparative and competitive positions. This cemented the assumption that they could be defended without much cost, which indeed proved to be the case until the system started to crack under the weight of large imbalances in the US economy in the late 1960s.

For a long time currency rates were not a topic for economic and monetary policy. They were where they were and few, if any, contested this state of affairs. Before the middle/late 1960s, when economic globalization emerged and made fixed rates obsolete, international trade and investment were not large enough to rattle the central banks.

From the early 1970s and for 20 years plus, currency upheavals became almost the order of the day. Global speculation unsettled the US dollar or the Japanese yen or the Deutschmark, as it was then. The major central banks had chosen to operate a system of managed currency rates vis-à-vis other currencies.

There were many reasons for adopting such a policy. The determining one was that fluctuating currency rates were thought to undermine trade and investment, thus jeopardizing economic growth. It didn't work out that way, though. The market did not believe in the currency rates pursued by the authorities and repeatedly pulled the carpet from beneath them, leaving the central banks hanging in the air.

Today the global economy is in the third stage. The world has lived happily for about 15 years under inflation targeting and without a major international currency crisis. But omens indicate that this may not last.

Since the early 1990s, almost all central banks have pursued inflation targeting with the goal of approximately 2% inflation. They have been successful. Global inflation has been kept at that level for nearly 15 years. Looking at the results, the market came to believe in the system. It is irrelevant whether this happy state of affairs was brought about by the central banks and their policies or by other factors. It happened, and that is what matters.

Now things are changing. A string of factors have entered the picture and pushed inflation above the targets. China may not be able to secure manufactured goods at the same low prices as it has over the past 15 years. Oil prices are hovering at a record high. Agriculture prices are beginning to rise, pushed by demand from the growing

Asian middle class. This does not automatically mean higher inflation, as productivity gains in China and India are in the pipeline. What it does mean, however, is a rising belief that the era of automatic low inflation may be over.

As the central banks have nailed their flags to inflation targeting and unscrupulously claimed credit for its success, the market will — not surprisingly — expect them to prevent inflation from moving beyond the acceptable range. The central banks, however, had limited influence in trying to achieve low inflation rates and they will have similarly little effect in stemming the tide of higher prices.

The economy will suffer from higher interest rates. This will bring the era of excessive global liquidity to an end and stoke the market's skepticism of central-bank policies. This may shatter the market's confidence in central banks and the policies they have chosen and, ultimately, destroy confidence in the international monetary system.

It is the duty and prerogative of central banks and monetary authorities to give guidance to the market; to let it know what the currency-rate policy is. The market sizes these signals up and follows such guidance if, and only if, it believes in the policies. If that belief crumbles, market forces may become strongly destabilizing.

Slowly rising inflation, creeping interest rates and doubts about inflation targeting may produce exactly such a situation, one asking for strong global leadership, and it is highly doubtful whether the International Monetary Fund has the strength and reputation to step in and fulfill that role.

The outcome may be a global monetary system that is much less global but more regional, with large currency groups accumulating sufficient size to withstand international, disruptive capital movements. Very few if any currencies can — alone and isolated — withstand the onslaught of speculators.

For Asia and especially East Asia, having learned painful lessons in 1997–98, this signals a need for much stronger regional currency cooperation. The first steps have been taken with various schemes for currency credits, but as the potential storm gathers, it is high time that Asia gets its act together and moves beyond the embryonic stage.

The lesson from Europe's three decades of hard work toward an economic and monetary union, the secret of central banking and how to counteract speculative capital movements, is found in three key sentences easily forgotten, but nonetheless priceless, in a crisis or in preempting a crisis:

- The larger the currency area, the more resistance disruptive capital movements will meet (the larger the pond, the bigger a stone is needed to make ripples).
- The value of a currency depends on confidence, and confidence lasts only while it lasts.
- It is earned by actions and the implementation of policies, not by declarations of intent. What counts is what you do, not what you say.

This article was first published in *Asia Times Online*, 18 July 2007 (www.atimes.com).

The Holy Grail of Central Banking

WHEN THE G-8 LEADERS MEET THIS WEEK THEY CAN CONGRATULATE themselves on high global growth, low inflation and a stable international monetary system. A similar picture has not been seen since the economic globalization of pre-1914 vintage. The current inclination is to credit central bankers, not political leaders, for these successes. The impression is that monetary policy is in the hands of the proper people, who possess the confidence necessary to steer a course round the rocks that shipwrecked predecessors. A golden age of central banking has arrived.

It is true that the central bankers' scoreboard looks impressive. Since 1993, the world has not experienced one single global monetary crisis on par with the turmoil of the 1970s and 1980s. Recent crises — in Asia in 1997 and 1998, in Mexico in 1994 and in Argentina in 2000 — have all been regional. These, with the possible exception of the 1998 Russian financial crisis, did not profoundly destabilize global financial markets. At the same time, the world has moved from comparatively high inflation rates in the 1980s into a bracket of 2 to 3 percent for most industrialized countries. Wage increases have been kept in check, despite persistent high economic growth.

The switch to inflation targeting as the central bankers' main policy objective is normally singled out to explain why the impossible — high economic growth and low inflation — suddenly has become possible.

In fact, central bank policies have had very little to do with producing such a string of splendid economic figures. In a recent interview, former Chairman of the Federal Reserve Alan Greenspan admitted that "the prevalence of low interest rates throughout the world was one of the things that surprised him."

Indeed, the world economy owes its current vitality to the emergence of China and other low-cost producers. These countries offer manufactured goods at low prices and welcome outsourcing. The direct effect is lower costs, which is multiplied by the indirect downward pressure on industrialized countries' domestic wages. In these circumstances, the central banks' tweaking of interest rates and money supply has been — albeit not irrelevant and not without policy impact — much less powerful and much less necessary than it was before the early 1990s.

As China and comparable countries have built up production capacity to meet strongly increasing demand, the boom in private consumption in the United States has not led to what conventional economic theory predicts: a rise in prices. Instead, low-cost production in the developing world has kept inflation in the developed world in check. This unexpected price stability — and in some cases, falling prices — has created a consumer's paradise, encouraging consumers to spend even more on goods and services.

Since a rise in consumer demand has not been accompanied by an increase in the inflation rate, central bankers believe that there is no reason to put the brakes on consumer spending — regardless of growth, employment and balance of payments. Inflation targeting means that as long as the inflation rate is kept at around 2 percent, everything is fine, and all other traditional economic warning signals should be disregarded. Consequently, monetary policy has not been adjusted, and central banks continue to stimulate their respective economies with loose, liquidity-creating monetary policy. Only recently and half-heartedly have central bankers around the world tightened up monetary policy — but not by very much.

The economy is a complex machine, so the excess liquidity pumped into the system by central banks has to go somewhere. That "somewhere", as of late, has been assets: stocks, bonds, gold, property. As liquidity flows into these assets, asset prices rise out of proportion to the actual value of the assets, creating speculative bubbles.

The very central bankers whose monetary policies create these bubbles have enhanced their reputations by warning against the potential negative effects of such bubbles — as was the case in 1996, when Alan Greenspan spoke about the stock market's "irrational exuberance."

Fortunately for central bankers, the foundation that supports their inflation-targeting strategies — the ability of low-cost producers to meet demand without increasing producer prices — appears to be in no danger of collapse. The number of people in the working age in China will continue to rise for a decade and in India, even longer. Information and communications technology has been coming to these countries, bringing with it a jump in overall productivity.

For now, protectionism in the United States and Europe represents the principal threat to the inflation-targeting strategies of central bankers. If protectionists succeed in setting up obstacles to imports from countries like China and India, inflation rates in Europe and the United States will certainly increase, causing confidence in central banks to fall.

Worse, this chain of events will eventually lead to the popping of asset bubbles, generating a possibly severe economic downturn. For the first time in 15 years, central banks will see inflation-targeting strategies jeopardized.

Alternatively, financial systems could become complacent and start lending to excessively risky borrowers because other assets have become too pricey, and thus out of reach. Non-performing loans may gobble up an increasing share of asset portfolios, threatening systemic stability in the case of loan defaults.

The recent troubles of the subprime-mortgage market in the United States are a perfect illustration of this problem. When large numbers of subprime — that is, risky — borrowers proved incapable of paying off their mortgages, several subprime-lending institutions collapsed. Some experts have predicted that the implosion of the subprime-mortgage market will eventually prompt an economy-wide recession in the United States.

While the goal of containing inflation is commendable, central banks' inflation-targeting strategies can stoke asset price increases, thereby destabilizing the economy. Perhaps central banks should supplement their inflation-targeting strategies with an asset-price yardstick. After all, the principal challenges to economic stability over the last 15 years have been asset bubbles, not inflation.

This article was first published in *The National Interest*, 6 June 2007.

Leave the Yuan Alone

IN JULY 1927, THE GOVERNOR OF THE BANK OF ENGLAND, NORMAN Montagu, visited the governor of the New York Federal Reserve Bank, Benjamin Strong. He had a mission.

In 1925 Britain had gone back to the gold standard, but at a rate overvalued by about 10 percent. Gold was flowing out of London, threatening the British gold reserves and consequently the international monetary system.

To prevent a run on the pound sterling, Montagu had to raise interest rates, but that would have killed the fragile British economic recovery, with potentially unenviable political and economic repercussions.

Montagu found a way out of his predicament. If he could persuade the Federal Reserve Bank of New York to lower its interest rate and adopt an easy money policy, the drain on the British gold reserves would stop.

He succeeded in talking Strong into such a policy. The effect proved to be disastrous, to say the least. The lax monetary policy in New York fuelled a stock market boom that crashed in 1929, taking the world into the Great Depression of the 1930s.

In December this year, a high-powered U.S. delegation chaired by the secretary of the Treasury, Henry Paulson, will go to Beijing. The chairman of the Federal Reserve, Ben Bernanke, will be among the members of the delegation.

The U.S. Treasury has already stated officially that one of the purposes is to exercise pressure on China to allow the yuan to fluctuate more freely.

The economic situation in the mid-1920s and the middle of the first decade of the 21st century are not comparable, but the scenario of one major economic power pushing another one into inappropriate policies later to be judged wrong looks disturbingly similar.

The American delegation will try to persuade China to solve a predominantly American domestic economic problem — to redress the imbalances of public finances and the balance of payments that has run out of control because of the lack of saving by American households, stimulated by the Fed's cheap money policy a couple of years ago.

This problem has very little to do with U.S. competitiveness and even less with the rate of the yuan.

A revaluation of the Chinese currency will not help much. When the United States in the mid-1980s forced Japan to make a dramatic revaluation of the yen (the Plaza agreement), the effect on the U.S. balance of payments proved to be negligible.

But the negative effects on the Japanese economy were significant, as this policy contributed to slow growth in Japan from 1990 onwards. It is still holding Japan in its grip.

The world needs strong and sustainable growth. With a U.S. growth rate definitely lower in 2006 than in 2005, and expected to be even lower next year, high growth is not coming from the United States.

Europe is showing growth of around 2 percent — insufficient to pull the rest of the world along. Japan is likewise operating at a growth rate of about 2 percent, and recent figures indicate it is slowing down.

So where is global growth to come from in the next couple of years? From China, India and Southeast Asia, all seemingly steady on growth patterns of between 5 and 10 percent.

The last thing the world needs at this time is lower growth in China, forced on it by the United States, with the inevitable result that global growth will head downwards in 2007. This is precisely what a forced revaluation of the yuan will lead to.

Companies operating in China will probably react in the same way Japanese companies did in the 1980s after the Plaza agreement — that is, they will maintain prices in yuan by cutting profit margins and/or squeezing labor costs.

Many of the companies operating in China and exporting to the United States are not Chinese, but American, European and Japanese.

A profit squeeze will affect their investment plans in a negative way. A downward pressure on wages for the Chinese labor force will tend to reduce private consumption in China at a time when rising domestic demand in Asia is crucial for maintaining a persistent pattern of high global growth.

So history may repeat itself in the way that a major economic power, facing difficulties of its own making, forces another one to adopt a policy that is eventually harmful not only to that country, but also to the global economy.

This article was first published in the *International Herald Tribune*, 29 November 2006.

Growth in Asia Propels US Stocks

IT LOOKS LIKE SOMETHING IS WRONG. WALL STREET IS NOT BEHAVING in accordance with conventional economic theory. It goes up when it should go down.

All omens point to a sluggish US economy in 2007. The latest revised growth predictions forecast a fall from 3.6% in 2006 to 2.9% in 2007. The increase in labor force plus growth in productivity, the instrumental forces behind the high growth for a number of years, will be less favorable in the years to come and bring the economy down to a trend growth of around 2.5% [1]. Admittedly, such figures are full of uncertainties, but all indicators announce a lower trend growth in the coming years.

Stock markets should react to such predictions by falling or at least not moving very much, but contrary to conventional wisdom, Wall Street and Nasdaq are actually rising. Not even 16 consecutive increases by the Federal Reserve of the short-term interest rate, bringing it to 5.25%, has dampened the market.

When analyzing behavior out of tune with theory, the observer can say that the theory is correct and the stock market will realize that sooner or later, or that the stock markets know or react to factors most of us do not incorporate in our analysis.

Let us go straight to the second option. The stock market knows that we are living in a global world. Most of the companies listed on Wall Street get most of their profits from the domestic US market, but less so every year. Revenue from the US market is still very high, but growth in revenues and profits from Asia outshines US figures. Such companies as Microsoft, Oracle, General Electric and Dell switch more and more to the buoyant and unstoppable growth machines in Asia — China, India and the majority of Southeast Asian countries. They sell to these countries, they invest in them, and they move more and more of their research and development to them.

This has the following consequences for stock prices on Wall Street.

When investors look at buying stocks, they among other things focus on price/earnings (p/e) ratio. Basic arithmetic tells us that with 1.2 billion people in China and an annual economic growth rate of about 10% in the years to come, the increase in purchasing power will be of a magnitude not yet seen. Add to this 1 billion Indians and about 500 million people in Southeast Asia, and they far outweigh any increase in US purchasing power. This is in particular true as a rising middle class with strong purchasing power emerges.

A stock may show a traditional p/e of, let us say, 15, but if we add in the growth prospects from Asia, a p/e much higher does not look out of tune. If p/e is above the average or normal level, the question is how long it takes for earnings to catch up — to produce earnings higher than estimated, thus bringing p/e back to normal. That depends on growth prospects and, as just outlined, the huge and fast-growing Asian markets will sharply reduce this length of time in the future.

A large part of the investors operating on Wall Street may still be American, particularly where pension funds are concerned. They want to buy a share of tomorrow's production to finance future payments, and to achieve such a performance, they look to companies getting an increasing share of profit on growth markets. This is where money is earned and production will take place. The pension claims from a growing number of people above 65 years of age dwarfs a fixed return from bonds, hence in reality eliminating bonds as a viable competitor to stocks, which explains why pension funds will gradually swing their portfolios from bonds to stocks and opt for overweight in companies having gained a firm foothold in Asia.

It is actually quite rational for stock markets to go up even in the shadow of a short-term economic slowdown and a growth trend falling to 2.5% for the US, because the market has concluded that this is not where growth is going to take place anyway.

As long as growth prospects for Asia remain bullish, there is no reason to expect falling stock prices on Wall Street for those companies acting as global players.

There are three key observations to learn from this analysis:

- To realize that an increasing number of American companies are only American by name and legal status but in reality global companies having chosen for historical and other reasons to maintain their headquarters in the US.
- To understand that pension funds are buying stocks expected to produce high earnings in the future, giving the pension funds the money they need to honor claims. Pension funds cannot live with a fixed income from bonds. They need to opt for a share of future production, and the answer is to buy growth stocks.
- To look at future stock prices not on the basis of an X-ray picture telling how the situation is right now but a flow — dynamic — analysis telling which markets will be decisive in the future.

Endnote

1. *The Economist*, October 26, 2006.

This article was first published in *Asia Times Online*, 29 November 2006 (www.atimes.com).

Part 5: Asia in the World

THE RISE OF ASIA WAS BOUND TO FOCUS UPON THE TWO LARGEST COUNTRIES, China and India. Many observers searched for and many thought they found good reasons for a forthcoming conflict even war. It is, however, much more likely that the future will be inscribed in an equation of China and India instead of China or India. Basically these two countries may be rivals, but do not threaten each other's vital interests and do not see each other as the main or arch enemy. There is only one factor that could initiate an armed conflict and that is access to water. A large part of India's water supply come from the Tibetan plateau and if China decides to divert this water for its own use India may well regard it as *casus belli*.

Trade is growing fast among the Asian countries auguring that we may soon see some kind of institutional framework for economic integration, albeit in a weaker edition than the European construction. Investment among Asian countries is lagging far behind and as long as that is the case the ardor for strong integration will be measured. Politically the course will be determined by the willingness of the fastest growing countries to share the wealth with less fortunate countries. If that is the case Asia may well look forward to decades of peaceful growth.

Peace and prosperity have reigned in Asia apart from local conflicts and superpower intervention in a couple of cases, but broadly speaking Asia has benefited from peace in forming its own phenomenal economic growth. Many Asians may think that this will continue to be the case, but such negligence of historic lessons could prove hazardous. Only a strong and determined effort based upon a sincere analysis of the problems and potential conflicts — domestically as well as between countries — will cement peace as a foundation for continued economic growth.

The American presence, including its military presence, has been vital as it was for the European reconstruction after World War II. It does not matter why the US pursued such polices, it did, and Asia benefited enormously. Now things are changing. The Asian countries are getting richer; the US is mired in economic difficulties. A continued American presence cannot be taken for granted. Even more the US has to make up its mind how it evaluates the new Asia and in particular Asian economic integration. Is it a potential threat, a nuisance, can it be neglected, or is it a helping hand for the US solving its own economic problems? What is Asia's role in shaping embryonic global governance for the next decades? These are key choices for the US, but equally crucial for Asia. The future of economic globalization may depend upon what the US decides and how Asia reacts. Both should put in a strong effort to understand each other. The US cannot stop the rise of Asia; the challenge is to handle it adroitly. Asia must recognize that the American transition from global superpower to something less although still extremely powerful is an agonizing process calling for adept diplomacy and readiness to shoulder more of the global burden from partners.

The global financial crisis poses a conceptual problem for Asia: Which model to follow? Asia has been attracted by the capitalism more or less in its American edition because it delivered what Asia wanted, high economic growth. Now the downside has been bared for all to see and it is regrettably not a pretty sight.

Both ethically and economically the model is being questioned. The financial institutions at Wall Street was encouraged and/or forced to go along with risky transactions even if they knew that was the case because the drive for short term profit did not allow them to step on the brake. If so, they would have lost market shares to competitors and the managers advocating and implementing such policies dismissed.

It may not be only a question of economic model, but what kind of society this will bring about. Certainly not a liberal economy and a market state with the invisible hand and the individual in the driver's seat. The world may enter an era of institutionalized economics with capital, money, ownership and power to steer the economy according to the wishes and preferences of institutions.

It would be one of history's whims if Asia swings towards the market economy and private ownership at the very moment these long-cherished assets have been undermined precisely by those who were supposed to be their custodians.

The Asian economies are faced with unexpected problems after several decades of high growth. The cards still look positive for persistent high growth, but it will not come as easily as was the case from 1978 to the beginning of the 21st century. Industrialization has brought about higher income per head and millions have been lifted out of poverty. China has accumulated the world's largest currency reserves while emerging as the biggest manufacturing country. India is a powerhouse with regard to software. The assets are there for everybody to see. So are the problems. One of them is divergent demography. Japan and Korea have falling population, China enters into stagnating population and an uneven gender proportion. The whole of South Asia plus Indonesia, The Philippines and Vietnam will continue to register rising population. Inequality is reaching high levels. Pollution may hamper growth more than it costs to reduce it.

All this poses challenges and political choices to Asia. They can only be solved in a global framework with Asia as a full partner in globalization and the rest of the world engaged in Asia's development. Asia's economy is now so powerful that it gradually replaces the US economy as the pacesetter for the global economy; we are not yet there, but well on the way. How Asia tackles the opportunities, challenges, and problems may well determine the future of globalization.

Asia: The New Global Economic Powerhouse

The US Economy

Until recently, the US was the decisive factor in the global economy — the trendsetter or the pacesetter. The rest of the world followed the American business cycle with a time-lag. That is no longer the case. When discussing Asia, the starting point must therefore be a short analysis of why and how the American economy has lost this position. Even if it may look a bit out of context to compare the US and Europe, it reveals the weaknesses of the US economy opening the door or rather inviting Asia to take over.

The US economy is generally perceived as much stronger than the European one, indeed the pacesetter for the global economy. This perception is wrong.

In an article published November 19, 2005, *The Economist*[1] punctures some of the myths and comes to the conclusion that the decisive factor behind the stronger US economic performance compared to the European one is "that America's population is increasing much faster than the euro zone's".

Nobel laureate Robert Mundell comes to the same basic conclusion — that the main difference between the US and Europe is population growth. In an interview in September 2006, he says "some say that Europe has performed badly compared with the US over the past 10 years, but they forget that Europe has zero population growth and that European per capita income isn't much below the US figure."[2]

The high US growth rate of approximately 3.5% per year over the last five years cannot be counted upon to continue, even if we put the subprime crisis aside for a while. A lower trend growth is in the cards, as the proportion of the US population available for work will not continue to rise — on the contrary, it is falling.[3]

US consumption has pulled the rest of the world along, but rested upon debt with property as collateral. This was fine, indeed splendid, as long as property prices continued to go up, but as we now know and was predicted by a number of people the property bubble would burst. Former FED chairman Alan Greenspan has calculated that approx 3% of personal consumption expenditure rests on this particular kind of borrowing.[4]

There is no reason to elaborate on the subprime crisis apart from stating that this is a mess bringing home to roost all the birds let loose by an irresponsible loan policy by a long list of US financial institutions, almost representing a who is who in global finance.

The point in this context is that the calamities in the slipstream of the subprime crisis will not be a short-term matter, but a long drawn out affair putting a ceiling on US growth for a number of years. The argument behind this statement is that — as shown in a paper by Edward E. Leamer of the UCLA — housing is not a price cycle, but a volume cycle.[5]

This explains why:

- We cannot count upon the US economy as the pacesetter any longer and if we could it would point downwards.
- It will take a while before we see economic growth in the US much above 1.5–2% on an annual basis.
- Much effort in the coming years will be devoted to redress economic imbalances accumulated in the US over the last decade or so.

These three elements tell us how important it is to look at the strength of the Asian economies, as neither Europe nor Japan will be able to step in and fill the vacuum created by the US. Either Asia makes it as the pull factor in global growth or no one does.

US Imbalances, Economic Policy and the Role of Asia

The US economic imbalances need to be redressed and they will be. The question is how and when. The well-known economic theory about adjustment of imbalances on the balance of payments tells us which instruments are available, but politics determine the mix to be applied.

It is all about transfer of purchasing power from the US to Asia. In other words the US Gross Domestic Product (GDP) per head must go down (at least relatively compared to Asia) and the GDP per head in Asia must increase.

US fiscal policy might be mobilized, but few will expect the Bush administration to increase taxes. The room of maneuver to reduce spending is almost nonexistent after a number of years with cuts, except for the military sector which is not likely to suffer cuts. The most effective instrument thus does not look suitable in light of the political situation.

Monetary policy could also do part of the job, but the misguided policies of former FED Chairman Alan Greenspan — waiting too long to push the interest rates up — has left the FED with almost no options and if it had any the subprime crisis has taken them away. Now it is a foregone conclusion that rates will be lowered to stimulate the US economy, ruling it out of the game to transfer purchasing power from the US to Asia. That leaves three options, each of them not very attractive.

First, the currency rate through a depreciation of the US Dollar: That will certainly take place, actually it has already has, but more vis-à-vis Europe than vis-à-vis the Asian currencies. In the summer of 2000, the US Dollar-Euro rate was close to 82 US Dollars per 100 Euro, in the beginning of 2008, it is close to 160. This translates into a depreciation of the US Dollar vis-à-vis the Euro of more than 50%, and still the US balance of payments has not improved. The depreciation vis-à-vis the Asian currencies is less, as Asia has chosen to be a Dollar zone.

The problem, as the US-Euro development shows, is that currency rate changes do no longer hold the same sway over the balance of trade. The reason for this has something to do with Asia. Almost all price-sensitive production has been outsourced to Asia. Production left in Europe or the US competes on other parameters than prices and costs. How relevant is a depreciation of say 10 or 20% if the unit costs in China are between 5 and 10% of costs in Europe or the US?

Second, semi-protectionism or even worse a swing towards outright protectionism: This is, unfortunately much more relevant. The shifting trend is more visible in the US than in Europe. Clearly the mood is changing. The seminal change in the US attitude towards the rest of the world since 9/11 — shifting from openness to seclusion — has cast the rest of the world in the image of an enemy, may be not militarily, but rather psychologically and economically.

The ongoing campaign to win the nomination for the Presidential race has legitimized attacks and accusation on other countries and 'America first' is commonly used by the candidates. Even Republicans display fewer ardors than usual in defending free trade and among democrats free trade is game for everybody to shoot at. One of the leading candidates [at the time of writing], Senator Hillary Clinton, stated in an article in the *Financial Times* that "she believed that theories underpinning free trade might no longer hold true in the era of globalization".[6] Later in the same article, she spoke about America's "economic sovereignty". In February 2006, a number of Senators from both parties confronted a Dubai-based consortium's purchase of US harbors and announced the intention to introduce legislation to prohibit companies owned or controlled by foreign governments from running port operations in the United States.[7]

Third (and probably the most likely outcome), a worn out and tired US might not manage to find the time and resources to tackle the problem, leaving it to market forces. If so, a correction will certainly take place, but under circumstances, which may be very unfavorable, dominated by abrupt and violent swings in economic fundamentals.

Asia Confronted with Rebalancing of the US Economy

Two factors determine whether a regional economy has moved into self-sustaining growth:

- A supply chain (trade with semi-manufactured goods finally transformed into the end product) linking the countries together in supporting each other and being more dependent on each other than on other regions in the world.
- The strength of domestic demand and private consumption emerging as the main driver behind the regional supply chains, that is countries export to each other to prop up domestic demand instead of consumption in non-regional countries.

Europe has some time ago moved into the stage of a self-sustaining economy with a declining dependence on the US. Economic statistics show that exports to the United States account for less than 3 percent of the euro zone economy.[8] Private consumption gobbles up between 50 and 60% of total Gross Domestic Product depending upon the business cycle.

Over the last decade or so, China's share of US imports has risen strongly, while most other Asian countries' shares have gone down. An analysis of export figures from 1996 to 2003 shows that China's share of the US market has gone up from 8.5 to 22.4%, while most other Asian countries' shares have been reduced to approximately one third of their size in 1996.[9] This points to the observation that the share of exports from Asia to the US has not changed visibly, but that China has emerged as the end-producer. It imports semi-finished products from the rest of Asia to export the final product to the US. If this were still the case, Asia would not be a self-sustaining economy.[10]

What has recently happened, however, is that when China's exports go up with 1%, imports to China from other Asian countries go up with 1.3% for semi-manufactured goods and 2.8% for investment goods.[11] Goldman Sachs has calculated that in 2007 only approximately 1,6 percentage points of Chinese growth (estimated at 10%) came from exports to the US compared with 2.7 points in 2005.[12] Deutsche Bank figures that a 1 percentage point slowdown in the US would trim China's export growth by 4 percentage points and reduce Chinese GDP by 0.5 percentage points.[13]

If we add the observation that intra-trade in East Asia amounts to approximately 54% compared with approximately 64% for the EU and approximately 46% for NAFTA, the conclusion becomes quite different.[14] It looks like a supply chain is building up geared more to Asia's own needs than exports to the US. The preliminary growth figures for Asia in the third and fourth quarters of 2007 connote that the slow-down in the US economy had some, but no major impact on growth in most Asian countries. Growth forecasts for 2008 published by the World Bank in the beginning of January 2008 support this view.[15]

Figures published by the Asian Development Bank reveal that in the five year period from 2001 to 2005 Chinese growth was steered by investment, with a little more than five percentage points followed by private consumption with a little less than three percentage points, while government consumption and net exports had no significant impact (The impact of net exports was even negative in two of the five years, 2001 and 2002, and negligible in 2004.)[16] Taken together, private consumption and private investments account for approximately 90% of total Chinese GDP.

In a macroeconomic context, China is the dominating economy in Asia and the figures mentioned above indicate that Asia (or at least East Asia) is turning onto the path towards a more self-sustaining economy.[17]

Various analyses of private consumption in China warrant this statement. Two elements are of particular importance: trendsetters and mass consumption.

Global cities emerge as a possible determining parameter for future trendsetters with regard to taste, style, preferences, brains and the likes, telling us where the strongly rising revenues and profits are to be found.

Almost all the new global cities or hubs will be found in Asia. Suffice to mention Shanghai, Beijing, Mumbai, Guangzhou-Hong Kong, maybe Singapore-Johore, maybe Saigon and in a long-term perspective cities like Chengdu, Chongqing, Bangkok and Sydney.

A few months ago, the theory about the spiky world — setting this out with utmost clarity — was published by Richard Florida.[18] The global elite asks for a common environment with regard to taste and preferences making its members at ease and at home and it will not be confined to one geographical place. It will move around the globe and choose geographical places with a congruous stylistic environment. Wealth is gradually transferred from the US and Europe to East Asia, which tells us that the future global elite will strike roots in Asia and consequently new consumption patterns emerge there. This also means that companies shooting for this extremely lucrative segment of the market will either be born in Asia or be Western companies having felt where the wind is blowing and migrated from Europe and the US to China, India and the other economic power centers (migrated in the sense that the 'brain' of the company has moved from former headquarters to be in touch with new tastes).[19]

China is today the world's third largest luxury goods consumer and prognosis tells us that by 2015 it will be the number one worldwide.[20] The total number of households in the income bracket driving demand for luxury goods will rise in the Asia/Pacific region from approximately 100 mio. in 2006 to almost 250 mio. in 2016 with China as the main source, opening up for a purchasing power of almost 260 billion US Dollars in 2016 after an annual 12% rise from 2006.[21] A similar trend is emerging in India with a growing middle class and a growing number of people moving into the segment of luxury goods.

In 2004, China's consumer market was number seven on the global hit list and Credit Suisse First Boston has calculated that in 2014 China will be the number one market with an annual growth in consumption of 18%.[22] The prognosis points to a share of Chinese urban households with an income of 5,000 US Dollars will rise from 17.4% in 2004 to 90% based upon an annual growth rate of 24%.[23]

The Main Drivers Behind the Rise of Asia

Supported by the strong and buoyant domestic economy, Asia is moving fast to overtake the US (and Europe) as the pull factor in the global economy. Five elements illustrate this and expose how Asia is gradually controlling the global economy.

1) *Skill content of exports*

Economists have long looked for signs of Asian exports moving into high value. That would signal a much more mature status for the Asian economies and would again cement the belief that Asia is becoming a self-sustaining growth area.

The International Monetary Fund has analyzed Chinese exports from 1992 to 2005 to find out whether they have more skill content or are still kept in the traditional mould.[24] The findings are that measured in per cent of manufacturing export the following sectors have fallen in their share: textiles, apparel, footwear and miscellaneous manufacturing.

The following sectors, however, have increased their share: industrial machinery, office machines, telecommunications and electronic machinery. That leaves little doubt that China is changing track from cheap labor to skills-based exports. The question remains, however, how much that is due to China's own performance or China, as mentioned earlier, is the end link in the supply chain, thus merely reflecting imports with higher skill content which are assembled for re-export. The study concludes that by excluding skills from imports the figure is much less visible, thus indicating that imports with higher skill content account for a considerable part. However, as these imports primarily come from other Asian countries, it may tell us that China is slowly moving towards higher skill exports, while Asia as such is moving faster.

The latest figures for 2007 tell us that China's high-tech exports in the first three quarters rose with 24.7% to 244 bn. US Dollars accounting for 27.8% of total exports. The figures for imports show a similar picture with a total value of 208 bn. US Dollars after a hike of 16.7% accounting for 30.1% of total imports.[25]

2) *Economic integration*

So far, the Asian market has largely been fragmented in the absence of genuine economic integration. The verdict is still out whether Asia is capable of shaping a large Asian market more or less in the same vein as the Single Market in Europe.

There is no doubt, however, that the intention is there. China is aware of the political imperative to spread its newfound wealth among other Asian countries in order not to be seen as dragging wealth away from them with inevitable negative political repercussions. The Southeast Asian countries are trying hard to create a kind of economic community in ASEAN. They know perfectly well that compared to the juggernauts China and India they cannot attract foreign direct investment unless they offer a common Southeast Asian market. For these countries, economic integration is a question of staying in league number one or be relegated to league number two. The ASEAN Charter, recently agreed upon, bears witness to that.[26]

India is reluctantly warming to internationalization of its economic links with other Asian countries in a market economy framework.

Right now, China negotiates a free trade agreement with ASEAN and ASEAN negotiates a similar agreement with India. Recently, China and India have agreed to start negotiations about a free trade agreement. If all these efforts are successful, and it is more likely than not, Asia will in about ten years from now see some kind of single market, albeit less ambitious than the European one, but it will broadly speaking offer many of the freedoms associated with a single market. Just think of such an economic powerhouse with approximately 3 bn. persons, growth rates around 7–8% and income per head moving into the bracket of 5.000 US Dollars. It constitutes a watershed in economic history. Enterprises will be offered freedom of localization and goods plus not all, but some services will cross borders without barriers. The high productivity in Asia will get a boost and the purchasing power will jump.

The drivers will probably be China and India. Much has been written about the rivalry between these two powers. There are two things to say about this.

First, they may be rivals, but they do not constitute a threat to each other's vital interests. For China, Japan fills this role and for India Pakistan does, but the absence of conflicting vital interests opens the way for economic partnership.

Second, over the last year bilateral trade has increased phenomenally. From approximately 150 mio. US Dollars in 1992, it surpassed 20 bn. in 2006 and is expected to reach 50 bn. in 2010. Direct investments between the two countries are still embryonic, but rising fast.[27]

3) *Asian multinational companies (AMC)*
The global market has been dominated by multinational companies originating in the West, framing business culture by corporate governance, corporate compliance and corporate social responsibility.

This will not last. So far, the only Asian multinationals have come from Japan with a handful Korean and one or two from a few other Asian countries. The Japanese multinationals, however, are not — with the exception of Sony and may be Toyota — genuine multinationals, but Japanese companies operating internationally.

The Chinese companies realize that their limited exposure to the market economy and seclusion from international and global trends forces them to buy — not market shares — but knowledge and skills about how to operate internationally. Having grown up in a strictly controlled Chinese economy, in an incubator controlled by state banks far from market conditions and with state-owned enterprises as their role models, they are handicapped in the global competitive game from the beginning. It will take too long to learn by doing, so they opt for buying this expertise by purchasing well-run and well-known Western enterprises. The classic illustration is the Chinese PC maker Legend's purchase of IBM's computer division with the new company operating under the name of Lenovo with its headquarters in the US. The large Chinese oil companies like Petrochina and CNOOC are following the same trend. In the beginning of 2008, the Australians did not only wake up to a new year, but also to a new world. After several years worth of effort by Australian banks to enter the Chinese market, it suddenly dawned on Australia that China had bought stakes in the three leading Australian banks![28]

In a few years time, the world will see Chinese multinational companies challenging the established Western companies. They have a large domestic market, they know better than many Western companies how to fit into the demand patterns of newly industrialized countries or developing nations, having done so on their home turf, while Western companies are controlled by the philosophy in the US and Europe — not necessarily an asset as growing markets are to be found elsewhere.

The Indian companies have to a large extent grown up in a market economy, thus knowing well how to function under such circumstances. They do not need any learning process — witness the emergence of Arcelor-Mittal as the world's largest steel producer and the Tata Group as one of the few successful diversified corporations now contemplating to buy Jaguar, one of the household names in British motoring.

The world has already seen Wipro and Infosys in the software sector and it has not gone unnoticed how well-managed companies like Ranbaxy and Dr Reddy's Lab have been in the generic pharmaceutical industry.

4) *Capital productivity*

China and India are supplementing each other with regard to labor and capital productivity.

China has a comparative advantage in labor productivity, being approximately 50% better than India in this regard, while India's capital productivity is approximately 30% better than China's.[29]

In economic terms, the implication of this is not difficult to figure out. Multinationals can allocate their activities, taking advantage of the two countries' respective advantages to enhance competitive advantage. When companies from the two countries find out what this means the coming free trade agreement opens the door for a similar effect. The companies doing this in a market with approximately 2.3 bn. persons and high growth rates will see their unit costs nosedive, strengthening their competitive positions.

This is, however, far from the whole story. The International Monetary Fund (IMF) has analyzed China's capital productivity.[30]

The starting point is a rising proportion of investments as share of GDP from 1995 to 2005: for China from 33% to a little more than 40% and for India slightly rising from 25% in 1995 to 28% in 2005.

The IMF then looks closer at China. 41% of manufacturing assets are held by domestic non-state-owned companies, 32% by state-owned and 27% by foreign-owned ones. The point is that a given amount of investments by state-owned companies generates much less value added than other types of companies. Compared to domestic private companies, the figures say 32% less for wholly state-owned, 14% less for majority state-owned, slightly less for wholly foreign-owned companies and 10% more for majority foreign-owned ones.

If state-owned companies are turned into non-state-owned companies and if the assumption is made that they will then catch up with productivity in the non-state-owned sector, China then faces an enormous jump ahead in capital productivity.

This may or may not be the case, but we do know that the Chinese government is acting fast in promoting precisely such a conversion. It is not the same as saying that it will be successful nor that it will bring about a jump in productivity as mentioned, but it is likely that it will increase productivity markedly, albeit the size may be uncertain.

Taken together, this points to a strongly rising productivity in Asia, not leaving much time to pause and reflect for Western companies.

5) *International investment*

The key sentence when talking about international investment is simple: There is only one place in the world where savings take place — and that is Asia.[31] The world is financed by Asia. So far this fact does not seem to have sunk in among Americans and Europeans because Asia has allowed Western financial institutions to shuffle around with its savings. This is no longer the case.[32] The subprime crisis revealed that the Western financial institutions behaved recklessly and in stark contradiction to all prescriptions of corporate financial governance. An Asian offensive to gain influence on ownership of the institutions investing Asia's savings is gaining speed.

It is a safe bet that from now on Asia will demand a say in how its savings are invested and not surprisingly Asia's own preferences will get higher, much higher, priorities. The next thing to happen is the emergence of Asian financial institutions getting stronger, not only in their domestic markets, but also abroad. Names such as ICICI from India and ICBC from China will be known around the world in a few years time. Insurance companies like China Life and Ping An are already on the offensive.[33] No wonder. When you sit on the worlds savings with an economy predicted to continue in the fast lane you will gradually, but surely get your hands on the wheel.

A phenomenon attracting more and more attention worldwide are the sovereign wealth funds (SWF; investment funds owned by governments). They have been known for a long time operating out of oil exporting countries, but Asia is now starting to flex its muscles as well. China is setting up the CIC (China Investment Corporation), which earlier this year bought a stake in Blackstone but now redirects its interest more towards Asian and Chinese investment opportunities.[34] There is a strong interest among Western politicians and financial institutions about which policies these sovereign wealth funds are going to adopt. Regardless of that, their sheer size will revolutionize the international capital markets, with the inevitable result that Western financial institutions will loose market shares.

Morgan Stanley has calculated that in 2015 the SWF will control 12 bn. US Dollars (the size of US GDP in 2006) surpassing total international currency reserves in 2011, with a Chinese fund as the biggest single operator.[35]

The Risk Factors

No rose without a thorn. Admittedly Asia is facing a string of problems posing question marks whether growth will continue.

1) *Productivity*

Inside the box of economics, Asia needs to shift from ample supply of production factors to higher factor productivity. Over the last decades, labor and capital has been abundant. Labor supply has grown with a rising population and a favorable age pyramid. Savings have been strong, especially in China and India is catching up now. That has stimulated growth and in some cases has led to the question of inoptimal allocation of production factors.

This trend will not be broken, but it is unlikely that growth in factor supply will continue to be as favorable. China will reach a maximum of people in the bracket 19–60 years in about 2015 and savings cannot continue to go up. India will see a continued rise in population in the active age bracket for at least 25 years and the savings rate is on an upward trend, but in both areas it is unlikely that India can fully compensate for China.

As in all other examples of transition from developing economy to industrial or service economy, the shift must take place from growing supply of production factors to higher factor productivity. Will Asia be able to do that?

The answer depends on three main issues:

- Asia's ability to root out many of the inefficiencies in the form of corruption, nepotism, distorted markets and politically motivated investment. In short, Asia needs to get better governance.
- The Asian capital market has markedly improved over the last decade, not least bearing in mind the lessons from the financial crisis in 1997–98, but markets are still not working in an optimal way. One of the keys — and maybe the most important one in order to analyze whether Asia will be able to squeeze higher productivity out of production factors — is the reform of the financial system. Financial institutions scrutinize investment projects and decide where to channel the savings. It is also bell weather for social capital perceived in the way that trust in governments makes it more likely that people switch from gold and cash (foreign currency) to bank accounts.
- It is an open question how good Asia's corporate governance is compared to many Western companies. Many Asian companies are still anchored in family ownership. There is nothing wrong with that except that experience both in Asia and abroad tells us that transition from the first and maybe the second generation is an acrimonious process, which many companies have not been able to survive.

2) *Political systems*

In many respects, Asia's political systems have mastered economic growth remarkably well. For the populations of Asia, higher living standards are on top of the list of priorities and the political systems in almost all countries have delivered. In a way, they legitimize themselves by rising living standards year after year.

Meritocracy is one of the key words. Many Westerners seem to take the view that sooner or later transition towards a model more like the Western one will take place. That may or may not be the case. There is no law to history, however, saying that continued economic growth requires a political system like the one we see in Europe and the US.

Even though there is no agreement that democracy is the 'ideal' or 'the best possible' political model, there are today 'rising expectations' among the deprived or the youth, which are principally fuelled by information spread through globalized networks. There is a growing demand for good governance, accountability and transparency. This cuts across any 'brand' of democracy and is not associated with a particular model.

The problem for Asia is not whether it can or will shift to democracy as defined in the Western mould, but whether the political system can intercept the growing preferences for fundamental rights of freedom and deliver on that issue as it has on rising living standards.

Behind the scene looms a problem which in unfavorable circumstances may overshadow most of the other question marks: What about the 'social losers'? Asia has gotten used to high growth and rising employment. Much social welfare is still invested with the family. The concept of 'social losers' is not on the agenda, even if it goes without saying that Asia has its fair share of those not able to cope with the challenges. As long as growth is high, the number of social losers may be sufficiently small to keep it on the lower rungs of the ladder of political priorities, but if the business cycle turns it may pose a nasty challenge to Asia's political system.

3) *Sustainable growth*

Energy, the environment, water and inequality pose tremendous challenges for Asia, its political systems and economic model.

With the switch from growing factor supply to higher productivity, it ranks as challenge number one.

As in all other cases of transitional economies, Asia has given low priority to the environment and accepted inequality. Now they are high on the agenda as the Asian countries realize that unless something is done quickly with tangible effects growth may continue for a couple of years, but soon be brought to a halt.

Energy is said to be in short supply for China and India. This is not true. Both countries have an ample supply of energy, but do not want to use what they have: coal.[36] The reason is the deterioration of the environment which pushes both countries towards other energy sources such as oil, LNG, nuclear power and renewable energies. So the problems of energy supply and the environment are linked and cannot be solved separately.

Water may be a vital problem for China in the longer run while it is not a problem for India.

The good news is that primarily China seems to be aware of these problems and pushes them high on the political agenda.[37] The bad news is that we simply do not know how responsive the lower echelons of the political system, the enterprises and the ordinary citizen are to these political signals.

In conclusion, we can say that the threats to Asia are there for everybody to see. What gives rise to guarded optimism is that the political leaders in most of the Asian countries have spotted the dangers and are trying hard to implement appropriate policies.

Europe's Response

The reaction to Asia's emergence as a global economic power has gone in two almost diametrically opposite directions. Some politicians, business leaders and academics take the view that the Western world cannot compete and needs to defend itself by barriers against outsourcing and imports combined with strong pressure to erode Asia's competitiveness, among other things trying to force an appreciation of the Asian currencies. The opposite camp is composed by those thinking that Asian growth is an ephemeral phenomenon, sooner or later to be unmasked, stopped in its tracks by the inability to achieve higher productivity and cope with the environment, energy, water and inequality.

To my mind both of these positions are wrong and untenable.

First, the law of comparative advantage is still valid, meaning that the US and Europe have to find their competitive advantages under new circumstances.

Second, globalization opens the door for high growth and increasing wealth, but it is not confined to one or two geographical regions. The transfer of purchasing power from the US and possibly also Europe leads to a narrowing of the gap in income per head, but without depressing income per head in the US and Europe. In absolute terms, all three regions may gain, but in relative terms Asia is the winner.

The US and Europe face a painful process, but they are far from being without hope and it is far less painful in the long run than doing nothing. The British historian Arnold Toynbee coined the phrase 'response to challenge', and this is precisely what the US and Europe face — economically and politically.

Economically, the Western world must realize that it cannot compete on costs. Trying to do so is a losing battle, increasing the burden and prolonging the pain. Instead, a shift towards performance and comparable competitive parameters must take place. The US and Europe need to analyze and define where their competitive advantages lie in today's and tomorrow's world. If the battle is fought on terms defined by the industrial era it is a lost one before it has even started. If the US and Europe are capable of choosing the ground where the competitive battle is to be fought it is not yet lost.

One of the encouraging omens is that one factor that may be decisive is the skills factor and this is where Europe rather than the US stands a fairly good chance to carve out a position for itself. The education sector with traditions and experience and a well-managed system is a sector where Europe and to a certain extent also the US are second to none.

The problem for the Europeans and the Americans is that use of this competitive parameter requires structural changes, not only in the education system, but in the social fabric in the societies as a whole. Darwin's key sentence that those who survive are not the strongest ones, but those best able to adapt will prove true.

One illustration is the combination of hardware and software as competitive parameters.[38] In this context, they are not perceived in the information and communications technology framework (ICT), but in general terms. Machinery and investment goods are nowadays rarely sold without a whole string of services like upgrading, training of personnel, maintenance, guarantee of assistance within a specific time period in case of breakdowns etc. All indications point to a strong lead for Western companies in offering this complex of machinery and services.[39]

For Europe, as an 'old' continent there is no other way ahead than to change track, seek its competitive advantage and marshal the resources to support the sector(s). The competitive advantage is to be found in societal structures improving skills, competences, creativity and ingenuity, marshalling the society as a whole behind a production structure favored by the business and, to an even larger degree, technological cycle. Countries performing well in the industrial age will not necessarily be on top in the ICT age; witness the problems Japan, Germany, Switzerland and Sweden face — all of them envied 30 years ago — while countries like Finland and Denmark, which were in the relegation zone in the 1970s, have swung into gear, spurred on by ICT, and are now referred to as role models.

In a way, it can be put in quite simple terms: Europe must let die what cannot survive and strengthen those sectors already doing well. The slogan 'Do what you are best at, only that and nothing else' is the key for Europe's survival. The more money is sent to non-profitable sectors, the more unlikely it is that the turn-around will succeed.

Europe should also sense that the opportunities to get a foothold on the Asian markets are still open. European companies are welcome, they still bring along knowledge that is needed. Asian multinationals search for European partners. This may not last as Asia's economic power may be overwhelming some years from now. Politically, the Western world lives in bubble, unable to comprehend that as economic clout changes so must political influence. It can be said quite clearly: So far, the rising Asian economic powers have wished to join the existing global system and the world should be thankful for that. Just imagine the political turmoil if they had tried to set up a competing system. The quid pro quo is that the Western powers must accept this gracefully and accept that the system is adapted to accommodate the Asian powers. It is laughable to look at the International Monetary Fund and other institutions and the G-7 and/ or G-8 trying to control the global economy as if most of the Asian economic powers did not exist.

Conclusion

It may be a long shot, but omens point to a seminal shift in economic and political power. Asia is starting to roll back what it lost to the Western industrialized world over the last 200 years. The drivers behind Asia's growth continue to be strong, although growth will not be as easy to come by like it was the case from 1979 until now. Asia's policy makers face harder choices, but basically the economies look set to produce high economic growth, delivering the financial resources needed to address problems and imbalances. We will see a new economic pattern with higher technology and Asian multinational companies shaping the growth patterns and emerging as robust global players. It will be fascinating to watch whether Asia is capable of designing its own pattern of economic (and maybe political) integration to serve as a framework for Asian growth and safeguard Asia's global economic and possibly also political interests. History tells us that economic power leads to political power, albeit the time lag may differ from case to case. The crucial point is whether the rise of Asia will be accompanied by a decline of the West or whether a new tandem will emerge to solidify globalization in more or less its present form.

Endnotes

[1] *The Economist* 2005, 'Seeing Europe the right way up', November 19, p. 71.

[2] **Wallace, L** 2006, 'Ahead of its time', *International Monetary Fund*, Interview with Robert Mundell, September, viewed 25 June 2008, <http://www.imf.org/external/pubs/ft/fandd/2006/09/people.htm>.

[3] *The Economist* 2005.

[4] **Greenspan, A & Kennedy, J** 2005, 'Estimates of Home Mortgage Originations, Repayments, and Debt on One-to-Four-Family Residences', Federal Reserve Board, *Finance and Economics Discussion Series Paper*, no. 41, viewed 9 July 2008, <http://www.federalreserve.gov/pubs/feds/2005/200541/200541abs.html>.

[5] **Leamer, EE** 2007, 'Housing and the business cycle', *paper to symposium*, Jackson Hole, Wyoming, 30 August–1 September 2007, viewed 25 June 2008, <http://www.nber.org/papers/w13428>.

[6] **Luce, E** 2007, 'Clinton doubts benefits of Doha round revival', *Financial Times*, 3 December, viewed 25 June 2008, <http://search.ft.com/ftArticle?queryText=clinton+samuelson+free+trade&aje=true&id=071203000069&ct=0&nclick_check=1>.

[7] *International Herald Tribune* 2007, 'Dubai company vows not to sell 6 U.S. ports', 24 February, viewed 25 June 2008, <http://www.iht.com/articles/2006/02/23/news/ports.php>.

[8] **Bennhold, K** 2007, 'Reports in U.S. and Europe dent confidence in economy', *International Herald Tribune*, 27 September, viewed 25 June 2008, <http://www.iht.com/articles/2007/09/26/business/econ.php>.

[9] **MasterCard & CLSA** 2004, 'The Twin Revolution: Asia-Pacific as High-Performance Region', Special Report, *Asian Economics Research*, September, p. 15.

[10] **Song, K** 2006, 'China's Fast-Changing Economic Structure and Its Implications for East Asia', viewed 25 June 2008, <http://www.smu.edu.sg/research/knowledgehub/apr2006/microsite/smukh_enews_5china.asp>.

[11] **Master Card** 2006, 'China and the New Global Economy', *Insights*, 2nd Quarter, viewed 25 June, <http://www.masterintelligence.com/ViewInsights.jsp?hidReportTypeId=1&hidSectionId=89&hidReport=152&hidViewType=null&hidUserId=null>.

[12] *The Economist* 2007, 'Switching Engines', 22 February, viewed 25 June 2008, <http://economist.co.uk/opinion/displaystory.cfm?story_id=8740223&CFID=10907378&CFTOKEN=96605982>.

[13]**Kennedy, S & Yanping, L** 2008, 'China Growth May Slow at Worst Time for World Economy', *Bloomberg.com*, 13 January, viewed 25 June 2008, <http://www.bloomberg.com/apps/news?pid=20601087&sid=apMSMBqLTGI w&refer=home>.

[14]**Hew, D** 2006, 'Economic Integration in East Asia: an ASEAN Perspective', *UNISCI discussion paper*, May, no. 11, viewed 25 June 2008, <http://redalyc. uaemex.mx/redalyc/pdf/767/76701105.pdf>.

[15]**World Bank** 2008, 'Global Economic Prospects 2008: Technology Diffusion in the Developing World', *World Bank report*, viewed 25 June 2008, <http://econ. worldbank.org/WBSITE/EXTERNAL/EXTDEC/EXTDECPROSPECTS/ GEPEXT/EXTGEP2008/0,,contentMDK:21603882~menuPK:4503397 ~pagePK:64167689~piPK:64167673~theSitePK:4503324,00.html>.

[16]**Asian Development Bank** 2006, 'Asian Development Outlook', *Asian Development Bank study*, viewed 25 June 2008, <http://www.adb.org/ Documents/books/ADO/2006/prc.asp>.

[17]The Chinese economy may be smaller than the Japanese economy, but looked at through the prism of influencing economic trends the Chinese economy is by far more important, as Japans economy is showing a trend growth of approximately 1.5–2%.

[18]**Florida, R** 2008, *Who's your city?*, Basic Books, New York.

[19]Armani considers Shanghai an important world city and has opened its show, 'Giorgio Armani: Retrospective' at the Shanghai Art Museum. Armani has 35 stores in operation, and there will be 40 by the end of the year (**Enterprise One** 2006, *Enterprise Focus*, May 2006, viewed 25 June 2008, <http://209.85.175.104/search?q=cache:XkjsKXVzR5cJ:www.business.gov.sg/ NR/rdonlyres/0423693D-18D4-45E1-BFFF-2FFAA225D861/9503/ EnterpriseFocusIssue0507.pdf+china+market+for+luxury+goods+2015+6+bn &hl=en&ct=clnk&cd=1&gl=sg>.

[20]**Master Card** 2007, 'MasterCard Worldwide Index of China's Affluent — Discretionary Spending and Lifestyles', *Insights*, 3rd Quarter, viewed 25 June 2008, <http://www.masterintelligence.com/upload/181/116/China_Affluent-Lifestyles-S.pdf>.

[21]**Master Card** 2007, 'The Demand for Luxuries in Asia/Pacific', *Insights*, 3rd Quarter, viewed 25 June 2008, <http://www.masterintelligence.com/ ViewInsights.jsp?hidReportTypeId=1&hidSectionId=117&hidReport=181&hi dViewType=null&hidUserId=null>.

[22]**Xinhua** 2005, 'China on way to 2nd biggest consumer', *China View*, 13 October, viewed 25 June 2008, <http://news.xinhuanet.com/english/2005-10/13/content_3612155.htm>.

[23]**Dyer, G** 2005, 'Young seen as leading Chinese consumer drive', *Financial Times*, 12 October, viewed 10 July, <http://us.ft.com/ftgateway/superpage.ft?news_id=fto101220052036192933&page=2>.

[24]**Amiti, M & Freund, C** 2007, 'China's Export Boom', *Finance and Development Quarterly*, vol. 44, no. 3, viewed 25 April 2008, <http://www.imf.org/external/pubs/ft/fandd/2007/09/amiti.htm>.

[25]**Digitimes** 2007, 'China high-tech exports valued over US$244 billion in January-September 2007', *Digitimes Press release*, November 22, viewed 25 April 2008, <www.digitimes.com>.

[26]**ASEAN** 2007, 'The ASEAN Charter', December, viewed 25 April 2008, <http://www.aseansec.org/ASEAN-Charter.pdf>.

[27]**Wei, J** 2006, 'China, India trade to hit US$20b this year', *China Daily*, 22 November, viewed 25 June 2008, <http://www2.chinadaily.com.cn/china/2006-11/22/content_739381.htm>.

[28]China's State Administration of Foreign Exchange has acquired through a Hong Kong subsidiary, SAFE Investment Company, small parcels of shares in ANZ, Commonwealth and National Australia Bank (**John, D** 2008, 'China buys Australian bank stakes', *Sydney Morning Herald*, 5 January, viewed 25 June 2008, <http://business.smh.com.au/china-buys-australian-bank-stakes/20080104-1k8w.html>).

[29]**Master Card** 2005, 'The Corporate Superpower of the 21st Century: Synergy between Chinese and Indian Business', *Insights*, 3rd Quarter, viewed 9 July 2008, http://www.masterintelligence.com/ViewInsights.jsp?hidReportTypeId=1&hidSectionId=80&hidReport=129&hidViewType=null&hidUserId=null>.

[30]**Dollar, D & Wei, S** 2007, 'Under utilized Capital', *Finance and Development Quarterly*, vol. 44, no. 2, viewed 25 June 2008, <http://www.imf.org/external/pubs/ft/fandd/2007/06/dollar.htm>.

[31]I omit the Middle East because savings or non-savings in that region wholly depend on the oil price, making it less interesting in an analysis of competitive advantages.

[32]**Ørstrøm Møller, J** 2007, 'Lessons from two financial crises: Chances for Asia to seize the day', *The Straits Times*, 29 December, viewed 25 June 2008, <http://www.oerstroemmoeller.com/photogallery/STChanceforAsiaDec2907.pdf>.

[33]In October 2007, it was announced that ICBC was buying a 20% share of South Africa's Standard Bank for 5.6 bn. US Dollars, the largest foreign investment in Africa. Standard Bank operates in 18 other African countries and globally in 21 countries: "This acquisition will help to build a foundation for ICBC to become a global bank," Chairman Jiang Jianqing told reporters

in Beijing (**Reuters** 2007, 'ICBC to buy $5.6 billion stake in South African bank', *International Herald Tribune*, 25 October, viewed 25 June 2008, <http://www.iht.com/articles/2007/10/26/business/26icbc.php>.

[34]**Powell, B** 2007, 'Sovereign Funds to the Rescue?', *Time*, 6 December, viewed 25 June 2008, <http://www.time.com/time/magazine/article/0,9171,1 691617,00.html>.

[35]**Morgan Stanley** 2007, 'Currencies: How Big Could Sovereign Wealth Funds Be by 2015?', *Morgan Stanley Research Global*, 3 May, viewed 25 June 2008, <http://www.morganstanley.com/views/perspectives/files/soverign_2.pdf>.

[36]China has the second largest and India the third largest coal reserves in the world (**International Energy Agency** 2002, 'Coal in the Energy Supply of India', *International Energy Agency Papers*, viewed 25 June 2008, <http://www.iea.org/textbase/publications/free_new_Desc.asp?PUBS_ID=1101>).

[37]Morgan Stanley's Chief strategist Stephen Roach said 28 March: "There's a broad consensus in Beijing that what has worked very successfully for nearly three decades will not work going forward. And while the economy certainly performed very impressively last year, there is a growing sense of concern in official China that may not be the case for much longer." (**Chandler, C** 2008, 'Forget subprime: In Asia, the big fear is inflation', *Fortune/CNN Blog*, 3 April, viewed 25 June 2008, <http://chasingthedragon.blogs.fortune.cnn.com/category/wen-jiabao/>.) China's Prime Minister Wen Jiabao used a large part of his speech to Fifth Session of the Tenth National People's Congress (NPC) on March 2007 to address these problems. (Xinhua 2007, 'NPC starts session with focus on social harmony', *China Daily*, 3 May, viewed 25 June 2008, <http://chinadaily.com.cn/china/2007-03/05/content_819778.htm>.)

[38]**Ørstrøm Møller, J** 1995, *The Future European Model*, Greenwood Publishing House, Westport, CT, pp. 17–18.

[39]Although Boeing does not compete with Asian companies its Gold Care Service (see **Boeing** 2008, 787 *GoldCare — Airplane Business Solutions*, viewed 25 June 2008, <http://www.boeing.com/commercial/goldcare/index.html>.) is an illustration of this offering precisely what is described in the text. You may go so far as to say that purchasing a Boeing 787 is more like long term leasing.

This article was first published in *Politik*, Vol. 11, No. 2, 2008.

Securing Peace in Asia for the Next 25 Years*

THE YOUNG PEOPLE OF ASIA ARE ENDOWED WITH THE RESPONSIBILITY, an awesome task, to ensure that peace will reign in Asia over the next 25 years. Be ambitious on behalf of peace, human dignity and a civilized mindset. Do not go for the second best that would many others, but you should not. These objectives are so worthy that they deserve the best of you and you are so worthy that you deserve the best.

The philosopher John Locke stated more than 200 years ago that freedom depends upon self-discipline, knowing how far you can go in pursuit of your own objectives without harming others. Strike the right balance between your freedom and respect for others, then freedom will grow in a harmonious world; if not conflicts nourished by deliberate self-interests or in some cases misunderstandings will take over and steer us towards a confrontational world.

You must be strong in your own beliefs. You have the right to tell others why you have chosen those views, why they are the right ones for you, why you think they may also hold values for others. But you can only expect others to listen to you if you listen to them. Broaden your horizon and people may come to appreciate the virtues embedded in your values, because they sense that you have rejected narrowness to opt for an open mind. We should resist the growing tendency towards a blown up self-righteousness and a world governed

---

*Eighth Daisaku Ikeda Annual Lecture, 29 June 2008.

by mutual arrogance of ignorance initiated by erroneous belief that we alone have found the pillars of wisdom. No one has the right to monopolize truth.

"*All for one and one for all*" is an oath taken by the Musketeers 350 years ago in Europe. It is still valid. Maybe even more so in a society challenged by economic globalization and individuals exposed to pressure of impression by modern technology making it impossible to ignore what other people around the globe think and why they do so. You hold your destiny in your own hands, but do not forget that your actions and decisions may frame the destiny of others.

Let me tell two anecdotes, both about the conqueror Alexander the Great who lived around 325 B.C.

The first one. When Alexander the Great reached India setting out from Greece, he met a group of jain philosophers and asked why they were neglecting to pay any attention to greet the conqueror. He received the following reply:

King Alexander, every man can possess only so much of the earth's surface as this we are standing on. You are but human like the rest of us, save that you are always busy and up to no good traveling so many miles from your home, a nuisance to yourself and to others! … you will soon be dead, and then you will own just as much of the earth as will suffice to bury you.

The core of the jain philosophy, at that time already more than 500 years old, was that all life is considered worthy of respect, the focus was upon spiritual independence by developing your own personal wisdom and self-control.

The second anecdote. Alexander the Great met Diogenes, at that time the world's most renowned philosopher and an old man. The powerful young conqueror, being solicitous of the old philosopher, asked what, if anything he could do for him. Diogenes, whose worldly needs were so humble that he lived in a huge clay jar, replied, "*I have nothing to ask but that you would remove to the other side, that you may not, by intercepting the sunshine, take from me what you cannot give.*"

"*You cannot take from me what you cannot give.*" Let that sentence rests in your mind.

These two anecdotes set out the main thesis of my speech:

— Use of force will do no good.
— Greed will risk undermining genuine human values.
— Tolerance and respect towards others are indispensable to safeguard your self-respect.
— Natural resources is a gift to be husbanded with care, humility and bearing in mind the need of future generations. The world and Mother Nature has been entrusted to our generation, not given to us for our indiscriminate consumption.

Recall the United Nations definition of sustainability: "meets the needs of the present without compromising the ability of future generations to meet their own needs."

Asia can be proud of its civilizations and culture going back several thousand years and in many ways outshining Western civilization. Until around the 15th century A.D. Asia was leader in research, technology and innovation. It was first around 1800 A.D. that the European economies replaced China and India as the largest and most powerful global economies.

Asia, however, is a comparatively newcomer in economic globalization. Until about 20 years ago the main Asian economies were held in a grip of poverty, low growth and backwards technology. A European economist, Gunar Myrdal, was awarded the Nobel Prize in 1974 for his analysis of Asia called 'Asian Drama', setting out the problems the Asian nations and economies faced.

Today, the world gasps for breath by watching not an Asian drama, but an Asian renaissance, which is the label, used by the World Bank describing the phenomenal economic growth and the successful fight against poverty.

It is, by any account, the greatest success in history. If it continues for the next 25 years Asia will have transformed itself from being backwards to pace setter in less than a generation. Asia will not only be an economic powerhouse, but also spread its wings to new technology, innovation, governance and cement multicultural and multiethnic societies.

I say IF.

Because there is no guarantee that it will happen. Neither Asia nor the rest of the world can buy prosperity and peace for the next 25 years accompanied by a guarantee warrant to be redeemed if it does not work as expected and planned.

Prosperity, peace, stability and human security are gifts from heaven whatever God we worship, but only if we put in a laudable, civilized and dignified effort ourselves. That goes for every human being as it goes for countries, nation-states and group of countries.

Let me enumerate some of the policies that, according to my mind, can be put to use by Asia, Asian nations and people living in Asia to pursue these goals. They will ask everybody to weigh egoism against the need of others, how to manage the resources of the earth put in our custody and to demonstrate that the phrase *"all men are born equal"* actually means what these words say. If successful, the future leaders of Asia can proudly say that they rose to the challenge and opened a door to a better future for their children and a better world despite the obvious difficulties.

The first policy is to distribute benefits in an equitable way.

Economic globalization is a hard task master, some countries will fare better than other ones, some markets will be more attractive than others and the guide that nothing succeeds like success and nothing fails like failures have proven itself correct time and again. China and India are by any standard Asia's most lucrative markets, by size, purchasing power and access to labor force and capital. They do not need much help to maintain high growth rates. Their competitiveness is reasonable guaranteed unless political leaders make mistakes and that is unlikely.

The same is, however, not the case for all other Asian countries. ASEAN positioned itself remarkably well as an attractive market before the Chinese and Indian miracle hijacked the attention and still possesses many assets, but it is no secret that compared to China and India ASEAN's home market is comparatively small. And that is even when putting all ASEAN countries together in the analysis. Japan is facing an extremely difficult demographic situation with falling population while Pakistan and Bangladesh is starting several decades of rising share of the population in the work age bracket.

Asia may be different from other regions around the world and Asians may be ready to live with an uneven distribution of benefits. But I do not think so why should that be the case? On the contrary, it is much more likely that the indispensable prerequisite for a peaceful development is a fair share of the growth to everybody. This is the lesson from Europe. Growing economic convergence oils peaceful relationship; diverging economic trends show discontent, enmity and ultimately confrontation.

Fortunately, Europe has also invented the instrument to distribute benefits: economic integration. ASEAN is on its way with the ASEAN charter. The rest of Asia is contemplating how far and how fast to go.

The question is often posed: why do we need to integrate and what are the virtues? It is a good question. Fortunately, there are good answers too.

Economic integration is not an end in itself. It is an instrument to pursue political objectives, set by the member states for their domestic development. Without integration these objectives could not be achieved or less efficiently.

Economic globalization means that trade, services, technology, investment, capital movements have jumped from the national level to the international even global level. None of these fundamental elements confine themselves to the national framework. But the governance or political control is still basically national. To rebalance, governance and political control must be moved to the same level as the elements they are there to control. So they must be lifted upwards to the international even global level. Integration is thus nothing else than the rule of the law for economics on international level exactly as is the case for the national society.

By joining forces nation-states grab bigger and stronger influence than if they prefer to sail alone in the stormy waters of globalization. There are different stages of integration and it may take a while before Asia comes to the point of pooling sovereignty to exercise it in common. But do not forget that all 27 member states of the European

Union has done so by their own free will. At first glance you would think that pooling sovereignty diminishes influence, how can it be otherwise when you are not in charge of your own sovereignty? But the answer is that you actually enlarge influence by acting together.

This can only work if there is a strong sense of trust among the members and a perception of a common destiny. It works both ways. When you have tried, you come to trust your partners. If you do not have such trust it is difficult, but when the French and the Germans, busy killing each other and extremely successful in doing so for centuries, can do it, so can other nation-states around the globe.

The second policy is even more difficult: burdensharing.

The last 25 years have offered an extremely propitious environment for economic growth in Asia. US, Europe and Japan have for most of the period been good markets. An increasing labor force in China has kept wage levels low and stimulated outsourcing that provided jobs for Chinese workers, increasing purchasing power. The savings rate has been high keeping cost of capital down. Energy, raw materials, food were plentiful with low prices. Water had not yet manifested itself as a scarce resource, and there was no price on clean environment.

All these are changing and not for good. Growth will be lower in the US, Europe and Japan. Some years down the road the workforce in China will shrink, pushing up wage costs and probably reduce the savings rate, augmenting cost of capital. In short, production factors will turn from increasing to decreasing in numbers. Food, energy and raw materials will be less plentiful with the inevitable consequence of higher prices. Water is already knocking on the door in many countries announcing scarcity. There is now a price to be paid for clean environment and it is going up, steeply: we meet it under the brandname of climate change and/or global warming.

For Asia, policy makers and the population that signifies a shift from managing economic growth to creating the conditions for economic growth.

Suffice to mention two illustrations of the potentially disruptive forces ignited by wrong handling of burdensharing.

For the first time over many years, export restrictions have been applied and by food exporters. Argentina in South America, the world's two biggest rice exporters, both in Asia, Thailand and Vietnam.

Similar actions inside nation-states in Europe with fishermen blockading harbors, truck drivers blocking highways and milk producers withholding supply.

Both in Asia and other parts of the world riots triggered off by food scarcities have shown, if we did not already know it, that the scarcities have started to hit and hit hard on the most vulnerable group, those who find themselves at the bottom of the social strata.

The signal is terrifyingly clear. Everybody wants more, but there is less to give. The ugly prospect of cracking consensus and lacking trust in the ability of the authorities to respond have emerged telling us that unless convincing schemes to tackle the problems are launched, people may start to take the law into one's own.

To get burdensharing right, so to speak, Asia needs to look at two issues: societal solidarity and stakeholder in the global system.

The third policy: Societal solidarity.

Economics have started to analyze what is termed social capital. It stands for mutual trust among individuals and between individuals and institutions.

High social capital means that citizens know by instinct, upbringing and tradition how to behave, what is right and what is wrong. This stimulates productivity because there is less need for supervision and control. Resources can be channeled into productive use instead of enforcing laws, regulations and rules. Laws transform into legal texts what is common knowledge. The judicial systems role is to rule in the few cases where people disagree about societal norms. Society is governed by a set of common values.

A low social capital means no common denominator laying down how to behave, what is good and what is bad. A behavioral set of rules must be provided by a blown up and cumbersome legislation. The judicial system is overburdened to settle the many cases of disagreement. Resources are diverted from productive use to ensure complicity with the written texts instead of relying on embedded values.

The future challenge is to convey to each individual that he or she is better off inside than outside society, more comfortable with a common set of values than enforcing of rules and less preoccupied by what is our right than how we make society function.

If not there is nothing to lose by breaking societal solidarity. Economically by ignoring fair distribution of benefits and burdensharing, politically by opting for populism combined with neglecting the right of minorities, ideologically by opening the door for terrorism as terrorist organizations convince some people that they are better off inside terrorist organizations than inside the societal caucus.

The fourth policy: stakeholder in the global system.

The global system has been fundamentally unchanged since its conception in the late 1940s. Good. It has delivered outstanding service to the world. The plain truth is, however, it cannot survive the switch from the era of plenty to the era of scarcity unscathed.

International meetings and domestic policies including the campaign prior to the presidential election in the US augurs a much harder climate for economic globalization and the accompanying political steering mechanism at the UN, the G-8 meeting among the major economic powers, the World Trade Organization, the International Monetary Fund and the World Bank.

The unpleasant truth is that an increasing number of politicians, a larger share of populations and some business people start to ask the awkward question: is economic globalization really the best model for us? They find ammunition from many sources, but regrettably the foremost economists of our time, the MIT Professor Paul Samuelson, who in the late 1940s carved out theoretical economy's uncompromising statement that free trade increased welfare, has now opened the door for the argument that this need not be the case in all circumstances. All the skeptics have turned this theoretical analysis to support their own political views even if that never was the intention of Professor Samuelson.

The United States accompanied by Europe, but primarily the US has shouldered the burden of the global system for more than 60 years. We must not forget that. Nor, however, should it escape our attention that the US nowadays and again accompanied by Europe does not show the same ardor when asked to uphold the system. It would be nice to believe that we can still appeal to the US and it will respond to our call, but it does not look so easy nowadays. And we cannot or should not criticize the US, why expect even demand that the US reports for duty all the time?

Asia can close its eyes and trust fate to produce a solution, but I would be immensely reluctant to recommend such a course. Asia has to prepare itself for circumstances where leadership, courage and responsibility are called for. For two reasons:

First, Asia is the part of the world, which has benefited most from economic globalization and consequently the part of the world having the strongest interest in keeping this model alive.

Second, you may believe economic globalization is so firmly rooted that my fear for its future is unfounded? You are wrong. About 100 years ago the world lived in an era of economic globalization, which was just as deep and strong as the one we see today. Only a decade later soldiers slaughtered each other in millions opening the door for an economic depression with over one-third of the population in the US and Germany, just to mention two countries unemployed.

Economic globalization is worth to defend because it is a bastion against war and armed conflict. It has its flaws and some of them have been allowed to run wild, but it is way ahead compared to how a non-global world would look.

I believe in Asia's will and capability to rise to the challenge. The greatest asset is the people of Asia; the future lies in your hands. Looking at you my confidence gains.

Let me finish with a small verse written by a Viking descendant.

When the storm gathers and the seas get rough
The firm grip of the helmsman

And the oarsmen turning tough
Takes the boat through to calm waters

The strongest timber, rope, and rivet
May not repulse the waves
Compassion and love for your neighbor
Beat down even the mightiest gale

Let selfishness guide you
The rock, you might strike
But join hands with your neighbor
A friendly coast will be your anchor

Dutch Way, Muslim Way

'FITNA', THE FILM, MADE RECENTLY BY DUTCH MP GEERT WILDERS, AND the cartoons about Prophet Muhammad that were published by several Danish newspapers some time ago have made headlines and caused controversy.

Why is this so?

First, people speak generally about the Dutch or the Danes when referring to the film and/or the cartoons. To classify all Dutch people and/or Danes as having the same opinion is a gross oversimplification.

The film and the cartoons ignited debates and revealed disagreements inside both countries. They divided the nations in two camps, one supporting, and the other opposing, the film and the cartoons.

Similarly, it is a gross oversimplification when the Dutch or the Danes speak of Muslims as a homogenous group of people holding uniform views about Islam's role in society.

The temptation to oversimplify issues has undoubtedly added fuel to the fire. The extremists have attracted the lion's share of attention and crowded the moderates out of the picture.

Second, in an era of globalisation, debates inside a country reverberate around the globe and resonate with foreign cultures. This is partly because news spreads so fast but a more sophisticated explanation is that many countries have moved from one culture to something like multiculturalism.

Neither the Netherlands nor Denmark had any Muslim population until about 25 years ago. They were genuine nation-states composed of one ethnicity and one religion (Christianity) that had forged behavioural patterns over centuries.

The arrival of a visible Muslim minority pushed them into uncharted waters. They now had to deal with citizens who brought along their own culture and societal patterns based on Islam and not Christianity, and who maintained cultural and family links with the countries where they were born.

Regrettably, the two camps in the controversy looked on each other with suspicion and hijacked most of the debate. Instead of opening the door (their mindset) to understand the other part, they closed it by clinging to preconceived perceptions and stereotypes of the other.

Such attitudes have made it difficult for what probably and hopefully are the overwhelming majorities in both camps, who seek better mutual understanding and wish to live in peace and harmony.

Third, the world has seen how large the gap can be between perceptions of good and bad behaviour. The main problem is the overlap between religious freedom and societal values. Religious freedom has not been a problem; societal values are.

Many European countries have Constitutions that were drawn up 150 years ago or earlier. They reflect the nation-state as it was then, transforming from absolute monarchy to some kind of democracy. As the kings had exercised censorship, it was of vital importance to secure freedom of expression without any exception.

The dilemmas that globalisation and immigration could pose for freedom of expression did not enter the mindset of the founding fathers of European democracies, as those dilemmas were unknown.

Instead, Europeans feared losing their newly-won freedoms. This fear was confirmed when Nazism, fascism and communism emerged in the inter-war period and solidified the belief that freedom of expression, without exception, is an indispensable bulwark against deviation from European democracy.

Immigrants from Muslim countries used to live in nation-states where the media respected religious feelings. Religion defined, on its own terms, what could and could not be said about religious issues.

Herein lies the reason for the clash. Europeans see freedom of expression as a cornerstone for the societies that they have built over more than a century; Muslim immigrants do not understand why their religious feelings are ignored or, in some cases, deliberately trampled on.

No one is really trying to begin a dialogue on the basis of knowing why the other camp takes the position it does.

If we look for a silver lining, it is encouraging that the two episodes have given rise to political statements about the need for better understanding and restraint. Those seeking violence and confrontation must not hijack the future.

The Europeans and the Muslim worlds fought each other for more than a thousand years, providing ample proof of the misery that war causes. Even in Bosnia-Herzegovina, there was war a little more than 10 years ago.

I hope this conflict will recede into history instead of dominating today's agenda.

This article was first published in *Today*, 19 April 2008.

Chance for Asia to Seize the Day

BECAUSE THIS YEAR MARKS THE IOTH ANNIVERSARY OF THE ASIAN financial crisis, observers were prepared for yet more studies on what went wrong and how to avoid another crisis.

Only a few expected another financial crisis, even though it was common knowledge that the property sector in the US and some other countries had entered a period of 'irrational exuberance' — to borrow the famous phrase used by former Federal Reserve chairman Alan Greenspan.

But even those who expected a reversal of the property cycle did not predict the emergence of a threat to global financial stability, with the likelihood of recession in the United States raising uncertainty about global growth.

There are four lessons to be drawn from these two crises.

Lesson No. 1 is that the world is actually less globalised than conventional wisdom tells us.

The financial crisis that began in Japan in early 1990, with nose-diving share prices and a property market locked in stalemate for 15 years, did not really affect other countries. This was so even though Japan's economy was the second biggest in the world.

Similarly, while the recession in the US in the first half of 1991 was felt by other countries, it did not drag the world into recession.

The Asian financial crisis in 1997 was the trigger, not the main reason, for a similar crisis in Russia and some Latin American countries. The US and Europe remained remarkably unaffected.

As for this year's subprime mortgage crisis in the US, we have to wait a bit before making a judgment, but so far its contagious effect also seems to be limited.

The conclusion one may draw is that while the world may look globalised, it is in fact regionalised. An economic slowdown in one country is felt by neighbouring countries, especially if they belong to the same economic grouping, but it has a limited impact on the global economy. The reason being that regional intra-trade as a share of total trade is high and growing, while dependence on other regions and/or countries is less important.

Intra-European trade comes to about two-thirds of all trade for the European countries. Exports to the US account for only 3 per cent of total European GDP.

Business Cycles

Lesson No. 2 is that while the business cycles of adjacent countries, and of countries inside the same grouping, tend to converge, the global picture is different.

Many observers expect globalisation and growing trade to synchronise business cycles, but the figures tell another story. International trade amounts to only 31 per cent of global GDP. For most countries, domestic consumption and investment are more important as economic pacesetters. The domestic business cycle is more insulated from outside effects than is widely believed.

This may change, as trade grows faster than GDP, but it will be some time before it rivals consumption and investment.

For the 15 years from 1991 to 2005 there were only four years (1993, 1994, 2001 and 2004) when economic growth in the three major economies (US, eurozone and Japan) moved in the same direction.

If the analysis is narrowed to the US and the eurozone, the business cycle moved in synchronisation in six years out of 15 (1993, 1994, 1995, 1997, 2001 and 2004). Economists may qualify these observations with theories about time-lag etc, but even that does not contradict the conclusion that, contrary to conventional wisdom, the global business cycle is a myth. The global economy is actually controlled by national and regional business cycles.

Lesson No. 3 touches on the vulnerability and fragility of financial systems.

The Asian financial crisis and the subprime crisis showed that, again contrary to conventional wisdom, the culprit is the financial system in core countries, namely the US and Europe.

They have been irresponsible over due diligence, financial management and corporate governance. Instead, resting on the laurels of their established reputations, they went in blind pursuit of profit and market share without balancing risks against gains.

The Asian financial crisis, as we know now, was due to short-term borrowings (denominated in foreign currencies) to finance long-term investments with income denominated in national currencies. Financial institutions in core countries lending to Asian countries were the guardians of the international financial system.

This role should have compelled them to act as good corporate citizens. Instead they started a race among themselves for short-term profit. When problems arose they jumped out and left the borrower and the international institutions to pull the chestnuts out of the fire, devoting most of their efforts to avoiding losses.

The subprime crisis reveals the same behaviour. Financial institutions stepped in to lend without performing the necessary scrutiny. They gambled upon continually rising property prices as collateral for revolving credits, as if the perpetual moving machine had finally been invented — by them!

In both cases, some of the world's most prestigious financial institutions allowed themselves to enter into deals which, by their own rules, were indefensible.

Lack of Judgment

Note the lack of judgment by all core financial institutions in core countries. It was not the financial systems in developing or newly industrialised countries which started the Asian financial crisis. Rather, it was lending from financial institutions in core countries.

Financial systems in non-core countries have so far — we do not yet know the whole story — weathered the subprime crisis far better than their supposedly renowned role models in core countries. To some extent, it may even be that that financial institutions in core countries dragged those in other countries into the mess.

Lesson No. 4 is that the prime movers of globalisation are the above financial institutions.

Global capital movements are growing faster than global trade. Over the past 10 years, new financial institutions such as hedge funds and private equity funds have entered the arena and are playing a bigger role.

While the spillover of domestic growth into other countries is limited, the opposite is true for financial operations. Financial institutions are interacting with each other across borders by selling and buying financial instruments. In theory, this distributes risk among many institutions, which in principle should make the system more robust and solid.

But in practice it works the other way, spreading panic as all institutions seek to get out as soon as they smell the risk, knowing that those that get out last will run up the largest losses.

My fifth point is more an observation than a lesson. Most of the world's savings are in Asia. These savings are now being used to rescue or bail out some of the core financial institutions that have had their fingers burnt.

It is not difficult to draw the conclusion that Asian financial institutions, courtesy of the subprime crisis, have been given a chance to buy influence in globally established institutions. This will give Asia much stronger control over how its savings are used.

Asia may not have liked seeing financial institutions in the US and Europe earning money while reshuffling wealth originating in Asia, and not being able to do much about it. But now, when these established institutions are on their knees, the chance is there — and it has been taken.

The calamities of the subprime mortgage crisis will be temporary. But the impact of the Asian move to gain control over its own savings will be permanent.

This article was first published in *The Straits Times*, 29 December 2007.

China's Model

THE CONVICTION IS WIDESPREAD IN THE WEST THAT THERE IS NO alternative to the combination of American capitalism as the global economic model and democracy as the ultimate political model. Eventually this model will reign albeit editions around the world may differ according to history and geography, but not much. Islamic Fundamentalism is the only barrier to pole position.

... [While] Islamic Fundamentalism may challenge the Western model, but is not deemed attractive by the non-Islamic part of the world. Another model though is being scrutinized and analyzed as an alternative: The Chinese model.

The two differ at the core. Islamic Fundamentalism seeks to destroy or obliterate the Western model in what is believed to be a God inspired historic mission. If successful only one model will be left: Islamic Fundamentalism. It cannot be a global model for two reasons: there is no room for non-believers and it cannot deliver economic development, which is what the world wants.

The Chinese model is a global alternative to the Western model. The two can co-exist in a duel or rivalry or in competition just like Socialism versus Capitalism did, vying for support and in the spirit of letting the best man win. It has delivered, it works and it has proved itself. It draws the logical consequence of global Capitalism and shies away from politics in the old fashioned sense of distribution of income, who owns production factors etc. All these questions harassing political life for a century or more have been settled. The job now is to manage the economy inside the existing framework. Many people name meritocracy as the prime gift of the US to the world, but the Chinese with more than one thousand years of mandarin rule got there first. And what they offer now is a mix and combination of meritocracy and management, an extrapolation of the Chinese system or model given finishing strokes and refined over centuries and now adjusted to the modern world.

It has worked extremely well in China since 1979 when Deng Xiaoping coined the phrase that 'Whether it is a black cat or a white cat, as long as it can catch the rat, it is a good cat'. This is the key to understanding politics in the future.

China and the Chinese do not explicitly offer this model in their political and economic offensive abroad. They do not follow the Western powers or Islamic Fundamentalists insisting that they alone know what is right not only for themselves, but for everybody else. They are not 'preachers', but 'doers'. The mere fact that China has succeeded disregarding the basic philosophy of Western political culture attracts the attention of many countries outside North America and Europe.

The Western philosophy overlooks that the principles (democracy, free elections and human rights all as defined by the West) may be sacrosanct for the Western world, but does not look equally attractive in the eyes of other nations with other traditions, history and circumstances. Part of this misunderstanding may be subscribed to the near monopoly of the Western media looking and reporting at the world through Western glasses. Another part, the almost Marxian belief in having history on its side. There may be set backs and disappointment, but the end result is known and given.

In comes the Chinese saying that what counts is economic growth, increasing standard of living and better human security, bringing along a better standard of living for everyone. It looks like a carbon copy of the prescription for the West's victory over Communism.

Certainly there are rising expectations especially among the young people in Asia, Africa, Latin America and other parts of the world to gain more fundamental rights of freedom enjoyed in the Western world. Certainly they want to be consulted to forward their input to the political decision-makers. The point is, however, that they do not associate this with a particular political model. In the West it is seen as two sides of the same coin. Not so in many parts of the world outside the West. Maybe, the grassroots whisper, it can be gained with a non-Western political model.

If the Chinese political model built around management and meritocracy captures this trend it will turn from potential challenger to a real alternative. It will need to 'universalise' its 'particularistic responses' to reach beyond China as a genuine global model.

If so the world will see a new duel just like the one we had between Socialism and Capitalism, but this time between:

A Western political model emphasizing human rights and a large degree of personal freedom and not the least these principles and the selection of political leaders through free elections as two sides of the same coin.

A Chinese inspired model focusing upon management and meritocracy without much emphasis on selection of political leaders as long as they live up to these expectations and offer the citizens personal freedom albeit not necessarily as defined in the Western model.

With luck the world may see no winner, but an amalgamation of the best elements from each of these two models. With luck. And if politicians and statesmen make an effort to get there.

This article was first published in *The Washington Realist*, 10 October 2007.

Energy and the Environment

THE FIGURES ARE CRYSTAL CLEAR. THE SAME GOES FOR THE MESSAGE they convey. Over the next twenty-five years — to 2030 — world consumption of energy will rise by approximately 55 per cent. Most of the rise will come from Asia excluding Japan, with an annual increase of 3.2 per cent, equal to a doubling of energy consumption by 2030. China and India are in the forefront.

Recalling an estimated annual economic growth rate of 5.89 per cent for this part of the world, these figures do not come as a surprise.

The price of oil reached more than US$90 per barrel in November 2007 irrespective of how one looks at it, the conclusion seems inevitable that future rising demand will continue to boost oil prices. A switch to other energy sources is possible depending on price and demand structure, but this takes time, required large sum of investment, and will sometimes be under political scrutiny as in the case of utilizing solar energy.

A forecast by the U.S. government with two scenarios for the oil price in 2030 — one at US$100 and another at US$34 per barrel — concludes that the total world energy consumption in 2030 will not differ much, but the composition of energy sources will. (See http:// www.eia.doe.gov/oiaf/ieo/world.html.)

With a lower oil price, the incentive to switch from oil to other sources will be feeble. The world continues to be heavily dependent on oil, which is a major source of greenhouse gas emissions. If the price of oil goes up, substitution will take place, but to a considerable extent to coal (coal will then overtake oil as the most important source of energy), which produces even more green gas emissions.

In the context of energy and environment, this is discouraging. A substantial reduction of emission levels would require a major switch into more sustainable energy sources, but that will not take place irrespective of the level of oil prices. Fossil fuels will continue to be dominant source of energy by far. This leads to the next conclusion that even with a continued drive to switch to clean energy sources, reduction of greenhouse gases must primarily come from higher energy efficiency and better anti-pollution technology.

Looking at energy efficiency, 2004 was a decisive year. Prior to that, economic growth rates surpassed the rise in energy consumption only for the OECD countries. After that year, non-OECD countries moved from equality between economic growth and rise in energy consumption to much more higher energy efficiency — economic growth clearly surpassing rise in energy consumption. This augurs more production per unit of energy used for the world as a whole.

It can be expected that energy efficiency will continue to improve until 2030 for both OECD and non-OECD countries. New equipment will be much more energy efficient than existing ones, not the least because of the growing environment awareness of greenhouse gas emissions and climate change opening the door for economic incentives and possibly regulatory measures to that effect.

Human activities are almost universally acknowledged as a driver of global warming, but scientists have not totally agreed upon the proportion generated by human activity and by other causes. The same vocabulary applies to climate change. Scientists agree that there will be climate change, but not totally on how much and how this will affect the globe. These differences or uncertainties are used and misused in political debate by some players to pursue their own agenda; not surprising in view of the economic and political interests at stake. Nation-states and enterprises have intervened in the debate to defend vested interests.

For most of the twentieth century, the annual rise in sea level was between 1 and 2 mm but it has accelerated at the end of the century to approximately 3 mm. A number of prognoses for the end of the twenty-first century are at hand. They vary from small changes to rises for over 1 metre or more in worst-case scenarios. Suffice to mention, a rise of 1 metre would submerge the Maldives and make parts of Bangladesh uninhabitable; hence these figures are of major economic and political significance.

Under the same scenario in Southeast Asia, part of capitals, major cities and important geographical areas may be threatened. Instability in weather conditions (El Nino, typhoons) could also be added. If some of the worst-case scenarios materialize, Southeast Asia may face unprecedented challenges. This cannot be overlooked by policy planners in Southeast Asia.

If the U.S. government study is correct, high oil prices will not in itself change relative prices sufficiently to solve the problem. We cannot count upon the market mechanism to combat global warming.

A deliberate policy primarily based on a combination of fiscal measures, subsides and restrictions seems to be what is needed to bring about higher energy efficiency and introduce incentives to switch into renewable energy sources where sun energy, wind power and bioethanol are on top of the agenda. The difficult item, however, is bioethanol, where a dive to convert areas to produce bioethanol could create a scenario of a jump from the frying pen into the fire. A sharp reduction in forests will cut into what is called the world's lungs and further diminish the global capacity to deal with greenhouse gases. It will also produce pollution in the form of haze has been seen several times. The ethical perspective of using farmland to produce energy springs to mind with the observation voiced in a hearing in the U.S. Congress that 800 million people behind the wheel of their car competes for land with 2 billion undernourished people in the developing world. If managed incorrectly, bioethanol may not be the blessing it has promised to be.

Meeting after meeting — for example the 2007 APEC summit in Sydney — have announced the imperative of doing something about the emission of greenhouse gases and global warming. These are often accompanied by objectives and goals normally measured by a quantitative reduction of emissions within a certain time scale or period. The same meetings are conspicuously more silent about how to go about achieving this.

Behind this hides one of the most brutal battles about burden sharing that the world has seen for a long time. The industrialized countries are ready to take the lion's share of cutting greenhouse gas emissions, but not to the extent wished by the newly industrialized and developing countries. These countries are willing to do something, but at the same time display suspicion — not that the issue is invented to keep them in check — but that the rich countries see it as an opportunity for doing so. In the years to come this battle unfold before our eyes.

Southeast Asia countries are at a crossroad. They have a leg in both camps. ASEAN has oil exporters and oil importers. It will not be easy to sketch a common position, but it will be even more difficult not to do so. After all, this is going to dominate the agenda in the years to come.

This article first appeared in *Regional Outlook: Southeast Asia 2008–2009* edited by Deepak Nair and Lee Poh Onn, pp. 74–76 (2008). Reproduced here with the kind permission of the publisher, Institute of Southeast Asian Studies, Singapore, <http://bookshop.iseas.edu.sg>.

The New Capitalism: Lessons for Asia?

THE WORLD IS MOVING AWAY FROM THE TEXTBOOK EDITION OF capitalism towards a new paradigm of which we know very little. Funds are transferred from place to place seamlessly. Reputable economies benefit. Economies not living up to the expected and/or required scoreboards are penalised by dwindling investments, auguring the prospect of an economic backwater in the making. Stock markets are at a record levels and judging by traditional theories, out of line with reality.

According to the financial dailies, the activities of investment funds constitute a major reason for the rising stock market indexes in the US and Europe. These funds are on the prowl to buy, often through unfriendly takeovers, of what used to be profitable, viable and well-managed enterprises. The bids are consummated through offers up to 30–40% above current market prices. The willingness of such institutional investors to pay a higher price makes stock market prices well above the historical average for price/earnings ratios of approximately 17, irrelevant.

This gives rise to some naive, simple albeit fundamental questions: Why do institutional investors think they can manage the enterprise in question so much better than the existing professional managements and boards, both of whom presumably know their business quite well?

The answer to that simple question is quite worrisome. Normally the typical "New Capitalism" transaction works in such a way that right after the purchase, the fund mortgages an enterprise through the roof, after which a large dividend is paid out, compensating the fund for a part of its investment. This manoeuvre suggests that the predator has limited its potential loss and is able to boast a short-term gain flowing from the take-over regardless of the capital outlay.

Now comes the tricky part of such transactions, of which, there are essentially two models:

The newly acquired enterprise may be broken up and its constituent components sold separately for a high price to other companies able to or expecting to generate higher revenue and profit. This model is on the table in the competition between Barclay's Bank and the Royal Bank of Scotland Group's take-over of the Dutch bank, ABN-Amro. Much of the interest revolves around the fate of ABN-Amro's American subsidiary, Lasalle Bank Corp.

The second option involves investing up front with a view to increase market share and profits in the years to come by running a **higher** risk than previous management. Such a model is pursued by the various American funds that have taken over English football clubs such as Manchester United, Liverpool and Aston Villa. To generate higher revenue and profits, these clubs need to win something every year and preferably, it has to be a major European trophy or the English championship.

Even an amateur investor knows that only one club can win and second place could well lead down a road towards bankruptcy. The argument runs that audio-visual channels are a big market, opening the window for virtual spectators and a larger fan base. Correct, but spectators and fans support the winning club. But very often, the overwhelming supporter base limited to the hard-core fans, thus not necessarily generating more revenue than before. In 2001, the English club Leeds United mortgaged itself to dominate the domestic league and succeed in the European Champions League. It failed, had to sell the best players (assets in the business vocabulary) to pay back loans and is now plying its trade in third division of English football, generating negligible income and remains largely forgotten — all in the space of five short years.

New capitalism, at least in the US and Europe, dictates that a considerable part of a business is mortgaged to generate a rise in revenue and profits, on the back of anticipated economic growth and accepting higher risks than were previously considered. If the US and European economies start to slow down, somebody down the financial chain will face heavy losses. In tandem, even with strong growth, the question remains as to how takeover funds plan to squeeze more profits out of an enterprise than was probably running optimally under incumbent management.

Lesson number one of new capitalism is not so much about economics, but concerns the social, the sociological and ultimately, the political. In 1965, private investors owned approximately 80% of US shares with 20% in the hands of institutional investors. The owners of such enterprises and employees were the average American. Owner's and employees' stake in enterprises were congruous — they owned the enterprises and they worked for these enterprises. This is not the case any longer. Private investors now account for less than 1/3 and institutional investors for more than 2/3 of total shareholding. The bond between owners and employees has been cut; they are not the same group of people anymore.

The institutional investor looks almost exclusively at profits. Investment may be steered abroad. Outsourcing is on the agenda. Both policies hit the employees. The risk for the institutional investor is negligible. This risk is further mitigated through diversification with regard to sectors and countries. The employees are burdened with all the risk through job insecurity and downward pressure on wages through outsourcing.

The second lesson to draw from new capitalism is that the relationship between owners and employees has become asymmetrical, no longer working in the same direction. This growing dichotomy may not be visible during periods with high growth, but will certainly surface when an economic slowdown calls for burden sharing. Lopsided distribution of benefits is one thing, unequal burden sharing another!

Lesson number three of new capitalism portends stringent rules about the origins of money channelled into funds not confined to terrorism and financial crime. New capitalism tends to make capital tracing difficult, creating a feeling of insecurity. Although financial surveillance and vigilance is believed to prevent whitewashing through these funds, global money can be earned in dubious ways without breaking rules or contradicting legal guidelines. Regardless of whether this is the case or not, the point remains that anonymous owners take control of enterprises with the sole objective of making more money without really bothering about the economic impact on nation-states or employees in affected companies. Sometimes a legal framework is created to permit risks at odds with good corporate governance.

The combination of the spread of capitalism in Asia, and the liberalisation of Asian financial markets accompanied by the rise of Asian companies may make it worthwhile for Asian policymakers to take a look at European and US experiences to pre-empt what in some cases may be classified as unexpected and sometimes unwanted behaviour in their markets with knock-on effects in the economic, social and political realms. If not, future operations undertaken by respectable and reputable investment funds, in many cases furthering growth in Asia, may well be looked upon with suspicion by the domestic population.

This article was first published in *OpinionAsia*, 11 June 2007 (www.opinionasia.org).

Whispers in the Wind

AT THE END OF FEBRUARY, A FEW DAYS BEFORE CHINA'S ANNUAL parliament session, Premier Wen Jiabao commented on China's political system and its future by saying, "The country has the full capacity to establish a nation of democracy governed by laws within the framework of a socialist system." He also stated, "China shall develop democracy in its own way."

At the opening ceremony for a new semester at the Party School of Chinese Communist Party Central Committee, Vice President Zeng Qinghong spoke about "education on democracy" and "inner party democracy".

These statements can be interpreted in various ways. As Wen Jiabao explicitly links democracy to the socialist model, while adding that it may take 100 years to reach a mature socialist system, the omens for political reforms may be deemed remote.

But the mere fact that the premier and vice president entered the stage and commented on democracy might reveal that the political leaders sense pressure from the grassroots for a more open political system.

This may not augur well for democracy in China, but it may be a first step toward a debate about values and principles associated with democracy in the Chinese political system. It may also confirm that China listened carefully when then-US deputy secretary of state Bob Zoellick invited it to become one of the stakeholders in the global political and economic system.

To influence global development, a stakeholder must be able to project an image of itself, projecting the values embedded in its political system.

Geopolitics over the past couple of years bears witness to that. Unilateralism has lost its magic. Cooperation and partnership is back in vogue. Military power does not deliver what policymakers seek: changes in political philosophy and political culture.

Ideas and ideals stand out as more suitable and more effective instruments to engineer alterations of political and cultural conditions, not the least in a global setting increasingly dominated by values and ethics.

Neither of these lines of thought was to be found in US President George W Bush's policy statement about the Iraq war or in the State of the Union speech. Although they are the key to ending the debacle in Iraq, the chosen instrument still seems to be found inside conventional wisdom focusing on military instruments for a non-military problem.

Only political endeavors making it worthwhile for the majority of Iraqis across religion, tribal connections and ethnicity to join and support a new political system will turn chaos into an orderly situation. And that will only last if accompanied by diplomacy and policies convincing the main powers in the Middle East that a neutral or even better supportive role is in their interest.

The Europeans were ridiculed by the US a few years ago when then-defense secretary Donald Rumsfeld spoke about "Old Europe" and "New Europe", rubbing in his contempt for the posture taken by a majority of Europeans, who said that the US might win the war in Iraq, but not the peace. There probably were a variety of reasons behind Old Europe's thinking, and some of the motives may not be praiseworthy, but at the end of the day Old Europe has been proved more correct in its assessment than the US.

Europe itself tasted the bitterness of self-conceit in 1991 when some Europeans spoke about the honor of Europe facing the crisis in the former Yugoslavia. The Europeans were, simply speaking, not capable of dealing with the rogues they faced. Only when the United

States decided to join a common US-European engagement was the stalemate unhinged and a political settlement negotiated.

The lesson learned by the Europeans and the Americans over the past 15 years — with no small cost in casualties and global prestige — reveals that a value-based approach is necessary to maintain balance, equilibrium and the stability that military power itself cannot bring about.

It is a watershed to come to this conclusion. Mao Zedong's famous phrase that political power grows out of the barrel of a gun has become a questionable guideline. Now power depends on the ability to reconcile cultural identities and in making societal models attractive for the larger majority of people, not just the part of the population constituting a majority.

Power is synonymous with the ability to persuade people to do the right thing measured against a moral yardstick that comes as close as possible to the international community's norm. A superpower necessarily leads the efforts to draw up this grade book but does not dictate how it should look.

The first page is to create common values that unfold their full potential when turned into universal values. People around the globe must embrace these values because they want to do so, because they have come to the conclusion that such a course offers them a better life, not because they fear for the consequences if they choose other values.

The US and Europe have their well-known societal model and political systems, although cracks and self-examination cast doubts over how robust the model is under the pressure of globalization and multiculturalism. The picture for Asia is not so clear.

There may be elements of convergence when looking at the economic models applied by the Asian countries, with market economies and to a large degree export-led growth being in the driver's seat. But no similar convergence is discernible looking at political systems and governmental style.

Some observers subscribe to the view that economic growth will stumble unless political systems are opened up for a democratic style of government. It may sound good, but there is no basis for such a theory. Asia and the Asian countries may very well continue the run of high growth without fundamentally changing the present political systems.

This is not the point. The point is whether the Asian population in due course will expect more than just high growth and an increasing material standard of living.

The young people growing up in the new economic powerhouses may not wish to copy the North American or European political model, but they certainly look for enhanced influence on the domestic political process and qualify transparency and accountability as issues to be taken seriously. They do not associate universal values with the exact form of government, but the principles governing the political system irrespective of its form.

Asia and its political leaders face the challenge of finding some kind of Asian political model founded on ideas and ideals attractive for the people of Asia. The crucial question is whether they can invent a model accommodating the wish for influence and transparency with the high degree of political stability enjoyed by a number of Asian countries.

If so, Asia may still be blessed with stability supported by high economic growth with potential foreign-policy confrontations under control. If no, the future looks a good deal more uncertain and risky.

This is the main reason that statements and policy declarations coming out from the annual session of China's parliament, taking place right now, and the 17th Party Congress scheduled for second half of 2007 will be scrutinized with a magnifying glass.

This article was first published in *Asia Times Online*, 9 March 2007 (www.atimes.com).

Asian Currencies and Globalization

THE INTERNATIONAL CURRENCY MARKETS LOOK STABLE AT FIRST GLANCE, but a closer look reveals potentially strong volatility even fragility auguring upheavals in the years to come.

The main problem is that a currency anchor is missing. A currency anchor is the currency commanding respect and credibility — a currency trusted by other countries, lending itself to be a safe haven in case of turbulence on the markets. When fluctuating it does so gradually and with small steps; the market takes the view that its value is largely correct.

For many years, the U.S. dollar has served the world as a currency anchor. When talking about fluctuations in a currency's value it was always seen vis-à-vis the U.S. dollar. The U.S. economy was without comparison the strongest, most buoyant and dynamic economy in the world. Even more important, economic globalization is apprehended as a global edition of American capitalism albeit with modifications and adjustment. This gave the U.S. dollar an unparalleled strength.

This is not so anymore. After many years, the deficit on the U.S. balance of payments seems to latch on to a size of 5 to 7 per cent of GDP. That is manageable to an economy like the American one in a short period, but not any more as it now looks more or less permanent. The fears are creeping into the soul of many investors that the U.S. real estate market is in for a real downturn pulling the economy along with the inevitable result that former high growth at 3 per cent per year or more will fall visibly, even dramatically. All in all, the picture of a less strong American economy appears on the horizon, making the U.S. dollar less attractive as an anchor currency.

But what are the alternatives? The euro has now been in place for about six years and survived its initial phases, which many observers expected to present the crucial test. It is doing well on the market. After having fallen to approximately US$80 to 100 euro in early autumn 2000, it rose to approximately US$135 in 2005 to stabilize around US$125 during most of 2006.

The euro is an attractive alternative to the U.S. dollar but is still new and to a certain extent unproven to the markets. The European Central Bank in Frankfurt has apparently gained a fine reputation for itself as a respectable central bank, but its takes a long time to build up a reputation comparable to that of the Federal Reserve System in the United States and the former German Bundesbank. Many countries may look to the euro, but not put all their eggs in that basket. The low growth in Euroland, problems for some of the major member states such as France and Germany to respect the ceiling for deficits on the public finances and numerous about political forces in Italy contemplating to the country out of the euro — though completely unrealistic — complicates the picture and puts a question mark on the future strength of the euro.

The Japanese yen is a serious contender on the market, but neither the Japanese economy nor the Japanese financial markets have reached a size and a strength making them a solid foundation for an anchor currency or, as it is sometimes called, a reserve currency.

Growth disparities among the three main economies and large imbalances in the United States and Japan gives further credence to expecting swings on the currency markets.

For the smaller currencies dependent on economic globalizations this is bad news. Experience indicates that the first victims in case of trouble will be the smaller and more vulnerable currencies not having the size and the strength to withstand speculation as it was seen during the financial crisis in 1997–98. They are the weak links in the chain and have to shoulder the first onslaughts.

Robert Mundell, who won the Nobel Prize for his work on optimum currency areas, once formulated this by saying that if you throw a stone in a small pond it will make heavy waves but if you throw it in a lake it will hardly be noticed.

For the Asian currencies, which apart from the Japanese yen, are exposed to the whims of the currency markets, the challenge is to create a lake instead of a small pond.

This is the background for the talk and various proposals about an Asian Currency Unit or a stronger cooperation among Asian countries with regard to currency rates.

The question may be asked right away: Why are stable currency rates preferable, why not let market supply and demand determine the rates?

The answer falls in two parts. Firstly, fluctuating currency rates convey an impression of a political system that is not able to control the national economy and lay down an economic policy. Experience indicates that highly volatile currency rate go hand in hand with weak political systems. So a large majority of politicians prefer stable currency rates, to inspire confidence in their political system instead of the other way round.

Secondly, even if the empirical evidence is neither uncontested nor unequivocal, there is a growing consensus that stable currency rates promote trade as industry knows the currency rates and regard them as fixed. Stable raises help in the planning and implementation of investment and trade runs without fear of unpleasant surprises stemming from fluctuating rates that may jeopardize the investment calculus.

For countries in Southeast Asia which are heavily dependent on economic globalization, strong volatility among their currency rates would unquestionably be determined to trade, investment, and economic growth.

This opens the door for ideas as to how to introduce currency rate cooperation among not necessarily all but most of the Southeast Asia countries. Such cooperation may at a later stage fit into a larger Asian cooperation, in this regard, there are three points to look at:

- Consultation about national economic policies to achieve, if possible, a higher degree of convergence. It is not imperative to have analogous economic policies but a certain degree of convergence is called for.
- Mutual credits among central banks to assist partners whose currencies are exposed to speculations. This is important because without international credits no individual country can withstand pressure emanating from the international markets.
- There should be a system based upon the keywords "fixed but adjustable currency rates" meaning that in principle the currency rates are fixed vis-à-vis each other but they can and should be adjusted if comparative competitive analysis warrants it.

The true test for currency rate cooperation comes when the system is under stress. The society will then depend on the willingness of the strong countries to lend and the readiness of the weaker countries to realize that strings and conditions for national economic policies will be attached to currency credits. The markets are not impressed by the size of currency credits. The markets look at economic policies to remove the underlying causes and only if these policies are judged effective will the storm blow over.

These are some of the valuable lessons drawn from the mechanism of European Monetary System (EMS) in the late 1970s and early 1980s. An Asian Economic and Monetary Union, like the European one, is not on the cards in the foreseeable future. But the lessons learned by the Europeans to achieve currency stability under difficult circumstances are available free of charge.

This article first appeared in *Regional Outlook: Southeast Asia 2007–2008* edited by Asad-ul Iqbal Latif and Lee Poh Onn, pp. 76–78 (2007). Reproduced here with the kind permission of the publisher, Institute of Southeast Asian Studies, Singapore, <http://bookshop.iseas.edu.sg>.

The US Facing Asian Integration:

A Policy Dilemma

The aim of this article is to highlight the crucial importance of integration in East Asia. At stake is not only the future of economic growth in Asia but the future of globalization — whether it will continue in its present edition, be adjusted to accommodate the rising Asian powers or give way to alternative economic models and political systems. Since the end of the Cold War the global operating system has continued as if nothing has happened. Obviously this cannot go on. The discussions in the United Nations Security Council in February/March 2003 removed any illusions left. The US are beyond all doubt the driver of globalization assuming the role commonly described as the American Empire. The jury, however, is still withholding its verdict whether US power is sustainable or sufficiently grinded down to open the door for a new power play to take place in Asia inside the triangle China, India and Japan with the US at the sideline pondering whether to interfere or not.

US Power?

At the pinnacle of its powers an empire confronts a choice: either to renounce some of its almighty power to shape a future global system reflecting its basic values thus securing influence in the longer term albeit not commensurate with its present power; or to exercise power without constraints making its reign absolute as long as it lasts but with the eventual fall so much more abrupt and so much more painful.[1] This is the dilemma for the Bush administration.

The first and indispensable parameter of imperial power and power projection is financial and military capability to enforce imperial order. The US economy has shown tremendous growth for the last 15 years. Few persons would argue that the US economy has stimulated a global boom almost unprecedented in strength and length since the beginning of the 1990's. The US have used the global institutions such as the International Monetary Fund, the World Bank and the World Trade Organization to cement a strong economic globalization.

US growth rates through the last 12 years (about 3.5–4% per annum) contributed more than anything else to global growth. The US have been criticized and heavily so[2] but without the US, global growth would have been negligible. Facing the question whether one would have favored another US economic policy leading to a less unbalanced US economy but lower growth the answer is almost unequivocally no, as lower US growth would have hampered the economic rise of powers such as China and India. For a long period the Chinese surge in economic activity was export-led and the export went to the US. And today, China's role in the Asian supply chain is to a large extent a consequence of her export to the US.

The US were for more than a decade *the* global growth engine. When the Asian financial crisis struck in 1997, a robust US economy stood as a bulwark against a global recession. Export growth to the US in the wake of currency depreciations was for a period the only buoyant part on the demand side for a number of Asian countries.

The unanswered and outstanding question is whether the imbalance in the US economy has infected the global capital markets thereby opening the door for a US recession to spread to the rest of the world. And if that happens, to my mind it is likely, what will be the political repercussions on the global economy shaped and framed by the US?

For years the external deficit measured as per cent of gross domestic product has amounted to 4% and is now approaching 6%. At this point of the business cycle, the deficit should fall yet it is still on an upward curve. And there are no policies or economic developments in sight to remedy the imbalance — not to speak of the external debt imbalance itself.

The US households have built up a colossal debt burden. Rising property prices (still holding) and the once booming stock market have supported a consumption boom without any precedent. The bright spot for a small number of years was the surplus on the public budget but this bulb is definitely switched off. The United States of America are heavily indebted — externally and domestically.

Despite its fragility the US economy has so far remained erect for two reasons. First, investors still believe that it remains more profitable to invest in US enterprises than in Europe and Asia's ones. When that prognosis proves to be false, as reported profits are not likely to live up to expectations, investment decisions will be reassessed. Second, all the major holders of currency reserves (China, Japan, Taiwan and Singapore) are in Asia. Their holdings are primarily in US dollar currency. China's political preferences have put production and jobs above everything else to ensure social stability. When domestic demand is matured enough to replace exports as a pull factor for the economy a shift in the allocations of the holdings is unavoidable.

Already a change in attitudes in the United States starts to exacerbate the dislocation of the US economy. For two centuries influx from abroad has been a strength not a threat, a blessing not a curse, a contribution to economic growth not a factor taking away jobs in the domestic economy. That is no longer valid.

September 11, 2001 may have produced an epic shift in the American attitude to the outside world. From openness to seclusion. From benevolence to distrust. From partnership to nationalism. There is a clue to possible impact on the US economy. Economists use as a rule of thump that more than 50% of the US economic growth since 1945 could be ascribed to new technology. The technological lead could be ascribed among other things to attracting talents from abroad. American universities and enterprises were a magnet for the best brains. Formerly Europe was the main source. Recently, Asia seemed to catch up and might well in the future outnumber Europe in that field.

Yet, a hardening of the US attitude towards foreign immigrants has increased the probability that a good number of Asians going back to Asia in the wake of the IT and electronics downturn are going to stay there. Foreign talents having oiled the technological surge in the US would partly be cut off. Instead they are likely to boost the economy and technology of US competitors. Suffice to mention in this context that in 2002 the number of foreign students in the US fell 8%, in 2003 10%, in 2004 3% while preliminary figures for 2005 indicate a rise of 1% over 2004. All in all, the total number has fallen in the course of four years from just under 300,000 to a little bit above 200,000.

US Empire?

For decades the US have been the global leader politically, militarily and economically. It has been an empire in the sense that the rest of the world followed where the US chose to lead it.

Genuine leadership reflects that others qualify the judgment of the leader as sound, opening the door for persuasive power. In such a case, the rest of the world follows suit because it feels the course is well argued and in conformity with common principles. Persuasive power presents the empire/super power with the option of solidifying its position (saving resources) instead of fighting wars (exercising power, a destructive and costly policy, using resources).

The ultimate secret of imperial power is to project power without winding down resources by putting moral and cultural power on top followed by economic power while military power is avoided as it bleeds the empire white, gobbling up manpower and economic strength. This is how the Roman Empire, the Chinese Empire and the British Empire survived. When they were called upon to defend their position in major wars, their empires crumbled.

The US have hitherto been able to play this game since WWII. The rest of the world looked upon the US as the uncontested leader. It trusted the US, followed their policies, sometimes not without grudging, but follow it did. The allies and friends all lined up. Not because they were afraid or scared, not because they felt compelled or coerced to do so, not because they feared for what would happen if they remained outside. But because they wanted to be alongside the

United States of America sharing basic principles about world politics, human rights and political systems.

This consensus does not seem so rock solid anymore. In fact it looks increasingly fragile. The US have slipped into some kind of unilateral multilateralism conveying the message that the US are a partner in international politics if it suits US interests. If not, they are not. Power projection and nationalism have replaced ethics and principles.

However, politics cannot be dichotomized. If the US look upon their commitment to the outside world solely in a power perspective, the rest of the world is bound to start to adopt a similar stance for its own stake. That will introduce a whole new ball game for internalization, globalization or internationalism — choose which label is preferable — where the common interests wither away to be replaced by hard nosed infighting won by the strongest, maybe even the most ruthless.

When an empire resorts to military might to force recalcitrant nations or even challengers to toe the line, power starts to trickle away. The US policy towards Afghanistan and Iraq has two sides. One reflects the strong and determined US policy to counterattack the terrorists and smoke them out. An overwhelming majority around the world sympathizes with that policy even if many question the method chosen. The other, as stated clearly in the Bush administrations foreign policy, is the determined effort to spread US style democracy around the world and to support US-style human rights. Though this vision is rallying widespread sympathy, many countries and people around the globe do not agree that the US have a monopoly to define human rights and democracy and even less the right to impose the US interpretation of both on other countries. On top of that comes suspicion that the US apply some kind of double standard, with their policy vis-à-vis Central Asia most frequently put forward as a proof of such practice.

It says something about the standing of US in the international community that two such praiseworthy and admirable objectives have not gathered more support. Instead the columnist Fareed Zakariah could write[3] *"George W. Bush's legacy is now clear: the creation of a poisonous atmosphere of anti-Americanism around the globe"*.

Globalization?

Globalization has not really penetrated our mindset and changed the way we think. The elite may have managed to transform itself into global citizens exactly as it was the case for the global elite 100 years ago when globalization was as widespread or maybe even more widespread than today among the privileged ones.

What might be termed internationalism as a kind of new philosophy has unfortunately not yet emerged. A large majority of the global population does not participate in globalization as they do not live in developing nations but belong to the overwhelming number of people still confined to the countryside with little if any links to the outside world. It is the case of the majority of the population of countries like China, India and Indonesia and all the African countries to name a few.

Globalization is without question the best model the world has ever seen if you look at it solely in the sole perspective of economic growth. But problems have raised their heads without finding appropriate answers, one of them being an increasingly inequitable distribution of wealth to the benefice of a minority of already well offs leaving the majority as on-lookers. This development is all the more looking worse that the majority of the people bought into globalization only to get their share of higher growth and to increase their wealth at the price, for some, of their national identity. The expected trade-off did not occur.

This unwelcome situation does not augur well for globalization. What will happen if, or, when economic growth declines, the people discover that their sacrifice of national, regional, cultural (religion, ethnicity) identity was in vain? There is no mental bulwark against a reversal of globalization. Solidarity on a global level congruous with national solidarity has not been built up. A large majority of people around the globe see globalization as an economic, technological,

transport and logistics phenomenon but do not see themselves as part
of a global system sharing more or less congruous values.[4]

The global institutions have failed to transform themselves from
steering committees working under the Cold War rules to the new
global world. Global values have not emerged to serve as some
kind of banister when mounting or descending the steps. Only the
US Empire emerged and whether it is popular or not to say so,
globalization currently stands exclusively for American capitalism and
nothing more. Furthermore, in that context, American political values
have proved themselves to be of dubious value when put forward,
as can be seen with the fiasco of the WDM of Iraq and this in an
uncompromising way. What would now happen to a world without
rudder if the sea becomes rough?

As a result, globalization looks dependent not only on the US
policies not failing, but the US economy not faltering either. For
better or for worse, the US economy stretched itself to become
a decisive parameter beyond its own local perimeter, taking on a
fundamental role for the future prospects of globalization. As we have
said, for better or for worse.

The verdict of history will be unanimous and unequivocal: since
1990 onwards a chance was at hand to shape a truly international
world, mirroring the perceived American ideals, principles and values.
But those values are now under scrutiny and unfortunately seem to
falter under the weight of the challenge.

Therefore, and it is unfortunate, the window of opportunity to
jump from a strictly economic model to an international one based
upon broader concepts is likely to close without the needed switch
happening. This is because the US chose to pursue globalization as a
"strict economic model" pushing its dependence on growth, and in
particular on US domestic growth, and nothing else.

All the rising powers be it China, India or Brazil could not and
did not wait to join the present political and economic architecture.
They have accepted more or less the market economy. They may still
hesitate or at least some of them may still hesitate about democracy,
but few will in earnest contest that their human rights record are far

better than, let us say 20 years ago. They may ask for and in some years time will demand adjustments in the decision making process within the global system. But they will do it as insiders, standing firm on the foundations of the structure. The US may have misgivings about China as a fellow player against terrorism, reining in rogue states, preventing the spread around of weapon of mass destruction (WMD). But just imagine the vast options if the Chinese political leadership really wanted to counteract US policy.

The well-kept secret is that countries like China and India are weak countries. They are rising powers but not yet there. Their economic growth remains fragile and dependent on outside forces such as foreign investment and access to foreign markets. Their social structure is threatening domestic stability. The recent election in India was swung to the advantage of the Congress Party because rural votes from mainly poor people made the difference. Reports about social unrest in China's rural districts or her Western underdeveloped regions or in the rust belt in her Northeastern part are common in the mass media.

Regardless of all the noise about the opposite, China and India are militarily weak and barely capable of defending themselves in case of a military conflict with the US. This is well understood by the political leaders steering a cautious course to avoid confrontations and skirting anything near adventurous foreign policy. The last thing they want is to be disturbed while they are trying to build up a permanent and solid economic base, which is some years away. They may look threatening from the outside especially viewed by right wing republicans in the US but they themselves are mostly scared by the risk of domestic social unrest.

The demand for economic growth in China and India removed any risk or possibility that one or both would try to shape another system based upon alternative or even opposite values and preferences. They chose the post-1945 system as their system and they are adjusting to it. The need for growth in these two large newcomers has sharpened globalization's dependence on growth.

The world has been incredibly lucky that the stand off between capitalism and socialism has not been replaced by another stand off with the rich countries as protagonists of globalization and the populous countries with a low income per capita as protagonists of nationalism or seclusion.

To fight rogue states and international terrorism, the US, with a strong emphasis on military power, believed they could do it alone. For a coalition of allies inclusive of the rising powers would raise a dilemma: the price would increase their political influence.

The US are extremely reluctant to pay that price. The alternative then is to go alone or form a so-called "ad-hoc coalition of the willing" with actually very few countries genuinely willing. Such an option drains US resources as the burden rests finally exclusively on the US shoulders. For them, the result whether they chose one or the other is in truth the same: reduced power. But for the rest of the world, it makes a substantial difference.

The first option augurs a peaceful, orderly and gradual adjustment of power and influences under the auspices of a benevolent US. The second option is likely to lead to conflicts and confrontation engendered by the US resistance to such an adjustment.

Judged by history no rising power is willing to wait indefinitely and no existing power has been eager to relinquish power and influence[5] easily and speedily.

Nowhere is this dilemma more visible than in the US policy vis-à-vis China. The Bush administration started with a rather belligerent attitude toward China but changed tack after September 11. In their fight against global terrorism, the US came to the conclusion that Taiwan was becoming a strategic liability, while a partnership with China would enhance the US projection of power.[6] China might see such a shift with irony.

The key to the future is to perceive US-China relations in the prism of Asian integration. Economic realities point to intra-Asian integration having more clout than Asia-Pacific economic links. From the mid-90's to 2003 China's share of US market tripled from about 8% to almost 25%. The rest of East Asia and most of the South East Asian countries saw a corresponding decline i.e. Japan from almost 30% to just above 10%.

For the last couple of years Japan, Taiwan and Hong Kong have seen China accounting for more than 50% of export growth. China has become the largest recipient of Foreign Direct Investment (FDI) with about 60 billion US dollars in both 2004 and 2005 surpassing the US. The politically sensitive issue of Taiwan has found an economic answer with Taiwan as a de facto part of China investing heavily and gradually becoming dependent on the Chinese market for her products and outsourced production to ensure her international competitiveness.

Asia Is Going to Institutionalize

Asia is starting to institutionalize itself not on the same lines as the model chosen by the Europeans since 1950 but it is clearly influenced by this only piece of inventive political engineering for a long time. The ten Southeast Asian countries in ASEAN have started talks about an ASEAN Charter. The same group of countries together with China, Japan, Korea, India, Australia and New Zealand met for the first time in an East Asian caucus in December 2005.[7] The group as constituted now includes 16 nations with Russia as an observer. It is no coincidence that the US were not invited, nor was the EU.

The strategic view is clearly to build integration among Asian countries. It would benefit them and provide them a platform for a higher profile in global political and economic negotiations. But how to proceed? Option one is to integrate along the pattern chosen by the Europeans that is an integration moving gradually from economics to foreign policy and rule based institutions while closing the door for non-Asian members. Option two is a looser construction, primarily or exclusively aiming at an improved Free Trade Area enlarged to economics spheres such as currency rate co-operation, while staying away from supranationality and rigorously respecting the character of intergovernmental co-operation. That would allow the door to be open along the road to the US. The US are not an Asian power but they do carry projection power in the region where they protect what they consider vital interest. Therefore they may consider that such a decision is not for Asia alone. Others may not agree.

Looked at through the spectrum of economic interest one would assume that China and Japan would steer the integration. There is no need to repeat the figures for bilateral trade and the Japanese investments in China. The problem is that neither the Chinese nor the Japanese see it that way. They are heavily integrated economically and it would be difficult for them to part ways but politically no bonds bind them together — on the contrary.

China wants the US to stay as a military power in Asia but not to be an Asian power. As long as the US provide a nuclear umbrella Japan may be tempted but not more than that to go nuclear. If the US quit, Japan would not hesitate to take care of her own security including the nuclear vector. So the Chinese perspective is to keep the US involved in Asia to prevent a militarily rising Japan.

China worries about Japan — not the US — and define her policy towards the US in that context. The Japanese position is to keep the US in Asia as a bulwark against a too strong Chinese power, which the Japanese cannot stop alone, a situation the policy makers in Tokyo are painfully aware of. Both China and Japan see the US presence in Asia as a pawn in the chess game to keep the neighbor down.

This difference in strategic perception makes it almost impossible for China and Japan to assume the role of drivers to the integration of Asia.

Commonality with regard to strategic outlook is much more likely to be found between China and India. Both of them see the US presence in Asia as stabilizing security. Yet, neither one sees itself as ally or on collision course with the US. Their security does not depend on the US. Even if long standing disagreements, quarrels and jealousy between them often find way to the headlines the basic fact remains that — contrary to China versus Japan — neither of them sees the other as a potential threat against their survival and development coming.[8]

The picture becomes even more transparent when looking at economics and trade where the two countries move fast towards identical interest in beefing up their co-operation. This explains why the flywheel for integration in Asia will be a closer, much closer relationship between China and India.

China and India will shape something like an integrated economy. Political stability is of paramount importance governing respectively 1,3 billion, and 1 billion people, and in both cases, with a relatively new (historically speaking) political system. Social stability is the uncompromising condition for political stability. And that can only be achieved by a large number of new jobs keeping pace with the increasing labor force. As the US economy starts to splutter a shift in economic pull factors, substituting US economy with domestic demand becomes indispensable, even imperative.

Their domestic economies are strong but not strong enough separately. In short: Either they get their economic act together to stimulate demand, or their primordial political objective — social stability — gets out of reach.[9]

Economic integration is already happening. In 2004 total trade between the two was about 14 billion US dollars compared with between 100 and 200 million US dollars about ten years ago. China is already India's largest trading partner. The number of businessmen visiting the other country is growing exponentially. The same goes for students albeit in smaller numbers. The flagship enterprises are investing in each other's markets. When the Chinese Premier Wen Jiabao visited India,[10] the two countries agreed to negotiate a bilateral free trade agreement (FTA). This clarifies the vision. The ASEAN countries have already established a FTA and are negotiating with China and India. Launching Chinese-Indian FTA negotiations means that a triangular FTA encompassing more than 3 billion people has moved from the talking stage to the negotiating table.

Both countries strive hard to get access to oil and natural gas. So far the skeptics have been wrong in their prediction that this would put them on collision course. What has happened is precisely the opposite. They have mapped out the framework for common activities in the energy area[11] and China repeated in January 2006 its support for India as permanent member of the United Nations Security Council[12] while holding back any such endorsement of Japan's candidature.

The US predicament boils down to the following question: will the US support, promote and facilitate some kind of Asian integration taking place under Chinese-Indian leadership with inevitable political repercussions for the role of the US themselves, not forgetting the chosen US partner and ally in Asia: Japan? Or will the US try to obstruct this course of events with unpredictable consequences not only for Asia, but also for the concept of globalization and internationalism? The third option is to ignore what is going on. It may be open for a while but their allies may prod it to clarify the policy line as they themselves will be engulfed in this economic and political restructuring of Asia.[13]

A US support would open the door for a continued US presence in Asia as a friend and a partner. Asia would become a solution to remedying the long term US economic imbalances. A reversal of roles would take place. Hitherto the US economic supported the phenomenal growth in Asia. In a few years time, the Asian economies may prop up a weakened US economy. The US would find it hard to sustain their growth without being an insider in the Asian integration. Two birds would be killed with one stone. The unpleasant prospect of an US recession would fade out of sight and global growth would serve as a barrier to prevent a backlash against globalization.

Even more important: it would signify political agreement among the major economic powers to solidify globalization and internationalism. The global model would be endorsed. Basically the world would be likely to continue in the tracks laid down since 1945–1950 that is more economic internationalization, more common decision-making, and congruous economic models.

The ride might be rough but the course would be set towards political systems more and more reflecting and inspired by principles embedded in the Western democratic model.

For this to happen, the US must acquiesce with a China-India leadership controlling the Asian integration instead of the US or a US supported Japanese leadership, which would not work.

But it is fairly easy to deduct that Japan will not be comfortable with such an outcome. Yet, very little room of maneuver is available to wriggle out of this straitjacket. To ensure a stable Asia and to avoid a sullen Japan diplomatic creativity is going to be in high demand. Without some prodding from the US it is most likely that

Japan will try to resist not necessarily an emerging Asian economic integration but its further development into a political vehicle for institutionalization more or less in the same vein as the European one.

A US obstruction would take the world into uncharted waters. US unwillingness, even resistance to trade-in short-term power for long-term influence might become blatantly obvious. In such a scenario, the risk of a US economic downturn would increase with negative repercussions for globalization. It might and probably would propel countries like China and India to consider other options.

A US obstruction would probably mean some kind of encouragement for Japan to pursue a more nationalistic course, even promoting Japan as part of a military shield for Taiwan. That would in turn lead to a predictable and in this scenario, aspired after Chinese reaction. China would then be depicted as an aggressive power, not eligible for Asian's trust.

The US decision to roll out the carpet for European integration was statesmanlike and instrumental in shaping a robust Western "global model". NAFTA seems to slide towards a stronger and larger framework. It may even grow into some kind of co-operation for most of the western hemisphere. The missing link is so far the Asian counterpart, and in particular, the interaction between these three large entities. Only the US can help to bring it about. If they want to. And only if such an interaction is provided can the world look with confidence toward consolidation of globalization and internationalism.

The interaction of a weakened US power, the emergence of China and India as rising powers operating inside the existing model and a Japan not really knowing where she wants to go make the game in Asia the great game for the next 10 years.

It is difficult to see a successful Asian integration worth that name with the US fostering the deepening rift between China and Japan and also alienating Australia from Asia by drawing it ever closer to the US. That would be a high-risk game undermining security and stability in the world's coming economic powerhouse.

The stakes are even higher when one realizes that China and India's acceptance of the present global economic and political system may not be unqualified and unconditional but rests upon them becoming stakeholders in the global system.

Conclusion

To shape a global system reflecting basically the free market model and a gradual maybe cautious development towards democracy albeit not necessarily defined as the European or American model is within reach. The battle is being played on the Asian pitch. The US have a decisive role as a catalyst for shaping such a global model mirroring American values. The alternative is to put a spoke in the wheel jeopardizing not only Asian integration but also the very future of globalization stimulating nationalism, incompatible with globalization.

Endnotes

1. This debate was actually started by Paul Kennedy in 1988 with his book *The Rise and Fall of the Great Powers* (New York, 1988) and followed by a number of books, for example Ferguson, Niall, *Empire, the Rise and Demise of the British World Order and the Lessons for Global Power* (New York, 2003).
2. For example Stiglitz, Joseph, *The Roaring Nineties*, London, 2003.
3. *Newsweek*, edition of May 14, 2004.
4. There is a long list of books on Globalization. Friedman, Thomas, *The World is Flat*, (New York, 2005) is generally regarded as the latest work praising the virtues of globalization. See also Møller, J. Ørstrøm, *The End of Internationalism or World Governance* (Westport, 2000) who offers a critical analysis of globalization and its shortcomings. A thoughtful analysis can be found in Bobbitt, Philip, *The Shield of Achilles* (New York, 2002).
5. When speaking about rising and declining powers what matters is the trend and not absolute figures. In absolute figures, the US will for many decades be the dominant economic power and at least until approx. 2050 be militarily dominant as it takes decades to build a military arsenal, but in relative terms the rising powers are closing the gap.
6. Mar, Pamela C. M. and Richter, Franz-Jurgen, *China: Enabling a new era of changes* (John Wiley & Sons — Asia), (Singapore, 2003) gives a perspective on China's role and the challenges facing China.

7. For a good and brief comment see http://www.atimes.com/atimes/
   Southeast_Asia/GLl7Ae01.html. For the conclusions see http://www.
   aseansec.org/18104.htm

8. An excellent book on China and India is Garver, John W., *Protracted
   Contest, Sino-Indian rivalry in the Twentieth Century* (Seattle and London,
   2002).

9. The Report from Asian Development Bank "Asian Economic Cooperation
   and Integration. Progress, Prospect and Challenges", ed Ippei Yamazawa,
   (London, 2000) is an interesting perspective on this and other issues
   linked to Asian integration.

10. April 2005.

11. See for example http://www.cnn.com/2006/WORLD/asiapcf/01/12/
    china.india.oil.ap/

12. http://sify.com/news/fullstory.php?id=14118146

13. Kyung-won, Kim, Koh, Tommy and Sobhan, Farooq, America's role in
    Asia (Asia Foundation report 2004) offers a splendid overview.

This article was first published in *Asian Affairs*, No. 27, 2006.

Globalisation Debate Threatens Asia

THE WORLD IS SUDDENLY FACED WITH A NEW ECONOMIC POLICY DISPUTE: National governments questioning the benefits and wisdom of cross-border mergers and acquisitions versus the imperative of economic globalisation relentlessly pushing such restructuring in the name of productivity and cost-cutting.

The depth and importance of this battle is not widely understood, despite its obvious importance for the future of globalisation.

The battle lines are visible both in Europe and in the United States, and are beginning to be seen in Asia. After the implementation of the single European market in 1993, the Europeans reaped considerable benefits from economies of scale, and restructuring of the continent's businesses was the next logical step. A truly European industrial structure, it was argued, should replace the out-of-date structures tailor-made to individual national markets.

Consolidation got off to a promising start. A wave of mergers and acquisitions swept through European nations. But the cross-border variety — which promised the largest efficiency benefits — proved a harder nut to crack. Admittedly, there have been some European cross-border mergers and acquisitions, but not nearly to the extent hoped for; and the apparent lag in productivity compared to the US has been partly ascribed to the lack of European restructuring.

Recently, several proposed deals have run into trouble with national governments in Europe: the plan by Italy's ENEL to purchase France's Suez; a planned merger of German energy and environmental giant E.ON and Spain's Endesa; the global steel giant Mittal's attempt to purchase Luxembourg-based Arcelor, itself one of the most prominent results of cross-border European mergers; a prospective union of Italy's Unicredito and Germany's HVB; and a merger between the Dutch bank ABN Amro and Italy's Antonveneta. That is not to mention the French government's uproar last summer when rumours circulated that Pepsi planned to buy the French food giant Danone.

In the US, the China National Offshore Oil Corp (CNOOC) was not allowed to buy the oil company Unocal. Chinese PC manufacturer Lenovo managed to get the green light to buy IBM's personal computer division, but only after a hard struggle. And now opposition has seemingly revived with the uproar over the US State Department's purchase of 16,000 computers from a Lenovo/IBM wholesaler.

An upcoming case is the French telecommunications giant Alcatel's bid for Lucent, where the delicate point is Lucent's defence and intelligence-related activities for the US government.

A political majority in the US Congress threw a spanner in the works for what the Bush administration thought was a done deal — the purchase by a Dubai-based organisation of a company running US ports — when commentators and politicians began to question the wisdom of allowing container ports to be managed by a company based in the Arab Middle East.

A deeper analysis reveals three motives that threaten not only restructuring of global industry but globalisation itself.

First, the fear of losing jobs and income has jumped from blue-collar workers to white-collar workers with higher education. Globalisation implies that no job is 100 per cent safe. Education, skills and even performance do not protect jobs from outsourcing.

Politically, that makes a difference, because white-collar workers have a potentially stronger political influence than their blue-collar counterparts. They know how to play the political game, because they form part of the political elite. Opposition from their side is thus far more dangerous for globalisation than resistance from blue-collar workers and trade unions. White-collar workers used to be the elite troops of globalisation. For them, it was almost entirely beneficial: No risk of job lost, but considerable gains from lower prices.

Now, these workers suddenly realise that their jobs may also be in danger, and they are reacting similarly to blue-collar workers and the trade unions. If this trend continues, globalisation may lose some of its most vocal supporters.

Second, governments worry about cross-border restructuring not because of the potential loss of jobs, which is manageable, but because of the potential loss of brainpower. After a merger, the purchasing company is not generally inclined to run duplicate planning staffs, strategic offices, research and development branches, financial headquarters, etc. These activities will be concentrated in one, or at most, a few places.

And in cross-border mergers, it is highly doubtful whether the "brains" of the purchased enterprise will stay in its original home country.

Thus, the loss for this country becomes two-fold. It loses the brainpower of the purchased company. Then, it loses the benefit of other companies either having or planning to establish brainpower to interact with the existing one now on its way out. Any ambition of creating an "industry cluster" or building up a high-performing group of enterprises can be swept away.

The government's position to fight to keep brainpower is logical. It cannot be brushed aside or labelled old-fashioned protectionism. It goes deeper than that. The coalition between white-collar workers switching their political view from staunch supporters of globalisation to scepticism and governments strongly motivated to keep brainpower at home augurs a potentially formidable and acute threat to globalisation.

The third motive is national security. After the end of the Cold War, the most serious threat to the West disappeared. Instead, terrorism, infectious diseases and international crime pose a threat against not the nation but the well-being of societies. If and when a cross-border merger or acquisition is perceived as a security threat, politicians hit the brakes. And after having stimulated awareness in the population over precisely this kind of threat, they find it difficult or politically inopportune to run any risks.

Potholes and Pitfalls

If the Europeans and Americans start to put on the brakes, Asia may end up the big loser, finding its easiest route into the big league of multinationals full of obstacles, or entirely blocked.

This explains the Dubai case and also explains why the first reaction to the Alcatel/Lucent case was the raising of national security questions, pointing out that Lucent is a provider of high-tech weapons and intelligence-gathering systems at the heart of the US defence system.

What are the implications for Asia of this new pattern of behaviour? The new scepticism over cross-border mergers is emerging precisely at the moment when many of Asia's largest and most vibrant companies plan to go multinational, and many of them look at mergers and acquisitions as the right way to obtain the expertise and management know-how they need.

CNOOC's failed attempt to purchase Unocal, in this light, may be considered an ominous sign. If the Europeans and Americans start to put on the brakes, Asia may end up the big loser, finding its easiest route into the big league of multinationals full of obstacles, or, in the worst case, entirely blocked.

A warning shot has been fired. If the momentum of globalisation is to be maintained, both business leaders and politicians must understand the underlying fear driving opposition to cross-border mergers and acquisitions. Even more, they must find ways to deal with that fear and anxiety to ensure an equitable distribution of globalisation's benefits, as developed-country economies transition from a manufacturing base with threatened blue-collar jobs, to a service or IT economy with white-collar jobs under fire.

This article was first published in *The Straits Times*, 12 April 2006.

Unified Asian Voice Will Sound Louder on World Stage

THREE MAJOR ECONOMIC ISSUES WILL DOMINATE THE EAST ASIA SUMMIT when the Asean+3 group meets India, Australia and New Zealand in Kuala Lumpur next month.

These include how to ensure that growth in Asia remains sustainable, how to distribute wealth that growth brings as well as how to translate the growing economic weight into global influence.

Asia's main driver of growth — exports to the United States — links its economies to the US business cycle. Though it has been a veritable engine of growth for the past 15 years, there is no guarantee that it will continue to be so.

Economists disagree over their forecasts for the US economy, though most feel that growth may continue, albeit at a lower rate. This will lead to lower growth in Asia.

That is, unless Asia can extricate itself from this by replacing exports to the US with domestic demand. This, of course, evokes the question of the Chinese economy. However, while domestic demand there is going up, it will probably not be sufficient to replace the US engine should its own exports falter.

Yes, with many Chinese families moving into the annual income bracket in excess of US$5,000 (S$8,500) a year and emigrating from rural areas into the cities, consumption will be stimulated. But for more robust domestic demand to sustain its growth, China must finetune its economic policy to shift consumption patterns upwards while also avoiding overheating and remaining cognisant of the ups and downs of US business cycles.

If the policymakers get it wrong, the Chinese economy may be derailed, which would jeopardise not just Chinese prospects but also most of Asia's.

Still, China is not synonymous with Asia. Japan still matters, so it is most encouraging to see it moving ahead, if a bit slowly. Its upturn is based primarily on domestic demand. However, the jury is still out as to whether its recovery is permanent or just a temporary blip of the same kind the world has seen a couple of times since 1990.

Can demand by the two major economies render Asia less reliant on the US economy?

The answer lies in Asian economies becoming more economically integrated. As they do so, they will become more interested in playing by the rules of the game. Yes, the lion's share of the benefits from growth will definitely go to China. But not exclusively.

Benefits accruing from economic integration will be shared by small and large countries, which should augur well for Asia in terms of it being an attractive place for investments. That is, this should increase the likelihood of more foreign investments. To promote further integration, Asia should be looking, over the longer term, at some mechanism to stabilise exchange rates since it may be too early to move towards a common currency or shared financial framework.

For a long time now, Asia has been punching far below its weight in the global economy as regional integration has not proceeded to a level for a common Asian position to be articulated in unison. The summit will not, of course, be a magic wand to conjure up such a position. What it can do is put the world on notice that when individual Asian countries speak up in international negotiations, they do so taking into account one another's views as well.

Such a simple message could well bolster Asia's influence and garner for the continent a higher profile globally.

This article was first published in *The Straits Times*, 30 November 2005.

China and India:

Rise of the New Global Powerhouses

FOR THE LAST 15 YEARS, THE AMERICAN ECONOMY HAS BEEN THE MAIN driver of the world economy. From 1990 to 2000, 60 percent of total global growth originated in the United States. No wonder, then, that the falling U.S. growth rate has hit the world economy hard. Growth in the Eurozone and Japan has not taken up the slack. A semi-recession has cast its spell over the global economy.

China and India constitute the only bright spots with annual growth of about 7–8 percent for China and 5–6 percent for India, but separately these two economies have not been strong enough to pull the world economy out of the doldrums.

What we see emerging now is a closer Chinese-Indian economic relationship. It has been in the oven for some time but held back by traditional animosities in both countries, primarily India, bureaucratic opposition and sheer geographical distance visible by the Himalayas.

Chances are that, in the next decade, or two China and India will create an economic powerhouse of unprecedented magnitude and effectiveness. World politics and world economics will be forced to adjust with a speed and to a degree not seen before in human history. With 2.2 billion people, a fast growing middle class, rising purchasing power, confident political leadership and competitive world class enterprises these, two countries will dominate the world economy.

Measured in exchange rates, they together account for 12 percent of global GNP. The share is almost double if calculated on the basis of purchasing power parity (PPP), which for these countries is a better yardstick. Calculated in PPP, the Chinese economy is already the second biggest after the U.S. economy. India and China display high growth, a high savings rate, an entrepreneurial class, large population and an age pyramid supporting growth with 24.8 percent the population below 14 years in China and 33.1 percent in India. Both are quickly adjusting to the market economy even if the social fabric and political structure shelter some impediments to an open economy.

The figures, especially for China, are staggering. China now has more than 400 million television sets — imagine the market for replacement and upgrading- and about 470 million telephone subscribers, equally divided between mobile phones and fixed lines. It also has 18 million millionaires, equal to the population of Australia. As for India, mobile phones amount to 16 million; up 50 percent year-on-year and rising one million per month.

High-tech industries account for more than a fair share of this strong economic performance. China is second only to the U.S. with regard to mobile phones, has 75 million people having access to the internet and is the world's biggest producer of personal computers. India is among the leading software countries in the world, attracting foreign direct investment (FDI) not only in manufacturing, but also for research and development from high-tech leaders around the globe, including the United States.

If we look at the 200 largest companies among emerging economies, we find 11 from India and 18 from China. A study performed by Credit Lyonnais in 2000 ranks India sixth and China nineteenth among 25 emerging markets.

This augurs well for Chinese and Indian companies entering as newcomers in the global market place and, even more importantly, as true multinational companies. Some examples from China include China Mobile, China Telecom, Legend, and Sinopec, while from India there is Infosys, Wipro, Reliance, and Hindustan Lever.

However, China and India face one common challenge — the creation of a large number of new jobs every year to match the cohorts entering the labor market. If that challenge is not met, social unrest may start and, if so, the established political leadership will feel the ground slip from under their feet. This may be more acute and visible in China, albeit still characteristic for the situation in India. The political elite needs to justify their grip on power by creating jobs and the indispensable condition for that is economic growth. As the U.S., European and Japanese export markets do not any longer deliver new jobs, a drive for a combined Chinese/Indian market will emerge.

It is true that the two countries have traditionally nourished reciprocal suspicion and distrust. However, geopolitics after September 11, 2001 has changed that. Common political interests now over-shadow this strange and defunct paranoia:

— They both want to be on friendly terms with the United States. but they do not want the U.S. to dominate Asia. By working together, they may curb rising U.S. influence without necessarily provoking a confrontation with the United States.
— China's power play — using Pakistan to irritate India — is out of date. Developments in the last two years have firmly established India's superiority on the Indian sub-continent. A more assertive and self-reliant India has managed to get sufficient room of manuever opening the door to a new relationship with China.
— They both face the threat of terrorism with roots in extreme Islamic thinking. India faces Pakistan, having to cope with the problem of Kashmir and more than 50 millions Muslims inside the country. China, with around 50 millions Muslims of its own in the western part of the country, is facing an autonomous movement in Xinjiang striving for an independent nation-state called East Turkestan.

Some people may fear that an Indian-Chinese entente might try to forcibly dominate the region. Maybe even worse, these two powers might go to war to eliminate the rival and establish supremacy in Asia. None of these scenarios are warranted if you analyze recent postures adopted by China and India. Neither are centralized empires. They are a conglomerate of individual nations, regions and ethnicities keeping their distance vis-à-vis the central government. SARS revealed many hitherto disregarded but known phenomena about China — one of them being that Beijing is not fully in control of the provinces. The central government is preoccupied with the task of keeping the nation together. Any distractions from domestic issues are most unwelcome. Risky foreign policy initiatives are simply not on the agenda.

The strong growth around these two countries will create stability and prosperity. A new kind of balance in Asia is coming to be sure, but it will not be one imposed upon the rest of the continent by military force or threats hereof. It will instead be a balance of power reflecting economic performance — an Asian system where all the siblings know their place in the family. If they adapt to this new hierarchy, stability will follow.

This article was first published in *In The National Interest*, 17 September 2003 (www. inthenationalinterest.com).

Threats to Asia's Stability —

and a Potential Solution

ASIA FACES TWO MAIN RISKS TO ITS STABILITY THAT COULD MUSHROOM into a sequence of events triggering confrontation and crisis, even leading to armed conflicts casting their ugly shadows over much of Asia.

The first main risk is Japan.

Japan was the economic success story until around 1990. Since then, its economy has been in almost continuous recession. That gives birth to three main problems for Japan, Asia and the rest of the world.

Psychologically the Japanese have lost belief in themselves. They have no trust in their ability to marshal changes through the political and social system. Japan was the only model successfully combining Asian culture with Western industrialization. That boosted pride and confidence inside Japan and gave the rest of Asia heart. When the model ran aground, the Japanese were at a loss — bewildered about what to do. The rest of Asia lost the model they looked up to — almost universally admired.

Economically, Japan is no longer "pulling" the rest of Asia along. The Japanese market may still be the biggest, but the Japanese economy is a secluded economy. According to the World Bank, Gross Foreign Direct Investment amounts to 0.9 percent of Gross National Product, compared to 4.3 percent for China, 5.1 percent for the United States, 13.3 percent for Germany, 16.4 percent for France and 38.7 percent for the United Kingdom. India is almost on par, with 0.6 percent. From 1990 to 2000, the percentage fell for Japan from 1.7 percent to 0.9 percent, while it rose between two and five times for the other main industrialized countries. In the mid-nineties, Foreign Direct Investment in Japan was $46 per capita compared to between $1500 and $3500 for the other main industrialized countries. There is a lot of talk but no real prospect of a fundamental economic recovery in Japan. Those who have the power to change the system are those who will lose if it takes place — so it will not happen. Deflation may be bad economic policy, but it boosts purchasing power among people living off their pensions. The Japanese age pyramid ensures that, electorally speaking, such bad economic policy will continue.

Politically, Japan does not know how to cope with its own problems. The rest of Asia does not know how to cope with a baffled and secluded Japan — almost invisible in world politics and world economics. Its power confers upon Japan a robust, if not leading, role. But politically, Japan sees the world through the prism of impotence. Japan and most of Asia is at a loss watching the failure of the Japanese model.

The Japanese island-mentality may direct the nation towards a nationalistic attitude, with the further risk of a more militaristic Japan. The trend may be initiated or strengthened by the rumblings coming out of North Korea. The U.S. request for a Japanese role in the Middle East may do the same. A more nationalistic and possibly militaristic Japan will destabilize the whole of Asia.

The second main risk is Islamic extremism.

A large, almost overwhelming number of Muslims want to live in peace with other religions, in conformity with the great tradition of Islam as a tolerant religion. In the 1999 Indonesian elections, the Islamic political parties that advocated the introduction of Islamic law (*sharia*) received only 14 percent of the votes cast. But that does not preclude the Islamicization of society. What has emerged in Indonesia — the largest Muslim country in the world — is a dichotomization, with a secular state but a society turning more and more towards Islamism. The risk is that moderate Islamic political parties are overtaken from within by small, fanatical groups opting for a theocratic state.

Southeast Asia is the fault line in the struggle between Islamist terrorism and modernity. In this part of the world, a string of countries have adopted Western-style societies and benefit greatly. If the West cannot win the struggle here, the West cannot win it anywhere.

Another area at risk is Central Asia. Central Asia used to be a forgotten part of the globe. Czarist Russia and the Soviet Union held sway over this large land mass without anybody really bothering it. Not so anymore. This is where some of the world's largest reserves of oil and gas are located. But to bring the crude into the industrial areas of the United States, Europe, Japan, China and soon India, it needs to be transported through geographically prohibitive and hostile territory.

The 'stan' states, as they are called, do not really have a national identity. They are embryonic entities vulnerable to outside influence. And several of them have a large majority of Muslims from which terrorist organizations can recruit. In contrast to South East Asia, dismal economic and social conditions provide an attractive base for potential terrorists.

To limit the effects of Japanese weakness and Islamic extremism, prosperity needs to be institutionalized. The focal point — the battleground so to speak — for any attempt to change Asia's direction is the process of institutionalization in Asia, like the EU in Europe and NAFTA in North America. There are two players in this game, a third one warming up and a fourth one with the power to tilt the balance in one or the other direction and holding the cards close to its chest.

China and Japan are the two players. China has proposed a Free Trade Area (FTA) with Southeast Asia and recently boosted this offer with the idea of a strategic partnership. Southeast Asia has responded to China's offer favorably. They welcome any stability and prosperity to be gained from economically strong China.

Meanwhile, the Japanese offer falls short of a FTA, primarily because Japan cannot or will not include agriculture trade in its offer. As usual, Japanese strategy is held hostage to less than 5 percent of Japanese society. However, membership should not be confined to

Asian countries but encompass the United States and Australia as well. The aim is a fairly loose integration of a group of countries without strongly congruous interests. This explains why the reception of the Japanese proposal can be described as lukewarm.

India is warming up, as its usual reticence towards engaging itself in international cooperation outside the scope of the UN has prevented India from entering the game, but India has recently shown strong interest in starting negotiations with the Southeast Asian countries about a FTA. The next logical step would be to combine the China-Southeast Asia and India-Southeast Asia negotiations.

The fourth player in this poker game is, of course, the United States. The U.S. with its economic clout, technological lead and military power can prevent Asia from organizing itself or steer the institutionalization in the direction U.S. prefers or lend its weight to a successful outcome.

Economics may provide a clue to the future U.S. policy. The figure for two-way trade across the Pacific is more than $700 billion, larger than across the Atlantic. During the 1990's, US exports to Asia rose 80 percent and Asian exports to the U.S. rose 150 percent. U.S. direct investment in Asia amounts to more than $200 billion. Uninterrupted deficits on the current account of the US balance of payments, now at the historically crucial ceiling of 5 percent of Gross National Product, have built up a colossal figure of U.S. foreign debt. The financiers are found primarily in Asia. One of them is China, ranking second with foreign currency reserves just below $300 billion.

The omens are crystal clear. The United States can prosper only if it chooses not only power-sharing, but also prosperity-sharing with the new economic powerhouse taking shape across the Pacific. If another policy is chosen (e.g. holding on to its existing supremacy no matter what happens), economic constraints will force an unwelcome and painful reappraisal upon policy-makers in Washington. The lessons of history do not need interpretations. A superpower is one only as long as it is able to pay for its foreign policy.

Power-sharing and prosperity-sharing will strengthen the U.S. economy, thus extending the scope for foreign and security policy. On top of that, such a policy enhances U.S. capabilities to pursue a number of its strategic objectives, of which the fight against terrorism is priority number one. Other U.S. policies toward Asia are risky, whatever they may be, as they augur strategic liabilities while at the same time overloading the economic resources of the United States.

This article was first published in *In The National Interest*, 24 September 2003 (www. inthenationalinterest.com).

Foreword[*]

AS A DANE LIVING IN ASIA FOR MORE THAN FIVE YEARS, WORKING IN international relations and married to a Vietnamese having lived with me in Denmark for a number of years, it is a privilege to write the Foreword to this book.

The Asia-Europe Meeting (ASEM) was born out of wedlock in the sense that when the Europeans and Asians — or should we say East Asians — met in 1996, the Europeans had got their act together through the European Union (EU) while the East Asians were, and still are, non-institutionalised. As many people saw it the purpose was to use the strength and buoyancy of the East Asian economies as a vehicle to shape some kind of mechanism for dialogue or cooperation between Europe and Asia.

Both with regard to substance and membership/participation, it is obvious that we are talking about a process. The substance has changed completely, as the financial crisis of 1997–98 has brought about a whole new set of parameters for economics and trade. And terrorism has changed the perception of security. Membership/participation of ASEM is almost embryonic in the sense that only seven out of the ten partners of ASEAN take part, while Northeast Asia is represented by three countries (China, Japan, Korea) and South Asia not at all.

---

[*]Published in *Asia and Europe: The development and different dimensions of ASEM*, Routledge, 2003.

ASEM is a tool. And to use a tool properly you need to know what objectives you are aiming at, how you are going to achieve them and how to ensure an equitable distribution of benefits (and costs, if any) — how to make it a positive-sum game for all participants.

This book explains in a scholarly, lucid and thoughtful way what ASEM is and what ASEM can be used for. Experts will appreciate it. The smooth language makes it accessible also for those not yet familiar with this special branch of international 'getting to know you'.

However, the main virtue is that it lays the following question squarely on the doorstep of those in power and those engaged in Europe-Asia affairs: do you want to deepen our cooperation and mutual understanding? If the answer is yes, then the book opens the door for finding out how it can be done.

Both Europe and the Asian partners feel the weight of the American superpower. They recognise that the US is calling the tune in today's world. But they do not want to be exclusively dependent upon the US. The main question they face is how to strengthen their cooperation without striking the tone of (cheap) anti-Americanism.

Even the Americans should appreciate a stronger European, Asian and European-Asian role on the world stage. For most issues it would be a friendly, albeit not necessarily echoing, voice. It would introduce some checks and balances without which no system is viable in the long run. The world badly needs a perspective other than the American one on many international issues. An initiative to do that taken by a group of nations sharing a large part of the principles governing the American model might contribute to a more stable international development. This will even more be the case if the main players base their relations on mutual respect and stretch out their hands to help those nations and/or groups of people asking for assistance.

This is what ASEM and its member states could do in the long term. This is what many nations around the globe would like them to do. And this is what most of them, being friendly to the US, want ASEM to do, making it possible for them to continue to be friendly to the US.

The ASEM partners must build up mutual trust and confidence in each other. This is the first step. Without such trust and confidence very few, if any, common endeavours stand much of a chance of getting off the runway and into the air. Taxiing up and down the runway may consume a lot of petrol but will not take us anywhere. Trust and confidence is also an indispensable step for promoting ASEM as a force whereby global issues can be discussed, and not necessarily a common position but a position having been discussed among ASEM partners can be floated as a contribution to global politics and economics.

So far ASEM has been somewhat reluctant about entering into a discussion on foreign and security policy. The European partners have been willing, but at least some of the Asian partners have argued that this was not really on the agenda for ASEM. Fortunately, this situation is changing. To a certain degree terrorism has put the spotlight on the fact that security is not an issue confined to the defence of sovereign national territory, but belongs to the list of questions imposing themselves on the international agenda. However, there is more than that on the plate. Some Asian countries, in particular China, are gradually abandoning their somewhat sceptical attitude to international cooperation. The stronger Chinese economy and the acceptance by the Chinese leadership that very few questions can be dealt with satisfactorily in a national context alone means that China has become not only more willing but also more interested in joining the international stage. In this respect, ASEM constituted a useful platform and has delivered in its own way. It was and is a good place for a country hitherto reticent about multilateralism to initiate a more active role in the international community. ASEM has opened the door for some of the Asian partners to discover the virtue and maybe also the pitfalls of multilateral diplomacy. For China and other Asian countries it represented a forum for serious business without being 'dangerous'. The water could be tested, experience gained — no reason for asking for a rain check here. In the long term, ASEM may well be praised for having played that role.

In the short term, the question remains whether ASEM is capable of striking the right balance between declarations and the exchange of views on the one hand and tangible results to the benefit of its partners on the other.

Useful steps in that direction were taken at the fourth ASEM held in Copenhagen in September 2002. Taking into account the loose shape of ASEM, it has done a lot of work in the area of declaratory diplomacy while resisting the temptation to confine itself to that role. Hopefully, the declaratory diplomacy can move towards a readiness to shoulder some of the burdens associated with crisis management, peace keeping and humanitarian tasks around the globe. Asian and European countries have a self-evident role to play, as many of the problems arise in the European and/or Asian theatre. We should not shy away from entering the fray. Otherwise the problems will not be solved, will not go away, but will have to be dealt with by somebody else with or without our consent.

Tangible results are indispensable if international cooperation is to survive in the longer run. Nation-states are not willing to put resources (financial and/or human) into meetings without, at some stage, reaping the benefits. Here again ASEM seems to be moving towards getting its act together. The projects concerning lifelong learning are a case in point. The initiative about trade policy falls into the same circle. And the idea to launch a conference for a better understanding between different cultures grows in the same garden. All of them are useful, modest, down to earth initiatives. If handled competently, ASEM may put forward ideas, guidelines or results worthwhile — indeed sufficiently worthwhile — to maintain momentum.

Let me finish by making three main observations.

First, the future of ASEM will, to a large degree, be determined by the stance of the US in international politics and economics. It is no use beating around the bush denying this. US policy will decide whether ASEM and its partners support the US in shaping a global environment in which the US, Europe and Asia see eye to eye or whether ASEM — at least some of the ASEM partners — feel the time has come to put a certain distance between themselves and the US. And this will also determine whether Asia, Europe and the

US move towards some kind of global governance or towards some kind of competition for influence, rivalry or even conflict, albeit not necessarily of a military nature.

Second, whatever happens, the crucial issue for ASEM will be whether the East Asian countries can overcome their international difficulties and scepticism towards closer cooperation and move towards some kind of stronger integration in accordance with the traditions, politics, economics and culture of East Asia. In short, can East Asia invent something like the EU, to do for East Asia what the EU did for Europe in the last half century? If it can, then the door will be opened for European-Asian cooperation to the benefit of both sides. If not, then the unbalanced partnership may go on as a marriage may go on without being consumed — a formality without much substance and no offspring.

Third, some Europeans, and probably some Asians too, think that East Asia can copy the European model. They are wrong. The European model has functioned remarkably well because it solved the question of minorities, first of all in Western Europe after the end of the Second World War and then in Central and Eastern Europe after the fall of the Soviet and Russian empires. It opened the door for the participation of the minorities in the international economy, removing the obligatory oath of allegiance to the national capital representing cultural imperialism. The European model avoided clashes between majorities and minorities inside nation-states and between different nation-states by weakening the nation-state — almost starting the process of letting it wither away. In East Asia, it is the other way round. There the nation-state, and a strong nation-state, is necessary for avoiding the situation whereby the minorities are marginalised and all the benefits flowing from the international economy are diverted towards the majority. A weakening of the nation-state would produce the exact opposite results of what we have seen in Europe. The basic thrust is the same, but strategists and thinkers have to go back to the drawing board to come forward with the Asian model and not content themselves by pushing the button marked 'copy'.

ASEM is a modest tool in the arsenal of international policy measures but it has its place. If used properly and wisely, taking it for what it is, neither more nor less, it can help Asians and Europeans in shaping their own destiny among the global players. Not bad.

www.ingramcontent.com/pod-product-compliance
Lightning Source LLC
Chambersburg PA
CBHW050328270326
41926CB00016B/3365